The Law of Business Organisations

The Law of Business Organisations

Andrew McGee, Christina Williams
and Gary Scanlan

LawMatters
PUBLISHING

Published by Law Matters Publishing

Law Matters Ltd
33 Southernhay East
Exeter EX1 1NX
Tel: 01392 215577
www.lawmatterspublishing.co.uk

British Library Cataloguing-in-Publication Data

A catalogue record for this book is available from the British Library.

ISBN 1 84641 000 2

Typeset by Pantek Arts Ltd, Maidstone, Kent

Printed by Ashford Colour Press Ltd, Gosport, Hampshire

Contents

Preface

This book is based on an earlier work by Professor Andrew McGee and Christina Williams, then a Lecturer in the Department of Law, the University of Liverpool, which was published by Oxford University Press. The present work, published for the first time by Law Matters Publishing, builds upon that first edition which adopted a radical approach to the teaching of the law of business organisations. The authors believe that the real distinction between business organisations is not that between the partnership and the registered company, but between the partnership and the private limited company on the one hand, and the public and listed company on the other. The book therefore places its emphasis and concentrates upon the close relationship between the partnership and the private limited company as the two forms of business organisation used by the vast majority of businesses carried on by groups of individuals and which operate in England and Wales.

The book seeks through a fictional group of characters to trace the birth, rise and eventual decline of a business. It follows the history of a business which started as a sole enterprise, through to a partnership, as the founder brought his children into the 'firm', and eventually its transformation into a private limited company, as third parties joined the enterprise during its days of expansion. The book then traces the business as a private limited company to its ultimate winding up, as the professional and personal differences between the parties destroy the business. In following this approach to the teaching and exposition of the subject, we hope to illustrate both the legal and practical reasons why persons choose these forms of business organisation to carry on their business affairs.

Thanks must go to Jeremy Stein for commissioning the work, for David Stott for his always careful and methodical approach in guiding the work through to fruition and to Catherine Minahan for a wonderful job in editing the book. As always thanks go to our families, but a special thanks must go to Kim Scanlan for putting up with a neurotic author during a too short leave of absence.

We have endeavoured to state the law as at April 2005.

AM

CW

GS

July 2005

Table of Cases

Table of Statutes and Statutory Instruments

Great Expectations Ltd – A History

In 1956, George, who had just left the Army after national service, started his own business as a furniture upholsterer. He had trained in this craft before his national service, but now wanted to be self-employed. He operated as a sole trader for many years, relying on his own high standards of work. His reputation became well-established and the business provided him with a comfortable living. His sons joined him in the business in the early 1970s when they left school. Bill was trained as an upholsterer, his father intending to pass the business on to him. Arthur, of whom his father had no very high opinion, was allowed to train as a bookkeeper so that he could make himself useful in the business. In due course both became partners in the firm (George 60%, Bill 30%, Arthur 10%). This rather uneasy partnership continued through the 1980s and early 1990s. It had always been understood that George would retire from the firm when he reached 65 (ie, 1994). Arthur was keen that at this point the firm should start to diversify into more general interior design work, and he had managed to persuade Bill that in preparation for this they should undertake a few small design contracts. Of course it was necessary to keep this information from George. One of the first such contracts was for a young merchant banker named Edwina, who was very impressed with the firm (the feeling was mutual).

Unfortunately George found out about this, and decided that he would not be able to retire after all, since Arthur and Bill obviously could not be trusted to uphold the traditions of the firm. Relations among the three of them became increasingly strained, and eventually Arthur threatened to petition for the dissolution of the firm, possibly citing George's alleged senility as a ground. This was around October 1997, and shortly afterwards Edwina lost her job following downsizing of her department at her merchant bank. Looking around for new projects, she thought of Arthur and Bill, and contacted them to discuss business opportunities. Arthur and Bill saw the prospect of developing the firm in many new ways, if supported by Edwina's energy and business acumen. George is outraged by the idea, but at nearly 70 he is tired and can no longer cope with the stress caused by all these new ideas and the threat of a petition for dissolution, so he reluctantly agrees to retire from the firm.

To mark the dawn of a bright new era in the history of the firm, Edwina suggests calling the business Great Expectations, and the three of them become equal partners, it being understood that management and development are to be left mostly to Edwina.

The business becomes reasonably successful, but the partners realise that further development will need additional capital. Edwina introduces them to Duncan, a former client of hers from her days as a merchant banker. Duncan is willing to invest a modest sum of money in the business in the expectation of getting a good return if the business succeeds. He also wants some control over the firm's activities in order to protect himself against the risk of loss, but does not want the full responsibilities of a partner.

Before long the practical difficulties of reconciling all these objectives lead them to the conclusion that the business will have to be incorporated, and in 2001 Great Expectations Ltd (GE) is formed, together with a 100% subsidiary, Great Expectations (Ideas) Ltd. The directors of both companies are Edwina and Bill, with Arthur as Company Secretary. Duncan becomes the major shareholder. Edwina, Arthur and Bill have lesser shareholdings. Bill also insists that Charlotte, his much-prized and long-serving secretary, should have at least a few shares. Further finance is obtained from the bank (Bus Bank) in the form of a term loan and an overdraft facility for which Edwina has given a personal guarantee to the bank. Table A is amended to give Edwina and Bill three votes per share on a resolution to remove them from the board, and to give Arthur similar rights in relation to any proposal to remove him as Company Secretary. Duncan is also given the right to attend board meetings, and in a separate Shareholder Agreement there is a provision for Duncan to require Edwina, Arthur and Bill to buy out his shareholding.

Initially the business is very successful, principally through the obtaining of a contract with Bleak House Ltd for the interior design of a very large block of flats in Central London. Arthur develops a taste for regular and lengthy holidays. Meanwhile Charlotte, who now acts as de facto Personnel Manager as well as covering for Arthur during his absences, persuades Bill that in view of the need to retain a skilled and highly motivated workforce, as much of the revenue as possible should be used to improve the lot of the workforce, rather than being kept for shareholders. Duncan has taken to exercising his right to attend board meetings, where he makes a nuisance of himself by disagreeing with the directors, and trying to rely on his power as the major shareholder. Edwina and Bill are forced to resort to reliance on the differing rules applying to board meetings and general meetings. They eventually resolve to look for ways of diluting Duncan's shareholding, so that they can change the Articles despite his opposition.

Edwina has introduced the company to the use of sophisticated contract terms and other financial management practices. Clients are always asked for a 10% deposit before any work is started, goods are always supplied under reservation of title clauses (many goods are bought by GE on the same terms, and GE always waits as long as possible before paying for these items) and as many as possible of the company's book debts are factored.

Despite these techniques it becomes apparent that the company has cash flow difficulties, and Edwina is advised by the company's accountant that very little profit is being made. On investigation it becomes apparent that Bleak House Ltd still owes the company substantial sums. The prospect of having to make a provision for an apparently bad debt is adversely affecting the final profit figure, as well as limiting the cash flow.

When the 2002 accounts are approved, only £80,000 is available for distribution. Edwina suggests getting round this through an artificial asset sales scheme. Alternatively it is proposed simply to return share capital to shareholders. Eventually a scheme is devised by which large salaries and/or consultancy fees are paid to the shareholders.

It is also apparent that further investment in the company is needed. Edwina is friendly with Frederick, a director of Ye Olde Curiosity Shoppe plc (YOCS), with which GE has done business. She persuades Frederick that YOCS should take a shareholding in GE, and Frederick sells this idea to the board of YOCS. The board of YOCS insists, however, on various amendments being made to the Articles of GE, including: a right to appoint two non-executive directors to the board and rights of pre-emption over and above their statutory rights. A Shareholders Agreement entered into at the same time gives YOCS the right to sell its shareholding to the existing shareholders within three years of the allotment. Frederick had already agreed in advance with Edwina (to whom he had taken a considerable shine) that in the event of YOCS passing over the opportunity, he would himself invest in GE. In the end YOCS does not take as many shares as GE would have liked. Frederick steps in and takes up the balance. Frederick's involvement was known to his father and brother (Chairman and Managing Director of YOCS respectively), although disclosure was never made to the board as a whole. This results in something of a scandal which is exposed at YOCS's next board meeting, the mood of which favoured instituting proceedings against Frederick for breach of fiduciary duty. Frederick's father and brother use their position and personal standing to avoid this, but the price is the removal of Frederick from the board.

Duncan at this stage exercises his rights under the Shareholder Agreement to have the others buy out his shareholding. Frederick, eager to leave the ranks of the unemployed, agrees with Arthur, Bill and Edwina to buy Duncan's shares in return for some financial assistance for the purchase from GE and a seat on the board. Even with this scheme they do not have enough money to buy all the shares, and GE buys them back.

When this new development in the history of GE becomes known to the board of YOCS, it resolves to use its best endeavours to retrieve its investment. The board is not feeling too sympathetic towards GE and, despite the interventions of Frederick's father and brother, the decision is made to pull out. Frederick's father, in a final gesture of family solidarity, introduces Frederick to a company with which he has connections and which specialises in corporate rescue, Hard Times plc.

Initial talks between GE and Hard Times were quite promising and a takeover seemed imminent. Unfortunately for GE, talks broke down when the 2003 accounts were published with a qualification as to the value of the stock.

The directors of GE have by this stage realised that there is very little hope for GE. In a last-ditch effort to save the company they applied to the court for an Administration Order. Bus Bank plc on the other hand have other ideas. They are heavily exposed where GE are concerned, and make the decision to appoint a receiver under their debenture.

For some time Edwina has been preparing for the worst. In 2003 she had set up a company, Great Expectations (Works) Ltd, which was created specifically to take on the more doubtful assets of GE, at book value, which included many bad debts. Charlotte and Frederick were appointed as directors, both of them being oblivious to Edwina's scheme. With her own immediate personal fortune in mind, Edwina is very concerned about the guarantee she gave to Bus Bank on incorporation. Naturally she wishes to see that her potential exposure is minimised. Bill is baffled – from being potential millionaire, he now discovers that he is penniless. Financial matters had from the start been dealt with by Edwina. Arthur is away on holiday. Frederick, the only director of any real wealth, is concerned with potential personal liability. He is attempting to distance himself from the whole affair.

The decision to place Great Expectations (Works) Ltd into a creditors' voluntary liquidation was made, it having served its purpose. At the same time it was resolved to wind up Great Expectations (Ideas) Ltd in a members' voluntary liquidation. Great Expectations Ltd is insolvent in every way, but Arthur, Bill, Charlotte, Edwina and Frederick are reluctant to let it die. They believe it has a future and decide to set up Great Expectations (2004) Ltd to help it overcome its liquidity problems. However, the creditors have lost patience, and Great Expectations Ltd is wound up on the petition of a creditor.

The liquidator dealing with GE is pleasantly surprised to find the accounts, including management accounts, in good order. He believes that there is a good chance of recovering money from the directors, both for maladministration and for misfeasance. In addition he intends to reopen certain transactions. He intends to send an adverse report to the Insolvency Service at the DTI concerning the conduct of GE's management.

A year later it became apparent that some of the work done by GE for Bleak House Ltd had been of very poor quality. Bleak House has now been restored to prosperity under new management, and wishes to sue GE for negligence/breach of contract. It therefore proposes to seek the restoration of GE to the Register, effectively to sue its liability insurers, since GE itself has no assets. It therefore becomes necessary to find the former shareholders of GE.

Charlotte and Frederick are living together and have set up a business as management consultants.

Duncan is busy with his trains.

Edwina has found another small firm, whose partners she is advising on the setting up of a company.

Bill is a self-employed upholsterer.

Arthur is on holiday.

THE PLAYERS

Arthur: born 1958. Bill's brother. Joined his father's business on leaving school, studied at night school (on his father's insistence) and is a qualified member of the Institute of Company Secretaries and Administrators. Married 1977, divorced 1982.

Bill: born 1956. Arthur's brother. Joined father's business on leaving school and was trained as an upholsterer with a view to succeeding his father. Has felt rather in the shadow of his father and is anxious to develop new ideas, so he is susceptible to imaginative schemes for this purpose.

Charlotte: born 1966. Left school at 15 without educational qualifications. Trained as a secretary. Married Walter in 1985. Two children, born 1987 and 1989. Involvement in business from 1990 transformed her personal and commercial skills, and made her aware of society's exploitation of women and more generally of the evils of the capitalist system. Divorced 1999. Active member of Greenpeace.

Duncan: born 1947. Started work in his father's business, but became frustrated and left to start his own business marketing a new kind of lintel which he had patented. The invention became very successful, and in 1995 he was able to sell the business to a public company for £3 million. Unmarried. A steam railway enthusiast, who spends most of his time engaged in this hobby.

Edwina: born 1965. Has a law degree and has worked as a merchant banker. Lost her job after the downsizing of her department in the merchant bank. A forceful and ambitious businesswoman. An early client of the interior design business.

Frederick: born 1963. Educated public school and Cambridge. Member of a wealthy family which controls YOCS (father is Chairman, elder brother is MD). Joined the firm on leaving university and became a director shortly afterwards.

Bleak House Ltd: Debtor of GE principally involved with developments in Docklands. Faced financial crisis in 2003.

Hard Times plc: Rescue specialist which considered assisting GE in 2004.

Ye Olde Curiosity Shoppe plc: Has business connections with GE in that it has consulted GE on various projects. Its business is mainly concerned with antiques, which are supplied to wealthy and discerning clients. Great Expectations has bought various items from YOCS on occasion.

Bus Bank plc: Edwina's former employers, who became involved with GE at about the same time as Edwina. Very much a hands-on bank, which has been in regular contact with GE management from the start. Monthly figures were part of the debenture contract, and cash-flow forecasts and creditor and debtor lists were regularly updated for the Bank's benefit.

Great Expectations (Ideas) Ltd: Created in 2001 to carry out promotional work for the GE group. 100% subsidiary. Directors Edwina and Bill.

Great Expectations (Works) Ltd: Created in 2003 to accept the group liabilities. 100% subsidiary. Directors Charlotte and Frederick.

1 Business Structures and Business Activity

LEARNING OUTCOMES

By the end of this chapter, you should understand:

- the definition and purpose of business law, and its relationship to business organisations;

- the various business structures adopted by small business enterprises, their form and relationship with the individuals involved in the business and with third parties dealing with those enterprises;

- business organisations which enjoy limited liability and those which do not;

- the evolution of and present role of the private limited company in business;

- the role of the European Union in the evolution of company law.

1.1 The purposes of business law

Business law is a term which has no clearly defined meaning in English law. It may be used to encompass much of company law and partnership law, as well as elements of the law relating to the sale and supply of goods and services, and such matters as intellectual property and even financial services. So wide a range of topics is naturally incapable of being readily subsumed within a single undergraduate course without unacceptable dilution of the depth of coverage, which may be one reason why English legal education has never developed a coherent notion of the meaning of the term. It is also true that neither the courts nor Parliament have made any attempt to delineate the subject as a fit topic for comprehensive legislation. Again, it would be difficult to do so, having regard to the range of subjects covered.

Despite this, there are good reasons for viewing these subjects as a related (if not necessarily coherent) whole. They all relate to the very important question of legal control of business activity. Developed Western societies are fundamentally reliant on business activity. Indeed, the great goal of economic growth, relentlessly pursued by virtually all governments in such countries, means no more than an increase in the level of business activity in the form of making, buying and selling goods and services. The notion of a recession, dreaded by all governments, is defined as two successive quarters in which the level of economic output declines. It is therefore clear that economic activity in the sense described is something which has to be encouraged, and our concern as lawyers must be to see how the law can help in that process.

At the same time it is readily apparent that not all economic activity is equally desirable. Some, such as the sale of hard drugs, whilst no doubt highly profitable, is generally regarded as entirely unacceptable and is punished with severe criminal penalties. In other cases the transaction itself may be acceptable, but the manner in which it is carried out may give rise to other problems – the sale of defective or dangerous goods provides an excellent example. Although criminal sanctions are not necessarily appropriate here – for example, the Consumer Protection Act 1987 may in some cases impose such sanctions, as may the Trade Descriptions Act 1968 in cases where the goods are misleadingly described – it is clear that the law has to intervene in some way in order to protect the purchaser. More difficult situations may arise where the seller of goods seeks to exclude liability for defects in them, under provisions such as those in the Unfair Contract Terms Act 1977.

The conclusion to be drawn from these examples is that the law must simultaneously facilitate desirable business activity and restrict, so far as possible, undesirable business activity. Telling the two categories apart is not always easy, and balancing the two objectives is frequently very difficult.

The examples above are readily understandable. What may be less obvious is the way in which the law relating to companies and partnerships fits into this overall scheme of business law. Two points need to be made. The first is that businesses of all kinds have both an internal and an external aspect. The internal aspect is concerned with the ways in which the business organises itself. It deals with matters such as who owns the business, who runs it (and how), who hires and fires workers, who ultimately receives the profits (if any). It is easy to see that questions about the structure to be adopted by any business, and about the legal rules governing the various structures, have much to do with this internal aspect of business. In recent years there has been growing interest in what are sometimes called the constitutional issues in connection with companies, or 'corporate governance', a term used mostly in relation to public companies. The second point is that the question of business structures also has implications for the external aspect of businesses. The external aspect is concerned with the way in which businesses relate to those not within the business. It deals with matters such as who has authority to enter into contracts on behalf of the business and who is liable if the business commits some breach of its legal obligations (including, but not limited to, such obligations in relation to the quality of goods supplied as were mentioned above).

The answers to many of the questions identified here (and others) depend at least partly on the form of business structure which has been adopted, and it is for this reason more than any other that the law regulating the different forms of business structure is worthy of serious attention.

1.2 The question of limited liability and disclosure

Perhaps the most important issue in relation to business structures is that of limited liability. An important theme of this book is the way in which the use of a company rather than a partnership can confer upon the owners of the business immunity from liability for the debts of that business beyond a nominal amount of their own capital which they have had to contribute in order to establish the business. This advantage is not available in a partnership, that is if we ignore the limited partnership and the limited liability partnership. It will be seen, however, that in practice there are many restrictions on the value of limited liability even in a company (see **Chapter 8**). At the same time, the requirement for companies to make public certain information about their activities, including accounts (see **Chapter 18**) and details of share holdings and directorships, has long been understood. Although such information must be made available to anyone interested, few people dealing with a company take advantage of it. Provisions in the Companies Act 1985 have reduced the auditing requirement for small private companies, and this reduces still further the effectiveness and importance of the disclosure requirements.

1.3 Companies in contemporary context

The legal structure which we now know as the limited company has been around since the middle of the 19th century in English law (the partnership, needing no formal structure, is much older). Although the basic legal form has not changed a great deal, the economic and social context within which companies operate has changed greatly. The Joint Stock Companies Act of 1856, perhaps the first recognisably modern company law statute, is clearly based on the much older idea that corporate status is a privilege, to be guarded jealously and given only to those who could satisfy restrictive criteria. Earlier statutes, such as the Joint Stock Companies Act 1844, did not recognise corporate personality, in the sense that they retained the unlimited liability of members for the debts of the company. The 1856 Act was also based on the notion of the company as a vehicle through which entrepreneurs might seek support from the public at large for some venture – often a very speculative one. A consequence of this was the expectation that those who had put up the capital for the business would not normally have any involvement in its day-to-day running. Naturally, they would not expect to have any liability for its debts either. Thus were born the modern notions of limited liability and the distinction between shareholders and directors. At this time it would have been assumed that a small business (perhaps typically a small family business) would have been run as a partnership.

The most important case in changing that perception was the decision of the House of Lords in *Saloman v Saloman* [1897] AC 22, HL, where it was held that the incorporation of a family business by Mr Saloman was effective to obtain the protection of the Companies Acts, notwithstanding that Mr Saloman remained the moving spirit behind the new business and was its main creditor. This recognition that the principle of limited liability was now readily available to anyone who could collect together the relatively modest amounts of capital needed to incorporate a company, may be regarded as the starting point of modern company law (as to this see further **Chapter 8**).

The century and more which has elapsed since that decision has seen a gradual transformation of legal and commercial attitudes to companies. In the present day the use of a company is very common, even for the smallest businesses. This has been encouraged by the emerging distinction between private and public companies, which has allowed small businesses to escape many of the more onerous regulatory requirements which are imposed on public companies. The rules on audit and certain of the rules relating to share issues and payment for shares may be cited as examples. There are more than 1 million companies on the Register of Companies, of which about 98% are private companies. This book concentrates almost entirely on the regulation of small businesses, and public companies accordingly receive only somewhat cursory treatment. A side-effect of the trend towards widespread use of the private company is that the partnership is in decline, though the limited partnership may be making something of a comeback after many years of disuse. Although many of the professions still require their members to practise individually or in partnerships (but with regard to solicitiors see the Administration of Justice Act 1985, s 59), the limited company is dominant elsewhere. This dominance presents its own problems for the application of company law. In many, perhaps most, private companies the directors and shareholders are the same people, a fact which renders redundant those aspects of the company law rules which seek to hold the balance between these two groups (see **Chapter 13**). One unfortunate consequence of this is that in many small companies there is no effective check on the behaviour of the directors, at least so long as the business remains a going concern (for possible liabilities when the business fails, see **Chapter 23**). However, these issues can begin to surface as soon as there is some disparity between the two classes. In practice this can often happen when a family company – perhaps founded originally by one person – reaches the second or third generation, shares having been left to various descendants of the founder, not all of whom wish to be actively involved in the management of the business. The business history which is used as the basis of this book conveniently compresses these and other developments into a shorter time span for the purposes of exposition and to improve the dramatic coherence of the plot. It will be appreciated that there are many other variations on this basic theme. Many of the issues discussed here can be understood more readily once the student has achieved some familiarity with the relevant legal rules. Accordingly, the final chapter of this book will discuss them again in the light of what is said in the intervening chapters.

1.4 Contract and status in partnership and company law

It is implicit in what has already been said that a partnership or a company is essentially a vehicle for the structuring and running of a business. The rules governing partnerships and companies should therefore be understood and evaluated in terms of their contribution to the objective of allowing the smooth running of businesses in both their internal and their external aspects. One question which must be considered in this context is the extent to which the rules governing these forms of business are, or ought to be, determined by the parties themselves and the extent to which the rules should be imposed by law. The former approach may be regarded as treating the business as essentially a contract, in which the parties are free to make their own terms; whereas the latter approach involves treating the business as an institution, in which the parties have a set status, which it is not open to them to alter. It would be naive to suppose that any business structure is exclusively a matter of contract or exclusively a matter of status. In fact, all such structures have elements of both, and the real question is which aspects of the business should be subject to which regime. Though adopting the contract theory in relation to single-member companies is clearly difficult, it is nevertheless important to understand that in such companies the single member determines many of the rules. The question of which regime governs the aspects of a business arises throughout this book, and the important point at this stage is that it should always be considered in terms of the objectives of business law discussed earlier.

1.5 International aspects of company law

All developed societies have some form of company law, or at least some law regulating business structures. In fact, in the Western world these rules are in their outlines conspicuously similar. This should not be regarded as surprising, since all these societies are grappling with the same basic economic and social questions as is the United Kingdom. At the same time there are important differences of detail, often arising from historical and cultural factors. These differences pose problems for those wishing to set up a business in another country (the European Union's response to these problems is discussed in **1.7** below). The alternative strategy of setting up a business in one's own country and then using it to do business elsewhere, is fraught with other difficulties. Such a business may find itself subject to the regulatory systems of two or more countries (since most countries, including the United Kingdom, exercise some control over foreign companies which do business in them). Questions about international business have become steadily more important in recent years as a result of the growing globalisation of world markets. Traditionally the issue was of importance primarily for a small number of very large multinational corporations, but it is now common to find much smaller businesses seeking to do business abroad. The question of the taxation of profits made in a foreign country is another important and difficult issue, but one which is beyond the scope of this book.

1.6 Some issues in modern company law

Company law is necessarily a dynamic subject. The underlying theme of this book may be said to be that a company (or any other business structure) is no more than a vehicle for facilitating and regulating the carrying on of business activities. In that sense the law relating to business structures should be seen as subservient to contemporary economic and social needs. As those needs change, so the rules and, more importantly, the practices of business law change. Thus, recent years have seen many changes in the practices of corporate finance, as well as in the relationship between shareholders and directors (see **Chapters 7** and **13**). At the same time there are always those who will seek to abuse for their own ends the opportunities and privileges which the law gives them. The fundamental point about companies is that they give their members limited liability for the company's debts, and this in turn results from the concept of corporate personality (see **Chapter 8**). An ongoing dilemma for company law is to what lengths it should carry these concepts. Their fundamental character cannot be denied, but difficulties arise where individuals use the apparent shield of incorporation as a means of carrying on fraudulent activities, often to the disadvantage of creditors. This may be dealt with either by disregarding the veil of incorporation and making members as such liable for the debts (see **Chapter 8**), or by imposing liability on directors as such (see **Chapter 23**). The statutory trend from the 1980s was in favour of greater personal liability of directors, though it is open to question how far the hopes of the legislators in this area have been realised.

The option of disregarding the corporate veil has always been available, but has not been the subject of significant legislation, except in the very narrow area of companies with one member, and even that has been overtaken by other developments. The courts have only rarely been willing to embrace this option, and there is little sign that this willingness has increased in recent years.

A more drastic way of dealing with abuse of corporate status is by preventing individuals from acting as directors of companies. This too became fashionable in the 1980s with the enactment of the Company Directors Disqualification Act 1986. The disqualification process is somewhat lengthy, and those charged with operating it have only limited resources.

These difficulties have led to more radical suggestions for reform, such as the introduction of a significant minimum capital requirement for private companies (at present these companies have no minimum capital rule, though rules of this kind are common in other Member States of the EC), or even the creation of a professional class of directors through requiring company directors to have some appropriate qualification before being allowed to act as such. Neither of these ideas found favour in the strong enterprise culture which prevailed in the United Kingdom during the late 20th century, but the continuing high level of company failure may bring about some change in the climate on this point.

1.7 The European Union dimension

Given the European Union's (EU's) essentially business and commercial orientation, it is not surprising that the questions about company law discussed at **1.6** above have attracted considerable attention at this level. There has been an extensive programme of harmonisation of company law rules, conducted through a series of Directives. Although some of the proposed Directives have stalled on controversial points, a good deal of progress has been made. However, a natural consequence of harmonisation by Directive is that differences of detail between national systems will remain, and it is clear that these differences are significant enough to be a problem in the conduct of trans-border business. In any event, it may be observed that even total identity between the various national systems of company law would not be sufficient to eliminate the problems, since companies also operate within the context of a more general private law regulating such things as contractual and tortious obligations, and these systems differ significantly between Member States. It seems unlikely that they can ever be harmonised.

Into this confused and confusing situation the EU has added two further complications. The first is the European Economic Interest Grouping (EEIG: see Regulation 2137/85), a form of unincorporated business entity which is intended to facilitate cross-border co-operation between small and medium-sized enterprises. Although EEIGs have been available since 1 July 1989, they have not yet made major inroads into business life within the Community, perhaps because of technical problems associated with them. The second complication is provided by the European Company or Societas Europea (see Regulation 2157/2001). The European 'Company' thus created is more or less the corporate equivalent of the EEIG. This corporate form is, however, intended for public companies, and is unsuitable as a business medium for any small businesses such as form the subject of this book; it is not considered further.

The question of the EU's involvement in company law is part of a much larger question about the completion of the Single European Market and the developing role of the EU more generally. Increased commercial pressure for the elimination of costly regulatory disparities may lead to greater uniformity in company law rules, but this trend is always liable to be impeded by a resurgence of nationalism within one or more of the Member States. The question is therefore not a purely technical one, and the uncertainties of the political process within the EU make predictions in this area very difficult.

FURTHER READING

O Kahn-Freund, 'Some Reflections on Company Law Reform' (1944) MLR 54.

G Scanlan, 'The Salomon Principle' (2004) Co Law 196.

A McGee and C Williams, *A Company Director's Liability for Wrongful Trading* (1992).

2 Partnership Formation and Relations between Partners

LEARNING OUTCOMES

By the end of this chapter, you should understand:

- the concept of the partnership as a business carried on in common with a view to profit;

- the sharing of profits and returns of a venture as evidence of the existence of a partnership;

- the relationship between the partners inter se, including the means by which the partners may conduct the business of the partnership and make management decisions;

- the fiduciary duties that all partners owe one another inter se;

- the dissolution of the partnership relationship – fixed term and partnerships at will;

- the dissolution of partnerships by operation of law and by court order;

- insolvency of partnerships;

- limited partnerships;

- limited liability partnerships.

SCENARIO

George trained in his youth as an upholsterer. In 1956 he left the Army and set up his own upholstering business, having decided that he was no longer prepared to work for others. George was a skilled craftsman of the old school: he believed in high quality work and providing a good service to customers. He also knew that upholstering was the only thing he could do, and that he must stick to what he knew. The business became successful in a small way and provided a modest living for George and his family. He had two sons, Bill and Arthur, and it was always his assumption that they would follow him into the family business. Neither was particularly successful at school, and in the early 1970s they came to work for the firm. Bill inherited some of his father's skills and proved a competent upholsterer. Arthur, by contrast, was useless with his hands. In fact, Arthur was a bit of a dreamer, who was always more interested in his leisure time than in his work. George rather despaired of the boy, but, in the hope of giving him something useful to do, made him go to night school to learn the principles of bookkeeping. After that Arthur looked after the firm's finances under George's stern supervision.

In the early 1980s Bill and Arthur were in turn taken into partnership with their father. Bill had to have a bigger stake in the business of course – he was the older brother, and anyway Arthur was just the bookkeeper. By 1992, George retained 60% of the profits, Bill 30% and Arthur 10%. Arthur and Bill were less than happy about this, but had always been too much in awe of their father to do anything about it. They had hoped that George would retire from the business in 1994, when he reached 65, but in the event George used the occasion of his 65th birthday party to announce that he intended to stay on another five years, since neither Bill nor Arthur was, in George's opinion, yet capable enough or old enough to be entrusted with the business. This uneasy state of affairs persisted, with George continuing to obstruct his sons in their work and Arthur and Bill for their part keeping secret the fact that they had begun to diversify into more general interior design work. It was at about this time that the brothers came into contact with a young businesswoman called Edwina, for whom they had undertaken a commission to design her apartment. George inevitably found out about their activities, and relations between the three of them became increasingly strained. Arthur, having exhausted his patience with his father, decided to resolve the situation once and for all. He threatened to petition for the dissolution of the firm on grounds of his father's senility. George, by this time worn out by the family rift, retired reluctantly from the business, having negotiated a modest annuity from the firm. Edwina, on the other hand, was so impressed by the abilities of the two brothers and the quality of the service provided that she decided to join them as managing partner, on the understanding that she would use her managerial and entrepreneurial skills to assist an expansion. It was agreed that they would all become equal partners in the new firm, the calculation of Edwina's contribution being based upon a book valuation of the assets of the firm. Edwina agreed to a further contribution of £15,000 to ease the firm's cash flow. Her first major accomplishment was to introduce them to a wealthy businessman, Duncan, who was looking for an up and coming business in which to invest. The second was to suggest that the firm be known henceforth as 'Great Expectations'. Duncan's investment, although modest, was enough to provide sufficient working capital to give the new firm a sound base from which to begin a period of steady expansion. The loan agreement executed between the firm and Duncan provided that Duncan's repayments would fluctuate with the success of the firm, an attractive feature to the partners as it presented an opportunity to avoid being unduly burdened with repayments until the firm was up on its feet. Thereafter, all parties agreed that it was highly desirable and beneficial for the business that all contributors, including Duncan, should benefit from its success.

OVERVIEW

We are dealing here with a business which has been in existence for some time, and which, like many such businesses, is run as a partnership, having started out being owned entirely by one man – George. It is unlikely that the choice of a partnership was a considered one; rather, it may be surmised that George took his sons into partnership because that seemed the obvious thing to do and because he had never had cause to be aware that any other form of business organisation might be suitable.

The most important features of a partnership are that it can come into existence without the need for any formalities, that it has no legal personality separate from that of its members (see Partnership Act 1890, s 4), and that the partners have unlimited liability for its debts. Legal intervention or regulation of the activities of a partnership is minimal, reflecting the essentially contractual nature of the relationship.

2.1 Sole traders

Before examining the implications of partnership, it is worth spending a little time on the position of the sole trader. A sole trader is a person who is in business on his own account, not operating through the medium of a limited company and not in partnership with anyone else, though he may of course have employees. A question of some importance in considering the position of those who work with or for a sole trader is to decide whether they are truly employees, or whether they in fact satisfy the tests for partnership as laid down in the Partnership Act 1890, so that a partnership has come into existence between the parties. Similarly, the question should be asked of those who have some financial involvement with the business – are they in truth a partner, or a financier?

Where it is decided that the apparent owner of the business is in truth a sole trader, the result is that he will receive all the profits of the business, but will also be liable without limit for the debts of the business. The status of sole trader is thus well suited to a person who likes to work alone and who is prepared to accept the pressures and risks which follow naturally from that arrangement. However, many of those who begin as sole traders in time decide that a partnership would be a sensible way to share the burden or to obtain additional capital, or to enable the business to grow through the importation of the skills and energy of a second person.

2.2 The Partnership Act 1890

The affairs of partnerships are in principle regulated by the Partnership Act 1890. This statute is largely declaratory of the pre-existing rules of the common law and equity. It is no doubt partly for this reason that the Act is mostly couched in straightforward language, relatively easily accessible even to non-lawyers. The common law rules were based upon the assumption that to a large extent the arrangements between partners could be dealt with quite adequately through contract, although it was recognised that such agreements would not always provide sufficient protection for parties who dealt with the firm. In any event, third parties would not be privy to the contract between the partners and the law had to provide a set of rules which regulated their dealings with such a business. It is possible for third parties to enter into contracts with the firm which provide expressly for such matters, though this is very uncommon in practice.

The Partnership Act rules may conveniently be divided into two types: those which can be excluded by agreement among the partners, and those which cannot. As might be expected, the former are generally those rules which relate to the relationship between partners, whereas the latter are those which relate to relationships between partners and outsiders. It is the former category of rules which is the subject of this chapter; the latter category is dealt with in **Chapter 3**.

2.3 The Existence of a partnership

Section 1 of the Partnership Act 1890 defines partnership as 'the relation which subsists between persons carrying on a business in common with a view of profit'. This simple form of words presents a number of difficulties. It is to be noted that s 1(2) then excludes from this definition any company registered under the Companies Acts, since these bodies have their own set of statutory rules.

The first point to be made is that the existence of a partnership is a question of fact. It does not depend on the intention of the parties to form a partnership, neither does it require anything in the way of formalities – there is no need for any written record of the fact of the partnership. This provides a marked contrast between partnerships and companies (as to this, see **Chapters 6** and **7**).

It is necessary that the persons concerned be carrying on a 'business', which is defined in s 45 as including 'every trade, occupation, or profession'. Furthermore, this business must be carried on 'in common' and 'with a view of profit' (see *Conroy v Kenny* [1999] 1 WLR 1340; as to when the business commences, see *Khan v Miah* [2000] 1 WLR 2123). Thus, associations of persons formed for a non-profit making purpose cannot in law amount to partnerships. Although these expressions in s 1 are not further defined in the Act itself, s 2 does give some guidance as to the factors to be taken into account when deciding whether or not a partnership exists in any given case.

First, joint ownership of property (whether under a joint tenancy or under a tenancy in common) does not automatically create a partnership, even where the co-owners share profits arising from the use of the property. In the great majority of cases, people who satisfy this definition will not be partners for the purposes of the Act. Such people might not be carrying on business in common, and the partnership framework is intended to be available to businesses comprising two or more persons who pool their respective resources for the benefit of the business itself (see s 2(1)).

Second, the fact of sharing gross returns from property or the provision of goods or services, does not of itself create a partnership. Again this does not suggest any joint enterprise between individuals, as expenses and costs would be borne after gross returns are shared out. The sharing of net profits by contrast would be very strong evidence of partnership (see s 2(2)).

Third, the receipt by a person of a share in the net profits of a business is prima facie evidence that he is a partner, but it is not conclusive. In particular, the payment out of the profits of debts or remuneration, or annuities to the dependants of deceased former partners, does not of itself make the recipient a partner in the business, neither does a payment out of the profits of an annuity in respect of the sale of goodwill, or payments of interest on a loan at a rate determined by the level of profits of the business. Schemes of this kind are a very common way of making provision for retired partners and their families, as was done for George when he retired from the firm. On the other hand, virtually all other cases of the receipt of a share of profits are in practice likely to be treated as creating a partnership. Receipt of a share of profits is without doubt the strongest and best evidence of a partnership. Such evidence is stated by the section itself to be prima facie evidence of the existence of a partnership, although the case law suggests that it will be treated as a factor which is necessary but not sufficient for the existence of a partnership (*Pooley v Driver* (1877) 5 ChD 458). The courts will look to the business itself and the nature of the relationship between the parties before applying the section. A debtor–creditor relationship will not give rise to a partnership, whereas a scheme whereby the financier intends to be involved in the partnership but does not intend to incur the liabilities of a partner may or may not, depending upon the substance of the matter (see s 2(3)).

The long and rather complex list of examples in s 2(3) may be taken as exemplifying a simple notion, itself contained in s 1(1), namely, that partnership depends on the fact of carrying on business in common, and that the recipients of the payments described in this list cannot be said to be carrying on business because they have no involvement in the management and running of the business, and do not in truth accept the liabilities of the firm. A more difficult scenario is presented when a financier seeks involvement in profits yet wishes to avoid any liabilities of the firm. Duncan is such an individual and, provided his position is not combined with any form of control over the business, the relationship would probably be recognised as one of debtor–creditor (see also *Re Megavand, ex p Delhasse* (1878) 7 ChD 511). It is suggested that involvement and control are the essential elements on which to concentrate when considering who is and who is not a partner. Thus, in the case of *Pooley v Driver*, noted above, Jessel MR noted the following:

> ... the person advancing must be a real lender; ... the advance must be a real loan; and consequently you come back to the question whether the persons who entered into the contract of association are really in the position of creditor and debtor, or in the position of partners ... the Act does not decide for you.

A further implication for Duncan is the effect this loan agreement will have on his position as creditor in the event that the firm is dissolved. Section 3 of the 1890 Act provides that a lender whose loan is in consideration for a share of the profits of the business will have his debt postponed to all the other creditors of the firm. This means that Duncan is incurring considerable risk in investing in this business, in that, if the firm were to become insolvent, he will be unable to recoup anything in respect of that proportion of the loan which is to be repaid out of a share of the profits until the firm's other debtors have been satisfied. In respect of the amount which is to be repaid at a fixed rate, Duncan's position will not be affected.

Charlotte, Bill's secretary (see **Great Expectations Ltd – A History**, above), provides another convenient illustration of these rules. She is an invaluable member of the firm, but it is reasonably clear that she is not a partner. She is paid a salary for her work, and this salary does not depend on the level of profits made by the firm. She does not take any part in the management of the firm and has not invested any of her own capital in it. Even if she were to be accorded the title 'partner', this could not of itself transform her role into that of a partner. Attempts to use the label as a convenience for taxation purposes or otherwise have failed (see, eg, *E Rennison & Son v Minister of Social Security* (1970) 10 KIR 65; *Saywell v Pope* [1979] STC 824).

It is, however, important to understand that the tests provided in s 2(3) are merely guidelines. Whether or not a partnership exists in any given case is a question of fact, which does not depend solely on the documents which the parties have executed or even exclusively on their intentions (*Northern Sales (1963) Ltd v Ministry of National Revenue* (1973) 37 DLR (3d) 612).

2.4 Using a business name

Although a partnership is not a separate legal person, it is usually convenient to adopt a single name for the firm as a whole. Section 4 of the Partnership Act 1890 expressly contemplates that this will be done. The choice of 'Great Expectations' provides an example of this. Because there is no longer a register of names used by firms, there is no need for the partners in Great Expectations to register their firm's name. Before 1982 a register was kept and all firms had to register at a central registry by virtue of the Registration of Business Names Act 1916. Some control is still exercised over the use of business names, however, by the Business Names Act 1985. These controls relate to the prohibition of use of certain business names (the 1985 Act, s 2) and the restriction on the use of certain words or expressions without first obtaining the approval of the Secretary of State or other government department specified by him (the 1985 Act, s 3). These words and expressions are specified in the Company and Business Names Regulations 1981 (SI 1981/1685) as amended, and include words such as English, European, King, Royal and Windsor.

Assuming that that particular pitfall is avoided and the business name chosen does not cause a breach of ss 2 and 3, the firm will find that it is subject to the disclosure requirements of the Business Names Act 1985 contained in s 4. This is an example of the law intervening where some regulation is recognised as being necessary for the functioning of this particular business activity. It simply ensures that third parties are aware of the identity of the person or persons with whom they are dealing, and requires the disclosure, in the case of a partnership, of the names of each partner (see the 1985 Act, s 4(1)(a)(i)) in legible characters on all business letters, written orders for goods or services to be supplied to the business, invoices and receipts issued in the course of the business and written demands for payment of debts arising in the course of the business. Furthermore, in any premises where the business is carried on and to which the customers of the business or suppliers of any goods or services to the business have access, the names and address of the partners must be displayed in a prominent position. The disclosure requirements will be satisfied by keeping a list of all partners at the firm's principal place of business where there are more than 20 partners (s 4(3)).

Recognition of the need to regulate disclosure in this way does not extend to a recognition that breach of these requirements should be the subject of any onerous sanction. Having made the matter one which should be in the contemplation of the parties, the law leaves it to them to see that it is complied with. Consequently, third parties who deal with businesses are, or ought to be, aware of the need to establish the identity of the other party. The sanction provided by s 5 for breach of s 4 lacks teeth. Section 5 provides that any legal proceedings brought by a person to whom the Act applies, to enforce a right arising out of contract made when he was in breach of s 4, shall be dismissed if the defendant to the proceedings shows that, by reason of the breach, he has been unable to pursue a claim against the offending business or that he has suffered some financial loss. So if, for example, Great Expectations was in breach of s 4 because it failed to disclose the names of the partners on its stationery, it would not be able to pursue a claim in contract against a customer who has failed to pay sums owing *provided* that customer could show that, as a result of the firm's breach of s 4, he was unable to pursue a claim against the firm or suffered some financial loss in connection with the contract, a fact which could be difficult to establish.

The Business Names Act 1985 does not prevent more than one business using the same or a similar name (see **Chapter 6**, where this function of the index of company names is discussed). Indeed, sole traders, partnerships and companies can all trade under a business name, subject of course to the disclosure requirements, and the same or a similar name could be used by many different types and sizes of business. A business which seeks to reserve the use of a particular name to itself, is unable to do so unless it can establish that for others to use it amounts to the tort of passing off, which may prove difficult to substantiate (see **Chapter 6**).

2.5 Relations between partners

The organisation of the business is very much a matter for the partners to agree between themselves. The framework provided in s 24 of the Partnership Act 1890 identifies the major issues which the partners need to resolve between themselves and provides a set of rules based upon the notion of equality in all matters. The provisions of the Act can be amended or excluded by the partners in this respect as they see fit for their own particular business and the individuals involved. Regulation of the partners' conduct is not, however, a matter which is entirely free from legal intervention. In addition to the contract between them, which may or may not adopt the various provisions of the Partnership Act which are applicable, the Act intervenes to regulate their conduct as partners to a considerable extent. This is because the relationship which subsists between partners is of a fiduciary character. In this sense it is similar to the relationship between solicitor and client and the relationship between trustee and beneficiary, though it is not identical to either of these relationships. A number of specific features of this relationship may be identified. Partners owe each other:

(a) a duty of good faith;

(b) a duty to account to each other in relation to their partnership dealings (see s 28 and *Law v Law* [1905] 1 Ch 140); and

(c) a duty not to make a secret profit out of their position as partners (see s 29 *Bentley v Craven* (1853) 18 Beav 75).

These obligations stem from the fiduciary duties imposed on fiduciaries by equity. The Partnership Act 1890, ss 28-30 merely stipulate expressly three fiduciary duties, although it is important to remember that equity knows no boundaries (see further *Floydd v Cheney* [1970] Ch 602).

Before turning to consider these equitable rules, discussion of the rules which govern the internal framework of the business, and which will therefore be of the utmost importance to the partners, is justified.

2.5.1 Management of the business

These are the rules governing the participation of partners in the management of the business and are contained in the Partnership Act, 1890 s 24. They are as follows.

2.5.1.1 Presumption of equal shares and equal liabilities

All partners are entitled to share equally in the capital and profits of the business, and must contribute equally towards the losses, whether of capital or otherwise sustained by the firm.

This rule exemplifies one of the most important assumptions made by the Partnership Act 1890, namely, that all partnerships are equal partnerships. It will be appreciated that this rule is very frequently excluded in practice in relation to capital, or profits or both. In the scenario, George, Arthur and Bill were far from equal in their respective interests in the firm. In some cases the profit shares may not even be in the same proportion as the contributions of capital. The rule that all partners must contribute equally to losses does not, of course, prevent outsiders from suing any of the partners for the full amount of any debts owed by the firm, in accordance with ss 9 and 12 of the Act (see further **Chapter 3**). It means only that, as between themselves, the partners are equally liable and must indemnify each other to the extent necessary to achieve equal contributions. This point may be deduced also from the next rule.

2.5.1.2 Right of indemnity

The firm must indemnify every partner in respect of payments made and personal liabilities incurred by him:

(a) in the ordinary and proper conduct of the business of the firm;

(b) in or about anything necessarily done for the preservation of the business or property of the firm.

In addition to emphasising the point made at 2.5.1.1 above, that as between themselves partners are equally liable for the debts of the firm, this rule entitles partners to defray legitimate costs and expenses out of partnership funds.

2.5.1.3 Right of interest in respect of payments in excess of agreed capital contribution

A partner making, for the purpose of the partnership, any actual payment or advance beyond the amount of capital which he has agreed to subscribe, is entitled to interest at the rate of 5% per annum from the date of the payment or advance.

The scope of this rule is more limited than may at first appear. It applies only to the case where a partner puts into the firm capital above and beyond that which he has agreed to subscribe. There is no right to any interest on the agreed *capital subscription*, but the position is different where additional capital is contributed. Interest is permitted in this situation because the partner in effect becomes a creditor of the firm to the extent of the further advance; he occupies two capacities in relation to the firm, that of partner and creditor, for as long as the further advance remains outstanding.

It is usual to provide for the payment of interest on additional capital, but a fixed rate of 5% per annum is not usually considered appropriate at the present day. Two distinctive features of interest rates over the past 20 years or so have been that they have been very variable and that they have nearly always, until the most recent past, been well in excess of 5% per annum. A more common provision in a modern partnership deed would be that the rate of interest was to be *x*% above the base lending rate for the time being of a specified bank. The value of x in this equation is of course a matter for negotiation, but it is appropriate to take into account the rate of interest which the lender could obtain elsewhere, as well as the rate of interest which the firm would have to pay in order to obtain the same funds from other sources.

2.5.1.4 Payments of interest on capital subscribed are payments out of profits

A partner is not entitled, before the ascertainment of profits, to interest on the capital subscribed by him.

This is the corollary to the rule discussed at **2.5.1.3** above, and makes clear that payments of interest on capital *subscribed* are in fact payments out of profits. This rule therefore has no application to additional contributions. In the scenario, Edwina is in the position of having agreed to become an equal partner in the firm; however, she has also agreed to contribute a further sum to the firm, and it is in respect of this further sum that she will be entitled to interest. A further significance of this rule is that interest should be paid according to the agreed profit shares, not according to the level of capital contribution, should that be different. In practice the first of these respects is the more important and the more problematic. It is usual to exclude this rule and to provide for the payment of interest on capital at a specified rate. This is of course especially important where the capital contribution ratios and the profit sharing ratios are not identical. The determination of the rate of interest is again a matter for negotiation, but it must be remembered that the firm is merely paying out its own capital to its own members. Obviously, a firm which regularly pays out more capital than it can really afford is soon going to get into financial difficulties, and this practical consideration tends to limit the rate at which interest is paid. Another instructive comparison in relation to this rule is that with the position in company law. Partners' capital contributions may be likened to the share capital of a company, but it is illegal for a company to pay interest on share capital, or in any way to return it to the shareholders (see further **Chapter 17**). The only payments which may be made in respect of share capital are dividend payments, which may only be financed out of profits available for the purpose (see **Chapter 16**).

2.5.1.5 Every partner may take part in the management of the partnership business

This is another fundamental rule of the Partnership Act 1890 (see s 24(5)). The assumption made by that Act is that all partners are active in the business. Given the prospect of unlimited liability to creditors, it is likely that all partners would wish to be active in the business, and it is not usual to exclude the *right* to participate in management, even where it is contemplated that some partners will take a relatively limited role in management. Where a prospective partner does not wish to manage and does not wish to accept the liabilities which accompany partnership, it is desirable to consider either a limited partnership under the Limited Partnerships Act 1907, or the formation of a limited company in which the inactive partner can be a shareholder but not a director. Consideration could also be given to a limited liability partnership. Although there is no one presently active in Great Expectations for whom any of these would be a realistic option, Duncan's modest investment in the firm was on a trial basis with a view to increasing both his stake and involvement in the business should it prosper. This issue is indeed raised in **Chapter 6**.

2.5.1.6 No partner shall be entitled to remuneration for acting in the partnership business

This rule (see s 24(6)) does not mean that no partner can ever receive any money from the business; it simply creates a presumption that partners receive their return exclusively in the form of profit share. Although the rule is sometimes excluded so as to give partners a certain guaranteed minimum income, it must again be remembered that such a scheme is unworkable in the long run unless the firm makes enough profit to support these payments. Whether such returns are called 'drawings' or 'salaries', the fact remains that they are in fact a return of profit.

2.5.1.7 No person may be introduced as a partner without the consent of all existing partners

This rule is perhaps best considered in conjunction with the rule discussed in **2.5.1.8** below. The two taken together illustrate the principle that day-to-day decisions may be taken by majority vote, but more serious matters require unanimity. This point is raised again in **Chapter 3** when we look at the scope of a partner's usual authority when acting on behalf of the firm (see *Rowella Pty Ltd v Hoult* [1988] 2 Qd R 80). The introduction of a new partner is naturally regarded as a matter serious enough to require unanimity. It is not usual to vary this rule (see *Highley v Walker* (1910) 26 TLR 685).

2.5.1.8 Ordinary matters – majority decision

Any difference arising as to ordinary matters connected with the partnership business may be decided by a majority of the partners, but no change may be made in the nature of the partnership business without the consent of all existing partners.

This is the basic decision-making procedure in partnerships, namely, majority vote of the partners on the basis of one vote each. The rules set out at **2.5.1.7** and **2.5.1.8** together create only two exceptions to that principle, ie changes in the nature of the business and introduction of a new partner, both of which require unanimity. It is again instructive to compare the corresponding rules in company law (see **Chapters 9** and **13**), where some matters require only a simple majority of the shareholders, whereas others require a three-quarters majority. At meetings of the board of directors, by contrast, everything is decided by simple majority. The simplicity of the rules adopted in the Partnership Act 1890 reflects both the culture of equality which the Act embodies and the refusal of the draftsman to enter into the calculation of detailed solutions which could then be undone by agreement among the partners. In practice it is quite common to see variations of these two rules. In large partnerships a system of weighted voting rights is often adopted in order to give more influence to the more senior partners (who may also have invested more capital in the firm), and occasionally certain questions are declared to be subject to their own specialised procedure.

2.5.1.9 The partnership books

The partnership books are to be kept at the place of business of the partnership (or the principal place, if there is more than one), and every partner may, when he thinks fit, have access to and inspect and copy any of them.

This is probably the least important of the s 24 rules from the point of view of the running of a firm. It merely ensures that full information about the state of the firm's finances is readily available to every partner, a desirable step in view of partners' unlimited liability for the firm's debts (see *Bevan v Webb* [1901] 2 Ch 59, where a valuer instructed by the dormant partners in a firm was held to be entitled to inspect the books in order to assist the dormant partners to evaluate their share).

2.5.2 Fiduciary obligations

So far we have looked at matters that affect the partners which can be varied by the partners themselves agreeing to a different strategy. What the partners cannot agree to exclude are the rules of equity which govern their behaviour towards each other. These rules spring from the relationship, which is of a fiduciary character, and impose a duty of good faith on all partners (see *Const v Harris* (1824) Turn & R 496).

2.5.2.1 The duty of good faith

This duty is explored again in **Chapter 10**, where we look at the duties owed by the directors and, to some extent, the shareholders of Great Expectations Ltd (see **Chapter 7**) to the company itself. Discharging this duty to the company requires the individuals to act in its best interests, which includes, *inter alia*, the interests of the other members. In partnership law, the requirement of good faith overrides all activities of the partners, including the exercise of any power of expulsion included in the agreement (see *Green v Howell* [1910] 1 Ch 495; *Peyton v Mindham* [1972] 1 WLR 8) and any decision to dissolve the partnership (see *Floydd v Cheney* [1970] Ch 602), and the three sections which concern the fiduciary duties of partners must be read with this in mind (see **2.5.2.2** to **2.5.2.4** below). These provisions simply deal with three aspects of the requirement for good faith, which as a duty springs from equity and which has no fixed boundaries.

2.5.2.2 Section 28: Duty of partners to render accounts

> Partners are bound to render true accounts and full information of all things affecting the partnership to any partner or his legal representatives.

This provision is illustrated by the case of *Law v Law* [1905] 1 Ch 140 where one of the two partners in the firm, who took a minor role in its management, sold his share to the other partner at a price which did not reflect the true value of his share. The court held that the true value should have been disclosed to him, and the failure to do so was sufficient to render the contract voidable.

2.5.2.3 Section 29: Accountability of partners for private profits

> Every partner must account to the firm for any benefit derived by him without the consent of the other partners from any transaction concerning the partnership, or from any use by him of the partnership property name or business connection.

The nature of this duty is discussed further in **Chapter 10** concerning the duties of company directors not to make a secret or unauthorised profit. It stems from the strict duty imposed upon trustees not to profit from their trust (*Keech v Sandford* (1726) Ch Cas 61). In the commercial context it refers to a profit which is secret and unauthorised, and which has arisen by virtue of the partner's position as partner, or from use of partnership assets or connections (or, in company law, from the director's position as director, or from the use of company assets or connections, see further **Chapter 10**). A good illustration is provided in the case of *Bentley v Craven* (1853) 18 Beav 75, where one partner kept for himself a discount obtained on the purchase of sugar for his firm which operated a sugar refinery. The court ordered him to account to his fellow partners for the profit he had made out of the transactions. Similarly, in *Pathirana v Pathirana* [1967] 1 AC 233, one partner in a firm, who had used a partnership asset to his own advantage, was required to account to his fellow partner for it. It is of course possible for the partners to agree between themselves some form of arrangement by which they consent to the receipt of profits by any of their number.

2.5.2.4 Section 30: duty of partner not to compete with firm

If a partner, without the consent of the other partners, carries on any business of the same nature as and competing with that of the firm, he must account for and pay over to the firm all profits made by him in that business.

This section can be used as an aid to interpreting s 29 (see **2.5.2.3**), which imposed a duty to account. It is useful in that it can limit the extent to which s 29 is applicable, for example where a partner has used partnership connections to make a secret profit but the use of it was in a different type of business. To make use of his position as partner to his advantage but without any competitive element affecting the firm, may therefore not amount to breach of duty (*Aas v Benham* [1891] 2 Ch 244). Section 29, however, does not require any form of competition where misuse of a partnership asset is concerned. It is likely that breach of the duty of good faith as exemplified in these provisions will result in some degree of overlap in these requirements (see further *Trimble v Goldberg* [1906] AC 494).

2.6 Dissolution of partnerships

2.6.1 Partnerships at will

There are various ways in which a partnership may come to an end. Under s 26 of the Partnership Act, 1890, every partnership is deemed to be a partnership at will; accordingly, any partner may dissolve it merely by giving the other partners notice of his intention to do so. The notice need not be in writing (though from an evidential point of view there are obvious advantages in written notice) and is effective as soon as it is received. The ease with which the 1890 Act allows the dissolution of partnerships is unacceptable to most firms because it creates uncertainty and makes any form of long-term planning for the firm very difficult, and this provision is therefore very commonly excluded. Any alternative version may be substituted, but there are a number of common arrangements which merit discussion here.

2.6.2 Fixed-term partnerships

It is possible to have a fixed-term partnership, ie one in which the partners are not at liberty to dissolve the firm within the fixed term, but which will automatically come to an end on the expiry of the term. Although this provides greater certainty, it is not normally considered adequate by itself, since it cannot usually be decided in advance that the partners will want to dissolve the firm at the end of the fixed term – if things go well, they are likely to want to continue. At the same time, the fixed term does lock the partners into the firm for the duration of the term even if things do not go well, though it is of course possible to abrogate the fixed-term element of the partnership if all partners agree.

Another solution is not to have a fixed term at all, but to require the giving of some period of notice where a partner wishes to dissolve the firm. Periods of three, six or 12 months' notice are commonly found. A solution of this kind allows reasonable flexibility for partners to leave the firm if they so wish, whilst also giving the remaining partners time to plan for the consequences of the change.

When a partnership is first formed it is quite common to combine the above two solutions. It may seem desirable that all partners should in any event give the firm a reasonable chance to succeed by committing themselves to the firm for an initial period of up to three years, but that thereafter any partner should be able to leave on the giving of reasonable notice, the period of notice required to be specified rather than being left merely as 'reasonable' notice.

2.6.3 Automatic dissolution

The Partnership Act 1890 provides for the automatic dissolution of a partnership in certain circumstances. These are listed in s 33 of the Act, and are as follows.

2.6.3.1 Death of a partner

Under the Partnership Act 1890, the entire firm is dissolved if any one of the partners dies. In practice this rule is obviously extremely inconvenient, and for that reason it is commonly excluded so that the firm can continue, though arrangements have to be made to buy out the share of the deceased partner, since the continuing partners will not normally want to be obliged to take the heirs of the deceased partner into the firm with them. (Insurance cover would be advisable on the lives of all partners so as to enable the deceased partner's share of the firm to be purchased with minimum financial disruption to the business.)

2.6.3.2 Bankruptcy

The bankruptcy of any partner is similarly a ground of automatic dissolution of the partnership. This rule too is commonly excluded in view of its unfortunate consequences, though it is usual to provide that the bankrupt partner shall cease to be a partner on becoming bankrupt.

2.6.4 Dissolution under s 34

Under s 34 of the Partnership Act 1890, where it is illegal for a particular person to be or remain a partner, the partnership is dissolved. The Act provides that the partnership is dissolved not only as regards that person, but also as regards the other partners. The most common instance of this happening occurs in partnerships of professional persons, where one of the partners ceases to hold the necessary professional qualification (see *Hudgell Yeates & Co v Watson* [1978] 2 All ER 363), perhaps as a result of disciplinary proceedings against him, though the same result would of course be reached if one of the purported partners were disqualified at the outset of the partnership. This result is obviously highly inconvenient, but it is not possible to exclude it. The best that can be done is to insert into the partnership agreement a clause to the effect that in these circumstances the remaining partners will immediately reform a new partnership excluding the person who is disqualified. This clause should be expressly declared to be one which will survive the dissolution of the partnership under s 34.

2.6.5 Dissolution by order of the Court

Section 35 of the Partnership Act 1890 allows the court to order the dissolution of a partnership on the application of any of the partners, or any creditor of the firm. This is a discretionary power, available only in the circumstances specified in s 35. These are as follows:

(a) that a partner, other than the partner suing, becomes permanently incapable of performing his part of the partnership contract;

(b) that a partner, other than the partner suing, has been guilty of such conduct as, in the opinion of the court, regard being had to the nature of the business, is calculated prejudicially to affect the carrying on of the business;

(c) that a partner, other than the partner suing, wilfully or persistently commits a breach of the partnership agreement, or otherwise so conducts himself in matters relating to the partnership business that it is not reasonably practicable for the other partner or partners to carry on the business in partnership with him;

(d) that the business of the partnership can only be carried on at a loss;

(e) that circumstances have arisen which, in the opinion of the court, render it just and equitable that the partnership be dissolved.

Section 35 needs to be understood in conjunction with other provisions of the Act. The first three grounds are all matters which are commonly the subject of express clauses in well-drafted partnership deeds. The reason for this is that the Partnership Act provisions do not allow any other satisfactory resolution of the problems to which these three grounds refer. Incapacity to perform, whether through mental illness or otherwise, does not automatically dissolve the partnership, neither does it give an automatic right to terminate a fixed-term partnership. Similarly, misconduct or other unreasonable forms of behaviour are not in themselves grounds for termination, and there is no right under the Partnership Act to expel a partner, however serious his breaches of the partnership agreement. Thus, s 35 provides a fallback solution for partnerships which have not dealt with these matters by means of an express clause. The disadvantages of being forced to use s 35 are obvious. The need to resort to litigation produces expense, uncertainty and delay, all of which can be avoided by proper drafting.

The fourth ground for dissolution by the court (see (d) above) is somewhat different from the others, in that it does not necessarily rest on any form of wrongdoing by any of the partners.

It deals with the situation where there is a dispute between the partners as to whether it is possible to make the business profitable. The wording of the provision shows that the petitioner must establish that making a profit is impossible, not merely that no profit is being made at the present time (see the comments of Farwell J in *Handyside v Campbell* (1901) 17 TLR 623). In many cases this fact will be obvious to the partners, who will be only too glad to dissolve the business. In others it may be possible to take advantage of a notice provision.

The final ground (see (e) above), which is clearly intended as a sweeping-up provision to deal with cases which cannot be foreseen in any detail, is to be regarded as a remedy of last resort, used only where the firm has become subject to irreconcilable differences which make its continued operation impossible. The exercise of this discretion by the court may be compared with the exercise of the similar power in relation to companies under s 122(1)(g) of the Insolvency Act 1986 (as to this, see **Chapter 14**). The analogy with the corresponding provision of the Insolvency Act 1986 in relation to companies suggests that the range of situations in which the provision may be invoked with respect to partnerships is potentially unlimited, but that in practice it will be used sparingly.

It is important to note that in all s 35 applications the court has discretion as to the best solution it may adopt with respect to a partnership. Thus, it is not sufficient to show that the circumstances specified in s 35 exist; the petitioner must also establish that in the light of those circumstances dissolution of the partnership is the best available option. However, the court does not have power to take alternative steps which are not authorised by the Partnership Act 1890. Thus, where the petition is based on serious breaches of the partnership agreement, s 35 does not empower the court to expel the miscreant partner (contrast the position in company law, where a petition under the Companies Act 1985, s 459 may be preferable to winding up due to the wide range of remedies available to the court). On the other hand, if the partnership agreement contains an expulsion clause, the court may well take the view that the other partners ought to use this clause, thereby keeping the partnership in existence as regards the remaining partners, rather than petitioning for the dissolution of the entire partnership.

2.6.6 Consequences of dissolution

Where the firm is dissolved, its assets are sold off and any surplus remaining after the debts of the firm have been settled is divided among the partners in the proportions in which the assets of the firm were owned by them before the dissolution (see Partnership Act 1890, s 39). Section 44 sets out these rules in detail. Losses, including losses and deficiencies of capital, shall be paid first out of profits, then out of capital, then by the partners in proportion to their profit-sharing ratio. The assets of the firm (including any capital contribution made by the partners under the rules just mentioned) are then applied in the following order:

(a) paying the debts and liabilities of the firm to persons who are not partners in it;

(b) paying to each partner rateably what is due to him from the firm in respect of advances as distinguished from capital (ie, advances made above and beyond the agreed capital contribution);

(c) paying to each partner rateably what is due to him from the firm in respect of capital;

(d) distributing any surplus to the partners in accordance with their profit-sharing ratios.

Any partner is entitled to announce publicly the dissolution of the firm and may require the other partners to join with him in doing any act for this purpose which he cannot do alone (Partnership Act 1890, s 37). Section 38 of the Act authorises the continuation of the business of the firm in so far as may be necessary for the purposes of winding up (but no further), and to that limited extent preserves the rights and obligations of the partners inter se, as well as their right to bind each other (this may be compared with the Insolvency Act 1986, ss 87 and 130, which achieve the same effect in voluntary and compulsory windings-up of companies). The exception to this rule is that the firm as a whole cannot be bound by the acts of a partner who has become bankrupt, though this exemption does not extend to anyone who has, after the commencement of the bankruptcy, knowingly allowed himself to be held out as being a partner of the bankrupt. This section will be important where a partnership terminates on bankruptcy, either under s 33 of the Partnership Act 1890 or because of a provision in the partnership agreement. So long as the former (and possibly continuing) partners do not allow themselves to be represented as being still in partnership with the bankrupt, they cannot be bound by his actions. If for any reason the bankruptcy does not terminate the partnership as regards the bankrupt, then it seems likely that the other partners will allow themselves to be represented as being in partnership with the bankrupt and will therefore incur liability accordingly.

2.6.7 Dissolution for fraud or misrepresentation

Because partnership is a contractual relationship as well as a statutory and fiduciary one, the ordinary rules of the law of contract apply to it so far as appropriate in any given case. In particular, a partnership may be rescinded on the ground of fraud or misrepresentation. Rescission is of course different from termination in the ways already discussed, because rescission is intended to operate *ab initio*, and the parties must therefore be restored to their original pre-partnership position. To this end, s 41 of the Partnership Act 1890 confers certain rights on a partner who has rescinded a partnership for fraud or misrepresentation, the aim of these rights being to put him in an advantageous position as compared with the other partners. These rights are:

(a) A lien on the surplus of the partnership assets after satisfying partnership liabilities for any sum of money paid by him for the purchase of a share in the partnership and for any capital contributed by him. This means that when it comes to distributing the net assets of the firm, the rescinding partner has first claim on those assets to recover his investment in the firm. To this extent he is allowed to promote himself above the other partners in the firm. However, as this right is merely a lien, it applies only where the rescinding partner is already by some means in possession of the property over which the right is claimed.

(b) The right to stand in the place of the creditors of the firm for any payments made by him in respect of partnership liabilities. Here the effect of s 14 is similar to that of the doctrine of subrogation. Having indemnified creditors of the firm for their claims against it, the rescinding partner is in effect subrogated to their rights against the firm; he stands in their shoes, so to speak. This is potentially an even more valuable right than that conferred by (a) above, since creditors of the firm have to be paid before there can arise any question of the distribution of surplus assets. On the other hand, the application of the right is more limited, since it arises only where the rescinding partner has personally paid out creditors of the firm.

(c) The right to be indemnified by the persons guilty of the fraud or misrepresentation against all debts and liabilities of the firm. This merely confirms the existence, in a partnership context, of a right which would exist anyway as a general point of the law of contract (see *Small v Attwod* (1833) Y 407; *Cruickshank v McVicar* (1884) 8 Beav 106). Those guilty of the fraud or misrepresentation must, as part of restoring the innocent partner to his pre-partnership position, indemnify him against any losses which he may have suffered as a result of their own wrongdoing, whether those take the form of losses in the course of the business or other losses.

2.7 Insolvency of partnerships

In addition to the possibility that an individual partner may be bankrupt (and may thereby cease to be a partner), there is also the possibility that the firm as a whole will be insolvent. This will occur where the firm is unable to meet its debts as they fall due. However, the unlimited liability of the partners is a significant element here. If the partnership assets are insufficient to meet the debts of the firm, creditors have a right of recourse against the separate assets of any or all of the partners. Thus, it will be possible to settle the firm's debts (and so to continue in business) as long as there is even one partner who remains solvent. Clearly, though, a partner who finds himself meeting all the debts of the firm because the other partners are without means is unlikely to be willing to see this state of affairs continue for any length of time. He is likely to seek to dissolve the firm, either by giving notice (if that is not precluded by the partnership agreement) or by applying to the court under s 35 of the Partnership Act 1890 (see **2.6.5**). A creditor may also petition for the dissolution of the partnership on the grounds of insolvency, if a debt of at least £750 is outstanding and remains unpaid for at least three weeks after the making of a statutory demand for payment.

2.8 Limited partnerships

The Limited Partnerships Act 1907 allows the creation of partnerships in which some partners are not liable for the debts of the firm. Such partners are known as limited partners and a firm of this kind is known as a limited partnership. Limited partners are not allowed to take any part in the management of the firm. If they do so, they lose their limited status and become general partners, thereby incurring the usual unlimited liability for debts. Every limited partnership must have at least one partner whose liability is unlimited. Such partnerships may be appropriate where it is desired to have one person inject capital into the firm (and to take a share of the profits of the firm accordingly), but that person is not prepared to accept the unlimited liability which comes with the status of a general partner. In practice, though, limited partnerships are very little used at the present day. The reason for this is that in the situation just described it is as easy to form a company and give all participants limited liability as it is to form a partnership under which only some have limited liability. In retrospect it can be seen that the 1907 Act was more or less obsolete even when it was passed, having been overtaken by the decision of the House of Lords in *Saloman v Saloman* [1897] AC 22 (see **Chapter 8**), which recognised the legitimacy of incorporation for even the smallest business.

2.9 The limited liability partnership

The Limited Liability Partnerships Act 2000 created a new form of business entity with limited liability. The Act was a response to large professional firms, which were concerned about the unlimited liability of partners facing very large legal claims, particularly for professional negligence. The limited liability partnership is an entity which has aspects or attributes which are similar to that of a company and also gives limited liability to its members, other than any negligent partner. This form of business enterprise is not a suitable business vehicle for the characters in this book and will not be considered further.

2.10 Advice to the parties

Partnership is not a relationship to be entered into lightly. It is remarkably easy in English law to find oneself in a partnership relationship without meaning to do so. The consequences of this can be serious, given that partners are agents for each other and have unlimited liability for all partnership debts. If there is to be a partnership, as seems likely, then careful thought is needed about who should be given the status of partner – trust and confidence between partners is most important, and these concepts relate to competence as well as to honesty. Once the identity of the partners has been decided, a further important question concerns the profit-sharing ratios and the amount of capital to be contributed. These do not have to be identical, though they often are, and in the present case it may well be appropriate to treat Arthur and Bill reasonably generously even if they are not able to inject much capital, since it will be largely their work which establishes the success of the firm despite the introduction of Edwina and Duncan.

Edwina has agreed to contribute her general business acumen to the firm. Although she has no expertise in interior design, and should satisfy herself as to the competence of Arthur and Bill, she does have managerial experience. It therefore seemed natural to make her the managing partner. This raises the question of her capital contribution. Arthur and Bill can contribute the assets of the existing business, but Edwina will have to make a cash contribution. She would be well advised to negotiate the lowest capital contribution she can in order to secure a one-third share, and then to offer additional capital contributions at rate of interest.

Duncan is in many ways more difficult to deal with. He will invest substantial sums in the firm, but does not intend to work in it. He is in effect a sleeping partner, although he may well argue that he is a mere financier for reasons relating to personal liability. One solution would be to create a limited partnership with Duncan as the limited partner – this would satisfy his desire not to be exposed to liability, whilst simultaneously giving him a share in the profits. On the other hand, Arthur and Bill may object to allowing him to share in the profits at all since he will not be working. They may prefer him simply to lend the money to the firm at interest, since that will confine him to the interest and will allow them to keep all the profits. This strategy again reduces Duncan's risk, but also reduces his potential profit. For Arthur and Bill it will seem attractive if they are confident that the business is going to prosper: if Duncan is not a partner, they cannot look to him to stand behind them should the business fail.

Charlotte's position is difficult for other reasons. Bill is anxious to protect her and may wish to give her the status of a partner, but an application of the principles already discussed would suggest that this is probably not an appropriate course of action. She has no capital to contribute, and at this stage it seems unlikely that she will bring in any work. Realistically, she is part of the support staff, and the natural status for her is that of salaried employee, though there is of course no reason why she should not be rewarded with appropriate bonuses if the business prospers. The business will be considerably strengthened by a committed and enthusiastic workforce.

The conclusion of this is that Arthur, Bill and Edwina should be partners – probably with equal status – whilst Duncan should be either a limited partner or a mere investor, and Charlotte should be an employee.

FURTHER READING

The law of partnership was subject to review by the Law Commission. See:

Law Commission Consultation Paper (No 159), *Joint Consultation Paper on Partnership Law* (2000).

Law Commission Report (Law Com No 283), *Partnership Law* (2003).

E Berry 'The Partnership Bill 2003: Unnecessary Tinkering or Much-needed Reform?' [2005] JBL 70.

On the limited liability partnership, see E Deards: 'Limited Partnerships: Limited Reforms?' [2003] JBL 435.

3 Liability of the Firm and Partners to Outsiders

LEARNING OUTCOMES

By the end of this chapter, you should understand:

- the firm's liability in contract;

- the authority of partners to bind the firm with respect to third parties;

- implied and ostensible authority;

- the liability of the firm in tort and criminal law;

- the liability of partners for the firm's debts – duration and nature of liability – the concept of joint and several liability;

- the doctrine of holding out.

SCENARIO

The new partnership is indeed prospering. Arthur, Bill and Edwina are finding that orders are flooding in. From time to time they have been commissioned to acquire antique furniture on behalf of clients. This latter activity brought them into contact with a company called Ye Olde Curiosity Shoppe plc, which appears to be taking a keen interest in the development of the firm. Arthur and Bill are experiencing great job satisfaction, and are delighted that Edwina seems to be willing to occupy the position of managing partner, a role Edwina has taken to with considerable enthusiasm: a great lateral thinker, she explores seemingly endless possibilities for expansion. As a businesswoman of some repute, Edwina is acutely aware of the need to keep the cash flow side of the business active in order to finance the longer-term expansion, and it is with this in mind that she entered into an exclusive contract with a national building company (Bleak House Ltd) to design a range of 'professional persons' apartments nationwide. The contract gives Bleak House Ltd 60 days to pay invoices from Great Expectations (the contract also included a retention of title clause, discussed in **Chapter 15**). As the first payments will not be due for two to three months, and Edwina will meantime have to recruit more employees to work on the project, she realises that the co-operation of the firm's bank will be needed to fund this initial expense. Undoubtedly, the bank would not have been forthcoming if it were not for the injection of funds into the firm from Duncan. Duncan's investment was modest and advanced on something of a trial basis, with a view to further investment, and involvement, if Edwina's predictions for success are realised. We saw in **Chapter 2** that Duncan had insisted on linking the repayments on the loan to the firm's success, although it is unlikely that this would change his status from financier to partner.

OVERVIEW

In **Chapter 2** we considered the nature of the partnership relationship and the rules which apply to partners inter se. We saw that, to a large extent, these rules can be amended, and indeed in many cases are, to provide for a workable framework for the particular business in question. This chapter, in contrast, seeks to present a clear insight into those rules which cannot be amended by the partners themselves, because they affect third parties who deal with the firm and who are not privy to the partnership agreement. Third parties are entitled to assume, unless otherwise notified, that all partners have equal power to bind the firm in relation to its normal activities. If they become aware of any provisions which indicate a contrary intention, it becomes more difficult for them to sustain an argument that they were relying on the appearances of a partnership. For the most part this chapter is concerned with the ability of the partners to bind the firm, and consequently each other, in contract. The extent to which each partner can incur liability in tort and under the criminal law, which can become the liability of the firm, is also considered. A related question concerns exactly who can be liable for a firm's debts and what the duration of that liability is.

The relations of partners to persons dealing with them are dealt with in ss 5 to 18 of the Partnership Act 1890. The Act provides for civil liability in contract, and otherwise there is also provision for liability to be imposed on persons who appear to be partners but who are in fact not partners. The nature and duration of such liability is also discussed under this heading. As a result, third parties who deal with a firm are able to discern the liability of the firm and of others involved with the firm. This may be particularly important where the acknowledged partners are men of limited means.

3.1 Liability of the firm in contract

3.1.1 Introduction

The point was made in **Chapter 2** that is important to take a great deal of care over the selection of partners, regard being had to the obvious requirements of honesty and integrity, and also to the perhaps less obvious requirement of competence. Unlimited liability of partners for the firm's debts could lead to a situation where a dishonest or incompetent partner's behaviour results not only in the insolvency of the firm, but also in the bankruptcy of his fellow partners. It is probably true that whereas sole traders and modest partnerships are able to keep fairly tight control over a firm's activities, the same cannot be said for larger partnerships, where specialisation and delegation of duties become necessary for the effective functioning of the business. Ensuring compliance with the partnership agreement becomes increasingly difficult as the business expands. Partners have extensive liability for the acts of fellow partners, even where these acts are unauthorised. Dishonest or incompetent partners can therefore impose significant liability on other members of the firm (consider the development of the ultra vires doctrine in company law, where the balance has shifted away from the protection of investors in favour of third parties who might otherwise find themselves with unenforceable contracts: see **Chapter 6**). Unlimited liability begins to look even more unattractive in these circumstances; business expansion may of itself be said to be one very good reason for incorporation (see further

Chapter 26), or for the adoption of the limited liability partnership. Arthur and Bill were both equally involved and informed during the firm's formative years in business, but to some extent the introduction of Edwina has changed this. Arthur and Bill had been looking to find a partner who would complement their design skills and who would be capable of managing the business side of the firm. This trend towards the partners creating niches for themselves and becoming specialists in their own sphere of activity highlights the need for openness and good faith on the part of all partners. Where one or more partner exceeds the common understanding as to the scope of his authority, and upsets the relations inter se, the firm's liability may nevertheless be beyond dispute. The inherent dangers of partnership as a business medium are not always fully appreciated. Indeed, in the scenario for Great Expectations, there is evidence that Edwina is moving at a tremendous pace; such activities may be causing the business to overtrade, which in turn will make the firm vulnerable to creditors; furthermore, Edwina's prize contract with Bleak House Ltd might not be in the firm's best interest. Would it then be possible for Arthur and Bill to countermand Edwina's promise, without the firm incurring liability for breach of contract? In other words, did Edwina have authority to bind the firm in contract with Bleak House Ltd?

3.1.2 Partners' authority

Edwina's authority as a partner stems from the common law rules of agency. Edwina was acting as an agent of Great Expectations in her dealings with Bleak House Ltd, the firm being the principal. As the firm is no more than a relationship between the partners, Edwina is also a principal with regard to her partners, who are also agents and principals. At common law we find authority for this in *Re Agriculturist Cattle Insurance Co (Baird's case)* (1870) LR 5 Ch App 725. Students with previous knowledge of the law of agency should find the study of a partner's authority easy to grasp. Authority may be based on consent, express authority being the result of an agreement between the principal and agent as to the activities which may be carried out. Implied authority also arises from consent, the firm and its partners agreeing that activities which are ancillary to the position of each partner should bind the firm – in recognition that many such activities cannot be provided for expressly. Ostensible authority, on the other hand, may arise without consent (although there is usually some considerable overlap between implied and ostensible authority) and occurs as a result of the doctrine of estoppel. Ostensible authority arises where the principal, by words or conduct, represents to third parties that the agent in question has the necessary authority to bind the firm. In partnership law this may be the result of granting partnership status, since by doing so the partner is not only given express and implied authority, he is given ostensible authority due to the representation made to third parties as to his status. In practice ostensible authority and implied authority will overlap, given that the usual authority of a partner depends very much upon the firm he represents.

The authority of a partner to bind his firm is provided by s 5 of the Partnership Act 1890, and from its drafting it would seem to indicate that a partner's authority is a combination of implied authority and ostensible authority; indeed, in *United Bank of Kuwait v Hammoud* [1988] 1 WLR 1051, Glidewell LJ refers to authority under s 5 as 'ostensible' (some commentators describe authority in s 5 as being implied; see Morse, 'Partnership Law'). Section 5 provides:

> *Every partner is an agent of the firm and his other partners for the purpose of the business of the partnership; and the acts of every partner who does any act for carrying on in the usual way business of the kind carried on by the firm of which he is a member bind the firm and his partners, unless the partner so acting has in fact no authority to act for the firm in the particular matter, and the person with whom he is dealing either knows that he has no authority, or does not know or believe him to be a partner.*

Three requirements emerge from this section:

(a) the act must concern *the business of the partnership;*

(b) it must be carried out *in the usual way;* and

(c) the third party must have *no notice of any limitation* on the partner's authority, or not know or not believe that he was not a partner.

These requirements are discussed in more detail at **3.1.2.1** to **3.1.2.3** below.

3.1.2.1 Business of the partnership

Great Expectations is an interior design business. It is a question of fact at all times whether a particular activity is concerned with this business. As with every other business, there will be some activities which are obviously within its sphere of activity, just as there will be those which are clearly outside of it. If we consider the scenario, an order from Arthur or Bill for wall coverings would almost certainly bind the firm, whereas an instruction to a landscape gardener may or may not be within the firm's kind of business depending upon the evidence available. Each case will turn on its own facts, and evidence may be adduced to assist the court in determining what is in fact the business of the partnership in question. In *United Bank of Kuwait Ltd v Hammoud* [1988] 1 WLR 1051, the Court of Appeal had to consider whether the giving of undertakings was in the ordinary course of business of solicitors for the purposes of s 5. Evidence was submitted by a former president of The Law Society that the giving of undertakings is often regarded as a key feature of the service provided by solicitors, and this was accepted (see also *Dubai Aluminium Co Ltd v Salaam* [2001] QB 113, a case concerning s 10 of the Act; see **3.2** below).

What is potentially problematic in our scenario is the contract Edwina has entered into with Bleak House Ltd to design flats. This would on the face of it appear to be within the kind of business carried on by an interior design firm, although the *scale* of the operation (remember it is a nationwide commitment) may suggest that in fact it is not the kind of business carried on by the firm. It will be a question of fact whether, having regard to all of the evidence available, the activity in question is indeed the kind of business carried on by this firm. The burden of showing that a partner has authority to act on behalf of the firm falls on the third party seeking to make the firm liable. Of course the more difficult scenario would be if the scale of the operations was in that grey area between the routine and the unthinkable. It may be that a court which found that a disproportionate contract was within the kind of business carried on by a firm would in any event find that it was not usual for one partner to commit the firm to such an arrangement. The rules of management to be found in s 24 of the Partnership Act 1890 (see **2.5.1.7** and **2.5.1.8**) illustrate the principle that day-to-day decisions may be taken by majority vote, but more serious matters require unanimity. For the purposes of s 5, the chief concern will be to discern what third parties understood the extent of the authority of each of the partners to be (see further *City Trust Ltd v Levy (United Bank of Kuwait v Hammoud)* [1988] 1 WLR 1051). This brings us on to the second requirement in s 5.

3.1.2.2 Carried out in the usual way

The second requirement under s 5 is for the partner to have acted in the usual way when entering into any given contract on behalf of the firm. What is it usual for one partner to have authority to do without the need to have express agreement from his co-partners? Suppose Edwina alone had entered into the loan agreement with Duncan on behalf of the firm. Is it usual for a partner to act alone in making decisions of this nature? Remember that Edwina is regarded as 'managing partner' by the others and herself (*Freeman & Lockyer v Buckhurst Properties (Mangal) Ltd* [1964] 2 QB 480; *Hely-Hutchinson v Brayhead Ltd* [1968] 1 QB 549). It is probably true that Great Expectations is a trading partnership; and as this is particularly relevant to the question of authority (*Higgins v Beauchamp* [1914] 3 KB 1192), this is therefore a matter of some importance. A definition of a trading partnership is to be found in *Wheatley v Smithers* [1906] 2 KB 321, which held that a trading partnership is one which both buys and sells goods. However, what may be regarded as a trading partnership in the 21st century would presumably reflect attitudes of today, and Great Expectations will no doubt qualify (see the comments of Staughton LJ in *United Bank of Kuwait Ltd v Hammoud* [1988] 1 WLR 1051, concerning the changing nature of the work of solicitors, and his cautionary note that expert evidence of today would be preferred over some of the elderly decisions available in deciding what is the ordinary authority of a solicitor).

Although not raised by the scenario, another potential issue is the authority of one partner to enter into a single joint trading venture. Suppose, for example, that Edwina had liaised with other firms to assist with the Bleak House contract, which was clearly larger than any previous contract negotiated by the firm and therefore involved more risk (although of course this may not amount to a contract at all, failing for want of authority). There is authority in *Mann v D'Arcy* [1968] 1 WLR 893, which states that although a partner has no authority to bring in a new partner or involve his firm in a venture which amounts to a new business venture, he does have authority to involve his firm in a single joint trading venture with another individual or firm, even if it amounts to a one-off partnership, always provided the venture is merely another method of carrying on the same business. In *Mann v D'Arcy*, D'Arcy was the active partner in a firm which entered into such a one-off transaction with Mann to buy and sell a large quantity of potatoes. The transaction was profitable, but when Mann failed to receive his share of the profit, he sued the only one of D'Arcy's partners to be in a position to pay him. It was argued that D'Arcy had not bound the firm because he had no authority to enter into a contract of this sort. The court, however, took the view that buying and selling potatoes was the kind of business of the firm, and further that it was carried on in the usual way; it amounted to no more than a method of mitigating the potential risk involved, in other words, a form of insurance for the particular deal. This approach has been applied in Australia in the case of *Rowella Pty Ltd v Hoult* [1988] 2 Qd R 80. There, a managing partner had entered into a joint venture, and the court held that if this had amounted to a joint venture which was within the normal business of the firm then it would have been binding on the firm. However, on the facts the venture amounted to an entirely different business.

3.1.2.3 Lack of authority known or ignorance as to status

Implied authority is at common law authority which arises due to the status of the agent in question; ostensible authority arises where a particular impression has been conveyed by a principal to third parties who have relied upon it. The authority of a partner under s 5 straddles both of these definitions and is largely a consequence of the doctrine of estoppel by conduct, whereby the authorising of an agent to act in a particular capacity includes the granting of authority to do any acts which are ancillary to such activity. Estoppel cannot arise where the third party has not been misled. So, for example, where the third party had knowledge of the lack of authority, or was not misled because he did not believe the agent to be such in any event, ostensible authority cannot exist. The Partnership Act 1890 applies this to partnership law by the final clause of s 5.

3.1.3 The doctrine of the undisclosed principal

At common law, an agent who acts within his authority but without disclosing that he is acting as an agent can bind the third party in contract with his principal. The principal can emerge and sue and be sued on the contract. This is known as the doctrine of the undisclosed principal and means that a third party may believe himself to be in a contractual relationship with one party only to discover that another has rights and obligations under the same contract. Although this may not be very popular, it is disapplied only in the limited circumstances where the identity of the contracting parties was crucial to one or other of them. (For example, if a buyer of goods wished to deal with a particular seller so as to set off moneys already owing between them (*Greer v Downs Supply Co* [1927] 2 KB 28), or if the decision not to contract with a particular individual was clearly understood between them (*Said v Butt* [1920] 3 KB 497.) It is important to remember that the doctrine is effective only if the agent had authority at the time liability was incurred. If the third party is unaware of the agent's status then such authority cannot be ostensible, since this would have required the principal to make some form of representation to the third party. It must therefore be express or implied.

Authority of partners under the Partnership Act 1890 is not express or implied in the same way as at common law; it requires the existence of ostensible authority by virtue of its drafting. Such an interpretation of s 5 leaves no possibility for the doctrine of the undisclosed principal to be applied in partnership law. The third party must at least have knowledge of the existence of a principal, a firm, even if he does not know the identity of it. Where the third party chooses to ignore this knowledge, preferring instead to deal with the partner in his capacity as an individual, then the partner's activities do not bind the firm (see *British Homes Assurance Corporation Ltd v Patterson* [1902] 2 Ch 404). The assumption that s 5 is concerned with a partner's implied authority as opposed to his ostensible authority cannot be supported by the language of the section itself; and furthermore, elsewhere in the Act the ability of partners to incur liability on the part of the firm is expressly stated to be where a partner is acting in the scope of his apparent authority (see s 11). In the *United Bank of Kuwait* case, Staughton LJ stated:

The promise of one partner binds the other members of the firm if it was an act for carrying on in the usual way business of the kind carried on by the firm: see Partnership Act 1890, section 5. A contract made by a servant or other agent binds the principal if it was made with the ostensible authority of the principal.

Those three propositions, or some or one of them, are crucial rules of law for the determination of the two appeals before the court. Although they are to be found in different compartments of the law, they all provide the same test, at any rate so far as these cases are concerned. Was Mr Emmanuel's undertaking given in his capacity as a solicitor? Was it an act for carrying on in the usual way the business of the firm? Was it made with ostensible authority? All three questions in effect are the same.

This approach supports the view that a partner's authority under s 5 is ostensible. The practice of the courts of using the terms 'implied' and 'ostensible' interchangeably reflects the substantial overlap between these two types of authority. It follows from the above analysis that the authority conferred by s 5 is not sufficient to make the firm party to the contract in cases where it is an undisclosed principal. It has to be said that judicial comment on this point has been far from clear. In *Watteau v Fenwick* [1893] 1 QB 346 (which was not a partnership case), Wills J considered the doctrine of the undisclosed principal at common law and suggested that it would apply in the same way under the law of partnership. The likely approach of the court in interpreting s 5 has been the subject of academic discussion (see **Further Reading**, below), focusing on the situation where a partner has implied authority but where the third party does not know him to be a partner. This tends to ignore the inclination of the courts to interpret s 5 as determining the scope of ostensible authority, as seen through the eyes of the third party, and it is this approach which should ensure that the doctrine will have no application where a partner is not known to be acting on behalf of a firm carrying out a particular type of business, unless he had express authority to act, as was the position in *Hexyl Pty Ltd v Construction Engineering (Aust) Pty Ltd* [1983] 2 NSWLR 624.

3.2 Liability of the firm for torts and crimes

The firm's liability for torts and the liability of each of the partners is stated in ss 10 and 11 of the Partnership Act 1890, thus:

10. *Where, by any wrongful act or omission of any partner acting in the ordinary course of the business of the firm, or with the authority of his co-partners, loss or injury is caused to any person not being a partner in the firm, or any penalty is incurred, the firm is liable therefor to the same extent as the partner so acting or omitting to act.*

11. *In the following cases; namely—*
    (a) *Where one partner acting within the scope of his apparent authority receives the money or property of a third person and misapplies it; and*
    (b) *Where a firm in the course of its business receives money or property of a third person, and the money or property so received is misapplied by one or more of the partners while it is in the custody of the firm;*

    the firm is liable to make good the loss.

3.2.1 Liability under s 10

Section 10 of the Act deals with a partner's capacity to incur liability on the part of the firm for a tort or a crime. The reasoning which we have seen with regard to contractual liability (at **3.1** above) is again applicable. The wrongful acts or omissions must be those of a partner acting in the ordinary course of the firm's business, or with the express authority of the partners if granted for a particular activity outside this permitted scope. It will be a question of fact whether the partner in question was acting in the course of the firm's business, and knowledge as to its activities on the part of third parties is not required (see *Dubai Aluminium Co Ltd v Salaam* [2001] QB 113). In other words, we are not concerned with ostensible authority. The law in this respect is more concerned with protecting third parties; the balance in their favour reflects this. A useful illustration is the case of *Kirkintilloch Equitable Co-operative Society Ltd v Livingstone* 1972 SLT 154, which concerned the activities of an accountant who, while professing to be acting on his own behalf and in a personal capacity for a client and not as a partner of his firm, carried out an audit negligently thus attracting liability in tort. The question was whether this resulted in liability for his firm. On the facts of the case the court held that he did have the authority, as required by s 10, to incur liability on behalf of the firm, as he was permitted to act on this client's behalf with the use of the partnership facilities (see also *Public Trustee v Mortimer* (1985) 16 DLR (4th) 404). The firm therefore was liable for his negligence.

A second case used to illustrate this provision is *Hamlyn v Houston* [1903] 1 KB 81. This case concerned a partner who had authority to compile information about his firm's rivals. He succeeded in obtaining this by bribing an employee of a competitor, using his firm's money. The Court of Appeal upheld the claim against the firm, on the basis that a tort had been committed by the partner in question while carrying out an authorised act. It was within the scope of his authority to procure the information, and it was immaterial that the acts he committed in order procure it were fraudulent.

A third illustration is the case of *Arbuckle v Taylor* (1815) 3 Dow 160, where a partner had initiated criminal proceedings, alleging theft of partnership property, against the plaintiff. The plaintiff was cleared of the charge, and he sued the firm for false imprisonment and malicious prosecution. Although the property relating to the criminal prosecution belonged to the firm, it was held that this did not give the partner authority to initiate proceedings on behalf of the firm. Such authority was confined to actions within the ordinary course of the firm's business, which did not include initiating a prosecution. The partner did not have the express authority of his firm, neither was there any implied authority (see also *National Commercial Banking Corporation of Australia Ltd v Batty* (1986) 160 CLR 251). In *Hamlyn v Houston* the partner had authority to find out about his firm's competitors. The fact that he did this in an unauthorised way did not prevent liability extending to the firm. The difference between this case and *Arbuckle v Taylor* is that, there, no authority existed to pursue the matter of theft.

Section 10 applies to crimes as to any wrongful act or omission, committed by a partner in the course of carrying on the partnership business ('... or any penalty is incurred ...'). There may therefore be some overlap between s 10 and s 11.

3.2.2 Liability under s 11

Section 11 covers the misapplication of money or property where the *partner* in question has received money or property within the scope of his apparent authority. If the partner in question had no authority then clearly the firm will not be liable.

For s 11(a) to apply, the third party must have dealt with a partner *qua* partner not *qua* individual; the capacity in which the partner acts is crucial, as can be seen from the case of *British Homes Assurance Corporation Ltd v Patterson* [1902] 2 Ch 404. There, Atkinson was appointed to act as solicitor for the British Homes Assurance Corporation Ltd. Atkinson later gave notice to the company that he had taken on a new partner, Patterson, and that the name of his firm had changed from 'Atkinson & Atkinson' to 'Atkinson & Patterson'. Despite this, the company continued to deal with Atkinson as though he were a sole practitioner, continuing to use his pre-partnership name of Atkinson & Atkinson on all correspondence, as payee of cheques and in accepting a receipt for moneys sent to the firm. It was only when a cheque was misappropriated that they chose to acknowledge Patterson as a partner in the firm by seeking to make him liable for the misapplication of the funds. It was held that Patterson was not liable because the company had not dealt with Atkinson as a partner in the firm; they had chosen to deal with him in his personal capacity, having elected to ignore the firm and to continue the contract as with an individual.

Section 11(b) covers the situation where the *firm* receives money or property which is subsequently misapplied. The firm will be liable to make good the loss only if the receipt is in the ordinary course of the firm's business. A partner who receives money within his ostensible authority under para (a), discussed above, indicates that in so doing the firm is receiving it in the course of its business, and will attract liability under both paras (a) and (b) (see *Rhodes v Moules* [1895] 1 Ch 236).

3.3 Liability of the partners for the firm's debts

Our discussion so far has focused on the firm's liability for the acts of its members. The firm is not, however, a separate legal entity, it is merely a relationship of individuals who have, by design or default, chosen to trade through the medium of a partnership. Consequently, when we talk about the firm being liable we mean the liability of the partners themselves, who are all liable without limit for the debts of the business. In other words, each partner is personally liable for all the debts of the partnership, regardless of any internal agreements reached by the partners as to the allocation of the firm's obligations. Of course such internal arrangements are binding between the partners inter se and can be enforced as between each other, but they cannot bind third parties who have a claim against the firm. Liability is joint and several, which means that claims against all or any of the partners can be contemporaneous or successive.

A distinction used to exist between liability for contractual obligations and liability for tortious obligations. Liability in contract under s 9 of the 1890 Act was *joint*, whereas liability under s 12 in tort was *joint and several*. The result of this was that contractual debts and obligations could only be the subject of one claim against the members of the firm. If a decision were taken to omit one or more partners from this claim, the third party's rights against those omitted would be lost. Several claims were not permitted. Claims in tort, on the other hand, could be contemporaneous or successive, more than one claim being permitted. The significance of this difference is illustrated by the case of *Kendall v Hamilton* (1879) 4 App Cas 504, where the plaintiff sued successfully all the members of a firm of whom he was aware, yet failed to obtain full satisfaction of his debt due to the lack of means of those partners. When he later learned of the existence of another, wealthy sleeping partner, it was held that as the debt was joint and not joint and several, the plaintiff's only cause of action had been used, thus he was not permitted to bring fresh proceedings against the newly discovered partner. Disclosure of the partners' names on letterheads, invoices, etc (see **2.4** above) does much to prevent this situation arising, as does the use of the procedure whereby the firm can be sued in the firm name (see CPR Sch 1, RSC Ord 81); however, the unfairness of allowing only joint liability as opposed to joint and several liability was addressed by s 3 of the Civil Liability (Contribution) Act 1978, which provides:

> *Judgment recovered against any person liable in respect of any debt or damage shall not be a bar to an action, or to the continuance of an action, against any other person who is (apart from any such bar) jointly liable with him in respect of the same debt or damage.*

As a result, the liability of partners for the whole of their firm's debts and liabilities is now joint and several.

3.4 Duration of the partners' liability

So far in our scenario we have seen George retire from the firm after a lifetime in the business of upholstery, the last 15 years or so of which were spent in partnership with his sons. Clearly many clients of long standing will have continued patronising the firm due to George's expertise and reputation for quality workmanship; his departure from the firm will have to be well publicised if future transactions are not to bind him. The change of the firm's name to Great Expectations will facilitate this transformation to some extent; nevertheless, the law still requires various procedures to be followed before George will escape liability for future transactions of the firm. Debts and obligations incurred by the firm before George's retirement will still bind him unless all parties affected by them agree to release him, through a tripartite agreement known as novation.

3.4.1 Retiring partner – liability for existing debts

The position is stated in s 17(2) of the Partnership Act 1890, which provides:

> *A partner who retires from a firm does not thereby cease to be liable for partnership debts or obligations incurred before his retirement.*

This is illustrated by the case of *Court v Berlin* [1897] 2 QB 396, where a solicitor engaged by a firm comprising three partners continued to act on the matter, on behalf of the firm, after the retirement of two of them. The court held that the solicitor was entitled to recover his costs from all three of the partners, notwithstanding the retirement of two of them. The obligation was a continuing one and had been incurred before retirement. It is possible, however, for any retiring partners to agree with those remaining that liability for all outstanding obligations shall cease at the date of retirement. Because third parties are not privy to such an agreement, they would not be bound by it. On the other hand, if they become parties to the agreement it becomes one of novation – a tripartite agreement between the retiring partner, the firm as newly constituted, and the creditor or creditors involved. All three parties agree that the obligation shall be borne by the firm as newly constituted, thus releasing any retiring partners from further obligation. The same principles will apply to a situation where the firm takes on a new partner and, as such, becomes a new firm. Third parties must by some positive act accede to the substitution; if they do not, preferring instead to treat the firm as it had been previously, they cannot later seek to make the new firm liable to them (see *British Homes Assurance Corporation Ltd v Patterson* [1902] 2 Ch 404, at **3.2.2** above), although of course their rights against the 'old' firm remain untouched. Novation is provided for under the Act in s 17(3), which states:

> *A retiring partner may be discharged from any existing liabilities, by an agreement to that effect between himself and the members of the firm as newly constituted and the creditors, and this agreement may be either express or inferred as a fact from the course of dealing between the creditors and the firm as newly constituted.*

3.4.2 Retiring partner – liability for future debts

Unless there is novation, George cannot be released from obligations incurred while he was a member of the firm. Once he has retired, however, his liability for future activities of the firm will cease, provided he gives actual notice of this to all the firm's customers (s36(1)). For persons who were customers on the date of retirement, a retirement notice should be placed in the *London Gazette* (s 36(2)). For persons who had no dealings with the firm before his retirement and to whom George was not known as a partner, no notice is necessary (s 36(3)).

3.4.3 Liability by 'holding out'

The doctrine of 'holding out' may result in liability for any person who holds himself out to be a partner, but it does not of itself transform such a person into a partner of the firm. For example, a retired partner, although no longer a partner in the firm, may continue to incur liability if he holds himself out as still being a partner, or suffers himself to be so represented by, for example, permitting the firm to continue using old stationery bearing his name as partner. George's repeated appearances could be interpreted as a comeback and, if he were to continue to involve himself in the business of the firm to such an extent that third parties believed he had not really retired at all, he could incur liability under s 14 of the Partnership Act 1890. He would be estopped, as against those persons to whom who he had represented himself to be a partner, from denying his liability.

It must be stressed that liability under s 14 is not by itself capable of raising the status of an individual to that of partner, and so it does not of itself incur liability for the firm. This is because an agent's authority to bind the firm, as opposed to merely binding himself, does not rest upon a representation made by the agent; such representation must be made by the principal. However, if the firm is aware of such a situation and does nothing to dispel the appearance of authority, liability on the part of the firm may be unavoidable.

The scenario does not suggest that the partners in Great Expectations have acquiesced in George's behaviour, but to continue to tolerate his interference may give rise to liability in that they will be estopped from denying his ability to bind the firm. Further, George may be able to go some way to support an argument that he again occupies the position of partner, albeit without the proper label, and should therefore benefit from the rights enjoyed by partners discussed in the preceding chapter (for an application of this to a retiring partner, see *Tower Cabinet Co Ltd v Ingram* [1949] 1 All ER 1033).

3.5 Advice to the parties

Changing the composition of a partnership after many years of trading raises all sorts of problems, mainly due to the nature of the relationship itself and the suitability of partnership as a business medium for an expanding enterprise. The scope of each partner's ability to bind the firm in contract and incur liability in tort highlights the need for the two most important attributes of any partner to be honesty and competence. As the firm expands and the number of decisions taken by the partners individually increase, it will become ever more difficult for each of them to be kept fully aware of the extent and (possibly also) the nature of their potential liability. If the firm were to introduce a new partner in the future in the shape of Duncan, it would be wise to give serious consideration to the question of incorporating the business and trading through a limited company. As the organisational structure needed to ensure the success of the business changes, so the legal framework to support its activities must change. The law of partnership cannot always provide a framework which minimises the risks to the business posed by its own expansion. No doubt Duncan's legal adviser would suggest that further financial involvement should depend upon incorporation. Indeed, he may suggest that incorporation is the only way to proceed (see further **Chapter 26**).

FURTHER READING

Professor JL Montrose, 'Liability of principal for acts exceeding actual and apparent authority' (1939) 17 Can Bar Rev 693.

JC Thomas, 'Playing word games with Professor Montrose' (1977) 6 VUWLR 1.

4 Obtaining Initial Finance

LEARNING OUTCOMES

By the end of this chapter, you should understand:

- the nature of share capital and the rules govening payment for shares;

- classes of shares – ordinary and preference shares – the deferred share;

- allotment of shares;

- share and risk capital;

- debt financing the debenture;

- registration formalities;

- pre-incorporation contracts.

SCENARIO

Arthur, Bill, Charlotte, Duncan and Edwina are now quite clear that they want to turn the firm into a company, and the procedures for incorporation are well under way. It has now become clear to them that they need to deal with certain financial questions. The company will have to have a share capital, though how much that should be and to whom it should be issued are as yet unresolved questions. Perhaps more important is the need to obtain the initial finance to get the business going.

4.1 Share capital

4.1.1 Introduction

In order to raise the initial finance some shares will have to be issued – a company must have an issued share capital (unless it is to take the extremely rare step of becoming a company limited by guarantee; see the Companies Act 1985, s 2(5)(b)). It is no longer necessary to have a minimum of two shareholders. The Twelfth EC Directive on Company Law has been implemented in the UK (SI 1992/1699), and it is now permissible to have only one shareholder. In the present case, however, it is likely that there will be more than one shareholder. The reasons for this have to do with the consequences of share holding.

The shareholders are the owners of the company – it is the ownership rights in the company which are represented by the shares. Consequently, the shareholders ultimately have the right to make decisions about the company's activities, though much of the day-to-day management of the company is delegated to the directors (Table A, art 70; see **Chapters 9** and **13**). Any profit made by the company is also likely to be distributed to the shareholders either as dividend (the rules as to the distribution of dividends are contained in **Chapter 16**), or in the form of an accretion to the value of their shares resulting from an increase in the value of the company's assets. When the company comes to an end and is wound up, the shareholders are entitled to share in the residual value of the company after payment of its debts in proportion to their share holding.

At the same time, shareholders are at risk of losing the capital which they invest in shares. If the company fails and is wound up while unable to pay its debts, there will be no residual value in the shares and the shareholders will receive nothing. It is for this reason that capital invested in shares is sometimes called 'risk capital' or 'venture capital'. However, it is important to understand that the risk which shareholders run is limited to the loss of the amounts due on their shares. They do not have any further liability for the debts of the company. Thus the holder of fully paid-up shares has no further liability for the debts, whilst the holder of partly paid-up shares is liable only for the sums outstanding on those shares. This is a fundamental aspect of the notion of limited liability, which is in turn perhaps the single most important feature of company law.

4.1.2 Rules as to payment for shares

Section 99 of the Companies Act 1985 allows payment for shares in a private company to be made in cash or kind (ss101 to 107 impose special restrictions in the case of public companies, but these are not examined in detail here). Section 99(4) also allows the issue of bonus shares from sums available for the purpose. These sums will normally be accumulated profits, so that this section is not relevant to the allotment of initial shares in the company. Bonus shares are explained in more detail in **Chapter 17**.

4.1.3 Prohibition on issuing shares at a discount

A point to be noted here is that in English law shares have to have a nominal value (see **Chapter 6**). This requirement probably serves little purpose at the present day, but while it remains in force it does have one important consequence. Section 100 of the Companies Act 1985 forbids the issuing of shares at a discount, ie for less than their nominal value. If this requirement is breached, the allottee remains liable to pay to the company the difference between the allotment price and the nominal value. However, no criminal offence is committed, and the company is not likely to exercise its right to the difference unless it goes into liquidation, in which case the liquidator will be under a duty to collect in all the assets of the company, of which this will be one (for liquidations, see **Chapter 23**).

Although shares must not be issued at a discount to their nominal value, there is no prohibition on issuing them at a discount to the current net asset value per share (*Hilder v Dexter* [1902] AC 474, HL). This does not diminish the company's capital, although it may prejudice the existing shareholders by diluting the net asset value and thus reducing the market value of their shares

4.1.4 Issuing shares at a premium

There is no prohibition on the issue of shares at a premium to their nominal value, though if this is done the excess of the allotment price over the nominal value must be transferred to a share premium account. As to this, see further **Chapter 19**.

4.1.5 Classes of shares

It is possible for companies to have shares of more than one class, though the presumption is that there will be only one class of share, and Table A is drafted on that basis (see **Appendix A**). There are various situations in which a company might wish to have more than one class of share, some of which are relevant to the formation of Great Expectations Ltd. One reason is to distinguish between rights to the income of a company and rights to the capital if the company is wound up. Where some shareholders, but not all, are working in the business, it may be thought desirable to give them the primary rights to income, whilst other shareholders who have invested money but who are not active in the management might have the primary rights to receive any capital surplus. This might be achieved by creating one class of shares which had no dividend rights (or very limited dividend rights) but whose holders received most of the surplus capital on winding up, together with a second class of shares which had all (or most of) the dividend rights but whose holders received little or no capital on a winding up. If this is done, it is usual to call one class of shares 'ordinary shares' and the other class 'preference shares', though neither term has any statutory definition (indeed, the term 'preference share' is not used in the Companies Acts). An arrangement of this kind may appear to offer advantages in the present case, since Duncan does not intend to work in the business. However, other factors may need to be taken into account. We are told that Duncan wants a good rate of return on his investment, and it is unlikely that he will be prepared to wait for some hypothetical future winding up of the company. Instead, he will expect to participate in dividends. The need to reward the active workers for their work can be addressed by giving them salaries, which are not awarded to mere investors.

A second possible reason for using different classes of share is to affect the decision-making process within the company. As is explained in **Chapter 7** changes to the Articles of Association require the agreement of holders of 75% of the shares. However, where there is more than one class of share, the requirement is for 75% agreement within each class. Thus, a member who holds all the shares of one class may be able to veto changes to the Articles even though he holds only a very small proportion of the total shares in the company. An arrangement of this kind may be used where one person is in a position of special influence, perhaps as the founder of the company or through possessing some special skill, but is not able to subscribe for a large proportion of the shares. Either Arthur or Bill might well be interested in using this device in the present case, but it is unlikely that Duncan will agree to the proposal, since he will see it as giving Arthur and Bill too much influence. It may be noted, though, that this version of the scheme would only give Arthur and Bill the power to block changes to the Articles. It has nothing to do with the day-to-day decision-making powers of the directors, so it is largely irrelevant to Duncan's power to influence the ordinary running of the company.

Another variant on the idea of share classes is the deferred share, whose rights are postponed to those of the holders of ordinary shares. These were at one time often given to company founders, but this practice is less common at the present day. Indeed, the use of deferred shares appears to be in decline.

Although different classes of shares are still sometimes found today, they are less common than they used to be, and for most small private companies they are unlikely to offer significant advantages. On balance it is suggested that Great Expectations Ltd would be better off without them.

4.1.6 Partly-paid shares

A shareholder's liability is to contribute to the assets of the company the sum of money which he has agreed to pay for his shares, a sum which may be more than the nominal value of the share but which may not be less than that nominal value (see **4.1.3** above). It is possible to issue the shares without receiving the full sum due at the outset. Shares which are issued on this basis are said to be partly-paid (or nil paid if nothing has been paid for them). Where shares are issued partly-paid or nil paid, it is open to the directors to make further calls on the outstanding sums at any time, and shareholders who fail to pay calls are liable to have their shares forfeited (Table A, arts 18–22; Companies Act 1985, s 143(3)(d)).

There are few advantages to the company in issuing shares on this basis. One possible situation is where it is desired to encourage a person's involvement in the company by giving him shares but where he is not in a position to pay for them in full immediately (in a public company context this approach has been used in recent years in a number of privatisations of nationalised industries). However, partly-paid shares are found less often in private companies now than in former times, and it is suggested that there is no good reason for Great Expectations Ltd to use them, unless it is desired to give Arthur and Bill a greater proportion of the shares than they can currently afford to pay for.

4.2 The process of allotment

The allotment of shares is a matter for the directors, and it is usual for prospective shareholders to make a formal application for shares, the purchase price being tendered simultaneously. The directors then resolve to allot the shares in accordance with the application, a share certificate is issued, and the new shareholder's name is entered in the Register of Shareholders with an indication of how many shares have been allotted. It is sometimes said that a person does not become a member of a company until his name is entered on the Register, even if shares have been allotted to him. This proposition is based on *Nicol's Case* (1885) 29 ChD 421, CA, where it was held that an allottee who had neither paid for shares nor been entered on the Register had not become a contributory for the purposes of a winding up. However, this case probably does not support the more general proposition. An allottee who has paid for his shares but who has not been entered on the Register is presumably entitled to rectification of the Register by the inclusion of his name on it. This implies that he is in fact a member, so that, for example, he is entitled to attend and vote at meetings. The same result would seem to follow where the shares are issued partly-paid, and the allottee could therefore in these circumstances be a contributory for the amount outstanding on his shares in the event of a winding up (see *National Westminster Bank plc v Inland Revenue Commissioners* [1995] 1 AC 119, HL).

Shares may sometimes be issued for non-cash consideration. In a private company this does not give rise to major difficulties (the position in relation to public companies is governed by the Companies Act 1985, ss 102–116), though there is always a question about the valuation to be placed on the assets. From the point of view of the directors, this is largely a matter of their duty to manage the company prudently. They need to ensure that the company receives proper value for the shares which it allots. The matter is of course especially sensitive where the directors are allotting the shares to themselves (for the rules requiring proper declarations of interest in these circumstances, see **Chapter 10**).

4.3 Debt financing

4.3.1 What is debt financing?

Debt financing means the practice of financing a company by taking loans. Every company will need working capital, and when a company is first formed there are likely to be initial costs – such as the purchase of plant and machinery – which have to be met at a time when no income has yet been received. Although it is sometimes possible to defer these by leasing equipment rather than purchasing it, other costs, such as initial marketing expenses, are not so easily delayed. Naturally, some of the initial working capital will come from the money invested by shareholders, but this is often insufficient. If the shareholders are not in a position to provide further capital from their own resources, it will become necessary to borrow the remaining money.

4.3.2 Finance from banks

In practice the most common source of debt financing for newly-formed companies is a bank. Indeed, all the major UK clearing banks advertise extensively the availability of this facility. It is likely that our newly-formed company will need to obtain finance from this source. Indeed, it is to be assumed that the pre-existing partnership had at least some bank borrowings, though the personal liability of the partners meant that little needed to be said on this subject.

Obtaining bank finance has a number of important implications for a company. First, banks offer at least two kinds of finance for businesses: loans and overdrafts. Loans are secured on the assets of the company and must be repaid according to a fixed schedule agreed in advance. Overdrafts are normally unsecured; they do not have to be repaid according to a fixed schedule, but the usual arrangement is that the bank may call in the overdraft at any time. Because loans are secured on the company's assets, they will be at a lower rate of interest than an overdraft. Most small companies will have both a loan and an overdraft. In practice loans are usually secured by means of personal guarantees given by the directors of the company, as well as by charges on the assets of the company (see further **4.3.2.1** below). A director's personal guarantee is frequently supported by a mortgage on the director's own home. This gives directors a considerable incentive to work hard to ensure the success of the company. At the same time it makes a very considerable breach in the principle of limited liability. Although the guarantees will normally be required of the directors as such rather than of the shareholders as such, there is in small companies often a considerable overlap between the two categories, with the result that the shareholders are often at risk of considerable personal loss if the company fails.

In the UK, unlike in many other parts of the European Community, it is virtually unknown for banks to invest in small companies by taking shares – the investment always takes the form of loan capital. It is open to debate whether this practice is entirely a healthy one – there is some evidence that it makes banks reluctant to continue to support companies through difficult economic times, since they find it more advantageous in the short term to withdraw the finance, thereby causing the company to collapse. It is interesting to note that the country in which the practice of banks taking an equity stake in companies is most fully developed is Germany, which was the most successful economy within the European Community over a period of many years. Although it is not possible to prove that the two facts are connected, it seems not unreasonable to suppose that the longer-term view which German banks are able to adopt is helpful to companies undergoing temporary difficulties.

4.3.2.1 Fixed and floating charges

Where the loan given by the bank is to be secured, two different forms of security are available. These are the fixed charge and the floating charge. The fixed charge is a charge over the fixed assets of the company – usually the land and buildings. The floating charge is a charge over the floating assets of the company, ie those assets or classes of assets which change from time to time. The most common examples of floating assets which can be charged are the stock-in-trade (for a trading company) and the book debts, ie the right to recover debts from persons to whom the company has supplied goods or services and who have not yet paid for them. It is likely that most companies will have some assets of both these classes at any given time, but the identity of the things within those classes will change on a regular basis. In the case of Great Expectations Ltd, the use of floating charges is further complicated by the facts that much of the stock-in-trade is bought under contracts which contain retention of title clauses, and that the book debts are factored so far as possible in order to aid cash flow. The implications of these policies are discussed further in **Chapter 15**.

4.4 Convertible debentures

Convertible debentures occupy an intermediate position between equity financing (ie, by allotment of shares) and debt financing. They are debentures which are capable of being converted, at the option of the debenture holder, into shares of the company. Thus, they start their life as a form of debt financing, but they may at some later stage be turned into equity. Convertible debentures provide a prospective investor in a company with a very convenient means of hedging his bets. If the company is not particularly successful, he can keep the investment in the form of a debenture, giving him a contractual right to interest, which is a first charge on the company's assets and does not depend on the existence of profits. On the other hand, if the company becomes successful, he can exercise his option to convert the debentures into shares, thereby becoming entitled to participate in the distribution of profits. None of this is proof against the risk that the company will fail totally, causing him to lose his investment.

Before exercising the conversion option the debenture holder would also be well advised to bear in mind three further points. The first is that even as a shareholder he is not certain of any dividend, since there is generally no obligation for the directors to declare a dividend at all. The second is that the level of influence which he wields in the company as a shareholder will depend on the size of his share holding, and this is something which he should calculate before exercising the option. The third point is that the option is not normally reversible. Once the debenture has been converted into shares, the ordinary principles of capital maintenance (see **Chapter 17**) will prevent the investor from converting the shares back to a debenture. It may be possible to circumvent this problem by including a clause in the original agreement to the effect that the company will upon demand re-purchase the shares, but this option will be effectively exercisable only if the company meets the requirements for re-purchase of its own shares at the time when the shareholder wishes to sell them. As one of these conditions is the availability of distributable profits to pay for the shares, and as the most likely situation for the attempted exercise of the option is where the company is making a loss, it will be apparent that the practical value of such a clause is likely to be limited.

Where convertible debentures are used, it is normal to make some provision in the debenture for the price at which the debentures are to be converted into shares. A common provision allows the debenture holder to subscribe for the new shares at par. This is in fact a very favourable deal. The option will be exercised only when the company is prospering, and in this event it is virtually certain that the net asset value of the shares will be greater than par, so that the debenture holder is effectively able to buy his shares for less than their true value. An alternative approach to the same question is to make the rate of conversion from debenture to shares vary over time; for example, each £1,000 worth of loan might be converted into 1,000 shares if the option is exercised within two years, but only 900 after two years, 800 after three years, and so on. This is an attempt to allow for the expected increase in the net asset value and thus to avoid the watering-down which might occur. It is necessarily an imperfect estimate, and the likelihood of the debenture holder exercising the option may well depend on the extent to which the estimate overvalues or undervalues the shares at any particular time.

It will be apparent from this discussion that convertible debentures offer many advantages to the debenture holder. At the same time they are potentially a problem for the other shareholders, who are in danger of having their shareholdings diluted at any moment and most probably just at the time when they become valuable. Many companies will therefore be reluctant to grant convertible debentures, and it will only be the prospective investor who is in a strong position – perhaps because the company is in desperate need of his money – who can hope to insist on such an arrangement.

4.5 Advice to the parties

It is obvious that the question of risk is an important one in this case. A number of the participants in the company have good reason for being very averse to risking their own capital in this venture – indeed that is a major reason for choosing to have a company in the first place. At the same time the company will need a reasonable amount of capital to get itself under way. The obvious compromise is to have a relatively small issued capital and to operate largely on the basis of loans. Within the issued share capital the question of the balance of power in the company is also significant, since shares represent not only a person's investment in the company but also the amount of influence which he has. This is because major disputes within the company will need to be resolved at a General Meeting of the shareholders. The detailed rules relating to meetings are outside the scope of this book, but it should be noted here that any important dispute will be resolved by a poll rather than by a show of hands. This is important, because on a poll each shareholder has one vote for every share held, whereas on a show of hands each shareholder has only one vote. On the other hand, share capital is risk capital in the sense that it may be lost entirely if the company goes into liquidation.

Another issue which needs to be considered briefly at this stage (and which is explored more fully in **Chapter 10**) concerns the role of the directors. Although the shareholders are the owners of the company, the day-to-day management of the company is in the hands of the directors, and it is not easy for shareholders to overrule directors on individual questions, though they can fairly easily take the more drastic step of dismissing the directors entirely. It is therefore a matter of some importance to decide who will be the directors. As the directors are responsible for day-to-day management, it is necessary to appoint people who will be willing and able to give the necessary time and commitment. It is also desirable to choose people who have some managerial experience.

A subsidiary issue within the question of choosing directors is that of the possible appointment of a Managing Director. Article 72 of Table A allows the directors to appoint such a person, and to delegate to him such of their powers as they consider desirable to be exercised by him. In practice this article is often used to give the Managing Director full executive powers on behalf of the company. This makes the proper choice of the Managing Director even more important than it might otherwise be, since the activities of the Managing Director can be crucial to the success or failure of the company.

It will be appreciated that the question of directorships is not at all the same as the question of shareholdings – a person with little capital to invest may by reason of personal qualities be eminently suitable as a director, whilst a person with substantial capital need not have any managerial experience or capabilities at all. This problem can be seen quite clearly in the present company. Duncan clearly has more money than anyone else and is therefore in the best position to provide the capital, but he has made it clear that he has no interest in running the company, and there appears therefore to be no reason to make him a director. Indeed, it is unlikely that he would accept appointment as a director, since this position involves legal duties and responsibilities which he would not wish to take on. By contrast, Arthur and Bill have relevant expertise and are going to be working full time in the business, which points in the direction of making at least one of them a director. However, neither has substantial sums of capital to invest, and neither can expect to have more than a fairly small proportion of the shares. Edwina is in an intermediate position. She has some capital available, though her major contribution to the starting of the business may be that she makes available her office premises. At the same time she does have managerial experience and would appear to be the obvious candidate for Managing Director. This leaves Charlotte, who is really in the weakest position of the five founder members of the company. She has no managerial experience and is not well placed to invest large sums of money in the company. She is unlikely to be a director, and there may even be a question about whether she should be a shareholder – certainly there is already evidence of hostility between her and Edwina. On balance, though, it is suggested that Bill's determination to protect her is likely to lead to her becoming a shareholder on a very small scale.

Perhaps the next question to be addressed is how much the total capital ought to be. By this is meant the total working capital which will be necessary to get the company under way – the question of the division of that capital between debt and equity will be considered subsequently.

The question of the possible cost of office premises is a very significant one here. The need to purchase such premises would significantly increase the necessary start up capital. A much better idea would be to lease the premises which Edwina owns. This would aid the cash flow of the company in the initial period. Ideally, Edwina should be persuaded to lease the premises at a nominal rent, at least for the first few years. Even with this substantial saving the company will incur the cost of buying materials (which can no doubt be acquired initially from the partnership whose business is being incorporated), as well as legal fees and the costs of publicity. Salaries for employees will also be a major charge on the company's resources, and it is desirable to have some spare capital in case business is initially slack and to deal with contingencies. It is suggested that an initial working capital of £100,000 would be sensible.

It is next necessary to decide who is going to provide that capital and how it is going to be divided between debt and equity, and how many shares each shareholder is going to have. Duncan is no doubt in a position to put up the entire sum himself if he were so minded, but this is not a good idea. In the first place it represents an unacceptable degree of risk for Duncan; in the second place it does not give the others enough incentive to work hard for the success of the company; in the third place it gives Duncan all the power in the company, and this is unlikely to be acceptable to any of the other participants. On the other hand, Duncan is clearly going to have a major role in the financing of the company, and if this is not going to be solely in the form of shares then a significant element of it will have to take the form of a loan. At the same time it may not be desirable for all the loan capital to come from Duncan, since this again threatens to give him too much power and too much exposure to risk. It would therefore appear sensible to obtain some of the initial finance from the bank.

When deciding how much of the £100,000 should take the form of equity there are a number of interlinked questions to consider. One problem is that the bank may well expect to see a reasonable amount of the participants' own money invested in the company so as to give them a genuine interest in its success. Another issue is that the balance of power between shareholders has to be carefully considered, and this is affected to some extent by the maximum amounts which the smaller shareholders can afford to invest. In the present case it is suggested that an initial issued share capital of £10,000 represents a sensible compromise among these various concerns. The remaining £90,000 will have to be obtained from Duncan and/or the bank as loans.

The next issue is to decide how the £10,000 will be divided among the five participants. Duncan, as the company's principal financier and the person with most money to invest in shares, is clearly in a strong position to insist on having a major share holding. He would be wise to do so, since this will give him a corresponding influence in General Meetings. On the other hand, the remaining participants should be wary of allowing Duncan too much influence in these matters; he has made it clear that he does not wish to participate in the management of the company, and it is therefore not desirable to give him so large a share holding that he can intervene on an occasional basis by giving the directors instructions which they must obey. For these purposes the crucial proportion of the shares is 75%. Such a holding allows the passage of a special resolution at a General Meeting (for more details on this see **Chapters 9** and **13**), and such a resolution is sufficient to give directions to the directors. The other participants, and especially the directors, should therefore resist very firmly any suggestion that Duncan should be given 75% of the shares. Alternatively, they might suggest the possibility of different classes of shares, though this is unlikely to be accepted, for reasons discussed at **4.1.5** above. At the same time Duncan is in a strong position to insist on a majority share holding, and this demand will probably have to be conceded. It may be noted that a majority share holding is sufficient to allow Duncan to dismiss the directors (subject to the possibility of what is known as a *Bushell v Faith* clause in the Articles; as to this see **Chapter 7**). However, a threat to do this is double-edged, since Duncan would then have to find replacements for the directors whom he had dismissed, and this would not necessarily be an easy task. It is therefore suggested that Duncan should have between 51% and 74% of the shares.

The next person to be considered is Edwina, who is likely to be second in influence to Duncan. Clearly Edwina cannot have a majority share holding if Duncan has one, so the first question for Edwina is whether she is to have 'negative control'. This term means having more than 25% of the shares, a total which is not sufficient to pass any resolution but which is sufficient by itself to defeat a special resolution proposed by others. Edwina will naturally want such a share holding, but it is suggested that the others would be wise not to give it to her; Edwina is clearly a rather difficult and prickly individual to deal with, and there are dangers in allowing her to obstruct the company's progress single-handed. It would be better to insist that she must get at least one of the others to support her in order to achieve negative control. This points to a share holding a little short of 25% for Edwina, but there is a further matter to consider, namely, whether Duncan and Edwina together should be able to pass a special resolution, ie whether their combined shareholdings should total 75%. Although Arthur, Bill and Charlotte will naturally see dangers to themselves in such an arrangement, it seems unlikely that they can resist it, given the financial muscle wielded by Duncan and Edwina. It may be noted at this point that some further balancing of power may be achieved later when appointing the directors if Edwina is not sole director

The scheme proposed so far leaves only a small proportion of the shares for Arthur, Bill and Charlotte, but this is inevitable given that they have relatively little money to invest. It seems desirable that both Arthur and Bill should, when combined with Edwina, be able to exert negative control, but it may be that Charlotte's share holding is intended to be purely nominal, in which case it would probably be preferable to require Edwina to combine with someone else for this purpose (though in practical terms this point may not be important, given the evident hostility between the two women).

Although there is more than one possible division of the shares which will achieve simultaneously all the parameters set out above, the arrangement set out in the table below is one which has the added advantage of being simple to remember.

Issued share capital £10,000 divided into 10,000 shares of £1 each

Shareholder	No of shares
Arthur	800
Bill	800
Charlotte	400
Duncan	6,000
Edwina	2,000

This is the allocation of shares finally decided upon by the participants, and will form the basis for the resolution of issues confronting the company in forthcoming scenarios in this book.

It still remains for the company to find a further £90,000 working capital. It is suggested that the bank might be asked to provide half of this, the remainder coming from Duncan. In practice the bank might well be prepared to provide the whole £90,000, but, as will be seen in later chapters, there are practical advantages in not being entirely beholden to the bank in matters of corporate finance.

This proposal does have certain associated problems, however. Loans to companies are normally secured by charges on the company's assets. Charges are of two kinds, fixed charges, which are over specific, fixed assets of the company (usually land and buildings), and floating charges, which are over classes of asset which change frequently. The examples most commonly encountered are the stock-in-trade of a trading company and the book debts of any company. At any given time there are likely to be assets within these classes, but the identity of those assets changes. It is nevertheless possible to charge the class of assets as a whole. Persons lending money to a company therefore have to decide whether to take fixed charges, floating charges or both. In practice banks usually take both types of charge, and it must be assumed that the bank in the present case would insist on doing so. For the same reasons Duncan too should insist on fixed and floating charges. However, this then gives rise to a second issue, which is about the priority of these charges as between Duncan and the bank. Where a company is unable to meet its liabilities to chargeholders, the charged assets may be sold in order to satisfy the debt. If these assets too are insufficient to meet all the debts, it becomes crucial to know which of the chargeholders has first claim on them. When the charges are created at more or less the same time, as will be the case here, it is possible to make a conscious choice as to which shall have priority (for the problems which arise where the charges are created at different times, see **Chapter 15**). Where the bank is one of the chargeholders, it must be expected that it will insist on having the first charge (see also **Chapter 22**, where the effect of Pt 10 of The Enterprise Act 2002 on the procedure for enforcing floating charges is considered).

The remaining question which needs to be considered is that of directorships and of the appointment of the Company Secretary, who is the officer of the company responsible for its administration, and in particular for ensuring its compliance with the regulatory requirements of company law. A private company such as this need only have one director (Companies Act 1985, s 282), but in practice it is usually found desirable to have at least two, if only to spread the workload. The Company Secretary may also be a director, but may not be the sole director (Companies Act 1985, s 283). In the present situation the filling of these posts is to some degree constrained by the availability of suitable candidates. Duncan can be ruled out since he does not wish to participate in management, whilst Charlotte lacks the necessary experience and qualifications. Edwina has the greatest managerial experience, and is a natural choice for a directorship. Indeed, the most obvious course would be to make her Managing Director. It is then suggested that Bill should become the other director, whilst Arthur acts as Company Secretary. The involvement of Bill and Arthur in managerial positions will go some way towards offsetting their lack of influence in the General Meeting of the company.

As a general rule directors are appointed by the General Meeting of the company, though there is also the possibility of the board of directors co-opting others to join them until the next General Meeting (Table A, art 79). However, the first directors will have to be appointed at the time when the registration forms for the company are submitted, and this will naturally be before the first General Meeting can be held. Consequently, the first directors are appointed using a special form signed by the subscribers to the Memorandum of Association.

4.6 Registration formalities

The company cannot come into existence as a separate legal person until it has been duly registered with the Registrar of Companies, who will issue a certificate of incorporation stating that the formalities have been complied with, and giving the name and registered number of the company. In order to obtain this certificate it is necessary to submit to the Registrar the following:

(a) the Memorandum (duly signed) and Articles of Association;

(b) the form for appointing the first directors;

(c) a declaration that all registration formalities have been complied with; and

(d) the fee.

Provided that all the paperwork is in order, it usually takes about six weeks for the application to be processed and the certificate of incorporation to be issued. Until this process is complete, the company has no legal existence, and the promoters should be careful not to suggest otherwise in dealing with third parties. On the other hand, once the company is formed it is essential that it should comply with the statutory requirement to disclose its name on all documents it issues (Companies Act 1985, ss 348(1), 349(1)). As it is impossible to be sure that the company name will be approved until the certificate is issued (and impossible to know what number will be allocated to it), there is a thriving business of company formation agents, who form companies with the intention of selling them to those starting in business who want to obtain a company at short notice. There is usually no difficulty in obtaining a company within 48 hours if this method is used. The disadvantages are that the company will already have a name, a Memorandum and Articles, which may not be entirely suitable for the purchasers' needs. Consequently, it may be necessary to expend time and effort in making suitable modifications, and this may offset the benefits of obtaining the company immediately. On the other hand, business can start without delay, especially if the company has a new-style objects clause allowing it to carry on business as a general commercial company.

4.7 Pre-incorporation contracts

Where the formation of a company is planned, it quite often happens that the promoters of the company want to enter into contracts on its behalf before it has come into existence, for example for the purchase of materials, or even for such important matters as taking leases of property. It is a natural and reasonable desire to want to get the affairs of the company under way as soon as possible, and to that end to seek to make arrangements even before the company is formed. Unfortunately this does give rise to some problems. Directors of the company normally act as agents of the company, but it is clearly not possible for them to do this at a time when the company is not even in existence, since it is a rule of agency law that the agent cannot take advantage of the contract unless he/it is in existence at the time when the contract is made. Similar difficulties arise in trying to enforce the contract against the company. In relation to pre-incorporation contracts made on behalf of a company, the Companies Act 1985, s 36C provides some guidance as to the position:

> A contract which purports to be made by or on behalf of a company at a time when the company has not been formed has effect, subject to any agreement to the contrary, as one made with the person purporting to act for the company or as agent for it, and he is personally liable on the contract accordingly.

Unfortunately this section is far from clear. Although the promoter is declared to be personally liable on the contract, the statute does not say expressly that the company itself is not liable, though it must be admitted that this appears to be the legislative intention, and the conclusion might be deduced from the reference to the contract 'which purports' to be made with the company and from the failure to state that the contract is deemed to be made with both the company and the person purporting to act for it. The point is important because of the common law rules which the courts had developed prior to the enactment of this legislation. These stated that the company could become liable, but only if, after incorporation, it entered into a fresh contract with the other party on the same terms. A distinction was drawn between this process and the attempted ratification of the earlier contract. This attempt was held to be doomed to fail because of the agency law rules alluded to above (*Kelner v Baxter* (1866) LR 2 CP 174; *Bagot Pneumatic Tyre Co v Clipper Pneumatic Tyre Co* [1902] 1 Ch 146). It is unclear to what extent s 36C still allows for the making of a fresh contract, but it is submitted that this possibility is unaffected by the section. A more difficult question is whether the company can now ratify the original contract. Although the distinction between ratification and making a new contract was at best an artificial and unsatisfactory one, s 36C does not appear to affect it, since it does not deal with the company's position.

The words 'subject to any agreement to the contrary' in s 36C also call for comment. It might be supposed that these words allow the parties to the contract to agree that the company is to be liable on the contract. However, it is submitted that this is logically impossible. First, the conceptual difficulty inherent in non-existent companies making contracts cannot be circumvented. Secondly, the company could in any event only become liable in contract, and this would require its agreement. The company is not bound by an agreement between the promoter and the creditor for the very good reason that the company is not and cannot be a party to that agreement. The only significance which can be assigned to these words in s 36C is that they allow the parties to agree that the promoter will not in fact incur personal liability. It is hard to see, however, why the other party would wish to agree to that, given that he would then be forced to rely on the goodwill of the company in agreeing to make a new contract on the same terms. This is a most unsatisfactory area of the law, in which over-technical adherence to the rules of agency law has apparently been allowed to prevent a commonsense solution. The law needs to find some way to make reasonable pre-incorporation contracts at least ratifiable by the company.

FURTHER READING

M A Pickering, 'The problem of the preference share' (1963) 26 MLR 499.
J H Gross, 'Pre-incorporation contracts' (1971) 87 LQR 367.

5 Taxation

LEARNING OUTCOMES

By the end of this chapter, you should understand:

- in outline, some of the rules relating to the taxation of partnerships as compared with the taxation regime applicable to private companies;

- the taxation of close companies and the taxation consequences of a company acquiring its own shares.

SCENARIO

While the members of Great Expectations are thinking about the idea of incorporating the firm, one issue which has been mentioned to them is that of taxation. For the most part they know little of the intricacies of tax law (though Duncan has had some experience of it in the past), and they are anxious to know how incorporation will affect their tax position.

OVERVIEW

Although the question of taxation is not directly part of partnership or company law, and is not always treated in textbooks on the subject, the way in which companies are taxed plays an important part in determining the circumstances in which they are formed and the ways in which they are used. It is for this reason that the subject is dealt with here, albeit briefly and somewhat selectively. For a complete explanation of partnership and company taxation, reference should be made to specialist texts on the subject. This chapter considers certain practical taxation issues which may arise for those involved in Great Expectations. After an explanation of the general principles, each issue is considered in reference to both partnerships and companies, the similarities and differences being highlighted.

5.1 The schedular system of taxation

For historical reasons which have now no more than curiosity value, the taxation of income in the UK is conducted according to a schedular system, under which income is divided into classes according to the source from which it is received. So far as Great Expectations is concerned, the important practical point is that the income of self-employed persons and of companies is taxed under Sch D to the Income and Corporation Taxes Act (ICTA) 1988, whereas the income of employed persons is taxed under Sch E. As appears later, there are some slight but important differences between these two systems of taxation.

5.2 Partnership taxation

As partnerships have no separate legal personality, it is not possible to levy tax on the partnership as such. Although the partnership is treated for the purpose of income tax liability as if it were an individual, the liability to income tax is that of each of the partners, based on their individual interests in the firm. The Commissioners may nevertheless require a nominated partner to make a partnership return (ICTA 1988, s 111).

Before 1994–95, partnerships were taxed on the preceding year basis, which meant that the taxable income for any given year was the income of the accounting period which ended in the preceding year of assessment. From the tax year 1997-98, the profits of a partnership, like those of a sole trader, are calculated on the current year basis.

5.2.1 Partnership taxation – the opening years

A new partnership is assessed for its first three years on the basis of the profits earned in each of the respective years; where the accounts for the first year commenced within any tax year, the basis of assessment is the profits arising in that tax year. For the second year the profits for the first 12 months of the business form the basis for the income tax liability. For subsequent years the income tax liability is calculated by reference to the profits earned during the current year of trade (ICTA 1988, s 62).

5.2.2 Change in partners

Where a new partner is admitted or a partner leaves the firm, the business is treated as continuing so long as at least one person who was engaged in that business before the change continues to be so engaged after the change (ICTA 1988, s 113(2)). This will most commonly be the case, since most changes involve the arrival and/or departure of one or more partners, with the other partners continuing. Only where all the partners retire from the business simultaneously is there a discontinuance of the business of the firm followed by the commencement of a new business (ICTA 1988, s 113(1)). This brings into operation the closing year rules followed by the opening year rules. It is not possible to avoid the happening of this discontinuance if all partners retire simultaneously. Such a discontinuance may be fiscally undesirable because of the closing year rules, and the only way to avoid it is to stagger the retirement of the partners, so that there is no one single change which brings the closing year rules into operation.

5.2.3 Capital gains

Capital gains are subject to capital gains tax (CGT) rather than to income tax. The governing statute is the Taxation of Chargeable Gains Act (TCGA) 1992. Taxable gains accruing on the disposal of assets are charged to tax at the disponor's marginal rate of income tax (TCGA 1992, s 4), subject to an annual exemption per person and to a notional uplift in the acquisition cost to take account of inflation since the date of purchase (TCGA 1992, s 20). Capital gains made by a partnership are treated as being made by each partner, and accordingly (TCGA 1992, s 59) are apportioned among the partners in the same way as income receipts.

5.3 Corporate taxation

Companies pay corporation tax on their profits, and in principle liability to this tax is calculated in the same way as liability to Sch D income tax (ICTA 1988, s 9, s70(1)). For companies there are three rates of taxation, namely, starting rate, small companies rate and standard rate. 19%, which is the small companies rate, and 30%, which is the standard rate, are the common rates. A company whose profits for any given year of assessment do not exceed £300,000 (ICTA 1988, s 13(3)) will pay tax at the small companies rate, whilst companies with profits of more than £1,500,000 pay tax at the standard rate. Between these two figures a tapering system operates to phase out the relief provided by the small companies rate (ICTA 1988, s 13(2)). No tax is payable on the first £10,000 profit and 23.75% is payable on the next £40,000 profit; this is the starting rate for companies.

Capital gains of companies are also subject to corporation tax (rather than to CGT), but the liability is calculated in accordance with the principles laid down in the TCGA 1992 for capital gains of individuals (TCGA 1992, s 8). Companies have, however, no annual exemption in relation to chargeable gains. This is a tax disadvantage associated with the use of a company. So far as Great Expectations is concerned, it may be doubted whether this point is of great significance, for the business has few capital assets, and is certainly not looking to sell them at a profit.

5.4 Taxation of groups of companies

If a company is set up, it may happen that at some later stage it will be thought desirable to create another subsidiary company (see **Chapter 4** and **Appendix E** for the eventual corporate structure of Great Expectations Ltd). In this event the rules relating to the taxation of corporate groups will become important. For these purposes, companies are in the same group if they have a common parent, or if one is the subsidiary of the other (ICTA 1988, s 413(3)).

5.5 Close companies

Great Expectations Ltd is a close company, ie a company resident in the UK controlled by not more than five people or by its directors, however numerous (ICTA 1988, s 414(1); the additional elements of the definition applicable to quoted companies (ICTA 1988, s 415) are not considered here). Such companies are subject to specially restrictive tax treatment, particularly in relation to loans made by them to their participators (ICTA 1988, ss 419–422).

5.6 Salaries

In the partnership of Great Expectations, Arthur, Bill and Edwina are partners, whilst Charlotte is merely an employee. The firm also employs a dozen or so others. Salaries which are paid to employees of the firm are taxed in the hands of those employees under the PAYE system. This means that the firm is obliged to deduct the tax due before paying the salaries to the employees. Salaries paid in this way are a deductible expense of the firm (see below) when calculating the taxable profits for the year. Remuneration paid to partners is not so deductible; instead it counts as a distribution of profit. Some difficulty may be encountered here in connection with so-called salaried partners. The concept of a salaried partner is from a tax point of view an impossible one. Either a person is a partner, in which case remuneration is profit distribution, or he is an employee. Identifying which applies in any given case is a question for partnership law (see **Chapter 2** for the concept of a partner). Arthur, Bill and Edwina are all partners in the proper sense of the term.

If the business is incorporated, there will of course be no 'partners'. It is to be assumed that Arthur, Bill and Edwina will be employed by the company, possibly as directors (for the details of the eventual arrangement, see **Chapter 4**). Salaries paid to directors are not profit distributions but deductible expenses. Although this may at first sight seem a desirable change, it should be remembered that the rules relating to deductible expenses are less generous for employees than for partners. The former important difference – that partners were taxed on the preceding year basis, whereas directors were taxed on a current year basis under Sch E – has long been removed.

5.6.1 Expenses

In relation to allowable expenses, there is a fundamental difference between the treatment of partners and the treatment of employees (including directors). The rules for Sch D require only that expenditure be incurred wholly and exclusively for the purposes of the business (ICTA 1988, s 74). Although it is not possible to apportion expenditure incurred for a dual purpose, this will allow the deduction of expenditure incurred more or less voluntarily for business purposes. By contrast, the rules under Sch E require the expenditure to be incurred wholly exclusively *and necessarily* for the purposes of the business. Thus, it is more difficult to obtain deductions for travelling expenses, for example, under Sch E (*Ricketts v Colquhoun* [1926] AC 1) than under Sch D. There is no doubt that, from the point of view of allowable expenses, Sch D taxation is to be preferred to Sch E taxation.

5.6.2 Losses

Where a partnership makes a loss in any given year, there will of course be no liability to tax. Losses may be carried forward and set against the profits of future years of assessment (ICTA 1988, s 385). Substantially the same rule applies to companies.

5.7 Purchase of own shares

In **Chapter 20** the possibility of the company buying back some of its own shares is considered. Apart from the company law aspects of this idea, the participants in the company would also need to consider the tax implications. A purchase of this kind is in principle a distribution of assets by the company. Consequently, the company would incur a tax liability on the payment and account for that tax to the Revenue. This consequence can be avoided if clearance for the transaction is first obtained from the Revenue. The relevant rules are to be found in ICTA 1988, ss 219-225. The company will need to show to the satisfaction of the Revenue that the transaction is entered into to benefit a trade carried on by the company and that it is not done primarily for the purpose of avoiding tax, or to enable an owner of shares to participate in the profits of the company without receiving a dividend (ICTA 1988, s 219.). In the case arising in **Chapter 20** it will be seen that there is no tax avoidance motive, the scheme being contemplated as as way of getting rid of Duncan for the greater benefit of the company.

5.7.1 Profit share

When partners receive money from the partnership, this is treated as a distribution of profit and tax is paid by the partners accordingly. The partnership itself cannot, of course, be subject to taxation, since it has no independent existence.

5.7.2 Undistributed profit

This is an area where there is a fundamental difference between partnership taxation and company taxation. The profit made by a partnership is attributed to the partners in proportion to their profit-sharing ratios. This attribution (and the resulting charge to tax) happens whether or not the profit is in fact distributed to the partners. Thus, there is no tax advantage to be gained by not distributing partnership profit (though of course there may be other good commercial reasons for re-investing the profits in the business rather than paying them to the partners). In a company, by contrast, corporation tax is paid on all profits, but the additional charge to shareholders which may occur on the payment of a dividend is avoided if the profit is retained in the company. It follows that, from the point of view of profit retention with a view to encouraging growth, a company has tax advantages as compared with a partnership. The tax liability may be further reduced where the company pays tax at the small companies rate (see **5.3** above).

5.8 Value added tax

The services and goods provided by Great Expectations Ltd are subject to value added tax (VAT) at the standard rate of 17.5% (Value Added Tax Act 1994). This sum will be added to all accounts rendered to customers and must be accounted for to Customs and Excise. However, where Great Expectations Ltd has paid VAT on good or services supplied to it which have contributed to the goods or services which the company supplies, such amounts, known as input tax, may be deducted from the amount to be paid to Customs and Excise. This system ensures that the company's liability to tax is only in respect of the difference between the price of the supply to the company and the price of the supply by it to the customer, ie the value added by the company's involvement in the process. So far as VAT is concerned there is no material difference between a partnership and a company.

5.8.1 Tax implications of the process of incorporation

If Great Expectations does turn itself into Great Expectations Ltd, the process of incorporation may bring with it certain tax consequences. First, there will be a discontinuance of the business of the partnership, so that the closing year rules will operate. Secondly, there is in principle a possible liability to CGT, since the transfer of the business to the company will involve a disposal by the partners of their interests in that business (the new business will belong to the company, not to the shareholders). However, it is possible to delay this charge by electing to roll the gain over into the company. In these circumstances the company is deemed to acquire the business from the partnership for such consideration as will ensure that there is neither a gain nor a loss on the transaction. The partners will not pay CGT, but if the company sells the business at some stage in the future, it will be charged to CGT on the basis of the deemed acquisition cost established when the company is set up.

5.9 Advice to the parties

It appears that the prospective shareholders in Great Expectations Ltd have been somewhat misled. A limited amount of tax sheltering may be available, for example, by means of keeping profits within the company so as to smooth the income flow. However, paying dividends rather than salaries may no longer be tax-efficient (see **Chapter 15**). It is nevertheless a mistake to suppose that there are generally substantial fiscal advantages to be derived from incorporation as compared with partnership status. It is sometimes said that no commercial decision should be made purely for tax-planning reasons, and this is good advice in the present context. Forming the business into a company was probably a good idea from the point of view of liability and finance, but tax could never have been a sufficient reason for doing so (though readers may by now be wondering whether these particular individuals were wise to go into business together at all).

OVERVIEW

Although we are concerned in this chapter with all the clauses in the company's Memorandum, the focus will be on the capacity of the company. It is only by determining this that we can predict with any degree of certainty which activities the company is empowered to engage in. It is therefore necessary to make a careful study of the objects clause in the Memorandum of Association, as it is this which indicates the parameters of the company's capacity.

The need for an objects clause within a company's Memorandum stems from the early days of company law, when it was envisaged that investors would have only a minimal interest in the management of the business being concerned more as to the nature of their investment. Having decided to invest in, say, the manufacturing of textiles or the railways, they could be certain that their investment would be used in that field until such time as they might wish to withdraw their support and reinvest elsewhere. The objects clause was descriptive of the activities for which a company had been incorporated, and investors could rely upon the company being restricted to its stated sphere of activity by the willingness of the courts to find contracts which fell outside of this to be ultra vires and void. This was enhanced by the doctrine of constructive notice, which provided that third parties who dealt with companies were taken to know what the capacity of a company was by virtue of the public nature of its Memorandum (*Ernest v Nicholls* (1857) 6 HL Cas 401; *Re Jon Beauforte (London) Ltd* [1953] Ch 131, [1953] 1 All ER 634). (However, see the Companies Act 1985, s 711A, which as yet has not been brought into force.)

Rapid changes in industry during the latter half of the 19th century, and the corresponding increase in the development of new markets, placed the law in something of a dilemma. On the one hand, companies were restricted in the scope of their activities by their objects clauses; and on the other hand, profitability often depended upon the ability to shift direction and expand into other areas of economic activity. The law had to balance the sometimes conflicting needs of the company, both as an investment proposition, which ensured that investors knew the nature of its proposed activities, and as a business medium, which required sufficient flexibility in order to keep abreast of economic developments and, of course, to maintain and increase profitability. Draftsmen of companies' Memoranda attempted, with some success, to address this problem through careful drafting of objects clauses which encompassed as many activities as possible. There are many reported cases which catalogue the development of the objects clause in companies' Memoranda and the judicial reaction to the various innovations in drafting, most of which were the result of claims that certain activities entered into by the company in question were ultra vires and therefore unenforceable against it (eg, *A-G v Great Eastern Railway Co* (1880) 5 App Cas 473; *Deuchar v Gas Light & Coke Co* [1925] AC 691; *Cotman v Brougham* [1918] AC 514; *Re German Coffee Date Co* (1882) 20 ChD 169; *Re Crown Bank* (1890) 44 ChD 634; *Bell Houses Ltd v City Wall Properties Ltd* [1966] 2 QB 656). The courts appeared to be construing objects clauses as widely as possible in order to avoid declaring activities ultra vires with the disastrous consequences this had for third parties. A useful example is to be found in the case of *Re Introductions Ltd* [1970] Ch 199, where a company's bank found itself in the undesirable position of being unable to enforce the repayment of a loan because it had been agreed for activities which were beyond the capacity of the company. The loan was therefore found to be ultra vires the company and void (banks routinely take copies of company customers' constitutional documents, and in this case the bank would have had actual, as opposed to constructive, notice of the company's capacity. Because of this the decision need not be viewed as inconsistent with the reasoning of later cases which distinguished between objects and powers; see, eg, the reasoning of the Court of Appeal in *Rolled Steel Products (Holdings) Ltd v British Steel Corporation* [1986] Ch 246; [1985] 2 WLR 908; [1985] 3 All ER 52.)

Eventually, accepted drafting practices for objects clauses meant that companies were competent to enter more or less any field of activity, but investors were left with pages and pages of objects from which to attempt to discern the nature of the business in which they had invested. The 1989 Act finally abolished the doctrine of ultra vires in relation to third parties dealing with a company (see the Companies Act 1985, s 35(1), as substituted by The Companies Act 1989, s 108(1)), although the right of a company's members to require the company to act in accordance with its stated objects was preserved (s 35(2)). Although the abolition of the ultra vires rule was prompted by the First EEC Council Directive (68/151), Article 9, the effects of the rule had already been recognised by the courts as failing to suit commercial needs. It became necessary to hold more of a balance between third parties who had dealt with a company and the company's members. A strict application of the ultra vires rule had inclined the advantage towards the latter group. The task of restricting its scope had initially fallen to the courts, which had already progressed to the point where the rule was of little practical value to the members in a situation where the company had been dealing ultra vires with a third party (see below). An interesting question is whether the courts will adopt a similar reasoning when construing a company's objects clause in an attempt to hold a different balance, ie that between the members inter se where some part of the membership is exercising its right under s 35(2) of the Companies Act 1985 to require the company to adhere to its stated objects. If they do, the ultra vires rule will be of little benefit to a company's members, since the company objects will invariably be stated in the widest terms, a practice which has long been accepted by the courts. Parliament too envisaged that companies would be relatively unfettered in respect of their capacity to engage in a wide range of activities. The 1989 Act provided the opportunity for a company to state as its object the carrying on of business as a general commercial company, which would empower it to carry on any trade or business whatsoever (Companies Act 1985, s 3A, as inserted by the Companies Act 1989, s 110). Great Expectations (Ideas) Ltd has adopted such an objects clause. Doubts have been cast on the effectiveness of this provision; see, eg, 'Modern Company Law for a Competitive Economy' London DTI 1998.

Duncan has invested in Great Expectations Ltd on the basis of its past success and future promise as a flourishing interior design business. If the company were to diversify into, say, the import/export business in order to facilitate its principal business, it is unlikely that he would object. However, an investor may have reason to object to diversification over which he has no control, and this might cause him to question the nature of his investment. In practical terms, the possibility of Duncan extracting his financial stake in Great Expectations Ltd in its formative years will be fairly remote, yet it is unlikely that he could successfully claim that the company was acting ultra vires for the purposes of s 35(2). At this stage in the company's development Duncan might consider using his considerable influence to negotiate the adoption of an objects clause which leaves the directors little room for manoeuvre but it is unlikely that he will succeed in getting the others to agree.

6.1 Form

Section 2 of the Companies Act 1985 requires the Memorandum to state:

(a) the company's name;

(b) its registered office;

(c) its objects;

(d) what the liability of its members is; and

(e) the amount and division of share capital.

For a private limited company there must be at least one subscriber to the Memorandum who must take at least one share (s 1(3)A)). Before July 1992, companies were required to have at least two subscribers (s 1(1)), and public companies must still comply with this requirement. The *form* of a Memorandum must conform with that specified by the Secretary of State, who has powers under s 3 to make such specification by statutory instrument. Table B of the 1985 Act must be followed for a private company and Table F for a public company. Tables B and F are noticeably similar, the only distinctions being that the company's name must end with 'limited' if it is a private company, and 'public limited company' if it is a public company and that a public company must state that it is a public company.

6.2 The company name

Choosing a company's name is more often than not a highly individual and personal act undertaken by the founders of the business. Even where a company has been bought 'off the shelf' (see **Chapter 4**), its name is very commonly altered by the members. Whatever the eventual choice, it will, it is to be hoped, enhance the activities of the business in some way, and of course lend itself to being marketed and advertised. A fairly common choice is often some derivation of the names of the founders, or a name intended to sound impressive (eg, Great Expectations Ltd!). In many cases the law will not intrude upon these deliberations, but when choosing a name for a company – this new legal 'person' – it is important to be aware that there are some restrictions and prohibitions which exist. Further, there is always the possibility that the use of a particular name, which is not of itself restricted or prohibited, may amount to the tort of passing off (**6.3 below** see, eg, *Direct Line Group Ltd v Direct Line Estate Agency Ltd* [1997] FSR 374).

6.2.1 The corporate name

6.2.1.1 Must indicate that liability is limited

Whatever choice is made as to the name for the company, it must always conclude with the word 'limited' (Companies Act 1985, s 25(2)). In keeping with the theme of disclosure, this indicates that the liability of the members is indeed limited to the capital fund already paid or promised (see **Chapter 17**). A public company's name must end with the words 'Public Limited Company' (s 25(1)). The abbreviations 'Ltd' and 'plc' are permitted in place of these required words (s 27). If the company were to be registered in Wales with its registered office in Wales, it would be entitled to use the Welsh equivalents of these words and their abbreviations (ss 25 and 27), although it will still be necessary to disclose in English that its liability is limited in every place where its name appears, ie letterheads, place of business and other publications (s 351(3)-(5)). Although it is an offence to use the words 'limited' or 'public limited company' where the user is not entitled to do so, such misuse does not invalidate any contracts made in the course of business (see *Cotronic (UK) Ltd v Dezonie* [1991] BCLC 721).

Non-profit making private companies engaged in work for charity or the public good are exempt from using the word 'limited' (s 30). All such companies wishing to omit the word must satisfy the requirements of s 30(3), which require the company's objects to be the promotion of commerce, art, science, education, religion, charity or any profession. The Memorandum or Articles must also contain provisions which require the company's prof-its, if any, or other income to be applied in promoting its objects and prohibit the payment of dividends to its members. There must also be a stipulation that if the company is wound up, its assets must be transferred to another body with charitable objects.

6.2.1.2 Must not include any prohibited words

Certain words are prohibited by the Companies Acts and by various other statutes, usually because they are words which are recognised as being capable of conveying a particular description of the business in question which is considered undesirable. So, for example, the use of words which would, in the opinion of the Secretary of State, amount to a crimi-nal offence is prohibited (Companies Act 1985, s 26(1)(d)). Thus, 'Tax Dodgers Ltd' or 'Queerbashers Ltd' are names which could never appear on the register of companies.

Other statutes prohibit the use of certain words which have an association with recog-nised charitable organisations. For example, s6 of the Geneva Convention Act 1957 prohibits the use of the words 'Red Cross' or 'Geneva Cross' unless the company has the authority of the Army Council.

Similarly, s 67 of the Banking Act 1987 prohibits the use of any name which indicates, or may reasonably be understood to indicate, that a company is a bank, or is carrying on a banking business, unless it has been authorised by the Bank of England under the Act and has a paid-up share capital and/or undistributable reserves of £5m or more. Section 107 of the Building Societies Act 1986 prohibits any representation by a company that it is a building society unless it is registered as one (other examples can be found under Company and Business Names Regulations 1981 (SI 1981/1685) as amended).

6.2.1.3 Restricted words requiring permission

Other words, although not prohibited, do require the permission of the Secretary of State before they can be used either because they are likely to give the impression that the com-pany is in some way connected with the Government or any local authority (Companies Act 1985, s 26(2)(a)), or because the word is one which is included in the list provided in the Company and Business Names Regulations 1981, which deals mostly with words asso-ciated with regulated trades or professions (SI 1981/1685, as amended by SI 1982/1653 and SI 1992/1196). These names must not be used without permission having been received from the relevant Secretary of State.

6.2.1.4 Name must not already be registered

A further limitation on the choice of corporate name would arise where another company has already been registered with the same name. If, for example, Arthur, Bill and Edwina were advised that a company was already registered as Great Expectations Ltd, they would have to choose a different name. If, however, they were aware of an *unincorporated* business with that name, as opposed to another registered company, they would not be prevented from registering their initial choice. This is because there is no central register of businesses. It is therefore possible to register a corporate name which is the same as that of another business, save for the potential liability for passing off (discussed at **6.3** below).

Having said that registration of a particular name depends upon the same name not already having been registered (see Companies Act 1985, s 26(1)(c) and (3), which describe minor differences which amount to no difference at all), this does not extend to situations where names of companies are similar, or indeed use many or almost all of the same words. So, for example, it was possible for a company to be registered as Star Eagle Ltd when a company already appeared upon the register as Eagle Star Ltd. The same words were used by both companies, simply in a different order. Many companies are registered with names that are very similar; similarity itself is not a ground for a refusal to register (although it must not be too alike for the purposes of s 28(2)).

The Registrar of Companies for England and Wales is required to keep an index of company names (Companies Act 1985, s 714), which includes, inter alia, all existing corporations which are incorporated by registration as companies under the laws of England and Wales, Northern Ireland and Scotland, and limited partnerships which are registered under the Limited Partnerships Act 1907.

6.2.2 Using a business name

Having chosen a corporate name, the corporators may nevertheless decide to carry on business using a different name. This is acceptable practice, although it must be remembered that the use by a business of a name which is not its true name will subject it to the disclosure requirements of the Business Names Act 1985 (discussed in **2.4** above). To trade using a business name rather than its corporate name does not enable the company to circumvent the rules governing the choice of corporate name. The Company and Business Names Regulations 1981, discussed at **6.2.1.3** above, apply equally to the choice of business name as to the choice of corporate name.

6.3 Passing off

Once the corporators have settled upon the choice of the company name, ensuring that all the various obstacles mentioned above have been avoided, the company will be registered with that name and will receive a certificate of incorporation. This document is conclusive evidence that all the requirements of the Companies Acts, in respect of registration, have been complied with (Companies Act 1985, s 13(7)). Erroneous registration is a matter which can be rectified in limited circumstances and, for the most part, in limited periods. Thus, s 28(2) of the 1985 Act permits the Secretary of State to order a change of name within 12 months of its being registered if, in his opinion, it is too like a name which already appears on the index. Section 28(4) and (5) also provide the Secretary of State with the power to order a change of name within five years of registration if, in his opinion, the company provided misleading information for the purposes of its registration with a particular name, or the company gave undertakings in order to be permitted to use a restricted name and these undertakings have not been fulfilled. There is no time limit on a compulsory change of name where the Secretary of State is of the opinion that a company is registered with a name which is so misleading as to the nature of its activities that it is likely to cause harm to the public.

The only remaining threat for the corporators therefore is the possibility that the use of a particular name may amount to the tort of passing off. A claim for passing off is concerned with the situation where one business is trading on the goodwill of another. It is not the form of business medium that is crucial but the nature of the businesses, coupled with the possibility of confusion between them which could result in loss to the complaining enterprise. A company which is formed with a name which is registrable, because it is not duplicating an existing corporation, may nevertheless be susceptible to a claim for passing off where the name is very similar to that of an existing business, which includes both companies (but not 'too like' for the purposes of s 28(2)) and unincorporated businesses.

Because the essence of passing off is the violation of another's goodwill, in most cases it will be necessary to show that it is both the business and the name which is similar. It is this combination of similar name and business, which together result in potential confusion to the public, that is required. An illustration is provided by the old but still useful case of *Hendriks v Montagu* (1881) 17 ChD 638, where the Universal Life Assurance Society (which was not a registered company) obtained an injunction to prevent Montagu from registering a company with the name Universe Life Assurance Association Ltd. It is extremely rare for a passing off claim to be successful in the situation where it is merely the name of the two enterprises which is similar. Nevertheless, such claims have been upheld in cases concerning the use of a particularly well-known name which, on the facts, can be shown to amount to passing off if used in any sphere of business activity, because there is evidence that its use involves trading on the goodwill of the original user. An illustration of this is the case of *Exxon Corporation v Exxon Insurance Consultants International Ltd* [1982] Ch 119, where the court granted an injunction which prevented the defendants using the word 'Exxon', and also ordered that the word 'Exxon' should not be allowed to remain on the index of companies. The defendants, although not ordered to change their corporate name, were left with two options, either to change it or to dissolve the company, despite there being no link between the nature of the two businesses. Although the court in *Exxon* held that there was no property in a name, and that the name 'Exxon' is too short to benefit from the law of copyright, the decision itself seems to suggest that where the original user is large and powerful, and perhaps (more importantly) where its name is very well known, a name can effectively be 'owned' (see also *British Telecommunications plc v One in a Million* [1999] 1 WLR 903).

Trade marks, by way of comparison with business names, identify a supplier rather than a retailer, the trade mark identifying the goods or services rather than the individual with whom the contract is made. Goods or services which emanate from a recognised and valued supplier may have a far higher value than other comparative goods or sevices made by an unknown. The Trade Marks Act 1994 allows for the registration of trade marks which distinctively identify particular products (be they goods or services), and applying the trade mark to products to which the registration does not apply is a statutory wrong giving rise to a claim for damages. However, as trade marks are applicable only to products, it seems unlikely that the unauthorised use of a corporate name could of itself amount to a trade mark infringement.

6.4 Statement of objects

6.4.1 Introduction

The objects clause details the activities for which the company was formed. Acting outside this statement of objects is described as acting ultra vires or outside the company's capacity. The binding nature of a company's stated capacity has already been discussed (see **Overview**, above) together with the implications this presented for third parties, who were deemed to have constructive notice of the content of a company's constitutional documents by virtue of the fact that they were registrable and available for public inspection. It is true that the harshness of this rule was alleviated by careful drafting of the objects clause together with the utilitarian approach of the courts, but it was the 1989 Act which finally removed the spectre of ultra vires, so far as third parties are concerned, from company law. Section 35(1) of the Companies Act 1985 now reads:

> The validity of an act done by a company shall not be called into question on the ground of lack of capacity by reason of anything in the company's memorandum.

As far as the members of a company are concerned, the statement of objects is still a live issue, although in practice this is unlikely to produce much litigation (see s 3A, below at **6.4.2.2**) not merely because the capacity of a company can be drafted in the widest terms, but also because any restrictive power relates to future activities of the company. When considering the construction of the objects clause in the situation where a member is seeking to compel the company to comply with a clause in its Memorandum, it must be remembered that the question is posed from an entirely different perspective. The reported cases were concerned with finding whether or not contracts were ultra vires in the context of their enforceability by third parties. For this reason these earlier decisions of the courts are probably best seen as illustrative rather than instructive. Where the company has already acted in an ultra vires fashion, a member is left trying to pursue a derivative action, which involves real difficulties (see **Chapter 14**).

6.4.2 Construction of the objects clause

6.4.2.1 Object or Power?

The distinction between objects and powers is no longer as important as it once was, following the abolition of the ultra vires rule, although some discussion is necessary given the ability, in theory at any rate, of the members to restrain the company and its directors from acting outside its constitution. A company has implied powers to enter into transactions which are reasonably understood to be incidental to the attainment of its objects (see *A-G v Great Eastern Railway Co* (1880) 5 App Cas 473). This was recognised in *Deuchar v Gas Light & Coke Co* [1925] AC 691, where a company formed to make gas from coal could manufacture caustic soda so as to be able to convert one of its by prod-ucts from its gas-making activity into a substance which could then be sold to dyestuff manufacturers. Again, in *Johns v Balfour* (1889) 5 TLR 389, the court accepted that the purchase of an estate of 17,000 hectares by a mining company was intra vires, as it would enable the company to continue to mine the land of which it had previously been a tenant. Other examples of implied powers include the right of a trading company to borrow money (see *General Auction Estate & Monetary Co v Smith* [1891] 3 Ch 432), and to give security for any borrowing (see *Re Patent File Co* (1870) LR 6 Ch App 83).

The model forms of Memoranda provided in Tables B and F conclude the list of objects with the words 'and the doing of all such other things as are incidental or conducive to the attainment of that object'. Despite this, the courts have on occasion shown themselves to be unwilling to interpret actions, although seeming to be conducive to the attainment of a stated object, as being intra vires. In *Peruvian Railways Co v Thames & Mersey Marine Insurance Co* (1867) LR 2 Ch App 617, it was held that a company did not have an implied power to issue negotiable instruments, a rather surprising decision given that it was a fairly common commercial transaction at the time. Unfortunately, this uncertainty was not limited to the 19th century. More recent cases indicate that it persists. A good example is the case of *Simmonds v Heffer* [1983] BCLC 298, where a donation to the Labour Party by the League against Cruel Sports was held to be ultra vires that association despite the fact that the elec-tion of a Labour Government would have seen the promotion of legislation advocated by the League. This case is somewhat difficult to reconcile with the earlier case of *Evans v Brunner Mond & Co Ltd* [1921] 1 Ch 359, where donations to universities and scientific insti-tutions for the furtherance of scientific education and research were held to be intra vires because they were incidental to the company's object of chemical manufacturing.

The early draftsmen of companies' Memoranda began a practice of including express powers in a company's objects clause so as to give greater certainty as to the legal validity of certain stated activities. This resulted in extremely lengthy objects clauses, which, although much criticised, are still the norm today. In *Cotman v Brougham* [1918] AC 514, Lord Wrenbury commented (at 522):

> The objects of the company and the powers of the company to be exercised in effecting the objects are different things. Powers are not required to be, and ought not to be, specified in the memorandum. The Act (CA 1862) intended that the company, if it be a trading company, should by its memorandum define the trade, not that it should specify the various acts which it should be within the power of the company to do in carrying on the trade.

Despite this and other criticism, the practice of incorporating powers in the objects clause persists. What is quite clear from the case law is that where an objects clause contains a mixture of objects and express powers, such powers cannot be raised from their status as mere powers. In *Re Horsley & Weight Ltd* [1982] Ch 442, CA, Buckley LJ said (at 552):

> It is now long been a common practice to set out in memoranda of association a great number and variety of 'objects', so called, some of which (for example, to borrow money, to promote the company's interests by advertising its products or services, or to

do acts or things conducive or incidental to the company's objects) are by their very nature incapable of standing as independent objects which can be pursued in isolation as the sole activity of the company. Such 'objects' must, by reason of their very nature, be interpreted merely as powers incidental to the true objects of the company and must be so treated ...

6.4.2.2 The main objects rule

The difficulties that arose with lengthy objects clauses which included powers as well as objects, were added to by the practice that grew of providing for many objects, although such a reaction was hardly surprising. Companies needed to be able to adapt to changing needs and markets without being restricted by an objects clause which was specific and thus limiting. Increasingly lengthy objects clauses, drafted for maximum flexibility, began to emerge. The courts' reaction to this practice was to adopt what was termed the 'main objects' rule. Dicta of Lindley LJ in *Re German Coffee Date Co* (1882) 20 ChD 169 illustrate how this operated (at 188):

General words construed literally may mean anything; but they must be taken in connection with what are shown by the context to be the dominant or main objects. It will not do under general words to turn a company for manufacturing one thing into a company for importing something else, however general the words are.

And in *Anglo-Overseas Agencies Ltd v Green* [1961] 1 QB 1, Salmon J said (at 8):

... where a memorandum of association expresses the objects of the company in a series of paragraphs, and one paragraph, or the first two or three paragraphs appear to embody the main object of the company all the other paragraphs are treated as merely ancillary to this main object and as limited or controlled thereby.

Clearly such an approach was not conducive to permitting companies the freedom to change direction and pursue another purpose. A possible answer to this problem was presented with the case of *Re Crown Bank* (1890) 44 ChD 634, where an objects clause which permitted the company 'to carry on any business whatever which the company might think would be profitable to the shareholders' fell to be considered. In 1890, the court held that this would not satisfy the requirement in the Companies Act that a statement of the company's objects be registered. In 1991, the provision in the 1989 Companies Act came into force, which permitted a company to register as its object 'to carry on business as a general commercial company'. This meant, according to s 3A of the amended 1985 Act, that:

(a) the object of the company is to carry on any trade or business whatsoever, and

(b) the company has power to do all such things as are incidental to the carrying on of any trade or business by it.

In the period between *Re Crown Bank* and the 1989 amendments, company Memoranda draftsmen had tried with some success to get around the problem of the main objects rule. One such approach was to draft objects clauses with separate objects provisions. These clauses concluded with a statement to the effect that 'each and every one of the above paragraphs states a separate and independent object of the company'. The validity of this practice was established in the case of *Cotman v Brougham* [1918] AC 514, as a result of which such clauses are often described as *Cotman v Brougham* clauses. Consequently, companies with literally pages and pages of provisions in their objects clauses became commonplace. The unwelcome position presented by the somewhat vague clause in *Re Crown Bank* was effectively circumvented by such lengthy objects clauses. Companies were empowered to do anything specified in their objects clause, which in practice meant any business the management believed to be desirable, assuming all desirable options had been included in the objects clause. *Cotman v Brougham* clauses have had rather a long lease of life, remarkable for an approach which started life as a loophole. The courts' willingness to recognise their validity probably coincided with their acknowledgement of the company as, inter alia, a business framework which of necessity had to accommodate the needs of the business. Other initiatives of the draftsmen were also successful. In *Re New Finance & Mortgage Co Ltd* [1975] Ch 420, it was held that an object to 'act as merchants generally' was sufficient to permit a finance company to enter into business as car dealers and petrol station operators (see also *Newstead v Frost* [1980] 1 WLR 135, HL). And in *Bell Houses Ltd v City Wall Properties Ltd* [1966] 2 QB 656, CA, a subjectively worded objects clause which permitted the directors to 'carry on any trade or business whatsoever which can, in the opinion of the Board of Directors, be advantageously carried on by the Company in connection with or ancillary to any of the above businesses or the general business of the Company' was held to be sufficient to permit a building company to enforce the payment of a commission earned through the introduction of another company to a financier, the only proviso being that the directors must believe they were acting within the objects clause and must hold their belief honestly. In that case, Salmon LJ stated (at 690):

> It may be that the directors take the wrong view and in fact the business in question cannot be carried on as the directors believe. But it matters not how mistaken the directors may be. Providing they form their view honestly, the business is within the plaintiff company's objects and powers.

6.5 Limited liability

The Memorandum must include a clause stating what the liability of the members is (Companies Act 1985, s 2(3)). Most companies are incorporated with limited liability, although it is possible, but unusual, to incorporate without limited liability (s 306(1)). Great Expectations Ltd has stated that the liability of its members is limited (see **Appendix C**).

6.6 Share capital

If the company is to be formed with a share capital then a clause must be included in the Memorandum stating its amount and its division (see further **Chapter 4**). Of course, it is possible to form a company without share capital, choosing instead to form a company limited by guarantee, but such companies are relatively rare. Great Expectations Ltd and Great Expectations (Ideas) Ltd have been incorporated with a share capital (see **Appendix C**).

6.7 Alteration of the Memorandum

6.7.1 Restrictions on ability to alter Memorandum

Section 2(7) of the Companies Act 1985 provides:

> A company may not alter the conditions contained in its memorandum except in the cases, in the mode and to the extent, for which express provision is made by this Act.

In *Ashbury v Watson* (1885) 30 ChD 376, 'conditions' were held to mean all the provisions contained in a company's Memorandum, whether they were required by the Companies Act to be there or not. The Companies Act 1985 also provides that any condition which is included in the Memorandum which could lawfully have been included in the Articles of Association instead can be amended by special resolution, subject to any conflicting instruction in the Memorandum itself (s 17(2)(b); and see also s 17(1), which provides that an alteration which is contested is of no effect unless confirmed by the court).

A company cannot contract out of the power given to it by the Act to amend the Memorandum. In *Russell v Northern Bank Development Corporation Ltd* [1992] 1 WLR 588, it was held possible for existing members to contract between themselves not to amend the Memorandum or agree to amend it subject to the fulfilment of certain conditions (shareholder agreements are discussed further in **Chapter 7**). However, it is crucial that the company should not be a party to any such agreement and, further, no remedy is available for breach of such an agreement which would amount to a restraint on the company's ability to exercise its statutory right to alter its constitutional documents.

6.7.2 Change of name

Section 28(1) of the Companies Act 1985 provides for the change of the company name, but this must be effected by a special resolution (ie 75% of the vote). The choice of a new name is subject to the same restrictions which applied to the initial choice (see **6.2** above). Once a change of name has been made, the Registrar will issue an amended certificate of incorporation and enter the new name on the index (see s 28(6)). That it is an amended certificate is important to note, because the company is still the same company it was before its date of incorporation – it does not change – the new certificate, for example, does not mean that the company has just been formed (see *Oshkosh B'Gosh Inc v Dan Marbel Inc Ltd* [1989] BCLC 507). One reason for such a change of name might be that the company has been subject to a successful claim in passing off (see **6.3** above), or is subject to a real threat of a forthcoming claim which cannot be settled without a change of name.

A change of name will be 'Gazetted' (s 711(1)(a)). Gazetting is the procedure for disclosure in the London, Edinburgh and Belfast *Gazettes*, published weekly, giving details of significant matters, eg, change of name, change of registered office, county court judgments against companies and individuals, appointments of receivers, etc.

6.7.3 Change of objects clause

Section 4 of the Companies Act 1985 permits the members of a company to change its statement of objects by adopting a special resolution to that effect. However, because historically this was recognised as being of extreme importance to all members, the Act provides for a smaller minority, that is the holders of at least 15% of the company's nominal capital (see **Chapter 4** for an explanation of nominal capital), or any class of capital, to apply to the court to have the special resolution cancelled. The resolution will be ineffective unless it is confirmed by the court (s 4(2)). This is a good example of the Act intervening to protect the position of minority shareholders (discussed in **Chapter 14**).

6.7.4 Changes in share capital

Section 121 of the Companies Act 1985 permits six types of alteration to the company's capital clause (see further **Chapter 20**). It is necessary for the company's Articles to authorise any such alteration (s121(1)), and Table A provides for this in art 32, with the exception of the amendments contained in s 121(2)(c) and (d), which are in any event now obsolete. The six types of alteration provided for in s 121(2) are as follows:

(a) increase of authorised share capital by new shares of such amount as the company thinks expedient;

(b) consolidation of all or any of the share capital and division into shares of larger amount than the company's existing shares;

(c) conversion of all or any of the company's paid-up shares into stock;

(d) reconversion of stock into paid-up shares of any denomination;

(e) subdivision of the company's shares, or any of them, into shares of smaller amount than is fixed by the Memorandum. If partly paid shares are subdivided then the ratio of amount paid up to amount unpaid must not be changed;

(f) cancellation of shares which, at the date of the passing of the resolution to cancel them, have not been taken or agreed to be taken by any person, and diminution of the company's authorised share capital by the amount of the shares so cancelled. Shares cannot be cancelled under this paragraph if a person has agreed to take them, but a mere unilateral expression of willingness to take shares if they were offered is not enough to render shares uncancellable (*Re Swindon Town Football Club Ltd* [1990] BCLC 467).

6.7.5 Alteration at the instance of the court

It is possible for the court to direct the company to alter its Memorandum under various provisions provided by the Companies Act 1985. This is just one of the wide range of powers given to the court to act where it is petitioned by dissentient members, eg following an application under s 459 (unfairly prejudicial conduct). The remedies available under this provision are prescribed under s 461(1), (2)(d) and (4). Dissentient members may also petition under the following further grounds, namely:

(a) s 5(4),(5) and (7) (minority objecting to an alteration to the company's objects clause);

(b) s 17(3) (minority objecting to the amendment of provisions contained in the Memorandum which could legitimately have been contained in the Articles); and

(c) s 54(5), (6) and (9) (minority objecting to a public company re-registering as a private company).

There is one instance where such a petition may be made by the creditors (see s 177 – creditor or member objecting to a payment out of capital for the purchase or redemption of its own shares). Further, the court is permitted to order a change to the company's Memorandum where it is a public company and its capital has been reduced below the threshold laid down for a public company, which is at present £50,000 (s 139(3)).

6.8 Advice to the parties

It is probably fair to say that in the 21st century most companies are empowered to enter into a wide range of activities. This is as a result of the continued practice of adopting an extremely lengthy objects clause which culminates with a *Cotman v Brougham* clause supported by a subjectively worded or *Bell Houses* clause (see **6.4.2.2** above). Indeed this position has been strengthened by the availability of the new s 3A objects clause (despite the reservations of the DTI on the effectiveness of this provision, see **Overview**, above). Even where a company does manage to enter into an ultra vires contract, this will no longer affect third parties due to the amendments made to s 35 of the 1985 Act by the 1989 Act. Members, on the other hand, are still entitled to require that the company in which they have invested adhere to its stated objects (s 35(2)), a remedy which may be of little use where the company is empowered by the Memorandum to engage in almost any activity (see **6.4.2.2** above).

For investors such as Duncan, who are participants in a small private company where no ready market exists for their shares should they disapprove of the company's activities and wish to invest elsewhere, the most practical advice would be for them to ensure that they can insist upon being consulted in respect of any important management decisions. It is true to say that this is possible, to a limited extent, but it would need to be reinforced in the organisational structure of the business itself, by way of an amendment to Table A. Duncan has availed himself of this protection (see **Appendix B**, special art 6). Another possibility may be to provide, through a shareholder agreement, that the other members be required to buy out a dissatisfied investor, although it is worth keeping in mind that this is likely to prove difficult to enforce in practice (see further **Chapter 7**). Duncan has availed himself of this opportunity by way of a shareholder agreement under which Arthur, Bill and Edwina are obliged to buy him out on demand (see **Appendix D**).

FURTHER READING

S de Gay, 'Problems surounding use of the new single objects clause' (1993) 137 SJ 146.

7   The Articles of Association

LEARNING OUTCOMES

By the end of this chapter, you should understand:

- the Articles of Association – their nature and contents;

- construction of the Articles;

- the s 14 contract;

- membership and outsider rights – the rights existing between the members inter se;

- alteration of the Articles and extrinsic contracts;

- restrictions on the exercise of voting powers – directors and chairman;

- shareholder agreements.

SCENARIO

Arthur, Bill, Charlotte, Duncan and Edwina have agreed to adopt Table A as the Articles of Association for Great Expectations Ltd, with some amendments (see further **Appendix B**) designed to protect the special nature of the investment provided by Duncan and the relative position of the founders of the business. It has also been agreed that they should enter into a shareholder agreement under which Duncan could require Arthur, Bill and Edwina, within three years of the date of the agreement, to buy his shares at a fair valuation immediately upon receipt of a formal request (see **Appendix D**). The understanding between the parties acknowledges that it is Arthur, Bill and Edwina's business about which decisions are being made, and it is for them alone to make provision as to its regulation, although they realise that there are rules about accounts and certain documents which must be disclosed under the Companies Act (see further **Chapter 18**), and Duncan's interest in the company's affairs has been given due consideration.

OVERVIEW

The introduction of Duncan into the firm, principally as a financier, provided the impetus for Great Expectations to incorporate. It also necessitated careful consideration as to the framework of the company's internal regulations and organisational structure. Given Duncan's fairly extensive financial involvement, it was acknowledged that his rights and expectations as far as the business was concerned would not be adequately protected by the provisions of the Companies Act 1985 and Table A. This is because shareholders as such have no right to take part in the management of the business, neither do they have any real power to control the directors to whom the management powers of the company are delegated by virtue of Table A. Certain powers are reserved to the shareholders to exercise at General Meeting, and these do provide some form of control over the management, but in reality the members are very much dependent upon the expertise and skill of the board in relation to profitability and future growth of the business. Prudence suggests that shareholders should take great care before placing an investment which, once made, might prove difficult to retrieve. Company law envisages shareholders selling their stake and reinvesting elsewhere should they become dissatisfied with the company's performance or find themselves at odds with its controllers. In practice, though, there is unlikely to be a ready market for shares in a private company. In any event the Articles will often contain restrictions on share transfers (see **Appendix B**). For this reason investors such as Duncan must seek further protection through the Articles and/or through a shareholder agreement. If carefully drafted, these measures can provide some degree of control over the activities of the firm, and possibly allow the transfer of the investment to other members of the company. Control necessitates the availability of management information, a practice insisted upon by other major financiers such as banks. It is for this reason that Duncan has insisted on the inclusion in the Articles of a clause allowing him to attend board meetings.

Turning to the founders of the business, it will be appreciated that neither the provisions of Table A nor the Companies Act 1985 provide sufficient protection for such individuals. It is therefore necessary for Arthur and Bill, and possibly Edwina, to consider including some provision to protect their interests. Under English company law, Edwina and Bill can be dismissed from their directorships by the passing of an ordinary resolution which requires only a simple majority vote. Any sense of unfairness as a result of them losing 'their business' is not recognised in company law, the business having become that of the company as a separate and distinct entity. An equitable approach has been taken, where companies are recognised as being quasi partnerships in some situations (discussed further in **Chapter 14**). The difficulties with this lie in defining a quasi partnership and, if so defined, in determining how long a company remains one so as to benefit from an application of these equitable rules. It is for the above reasons that adjustments are often made through the use of enhanced or weighted voting rights in an attempt to entrench the directors' position. Alternatively, certain shares could be designated non-voting so as to ensure that voting control is vested in the founders. An example of the former would be where the directors' votes were increased from one vote per share to 3 votes per share on a resolution to remove them from office (this has been done in the case of Great Expectations Ltd – see **Appendix B**). Careful attention to the arithmetic is required if such rights are to be effective, and they become increasingly difficult to preserve when the company issues more shares and expands its roll of members. An example of the latter would be where shares are issued as non-voting, though perhaps preferential, in respect of dividends. This would reflect an expectation on the part of the holder to occupy a position of mere investor.

Great Expectations Ltd and Great Expectations (Ideas) Ltd have adopted Table A, although they have opted to introduce a number of amendments. The first provides for weighted voting rights in favour of the directors, Edwina and Bill, and the company secretary, Arthur, on a proposal to remove them from office. Secondly, provision is made for Duncan to attend board meetings. In a separate shareholder agreement there is provision for Duncan to require Edwina, Arthur and Bill to buy out his share holding. The Articles of

Association for Great Expectations Ltd (those for Great Expectations (Ideas) Ltd are substantially identical and are not separately reproduced) and the shareholder agreement between Arthur, Bill, Duncan and Edwina are included in the appendices. It is the purpose of this chapter to demonstrate the enforceability of the Articles as a contractual document between: (i) the company and its members; and (ii) the members and each other. The provisions included, which were designed to give further protection to the founders of Great Expectations Ltd, will serve to illustrate the difficulties of enforcing provisions through the Articles of Association. We will also be considering the Articles as a constitutional document. The effectiveness of shareholder agreements, either as an alternative to amending the Articles or as a supplement to them, will also be explored.

7.1 Content of the Articles of Association – Table A

The Articles of Association govern the internal regulations of a company and provide a necessary framework for its operation. A model set of Articles is provided in the Companies Act 1985 (and the Regulations made thereunder), Table A, and this will apply to all companies formed post-1985 unless amended or excluded (s 8(1)). If Table A is not excluded then it is perfectly legitimate to read the company's own Articles alongside Table A to resolve any ambiguities. Table A will apply unless the company's own Articles are inconsistent with it (see *Fisher v Black and White Publishing Co* [1901] 1 ChD 174). Thus, it is not sufficient merely to register special Articles for a company – if Table A is not to apply, it must be expressly excluded. Companies formed prior to the 1985 Act will be governed by the Table A of the Act in force upon that company's incorporation, eg if incorporated in 1981, Table A of the 1948 Act. If the corporators of a company would prefer to adopt only part of Table A they are free to do so; indeed, they can choose to draft their own Articles and to reject Table A in its entirety (s 8(1)). If they do so then they must register their own set of Articles (s 7), which must be printed, divided into paragraphs numbered consecutively, and signed by each subscriber to the Memorandum in the presence of at least one witness who must attest the signature. If a company does not register Articles then Table A applies automatically (s 8(2)), and it for this reason that it is a good idea for all students of company law to become fully acquainted with its regulations.

The Memorandum of Association, as we have seen (see **Chapter 6**), must provide for certain matters, whereas the Articles, being management regulations, are very much a matter for the corporators to decide upon for themselves, although there are certain powers reserved to the General Meeting by virtue of the Companies Act 1985, and these cannot be amended by the Articles (see ss 9 and 303). In practice, however, most of the points covered by Table A will be provided for in a company's Articles. Even if Table A is not adopted, or if it is adopted in part only, the content of a company's Articles will provide for much the same topics as are provided by Table A. Table A is divided into the following parts:

(a) Articles 2–35 – shares and share capital;

(b) Articles 36–63 – general meetings;

(c) Articles 64–101 – directors and secretary;

(d) Articles 102–110 – dividends, accounts and capitalisation of profits;

(e) Articles 111–116 – notices of meetings.

If Table A is amended by statutory instrument (s 8(1)) then any alteration will not affect companies who registered their Articles before the alteration (s 8(3)).

7.2 Construction of the Articles

The relationship between the Articles and the Memorandum requires careful attention. The Articles are subordinate to the Memorandum (see *Guiness v Land Corporation of Ireland* (1882) 22 ChD 349), and clear provisions in the Memorandum will always prevail over the Articles, even where there is conflict with the Articles. This is so whether the provision in the Memorandum is one which is required by law to be there or not (*Ashbury v Watson* (1885) 30 ChD 376). Where there is ambiguity in either document, it is perfectly legitimate to refer to the other document in an effort to resolve that ambiguity, since the Articles and the Memorandum together make up the constitution of the company (*Re South Durham Brewery Co* (1885) 31 ChD 261). In addition to the requirement that the Articles must not be in conflict with the company's Memorandum, the Articles must not be inconsistent with the general law, which means that any offending provision will be void (*Welton v Saffery* [1897] AC 299, HL). Similarly, in so far as the Articles are inconsistent with the Companies Act 1985 they will be void (*Re Peveril Gold Mines Ltd* [1898] 1 Ch 122). The Companies Act 1985 expressly provides for limitations as to what can be contained in the Articles on certain matters, and if there is a conflict between these provisions and the Act then the provisions are void (see, eg, relief of directors from liability (s 310(2), length of notice of members meetings (s 369(1), time for delivery of proxy appointments (s 372(5), the right to demand a poll (s 373)).

A further point to note when construing a company's Articles is that they are a business document, as the courts have recognised. Because of this, the maxim 'validate if possible' applies, as stated by Vaisey J in *Rayfield v Hands* [1960] Ch 1. This means that the Articles should be interpreted in a way which makes the provisions workable. Jenkins L J, in *Holmes v Keyes* [1959] Ch 199, said: 'I think that the Articles of Association of the company should be regarded as a business document and should be construed so as to give them reasonable business efficacy.' It must be recognised, however, that the strict enforcement of the Articles may not always be in the best interest of the business, although an argument along such lines is unlikely to carry much weight in a company which is not a quasi-partnership (see **Chapter 14**).

Table A contains various provisions which are commonly excluded in small private companies, notably arts 73–75 on the retirement of directors by rotation and arts 84–86 on directors' interests in transactions with the company. These are frequently found to be inconvenient in such companies. On the other hand, some provisions which are commonly added to Table A may also be thought capable of working against the interests of the company. Perhaps the best example of this is the weighted voting rights clause protecting the position of a director. Great Expectations Ltd has such a clause, and it will be seen later (see **Chapter 21**) that this is capable of having undesirable effects. Nevertheless, it must be remembered that the Articles are a contract, and the traditional contractual approach of allowing the parties to make their own bargain is still applied quite strongly, though there may be exceptions to this in the case of quasi-partnerships, where the courts are more likely to view the business as an enterprise and to try to find a fair and reasonable solution to any problems which arise.

A further point is that in quasi-partnerships the force which holds the business together is the mutual trust and confidence between the participants, rather than the strict provisions of the Articles. When the participants are reduced to reading the Articles closely and insisting on the recognition of their legal rights, it is likely that this trust and confidence has already broken down. An example of this may be found in the special Articles of Great Expectations Ltd, where Duncan has obtained the right to attend board meetings. If Edwina and Bill begin to find his presence there unwelcome, they will simply hold fewer meetings, and ensure that most of the important decisions are made on a day-to-day basis and merely reported to formal meetings. In this way the special Article will be rendered largely valueless to Duncan. Such behaviour will of course be clear evidence that the mutual trust and confidence has been at least severely damaged.

7.3 The 'section 14 contract'

Section 14 of the Companies Act 1985 provides:

Subject to the provisions of this Act, the Memorandum and Articles shall, when registered, bind the company and its members to the same extent as if they respectively had been signed and sealed by each member, and contained covenants on the part of each member to observe all the provisions of the Memorandum and of the Articles.

This provision originates from the deeds of settlement of unincorporated companies formed at common law, and the drafting is somewhat problematic. The section makes no reference to the Memorandum and Articles being deemed to have been signed and sealed by the company, and in the absence of such signing and sealing it would appear that the company is not bound. Yet it is obvious that the intention of the legislation is to make the company party to the contract. The explanation of this quirk of drafting appears to be that the unincorporated companies to whom the clause previously applied had no separate legal personality, and would not have been thought capable of executing such a contract. It is, however, settled since *Wood v Odessa Waterworks Co* (1889) 42 ChD 636, CA, that the provision is to be interpreted as if it deemed the company to have executed the contract as well.

On this basis it might appear that the Memorandum and Articles form a contract between the company and members as to all the provisions contained therein, but the section has been construed to provide that it is a contract between the company and its members in their capacity *as* members, and not in any other capacity, therefore it does not follow that all provisions contained in the Articles and Memorandum create an enforceable contract. In *Hickman v Kent Romney Marsh Sheep-Breeders' Association* [1915] 1 Ch 881, Astbury J stated (at 900):

... no right merely purporting to be given by an article to a person, whether a member or not, in a capacity other than that of a member, as for instance, as solicitor, promoter, director, can be enforced against the company; and ... [only] Articles regulating the rights and obligations of the members generally as such do create rights and obligations between them and the company respectively.

And in *Bisgood v Henderson's Transvaal Estates Ltd* [1908] 1 Ch 743, Buckley LJ said (at 759):

> The purpose of the Memorandum and Articles is to define the position of the shareholder as shareholder, not to bind him in his capacity as an individual.

7.4 Membership rights and outsider rights

Membership rights, or rights which attach to a member in his capacity as a member, are usually those rights which are annexed to the shares held, so if, for example, the shares were sold on the market the rights would remain with them. Obvious examples are the right to vote and the right to a dividend. In *Rayfield v Hands* [1960] Ch 1, it was held to be an enforceable membership right for a member to be included on the register of members. In *Pender v Lushington* (1877) 6 ChD 70, a member's right to vote at meetings was held to be an enforceable right. However, where the Articles provided that the member should have the right to be the company's solicitor (see *Eley v Positive Government Security Life Assurance Co* (1875) 1 ExD 20), the Articles were not held to amount to a binding contract for these purposes as this did not apply to the member as a member but as a solicitor or an outsider. Similarly, in *Browne v La Trinidad* (1887) 37 ChD 1, Mr Browne could not rely on a provision in the company's Articles which provided that he should remain a director of the company for the four-year period mentioned in the Articles. In *Beattie v E & F Beattie Ltd* [1938] Ch 708, a provision in the Articles that disputes as between members themselves or the company and its members be referred to arbitration, could not be relied upon by a member who was seeking to refer a dispute between himself and his company in his capacity as a director, since in this capacity he was an outsider so far as the Articles were concerned.

It is possible for an individual to occupy the position of director as an insider not an outsider, which would mean that any articles affecting him in his capacity as a director would take effect *qua* member and not *qua* outsider (see *Rayfield v Hands*, above). It is, of course, also possible for a member who is also a director of the company to have further rights and obligations imposed on him by the Articles. Further, it is possible for such rights and obligations to affect him in his capacity as member, and so be binding as insider rights or obligations, rather than affect him only in his capacity as director or outsider. There is, however, authority which states that the usual obligation imposed upon directors contained in the Articles, requiring directors to hold qualification shares (ie, a minimum number of shares in order to hold office), is unenforceable as part of the s 14 contract (see *Re Wheal Buller Consols* (1888) 38 ChD 42).

More recently the trend has been to extend the rights and obligations which can be imposed by the Articles upon a member to include rights which need not necessarily be annexed to the shares. Instead, membership rights have been found to exist which attach to members themselves, provided *any* shares in the company are held. There have also been situations where directors have been held to constitute a special class of member, with the result that Articles which affect them in this capacity are enforceable as they are taking effect *qua* member not *qua* director.

In *Beattie* (above), the provisions in question were held to affect the directors in their capacity as directors only and not as members. In *Rayfield v Hands* (above), the Articles provided that the member/directors must purchase other members' shares upon request, and this was held to be enforceable against the directors in their capacity as members. This approach has been recognised more recently in *Cumbrian Newspapers Group Ltd v Cumberland & Westmorland Herald Newspaper & Printing Co Ltd* [1987] Ch 1, where membership rights which attach to individuals rather than to shares were found to exist; rights conferred upon such individuals were therefore held to be rights *qua* member not *qua* outsider.

7.5 'Constitutional' behaviour

There is a belief that a member of the company can compel the company to act in accordance with its constitution as a whole, which includes any outsider rights contained within it. This would in effect permit a member to compel compliance with all of the provisions contained in his company's Articles of Association (and, of course, its Memorandum). This thesis is that of Wedderburn (see **Further Reading**), who states that:

> ... a member can compel the company not to depart from the contract with him under the Articles, even if that means indirectly the enforcement of 'outsider' rights vested either in third parties or himself, so long as, but only so long as, he sues qua *member and not* qua *'outsider.*

Following this approach, unconstitutional behaviour could be challenged by a member, which would include any behaviour which contravened any provision of the Articles whether they were outsider rights or not. A counter-argument put forward is that only matters contained in the Articles which relate to membership matters are enforceable by the members. This reduces the Articles to a mere contractual document, which will then be analysed according to rules of contract.

This dilemma in English company law is perhaps in part due to the fact that English law does not have a developed concept of the enforcement of a constitution for an organisation, perhaps because the British constitution is largely unwritten.

There is some support for Wedderburn's argument in *Salmon v Quin & Axtens Ltd* [1909] 1 Ch 311, CA (affirmed by the House of Lords sub nom. *Quin & Axtens Ltd v Salmon* [1909] AC 442), where the majority shareholders, Axtens and Salmon, were also managing directors of the company, each with a power of veto of board decisions on a wide range of matters. Salmon exercised his power of veto, but the board ignored it and went ahead with a decision and obtained approval of the shareholders by ordinary resolution (an alteration to the Articles requires a special resolution; see **7.7** below). Salmon sued, successfully, for an injunction to restrain the company and the board of directors from acting on their earlier decision. In the Court of Appeal, Farwell LJ saw this as 'an attempt to alter the terms of the contract between the parties by a simple resolution instead of by a Special Resolution'. The application of contractual rules supplied the answer, but in effect the Court was preventing the company from acting unconstitutionally, which in this case was the failure to acknowledge Salmon's personal right contained in the Articles. The more recent decision in *Cumbrian Newspapers* (see **7.4** above) might provide an alternative solution to this particular problem.

In that case, rights given to certain members by the Articles were treated as enforceable membership rights accruing to them despite there being only one class of shares provided for in the Articles. It was possible in this case to divide the members into recognisable groups, one of which had enhanced membership rights which took effect *qua* member and not *qua* outsider.

The Companies Act 1989 amended s 35A(4) of the Companies Act 1985, which now provides:

> *Subsection (1) does not affect any right of a member of the company to bring proceedings to restrain the doing of an act which is beyond the powers of the directors; but no such proceedings shall lie in respect of an act to be done in fulfilment of a legal obligation arising from a previous act of the company.*

This gives members a right to sue for an injunction where the directors are proposing to act outside of the powers given to them by the Articles. It is not clear whether this affects all matters provided by the Articles, or just those affecting members *qua* members. The fact that the provision does not state its scope to be exclusively concerned with membership rights might be taken to indicate that *all* acts which are deemed to be beyond the scope of the directors' authority (as laid down by the Articles) can be restrained. Note, however, that legal obligations which have already arisen cannot be avoided. An aggrieved member would be left with no effective way of rectifying previous unconstitutional behaviour, and would instead have to seek a remedy on behalf of the company as an exception to the 'Rule in *Foss v Harbottle*' (see **Chapter 14**) or initiate proceedings under the Companies Act 1985, s 459 (relief from unfairly prejudicial conduct, see **Chapter 14**).

7.6 Contract between the members inter se

The interpretation of the Articles as a contract means that not only are the members and the company bound by the contract, but so are the members inter se (*Wood v Odessa Waterworks Co* (1889) 42 ChD 636, CA; *Automatic Self-Cleansing Filter Syndicate Co Ltd v Cuninghame* [1906] 2 Ch 34). The point has already been made at **7.4** above that members are bound only so far as membership matters are concerned. It is thought that where members seek to enforce the Articles inter se, this should be done through the company (*Welton v Saffery* [1897] AC 299, HL). It is normal for the Articles to contain only provisions relating to company management and the rights of the shareholders against the company and vice versa, rather than to the relations of the members between themselves. Indeed, Table A contains no provisions of the latter kind. In fact the courts have not often been called upon to enforce this contract in actions purely between one member and another: indeed, there has only been one reported case where the Articles have been enforced between one member and another, that of *Rayfield v Hands* [1960] 1 Ch 1, where the relevant Articles of Association provided that a member who intended to transfer his shares had to inform the directors, who would take the shares equally at a fair value. Rayfield wanted to transfer his shares but the directors refused to take them. The right to have the shares bought was a membership right, and the duty to purchase them was seen as a membership obligation and not as an outsider obligation imposed upon the directors. This obligation affected them in their capacity as members. Vaisey J made it quite clear (at 9) that the nature of the company was a material fact:

The conclusion to which I have come may not be of so general application as to extend to the Articles of Association of every company, for it is, I think, material to remember that this private company is one of that class of companies which bears a close analogy to partnership.

It may therefore be doubted whether the same result would be reached in relation to a larger company. Another relevant point is that at the present day provisions such as this might more commonly be found in a shareholder agreement rather than in the Articles. The matter is not one which directly affects the management of the company, neither does it affect all the members, since it may be that not all are party to the agreement. This was the situation in *Rayfield v Hands* and is also true in Great Expectations Ltd, where Charlotte is not party to the share buyout agreement. It is to be noted that in Great Expectations Ltd this arrangement has accordingly been incorporated in a shareholder agreement rather than in the Articles.

7.7 Alteration of the Articles of Association

It has been stated that the Articles form a contract between the members and the company, and between the members and each other. The point has already been made that an application of the rules of contract does not always deal adequately with the special nature of the Articles as a constitutional document (see **7.3** above), nor as an organisational structure for a business. A further difference between contract law and the Articles is that the Articles can be altered unilaterally. The company as one party to the contract can alter its Articles by a special resolution of the members, whereas under contract law one party to an agreement cannot unilaterally alter its terms. As the basis of the management structure of the company, it is crucial that the Articles can be altered from time to time as the needs of the business require. Provision is made in s 9 of the Companies Act 1985 for the Articles to be amended by special resolution, ie 75% of the vote.

Because any provision contained in the Articles which is in conflict with the Companies Act is void (see **7.2** above), it follows that a company cannot contract out of s 9 by inserting a provision in its Articles imposing further restrictions on this power to change them (*Allen v Gold Reefs of West Africa Ltd* [1900] 1 Ch 656, at 671). It is unclear whether it would be possible to provide in the Memorandum that the Articles could be changed by an ordinary resolution. On the one hand, this would not contravene the express words of s 9, since a special resolution would still be effective. On the other hand, it might be thought that s 9 is intended to strike a proper balance between the need to protect entrenched constitutional rights in the interests of fairness and certainty and the need to allow changes in at least some circumstances, and that allowing changes more readily contravenes this objective of company law.

The need for a special resolution to alter the Articles does not preclude the possibility of providing for certain voting rights to be enhanced or weighted in favour of one or more members, or indeed of a recognisable group of members, such as the directors (assuming that they are also shareholders) or founders, thus making it difficult to pass the requisite resolution by the required majority. For example, if certain shares are given multiple votes in certain specified situations, the majority of shareholders may have insufficient votes to pass a resolution. Weighted voting rights have been provided in the Articles of Association of Great Expectations Ltd in order to protect the positions of Arthur, Bill and Edwina (**Appendix B**). Without this protection, Duncan would have been in a much stronger position to secure a resolution which would be taken as expounding the will of the company as a legal person separate and distinct from the entrepreneurs who are its lifeblood. The concept of majority rule and shareholder control has long been recognised in company law, and weighted voting rights, depending upon the extent to which they are available to members of a company, place a substantial restriction upon this. Balanced against such shareholder control of a business is the recognition of the entrepreneurs, whose role is acknowledged in legal practice through, inter alia, the widespread use of weighted voting rights (balancing the various competing interests that make up the company is discussed further in **Chapter 9**). Their validity can be supported by the wording of art 54, which states that voting be 'subject to any rights or restrictions attached to any shares'. Both the Court of Appeal and the House of Lords upheld their validity in the case of *Bushell v Faith* [1970] AC 1099. The facts of this case provide a useful illustration as to how such rights can prove to be effective even in the simplest of forms. Faith held 100 shares in Bush Court (Southgate) Ltd, his two sisters also held 100 shares each. The Articles of Association of the company provided that in the event of a resolution being proposed at any General Meeting for the removal from office of any director, any shares held by that director would on a poll in respect of such resolution carry the right to three votes per share. Faith was thus able to record 300 votes to his sisters' 200 votes when they attempted to pass a resolution to remove him. The House of Lords, Lord Morris of Borth-y-Gest dissenting, held that this was a perfectly legitimate use of weighted voting rights, notwithstanding that it effectively circumvented s 184 (now s 303) of the Companies Act and made it possible for a director to prevent his removal against his will. The opinion of the court was that as the draftsmen of the section, and indeed Parliament, had chosen not to interfere with the practice of leaving to companies and their shareholders liberty to allocate voting rights as they pleased, then the courts would not do so. Lord Upjohn in the House of Lords stated:

> Parliament has never sought to fetter the rights of the company to issue a share with such rights or restrictions as it may think fit. There is no fetter which compels the company to make the voting rights or restrictions of general application and it seems to me clear that such rights or restrictions can be attached to special circumstances and to particular types of resolution.

Lord Morris of Borth-y-Gest, dissenting, believed that the unconcealed effect of such a device is to make a director irremovable and that to sanction such a provision would be to make a mockery of the law. These arguments concentrate upon the legal framework itself rather than on the business which it supports. It is unfortunate that none of the judges in this case considered the questions of policy which underlie the arguments. On the one hand it may be said that it is largely for the participants in a company to organise its internal regulation as they see fit, and that the courts should not intervene. On the other hand, it must be admitted that s 303 of the 1985 Act (see below) is an attempt to intervene in the internal regulation of companies by prohibiting the inclusion of certain provisions in the Articles.

Although the decision in *Bushell v Faith* is couched in such terms as to comply with the letter of s 303, there can be little doubt that it seriously undermines the apparent purpose of that section, which is to give a simple majority of the shareholders the power to dismiss directors if they see fit. The company in this case was clearly a quasi partnership, though that phrase does not appear in any of the judgments, and indeed had not come into common use in English company law at that time. It may well be that in a quasi partnership the use of such clauses is a perfectly legitimate contracting out of the strict company law rules, but it is surely clear that there must be some limit on the availability of such clauses. It would be objectionable, for example, to have a clause giving one million votes to the holder of one share! It is impossible to say definitively where the line will be drawn, and it seems that in the absence of statutory intervention the matter will have to be left to the courts.

A further check upon the ability of the company to alter its Articles is provided in the provisions which protect class rights. Sections 125–127 of the Companies Act 1985 provide that where an alteration to class rights is proposed then, unless otherwise provided for by the Articles or Memorandum, a three-quarters majority of that class must approve any such alteration.

7.8 Alteration of the Articles and extrinsic contracts

It is possible for an outsider to have a contract with the company and to have some of the terms of that contract included in the company's Articles. It is not the Articles that constitute the contract – they merely contain some of the terms of the extrinsic contract. We have already seen that if an outsider were to rely on a contract created by the Articles, he would find that the contract does not exist for his benefit (see *Eley and Beattie* at **7.4** above). In most situations of this kind the contracts concern directors of the company who are appointed by the company and have the terms of their directorship provided for in the Articles (see further **Chapters 10** and **11**). An examination of Table A will show the extent to which provisions for directors are provided for in the Articles – Arts 64–101. In the case of *Re New British Iron Co*, ex p Beckwith [1898] 1 Ch 324, Wright J stated at 326:

> In this case there is a provision in the Articles of Association which ... fixes the remuneration of the directors at the annual sum of £1,000. That article is not in itself a contract between the company and the directors; it is only part of the contract constituted by the Articles of Association between the members of the company inter se. But where on the footing of that article the directors are employed by the company and accept office the terms of (the Articles) are embodied in and form part of the contract between the company and the directors.

The disadvantage of including the terms of an outside contract in the Articles of Association is that the Articles are alterable both by their very nature (being a management structure) and by virtue of s 9 of the Companies Act 1985. As a result, it is possible for the terms of such a contract to be altered notwithstanding that this amounts to a breach of contract. The only remedy available for such a breach would be damages, given that the effect of an injunction would be to fetter a company's statutory right to alter its Articles. In *Southern Foundries (1926) Ltd v Shirlaw* [1940] AC 701, Lord Porter said (at 740–41):

> *A company cannot be precluded from altering its Articles thereby giving itself power to act upon the provisions of the altered Articles – but so to act may nevertheless be a breach of contract if it is contrary to a stipulation in a contract validly made before the alteration.*
>
> *Nor can an injunction be granted to prevent the adoption of the new Articles and in that sense they are binding on all and sundry, but for the company to act upon them will none the less render it liable in damages if such action is contrary to the previous engagements of the company.*

This dictum was approved in *Cumbrian Newspapers Group Ltd v Cumberland & Westmorland Herald Newspaper & Printing Co Ltd* [1987] Ch 1, *per* Scott J at 24.

More recently, in *Russell v Northern Bank Development Corporation Ltd* [1992] 1 WLR 588, it was held that a company cannot fetter its own statutory power (to increase its capital). However, provided an agreement does not fetter the company in this way then such an agreement between the shareholders will be effective, although only to regulate the way the shareholders exercise their rights as shareholders.

7.9 Restrictions on the exercise of voting power

7.9.1 'Bona fide for the benefit of the company as a whole'

The power to alter the Articles is to be exercised by a special resolution of the General Meeting. The power must be exercised '*bona fide* for the benefit of the company as a whole' (*Allen v Gold Reefs of West Africa Ltd* [1900] 1 Ch 656, *per* Lindley MR at 671–2). In other words, the members must act in the best interests of the company as a separate and distinct entity, which may not always coincide with what is in the members' individual interests. (In *Greenhalgh v Arderne Cinemas* [1951] Ch 286, at 291, Evershed MR stated that '*bona fide* for the benefit of the company as a whole means not two things but one'.) Such a commonsense approach is indeed persuasive; after all, the members acting by resolution in General Meeting are exercising a power as an organ of the company. On the other hand, to restrict members in this fashion is in many ways the equivalent of fixing them with a fiduciary duty when they exercise their right to vote. The traditional approach of English law has not taken this route, preferring to treat the right to vote as a personal right which may be exercised in a member's own self-interest, even where this involves a conflict between self-interest and the interests of the company. (In *Carruth v Imperial Chemical Industries Ltd* [1937] AC 707, Lord Maugham said that 'the shareholder's vote is a right of property, and *prima facie* may be exercised by a shareholder as he thinks fit in his own interest'; see also *Burland v Earle* [1902] AC 83.) This approach need not, however, be viewed as inconsistent with the existence of a general duty to act in the best interests of the company, although it does indicate that acting out of self-interest does not of itself amount to a breach of duty.

Until relatively recently, the prevalent view appeared to equate benefiting the company as a distinct entity with benefiting its owners, or the majority of them. Intervention by the courts was forthcoming only where there was evidence of clear abuse by the majority. Cases such as *Ebrahimi v Westbourne Galleries* [1973] AC 360 and the more recent decisions in *Clemens v Clemens* [1976] 2 All ER 268 and *Estmanco v GLC* [1982] 1 WLR 2, suggest that in certain circumstances the courts may be prepared to grant relief which would restrict the ability of the majority to act in its own self-interest where it would result in harm to the company as a whole. This is likely to be where the conduct of the majority amounts to 'fraud on the minority by those in control' at common law (as an exception to the Rule in *Foss v Harbottle*, see **Chapter 14**), or to unfairly prejudicial conduct for the purposes of a s 459 petition, or where it provides a 'just and equitable ground' for winding up under s 122(1)(g) of the Insolvency Act 1986 (see **Chapter 14**).

Establishing whether or not a power has been exercised *bona fide* in the interests of the whole company is by no means an easy task. The dominant trend is to adopt a subjective approach. If the members honestly believe that the action is for the benefit of the company then, provided there are reasonable grounds for such a view, the courts will not interfere. In *Shuttleworth v Cox Brothers & Co (Maidenhead) Ltd* [1927] 2 KB 9, it was stated that for an alteration to be otherwise than *bona fide* it would have to be 'so oppressive so as to cast suspicion on the honesty of the persons responsible for it, or so extravagant that no reasonable men could really consider it for the benefit of the company' before the courts would interfere. The courts are not willing to involve themselves in decisions taken by members, even if the court might have arrived at a different decision, provided reasonable men could come to that decision (*Shuttleworth, per* Scrutton LJ at 23). Much, however, depends upon the nature of the resolution and its effect on the specific company (*Sidebotham v Kershaw Leese* [1920] 1 Ch 154; *Brown v British Abrasive Wheel Co Ltd* [1919] 1 Ch 290; *Dafen Tinplate Co Ltd v Llanelly Steel Co* [1920] 2 Ch 124). The best interests of the company test has been qualified in other common law jurisdictions and suggestions made for its replacement (see *Gambotto v WCP Ltd* (1995) 182 CLR 432). It remains a cornerstone, however, of English company law.

7.9.2 Chairman and the directors voting as members

There is a view which has gained widespread recognition in Continental Europe, that the company is an enterprise comprising, first and foremost, a business and, secondly, a convergence of interests, which includes the entrepreneurs, the shareholders, the employees, the creditors and the consumers. However, these various groups receive little or no protection from English company law (see further **Chapter 26**) and the term '*bona fide* in the best interests of the company as a whole' does not require a consideration of any of these groups. Whenever members vote they ought to be concerned with whether or not the proposal is for the benefit of an individual hypothetical member (*Greenhalgh v Arderne Cinemas* [1951] Ch 286, at 291). Furthermore, directors' voting rights as *members* are not suspended even where the director concerned has a personal interest in the outcome of the vote which may be in conflict with the interests of the company. This is not the position with regard to listed companies. The Chairman of the company may also cast his vote as shareholder as he thinks fit, notwithstanding a conflict of interest, unless he is exercising his casting vote. The Chairman's casting vote is provided for in art 50 of Table A thus:

> In the case of an equality of votes, whether on a show of hands or a poll, the chairman shall be entitled to a casting vote in addition to any other vote he may have.

In serving this function there can be no doubt that the Chairman is acting as an organ of the company and should therefore be subjected to the same fiduciary obligations as directors. (As will be seen in **Chapter 10**, directors when acting as such must not put themselves in a position where their own personal interest conflicts with that of the company.) This should ensure that where the Chairman is taking his casting vote he must have regard to the interests of the company over and above his own personal interests.

7.10 The draft Fifth EC Directive on Company Law

The draft Fifth Directive is concerned with harmonising the law on shareholder voting rights in public companies in the European Community. If it is adopted, it will ensure that English company law is brought into line with the laws of the other Member States on the question of a suspension of voting rights where a shareholder has a personal interest in the outcome of a resolution. Differences will remain in the case of private companies.

7.11 Shareholder agreements

The companies legislation applies to all companies, including quasi partnership type companies, and very often these rules ignore the fact that in reality the needs of the members are often quite different and depend upon the enterprise with which they are associated, whether as investors or directors. To some extent this particular difficulty has been acknowledged by the courts, which have at times seen fit to resist a strict application of the company law rules (*Caratti Holding Co Ltd v Zampatti PC* (1978) 52 ALJR 732; *Ebrahimi v Westbourne Galleries Ltd*) or which have been willing to interpret the Act in such a way as to recognise the special position of the company in question (*Rayfield v Hands* [1960] Ch 1; *Bushell v Faith* [1970] AC 1099). However, commercial certainty cannot be satisfied in this way alone, with the result that shareholder agreements are becoming more commonplace amongst those involved in small to medium-sized businesses. Obviously this practice is a useful alternative to any attempt at predicting the outcome of a judicial interpretation or application of a company's Articles and, in the absence of a ready market for the shares, coupled with the likelihood of share transfer restrictions, it is a sensible one too. The company does not become a party to the agreement – and this is an important point, because the Northern Ireland Court of Appeal over a decade ago upheld the validity of a shareholder agreement, but only on the grounds that it was not operating so as to constitute a fetter on a statutory power of the company (*Russell v Northern Bank Development Corporation Ltd* [1992] 1 WLR 588).

When drafting a shareholder agreement regard must be had first and foremost to the company in question, as obviously the matters provided for vary from company to company. We have drafted an agreement for the members of Great Expectations Ltd (see **Appendix D**). A major benefit of contracts of this nature is that it does not matter if the rights conferred are not unquestionably 'insider' rights or membership rights (see the discussion of *Rayfield v Hands*, at **7.4** above). An extrinsic contract can be made to protect membership rights and also to protect rights of outsiders, whether or not they are members of the company. While alterations to Table A are very often sufficient to provide for the organisational aspects of the business and the respective rights of the members and directors, it is more common to include rights which are by their very nature more personal, and so at risk of being found to be 'outsider' rights, into a separate shareholder agreement. For example, it would not be uncommon to find provision as to the procedure for dealing with disputes between the shareholders and directors, requiring that they be submitted to arbitration. Unless this were included in the company's Articles, it would not bind the company and so would be ineffective. It would be wise to prevent a *Beattie* (see **7.4** above) situation from arising by including a statement to the effect that the agreement extends to situations between the company and members and includes them in any other capacity.

The Articles are probably a suitable place in which to include provision that voting rights attached to shares should, in specified circumstances, be exercised in a certain way or not exercised at all. This enhancement or restriction of voting rights is by analogy with *Bushell v Faith* (see **7.7** above) a clause which would be valid since it does not prevent the company from changing its Articles by special resolution, at least in theory. Agreements to vote in a certain way, or not to vote at all, to which the company is not party are clearly enforceable. Voting agreements can also be used to provide for powers of veto over certain specified transactions, or power to compel members to vote in a certain way on a given course of action, eg to wind up the company if, say, losses are incurred for a successive number of years or a shareholder is dismissed from a directorship.

Another important provision relates to protecting the financial position of certain shareholders, and was insisted upon by Duncan's solicitor. This provision allows a member to disassociate himself from the company should certain specified events occur. For example, where events suggest that there will be a serious diminution in the value of a member's share holding, any dissatisfied shareholder may require other shareholders or the directors to purchase his shares at a previously agreed price, or at a price arrived at on the basis of an agreed formula and subject to valuation by an agreed body (which would usually be the company's auditors). This eventuality is provided for in the agreement between Arthur, Bill, Duncan and Edwina (see **Appendix D**).

Another sensible provision, which avoids the need for costly litigation with an uncertain outcome or unsatisfactory settlement, is one which allows for dissentient minorities to divest themselves of their stake to the highest bidder, thus ensuring a competitive element to the proceedings.

Provisions of this kind, whether in the Articles, in an extrinsic contract or included in the Articles but deemed to amount to terms of an extrinsic contract, are necessary in private companies in order to provide for certainty for all parties and to avoid the expense of litigation. Such litigation, unless clearly within the narrow scope of the s 14 contract (see **7.3** above), would always come under the notorious 'Rule in *Foss v Harbottle*' or under s 459 (unfairly prejudicial conduct) or s 122(1)(g) of the Insolvency Act 1986 (winding up on the just and equitable ground), and although the courts have shown themselves willing to acknowledge the special position of small private companies by looking to the nature of the enterprise, when applying these rules the outcome could never be predicted with any real degree of certainty given the fact that the courts do not consider their role to include deciding matters of management. There is also the possibility that the corporate form and its attendant rules might be found to be more important than the enterprise itself.

8 The Consequences of Incorporation – Corporate Personality

LEARNING OUTCOMES

By the end of this chapter, you should understand:

- the concept of corporate personality – the *Salomon* case;

- piercing or lifting the corporate veil –sham companies and the use of the principles of agency;

- the identification theory;

- groups of companies – the concepts of economic and functional control;

- avoiding corporate personality by contract;

- statutory exceptions to the concept of corporate personality;

- the alter ego doctrine.

SCENARIO

Great Expectations Ltd and a subsidiary company, Great Expectations (Ideas) Ltd, have now been formed. The partnership business was bought by Great Expectations Ltd, whereas Great Expectations Ideas Ltd is concerned with marketing and advertising. This all seems a little confusing to Arthur and Bill, who continue to struggle with the concept of the separate legal status of a company. Limited liability and its implications for them as owners of the company seems to have been readily absorbed and understood, but the separate identity of the company for all other purposes presents potential confusion for our entrepreneurs. Business practice in many ways fuels such confusion; indeed, the company's bank, Bus Bank plc, continues to support the business on the basis that the distinction is a mere technicality, requiring the members of the company to furnish personal financial information in addition to that of the company (see further **Chapter 12**).

OVERVIEW

For the members of Great Expectations Ltd, the decision to trade through a company rather than continuing as a partnership has affected the power balance of the enterprise. We saw in **Chapter 4** how the various share holdings determine the members' ability to control the activities of the business now that it is a company. An immediate contrast can already be drawn with their original respective positions in the partnership, where equality among the partners was presumed by the Partnership Act in matters of management and in respect of the sharing of capital and profits. The division of capital as reflected in their holdings will of course determine the proportion of profits each member receives. The input of expertise and labour can be recognised through the payment of salaries.

Incorporation brings with it many benefits for the business and its members (discussed further in **Chapter 26**), due to the application of company law with its own detailed and extensive set of rules. The most notable feature of this is that it is now the company which is responsible for its own debts (see *Salomon v A Salomon & Co Ltd* [1897] AC 22, HL), which means that its creditors must look to the limited capital fund provided by the company's members, who are under no obligation to provide sums over and above those which have already been invested in, or which remain outstanding on, the shares they have agreed to take. If the venture fails, the legal consequences will be borne by the company alone rather than by the individuals themselves (see, however, **Chapter 23**).

At times, the acknowledgement of the company as a being separate and distinct from its shareholders might not be to the advantage of the company's owners, as accompanying disbenefits can arise where a strict approach is adopted. For example, to treat its owners as mere shareholders may in some circumstances fail to recognise any wider interests they may have in the company, such as in its property (*Macaura v Northern Assurance Co Ltd* [1925] AC 619; *Acatos and Hutcheson plc v Watson* [1995] 1 BCLC 218) or management structure (*Ebrahimi v Westbourne Galleries* [1973] AC 360). The rule is nevertheless fundamental to an understanding of company law as, once it is incorporated, a business becomes a legal person subject to detailed and extensive company law regulation.

Attempts to avoid the rule, or to seek to avoid any of the regulations which apply to companies, must be carefully thought out, as it is only in very limited circumstances that they will be successful. Where the courts have been persuaded to look behind the company to its owners, they have been described as 'piercing the corporate veil'; and where the consequences of company law regulation have seemed inappropriate for a particular company, such companies are often described as 'quasi partnerships'. The use of either of these terms is not particularly helpful in trying to predict whether or not a strict application of company law is likely to be forthcoming, and it is necessary first to identify the salient features of the cases in which the courts have not felt that the company is sufficiently separate and distinct to be subject to its own set of rules. One particular set of cases which presented the courts with something of a dilemma concerned the position of groups of companies which trade as one economic unit while each member company of the group retains its separate and independent status in law. For a short time it seemed that the economic unit argument might provide grounds to obviate some of the disbenefits which follow as a natural consequence of separate status. However, as we shall see at **8.4** below, where groups of companies are concerned to disregard the separate status of one member of a group for one purpose (in order to obviate a disbenefit), it could lead to the logical conclusion that separate status should also be disregarded for all purposes, which may not be to the group's advantage, especially if one company within that group found itself unable to pay its debts.

Perhaps a more difficult concept is that of the 'quasi partnership' type company which, if found to exist on the facts, might justify a departure from any company law rules which, if applied, would result in an unjust or inequitable solution. The lack of certainty generated in this area has been met by an increase in the adoption of shareholder agreements (see **7.11** above), where provision can be made to protect such rights and obligations of the members inter se as are thought to be appropriate for the business in question, keeping in mind that the company's constitution might be unable to provide a sufficiently secure basis from which to proceed.

8.1 Corporate personality

The recognition of a company as a legal person from the moment it receives its certificate of incorporation (Companies Act 1985, s 13(3)), separate and distinct from its members, can be described as a cornerstone of English company law. Because the company is a separate legal person, it is the company which enters into contracts (*Lee v Lee's Air Farming Ltd* [1961] AC 12, PC; *Secretary of State for Trade and Industry v Bottrill* [1999] ICR 592), the company which owns property (*Macaura v Northern Assurance Co Ltd* [1925] AC 619; *JJ Harrison (Properties) Ltd v Harrison* [2002] 1 BCLC 162), the company to whom the directors owe their duties (*Allen v Hyatt* (1914) 30 TLR 444, PC), and the company that incurs credit and becomes indebted. This new creation requires its capacity to be set out, and we have seen that this is done in its Memorandum of Association (see **Chapter 6**). Its internal regulations are provided for in its Articles of Association (see **Chapter 7**).

Examples of the application of this most fundamental rule are to be found throughout company law. For example, if a compensation order is made against a company's directors for causing it to trade wrongfully, it is to be paid to the company and not to the creditors (see **Chapter 23**). If some part of the membership complain that harm has come to them due to the activities of the majority or of the controllers, at common law that claim must be brought through the company, as it is the company which has been harmed (see **Chapter 14**). The 'best interests of the company' will not necessarily be considered solely from the situation of its owners, other interested parties, such as employees and creditors, having been recognised as having a right to be regarded when the 'interests of the company' are considered (see **Chapter 9**).

This most important and fundamental theme of company law has its origin in the case of *Salomon v A Salomon & Co Ltd* [1897] AC 22, HL. Mr Salomon had been in business as a bootmaker, trading as a sole trader before taking the decision to incorporate. He sold his business to the company created to carry on his business, A Salomon & Co Ltd, and took the bulk of its shares for himself. (At that time it was necessary to have seven subscribers to the Memorandum, and these were made up of Salomon's wife and children so that the formalities were complied with. Following the implementation of the 12th EC Directive on Company Law, it is possible to have a single member company; see **Chapter 4**.)

Mr Salomon therefore owned the company; the company owned the business. In order to pay Salomon for the business, the company issued him shares and owed him the rest by way of a debenture which was secured on the company's assets. This debenture was cancelled and reissued to a Mr Broderip, who advanced Salomon £5,000. The debenture holder was clearly in a better position than the company's other creditors (see further **Chapter 15**), which meant that when the company failed and went into insolvent liquidation, ie was unable to meet all of its debts, the company's creditors ranked behind the debenture holder. Although Broderip recovered his £5,000, there were insufficient assets to pay anything to the unsecured creditors. Acting on behalf of the company, the liquidator challenged the validity of the debenture on the ground of fraud. On the same ground he claimed rescission of the agreement for the transfer of the business and repayment by Salomon of the balance of the purchase money. In the alternative he claimed payment of £20,000 on Salomon's shares, alleging that nothing had been paid for them. The liquidator's claim broke down completely when it came for trial, but Vaughan Williams J suggested that the company had a right of indemnity against Salomon. From the outset the separate legal entity of A Salomon & Co Ltd was recognised, but almost immediately the court found grounds which it felt warranted disregarding a strict application of company law to this business, finding instead that the company had been a mere agent of Salomon who, as principal, was himself liable for the company's debts. The House of Lords refused to find that this was so on the facts; it was insufficient to demonstrate that a company was simply a 'one man company' in order to demonstrate that an agency relationship existed. It was held not to be contrary to the true intention of the Companies Acts to found a company with a predominant member possessing an overwhelming influence and an entitlement to practically the whole of the profits; neither was it found to be against public policy or detrimental to the interests of creditors. For a previous owner of a business to be carrying on the same business, having sold that business to a company of which he is the predominant owner, is insufficient to justify a finding of agency; the company is not in law the agent of its owners. Lord MacNaghten stated (at 51):

> When the memorandum is duly signed and registered ... the subscribers are a body corporate 'capable forthwith', to use the words of the enactment, 'of exercising all the functions of an incorporated company'. Those are strong words. The company attains maturity on birth. There is no period of minority – no interval of incapacity. I cannot understand how a body corporate thus made 'capable' by statute can lose its individuality by issuing the bulk of its capital to one person, whether he be a subscriber to the memorandum or not. The company at law is a different person altogether from the subscribers to the memorandum; and, though it may be that after incorporation the business is precisely the same as it was before, and the same persons are managers, and the same hands receive the profits, the company is not in law the agent of the subscribers or trustee for them. Nor are the subscribers as members liable, in any shape or form, except to the extent and in the manner provided by the Act. That is, I think, the declared intention of the enactment.

That one man companies are not an abuse of the Companies Acts has been recognised in many cases since this notable decision. Indeed, the rapid growth in private companies since *Salomon* is no doubt directly attributable to the courts' recognition of the 'one man company'. The decision has been described as 'calamitous' and calls have been made to check the widespread use of the corporate vehicle by the unscrupulous. Yet, despite this, *Salomon* remains largely untouched (see, eg, the Report of the Review Committee on Insolvency Law and Practice (The Cork Committee), HMSO Cmnd 8558; see **Chapter 23**);

and although to a limited extent it is possible to find that a company is in fact an agent of its subscribers (see below), this route has not been pursued, which is probably not surprising given the strength of the judgments on this point in *Salomon*. The Cork Committee, reporting in 1982, acknowledged as undesirable the potential abuse of the corporate form by those who incorporate with the sole objective of placing a high degree of risk onto unsecured creditors. Their recommendations, although not adopted in full, resulted in the wrongful trading provision of the Insolvency Act 1986 (s 214), which is often presented as an example of statute intervening to pierce the corporate veil.

Examples of the *Salomon* principle being applied in various situations are: *Macaura v Northern Assurance Co Ltd* [1925] AC 619; *Lee v Lee's Air Farming* [1961] AC 12, PC; and *Re Lewis's Will Trusts* [1985] 1 WLR 102. In *Macaura*, the owner of a timber estate, having sold it to a company of which he was the major shareholder, proceeded to insure the timber in his own name rather than in the name of the company. When the timber was destroyed by fire, it was held that he did not have a valid claim against the insurers, as he had no insurable interest in the property. Lord Wrenbury stated the position thus (at 633):

> My Lords, this appeal may be disposed of by saying that the corporator even if he holds all the shares is not the corporation, and that neither he nor any creditor of the company has any property legal or equitable in the assets of the corporation.

In *Lee's Air Farming*, Mr Lee had held 2,999 of 3,000 shares in Lee's Air Farming Ltd before he was killed in an accident flying one of the company's aeroplanes. He had also been the company's sole governing director. The Privy Council upheld a claim by his widow that he could nevertheless be a 'worker' of the company for the purposes of the Worker's Compensation Act 1922 (NZ), it being recognised that it was the company as a separate entity which employed him; Lee himself had simply acted as the company's agent in negotiating his own employment contract. In *Re Lewis's Will Trusts*, the owner of a farm sold it to a company, GR Lewis (Talygarn) Ltd, and held the majority of the shares. He left the farm in his will to his son; however, because it was not he but the rather the company which owned the farm, it could not be given to his son by virtue of the will and his wishes as contained in the will could not be read as transferring his shares in the company to his son. As a result the shares were divided between Mr Lewis's son and daughter under the rules on intestate succession.

A comprehensive statement on this important rule is to be found in the case of *Tate Access Floors Inc v Boswell* [1991] Ch 512, where it was emphasised that a company is separate and distinct from its members for all purposes. Browne-Wilkinson V-C said (at 531):

> If people choose to conduct their affairs through the medium of corporations, they are taking advantage of the fact that in law those corporations are separate legal entities, whose property and actions are in law not the property or actions of their incorporators or controlling shareholders. In my judgment controlling shareholders cannot, for all purposes beneficial to them, insist on the separate identity of such corporations but then be heard to say the contrary when discovery is sought against such corporations.

8.2 Piercing the 'veil of incorporation'

This probably presents one of the biggest problems in company law today, with little certainty and consistency emerging from the decisions of the courts. In reality the corporate veil is pierced through contract for the vast majority of small companies, through the practice of taking personal guarantees from their directors to support company borrowing or by insisting that the director incur joint and several liability with the company for credit advanced to the company. This practice enables certain creditors to look beyond the limited fund possessed by the company to the directors themselves, who in companies of this type are very often the major shareholders.

Piercing the veil very rarely involves a disregard of the company itself; more often the company will be recognised and the veil merely lifted in order to see who is behind it, sometimes to the benefit of the corporators and at other times not.

8.2.1 'Sham' companies

The company is more usually disregarded in situations where the company in question is recognised as being a mere 'sham'. This is because the facts point more to an intention on the corporators' behalf to create a mask behind which they can hide. There are two possible solutions for the courts in this type of situation: they can choose to disregard the company entirely; or, in the alternative, they can find the existence of an agency relationship. Either enables the court to look behind the falsehood of the company.

Two cases illustrate the courts' approach when dealing with 'sham' companies (these are simply two cases which have been selected by way of example, there are others which could be used under this heading). The first, *Gilford Motor Co Ltd v Horne* [1933] Ch 935, CA, concerned an attempt by Mr EB Horne to avoid a covenant not to compete by having his wife form a company, JM Horne & Co Ltd, which would carry on business instead. The Court of Appeal formed the view that this company was a mere sham – a device designed to disguise the breach of the covenant by Mr Horne. A similar finding was reached in the case of *Jones v Lipman* [1962] 1 WLR 832, where Mr Lipman sought to avoid a legal obligation to complete a sale of land to Jones by incorporating a company, of which he was a shareholder and director, and selling the same land to it. Russell J's judgment contained the following very visual, and therefore memorable, statement:

> The defendant company is the creature of the first defendant, a device and a sham, a mask which he holds before his face in an attempt to avoid recognition by the eye of equity.

In this case the company was seen to be a sham; but as an entity it was not disregarded, in so far as the court ordered both the company and Mr Lipman to complete the original contract of sale.

Other cases where the courts have found a company to be a sham have resulted in them finding it to be a mere agent of its owners, who are in fact the principal and thus the true party to the contract. For example, in *Re FG (Films) Ltd* [1953] 1 WLR 483, a company was incorporated in England but was controlled by an American company. It claimed that a film made by it was in fact 'British', in order to take advantage of a requirement that British films be given preferential showing in British cinemas. Vaisey J held that the British company was merely an agent for the American company and that this was not therefore a British film. In dealing with cases where companies appear to have been formed for non-legitimate purposes, or to avoid or take advantage of the law, the agency route may be preferable to an allegation that the company in question is a sham. This is because the sham cases, such as *Jones v Lipman* and *Gilford Motor Co Ltd v Horne*, tend to suggest an element of fraud and, given the difficulties associated with discharging the burden of proof required by such a suggestion, it may be simpler to argue the agency point. This argument was put forward by Schmitthoff, who said (see **Further Reading** at the end of the chapter):

In practice, it is easier to escape from the strict interpretation of the rule in Salomon *by the agency route than by relying on abuse of the corporate form. The latter argument always implies a degree of impropriety, though not necessarily fraud, while the former argument does not imply opprobrious conduct. The former argument is thus more readily available than the latter. Only in exceptional cases the argument based on abuse of the corporate form will succeed.*

8.2.2 The identification theory

Closely linked to the discussion above is the situation which necessitates an examination of the people behind the company in order better to understand the nature of the company itself. Recognition of the company as a separate legal entity does not necessarily negate the need to look at those humans who are the company; for example, it will at times be necessary to identify exactly who personifies the company in order to find it in breach of the law of tort or the criminal law. This is known as the identification theory, and through it companies can be prosecuted for a criminal offence even where *mens rea*, or intent, is required. This is sometimes known as the 'alter ego doctrine' and is considered more fully at **8.7** below.

The identification theory has also been used where the personality of the members is crucial in determining the nature of the company itself, where it is impossible to determine its business without looking to its members. For example, in *Trebanog Working Men's Club & Institute Ltd v Macdonald* [1940] 1 KB 567, becoming a member of the company meant becoming a member of the club. When the members bought alcohol at the club it was therefore not being sold to them by the company (which would have required a licence), since they were themselves the company in this instance. Another example is *Abbey Malvern Wells Ltd v Ministry of Local Government & Planning* [1951] Ch 728, where the company's Articles stipulated that the only persons who could be directors of the company must be trustees of a deed which required them to carry on the company's business for charitable purposes. The nature of the company could be established only by looking to the character of the directors.

8.3 Agency

Avoidance of the *Salomon* rule via the agency route has already been mentioned (see **8.2.1** above) in the context of the company amounting to no more than a creature or puppet of the individuals behind it. This approach has also been employed in the economic unit or group of companies situations, where the degree of control of one member of the group over another has amounted to an agency relationship. The judgments in *Salomon* itself did not exclude this as a possibility, although Lord MacNaghten was very clear in his judgment that the courts will take some convincing if they are to find that a company is in fact the agent of its subscribers or trustee for them. However, it is possible to show that the company was not in fact acting on its own behalf but was instead acting under the guidance and at the behest of a principal. In *Smith, Stone & Knight Ltd v Birmingham Corporation* [1939] 4 All ER 116, the business of a company was carried on through a subsidiary company which was to all intents and purposes a department of its parent. When Birmingham Corporation exercised its powers compulsorily to purchase land owned by the subsidiary, the parent claimed compensation. (Compensation which would have been payable to the subsidiary company would not have reflected the loss to the business which was in fact the parent company's business. It was therefore essential for the parent company to identify itself as more than a short-term tenant.) In deciding that an agency relationship existed on the facts, Atkinson J identified six factors to be considered:

(a) Were the profits of the subsidiary those of the parent company?

(b) Were the persons conducting the business of the subsidiary appointed by the parent company?

(c) Was the parent company the head and brains of the trading venture?

(d) Did the parent company govern the adventure?

(e) Were the profits made by the subsidiary company made by the skill and direction of the parent company?

(f) Was the parent company in effective and constant control of the subsidiary?

These six factors are concerned with functional control rather than capitalist control, with the possible exception of the first. Capitalist control is concerned with ownership control over the business, which is not of itself indicative of agency, whereas functional control is an indicator as to exactly who is in control of and running the business; it is this which can be used to support a finding of agency. Of course both capitalist and functional control will usually co-exist in most private companies where majority shareholders are in place as sole directors, at all times (and by most parties) considering the company as merely an extension of themselves. And it must be said that a finding of either kind of control as indicative of agency was not considered in *Salomon*, *Lee's Air Farming* or *Macaura*. It seems that this approach was 'invented' and justified where it seemed expedient to do so in the case in hand. The agency route has not to the writer's knowledge been used in order to find such individuals to be principals of their companies when their 'agent' cannot meet its commitments (however, see the statutory provisions which pierce the veil where fraudulent or wrongful trading can be established, without any need to show an agency relationship, discussed in **Chapter 23**).

8.4 Groups of companies – the 'economic unit'

Identifying the individual companies that exist in a group as separate and independent entities is not a true reflection of the economic reality. Very often such groups are so inter-twined with each others' affairs as to amount to little more than departments of one organisation or entity. A legalistic approach suggests that this economic reality be ignored, each company to suffer its own losses and be accountable for its own debts, not incurring responsibility for the debts of other companies within the group. This clearly benefits a group where one of its members becomes loss-making and can be allowed to be wound up insolvent without causing further harm to the other companies within the group. Cross-guarantees and letters of set off provide a practical solution to this dilemma for the bankers to such corporate groups. Further, some recognition of the special position of groups of companies can also be found in the Companies Act in respect of the accounting and disclosure provisions (see further **Chapter 18**).

The fact that Parliament has seen fit to recognise this situation has been used to promote the notion that it is a suitable approach for the courts to adopt (see dicta of Lord Denning in *Littlewoods Mail Order Stores v McGregor* [1969] 3 All ER 855, at 860). However, with the exception of the decision in *DHN Food Distributors Ltd v London Borough of Tower Hamlets* [1976] 1 WLR 852 (see below), the courts have been somewhat reluctant to follow this suggestion. In *The Albazero* [1977] AC 774, two subsidiary companies within the same group had owned a cargo of crude oil. When the crude oil was lost, the first subsidiary had in fact transferred ownership to the second subsidiary. When claiming against the shipowner, the court held that it was the owner at the time of loss who should bring proceedings and refused to entertain the suggestion that the wholly-owned subsidiaries should be treated as one because they were both owned by the same company. Lord Roskill said (at 807):

> ... each company in a group of companies ... is a separate legal entity possessed of separate legal rights and liabilities so that the rights of one company in a group cannot be exercised by another company in that group even though the ultimate benefit of the exercise of those rights would enure beneficially to the same person or corporate body irrespective of the person or body in those rights were vested in law.

This seems to be the prevalent view of the effect in law of an economic unit, although the decision in *DHN* the following year by a differently constituted Court of Appeal did result in considerable controversy for a number of years. The DHN case concerned the question of compensation as a result of a compulsory purchase order on land belonging to one company in a group which was actually used for business purposes by another of the group's companies. No question of agency arose (see *Smith, Stone & Knight* at **8.3** above) and it was necessary to recognise this economic unit as a single entity if compensation were to be recovered. The Court of Appeal obliged, Lord Denning making the following comments (at 860):

> We all know that in many respects a group of companies are treated together for the purpose of general accounts, balance sheet, and profit and loss account. They are treated as one concern. Professor Gower in Principles of Modern Company Law, 3ed. (1969), p 216 says: 'there is evidence of a general tendency to ignore the separate legal entities of various companies within a group, and to look instead at the economic

entity of the whole group'. This is especially the case when a parent company owns all the shares of the subsidiaries – so much that it can control every movement of the subsidiaries. These subsidiaries are bound hand and foot to the parent company and must do just what the parent company says. ... This group is virtually the same as a partnership in which all three companies are partners. They should not be deprived of the compensation which should justly be payable for disturbance. The three companies should, for present purposes, be treated as one, and the parent company, DHN, should be treated as that one. So DHN are entitled to claim compensation accordingly.

If the companies were indeed like partners then it would be possible for one company within such a group to bankrupt the others (see **Chapter 2**), a result which has never been contemplated by the courts. At the earliest opportunity, the House of Lords criticised the *DHN* decision, in the Scottish appeal *Woolfson v Strathclyde Regional Council* (1978) 38 P & CR 521. There, Lord Keith said that he had

Some doubts about whether the Court of Appeal in the DHN case had properly applied the principle that it is appropriate to pierce the corporate veil only where special circumstances exist indicating that it is a mere facade concealing the true facts.

The more recent decision of the Court of Appeal in *Adams v Cape Industries plc* [1990] Ch 433 has reaffirmed that the separate entity of each company in a group is to be presumed unless there is very strong evidence to rebut it.

The decision in *DHN*, although unsafe to rely on for such a wide application, may still be relevant where the facts suggest that the subsidiaries have no separate business operations and would be treated for *all* purposes as one with their parent (see Goff LJ in the DHN case at 861). This may pose a considerable threat to group enterprises. Suppose the two companies in our scenario, Great Expectations Ltd and Great Expectations (Ideas) Ltd were found in law to be one entity. Any hiving-off of higher-risk projects to Ideas would prove to be worthless, and Great Expectations Ltd would be found to be incurring such risks for itself. On the other hand, Great Expectations (Ideas) Ltd might find it easier to raise capital for its activities if it is believed to be part of a larger and more secure group.

The economic unit argument received short shrift from the Privy Council in 1987, in the case of the *Bank of Tokyo Ltd v Karoon* [1987] AC 45, where the defendants sought, unsuccessfully, to rely on it. Robert Goff LJ made the following statement (at 64):

(Counsel for the Bank of Tokyo Ltd) suggested beguilingly that it would be technical for us to distinguish between parent and subsidiary company in this context; economically, he said, they were one. But we are concerned not with economics but with law. The distinction between the two is, in law, fundamental and cannot here be bridged.

The most recent relevant case is that of *Adams and Others v Cape Industries plc* (see above), which came before the Court of Appeal. This case presented an ideal situation for the court to recognise the economic unit so as to serve justice in the interests of those who seek to claim against a company which is part of a larger group. The claim here was in tort, in respect of asbestos workers who had suffered illnesses as a result of exposure to asbestos at a factory in Texas. If the plaintiffs were to succeed in their claim, they had to persuade the court to pierce the veil of the companies active in America so as to find they were in fact part of the same economic unit with the parent company, Cape, which was based, along with its assets, in England. The Court of Appeal, although finding that Cape, as parent company, did have control over the policy directives of its subsidiary, held that this did not amount to the degree of control which it would be necessary to show in order to pierce the veil and find that the subsidiary's activities were in reality those of its parent (see *Smith, Stone & Knight* at **8.3** above). In conclusion, therefore, it would seem that, in the absence of an agency relationship, the courts will be unwilling to pierce the corporate veil where there is a group of companies, albeit carrying on business as an economic unit.

8.5 Contract

The possibility of avoiding the corporate veil through contract has already been mentioned at **8.2** above. In practice this is fairly commonplace; indeed, we saw in our scenario that Bus Bank plc, bankers to Great Expectations Ltd, have insisted on Edwina executing a contract of guarantee in support of the company's indebtedness to the bank. The bank's policy when dealing with companies such as Great Expectations Ltd is quite clear. The bank does not consider it to be acceptable to have recourse merely to the company's limited fund when it comes to repayment of a loan or settlement of credit. There are numerous devices by which this can be achieved: contracts of guarantee; letters of set off; cross-guarantees in groups of companies; and joint and several liability for company borrowing undertaken by members/directors, for example where a company credit card has been issued. The most commonplace method in the case of private companies is the taking of guarantees, whereby guarantors are jointly and severally liable with the company for its debts. This is an option much favoured by the bankers of many private companies.

Anecdotal evidence indicates that many suppliers of goods to such companies, who extend credit terms, have recognised the wisdom of adopting this approach, although much depends on their ability in the marketplace to insist on such a term. The benefits to the creditor are, first, the avoidance of the members' limited liability to the company, in that the member becomes liable for the amount agreed under the guarantee which may, in exceptional circumstances, be unlimited; and, secondly, the guarantor's fortunes become more closely tied in with the company. This of course may be beneficial to the company itself, and is often used as justification for requiring personal guarantees of member/directors (see **Chapter 12**). A side-effect which may be damaging to the company is that the added security may give rise to company expansion which is out of line with the company's capital base. In other words, the company's activities may become heavily dependent upon short-term finance which has been obtained other than as a result of the company's worth. Expansion, even if funded by greater involvement of the company's bank, is usually matched by an increase in credit from suppliers as more goods or services are supplied on credit. The capital cushion, recognised as so important to maintain in *Trevor v Whitworth* (1887) 12 App Cas 409, becomes increasingly inadequate for the level of the company's activities. Consequently, many of the company's ordinary creditors, those who are not able to look beyond the company for repayment of its debts, are extremely vulnerable (see **Chapter 23**).

8.6 Statute

It is difficult to predict with any degree of certainty the way the courts will proceed in dealing with the effect of the separate entity of companies, where they are asked to pierce the veil and consider the identity of a company's shareholders, whether they be individuals or corporate bodies, in situations where there is no clear precedent. The present trend seems to be to resist attempts further to erode the *Salomon* principle, which has the effect of promoting greater certainty perhaps at the risk of injustice in some cases. Mayson, French and Ryan, *Company Law*, 21st edn (Oxford University Press, 2004), 5.2.2.11, noted the change in attitude of the Court of Appeal over a four-year period as evidenced in the dicta from two reported cases: *Re a Company* [1985] BCLC 333, at 337–8 ('the court will use its powers to pierce the corporate veil if it is necessary to achieve justice') and *Adams v Cape Industries plc* [1990] Ch 433, at 536 ('... save in cases which turn on the wording of particular statutes or contracts, the court is not free to disregard the principle of *Salomon v A Salomon & Co Ltd* [1897] AC 22 merely because it considers that justice so requires').

Parliament has, however, been active over the last 20 years in legislating to provide for the piercing of the corporate veil in situations which had been recognised as being open to potential abuse, for example in the area of taxation and in the Insolvency Act 1986, where provision was made to permit the liquidator of a company, which had been caused to trade fraudulently (s 213) or wrongfully (s 214), to apply to the court for a compensation order against the wrongdoers. This to some extent takes away one of the most tangible benefits of trading through a company, limited liability. Any such order must, however, be applied for by the liquidator on behalf of the company, and any resulting compensation order must be paid to the company itself (s 212 permits any creditor contributory, etc to apply, but compensation received must still be paid to the company).

8.7 The alter ego doctrine

We have already established that, once incorporated, a company is a legal person in its own right. Clearly, it is impossible for the company to act as a person in all respects, it being hindered by its own lack of a physical being. This unavoidable defect is overcome by adopting an approach which identifies certain human agents to be acting as the company as opposed to acting on its behalf. Such individuals may find their actions and failings imputed to the company, becoming the actions or failings of the company itself (see *DPP v Kent & Sussex Contractors Ltd* [1944] KB 146).

The identification theory is a question of fact in each case, and any notion of a company being held accountable for a criminal offence due to actions or inactions on the part of such persons must be decided on a case-by-case basis (see *R v P&O European Ferries (Dover) Ltd* (1990) 93 Cr App R 72, at 84). The much quoted passage of Denning LJ in *HL Bolton (Engineering) Co Ltd v TJ Graham & Sons Ltd* [1957] 1 QB 159 provides a vivid description of the identification theory (at 172):

> A company may in many ways be likened to a human body. It has a brain and nerve centre which controls what it does. It also has hands which hold the tools and act in accordance with directions from the centre. Some of the people in the company are

mere servants and agents who are nothing more than hands to do the work and cannot be said to represent the mind or will. Others are directors and managers who represent the directing mind and will of the company, and control what it does. The state of mind of these managers is the state of mind of the company and is treated by the law as such.

It is clear from Lord Denning's comments that it is those who are the directing mind and will of the company who can be said to personify the company's mind. Simply to perform some of the functions of management, perhaps with a degree of discretion, will not of itself suffice to find that it is the company which is acting (see dicta of Lord Reid in *Tesco Supermarkets Ltd v Nattrass* [1972] AC 153, at 171). In *Tesco Supermarkets Ltd v Nattrass*, a store manager caused his particular branch to breach s 11 of the Trade Descriptions Act 1968. A defence was provided within the section, but this was available only where the company could show that the commission of the offence was due to the act or default of another person, and that the company had taken all reasonable precautions and exercised all due diligence to avoid the commission of such an offence by itself or someone under its control. Identifying the store manager as someone other than the company, ie as another person, was therefore crucial. In the event the House of Lords did just that; the store manager was one of 800 such managers and could not be said to have acted as the company. Similarly, in *R v Andrews-Weatherfoil Ltd* [1972] 1 WLR 118, a bribe made by an employee of a company, who was the manager of its housing department, did not amount to a bribe having been offered by the company. Note, however, that the alter ego doctrine cannot be used to provide a defence for company officers who commit an offence against the company, in that they cannot maintain or allege that the company authorised it (*A–G Reference (No 2 of 1982) [1984] QB 624*).

8.8 Conclusion

The separate legal entity created upon the formation of a company confers many benefits upon the corporators and is vulnerable to abuse. The trend emerging from the courts, which appears to be in favour of upholding the *Salomon* principle in almost all cases, suggests that it is for Parliament to tackle this problem. Is it necessary for small businesses to trade through limited companies; or is this potentially damaging for the economy, where struggling companies can be wound up enabling the business itself to trade through a newly-formed company? The domino effect of company collapses on creditors and creditors' creditors is all too apparent. Tackling the 'phoenix syndrome' (discussed in **Chapter 23**), which prevented a new company rising from the ashes of old with a same or similar name and continuing the same business, solves only part of the problem. Often risks are calculated and the company is used as a vehicle to provide a large income at an early stage, not necessarily out of profits (*Re Halt Garage (1964) Ltd* [1982] 3 All ER 1016); then, when the cash flow can no longer support the payments, the company dies and is written off as a victim of the recession, with bad management seen as merely a factor. It seems to be legitimate to ask why it is necessary to make incorporation so easy – surely businesses could start life without corporate form? The price for such benefits appears to be set extremely low, with no realistic minimum capital requirement provided for in English company law.

FURTHER READING

O Kahn-Freund, 'Some Reflections on Company Law Reform' (1944) 7 MLR 54; (1940) 3
  MLR 226.
C M Schmitthoff, 'Salomon in the shadow' [1976] JBL 305.
L S Sealy, 'Modern Insolvency Laws and Mr Salomon' (1998) 16 C & SLJ 176.
S Ottolenghi, 'From peeping behind the corporate veil, to ignoring it completely' (1990)
  53 MLR 338.

9 The Balance of Power

LEARNING OUTCOMES

By the end of this chapter, you should understand:

- the position of the directors;

- directors' duties and the enforcement of those duties;

- the position of the shareholders;

- relationship of the company with creditors;

- relationship of the company with employees.

SCENARIO

Now that the company is under way, the participants are beginning to understand that certain consequences follow from the decisions which they made earlier about who was to be a director and how the shares were to be divided up. They are also beginning to realise that the company's relationship with its creditors is not quite the same as the relationship which the former partnership enjoyed. Some specific problems have brought these issues to light. Duncan, who holds 60% of the shares (see **Appendix F**), has found that leaving the running of the company to the directors is not as attractive an option as he had previously thought. He has some reservations about Edwina; although he was initially impressed by her energy and enthusiasm, he cannot entirely ignore that fact that she is a woman, and Duncan has never really been convinced that women can be relied upon in business. Given that his is the major financial investment in the company, he is inclined to think that he ought to be able to give the directors instructions whenever he likes – that was of course one of the reasons for his insistence on the addition to the Articles of a clause giving him the right to attend board meetings (see **Appendix B**). He does this somewhat erratically, for he looks at the company's affairs only when he can spare time from his steam trains. As a result, he has taken to telephoning Edwina and telling her what he wants done. He seems to have views on most policy questions, including the quality control system, the level of wages paid to employees and the extent to which the accounts should provide for bad debts, to mention only a few. Edwina is not amused by this treatment. She points out that Duncan's views are not normally based on a detailed study of the company's position, and in her view they are usually quite misguided. In any event, Duncan is not a director, and Edwina thinks that it is for the directors to run the company. She has begun to consider the possibility of diluting Duncan's influence in the company by issuing more shares to others.

Charlotte has begun to cause other difficulties. She is a very small shareholder and an employee, but is not a director. She is acting as de facto Personnel Manager as well as covering for Arthur during his long absences (Arthur regularly indulges his taste for exotic holidays). She is becoming increasingly confident in her new position of responsibility and believes herself to be well informed on important matters concerning company policy. Charlotte disagrees with a number of the policies adopted by the company. In particular, she is concerned that the company imports certain rare woods from Brazil to use in manufacturing tables which it then supplies to clients. She regards this as ecologically undesirable and would like to be able to prevent it. She has also become something of a spokeswoman for the employees in general, and has become convinced that the company pays its workers too little and offers them inadequate fringe benefits, particularly in relation to pension rights.

Arthur and Bill have their own problems. They were not required to give personal guarantees to the bank to secure the loans to the company (Edwina did give such a guarantee) but they realise that if the business fails they will be out of work with no immediate prospect of finding other jobs. Arthur has developed a liking for frequent holidays, and Charlotte is increasingly expected to cover for him while he is away.

Meanwhile, some of the company's creditors are beginning to be awkward. Edwina has instituted a policy of waiting as long as possible before settling the company's debts to its suppliers. She justifies this to Arthur and Bill by saying that it aids the company's cash flow, keeps down the level of the bank overdraft and thereby reduces interest charges. However, some of the suppliers have begun to threaten further action to speed up payment, though they have not as yet specified what form that action might take.

OVERVIEW

The fundamental idea behind this chapter is that much of company law is about holding the balance between directors, shareholders and creditors (the employees of the company might also be mentioned, though, as is shown at **9.5** below, they receive very little protection from company law). Although company law does in principle *acknowledge* the interests of all these groups, it is not always prepared to enforce recognition of those interests by management, which is effectively left free to choose how much weight to give to them. This chapter serves as an introduction to these issues, which are then examined in more detail in the next eight chapters.

9.1 The position of the directors

This is a matter of quite fundamental importance in company law, and yet there is no provision in the Companies Acts which states in unequivocal terms the powers and duties of the directors. Instead, these must be deduced from a series of provisions.

The starting point is that the directors manage the company on a day-to-day basis. This conclusion may be derived from Table A, art 70, which states:

> Subject to the provisions of this Act, the memorandum and the articles and to any directions given by special resolution, the business of the company shall be managed by the directors who may exercise all the powers of the company.

Thus, it is not normally open to the shareholders to tell the directors how the company is to be managed (see *Towcester Racecourse Co Ltd v Racecourse Association Ltd* [2003] 1 BCLC 260). Article 70 provides an answer to a long-standing controversy in company law (see **Further Reading**, below), namely, the extent to which the appointment of the directors involved a deemed delegation to them of the powers which would normally be expected to belong to the shareholders as owners. It is now clear that there is an effective delegation. Such delegation is a practical necessity, since no business can hope to operate efficiently if every decision has to be referred to the shareholders for approval – Duncan is not involved in the day-to-day management of the company and cannot reasonably expect to be constantly consulted; if he wants this level of involvement, he must become a director. It may be possible to override this delegation in individual cases by means of a special resolution, so that it is only in cases where holders of 75% of the shares are opposed to what the directors are doing that the delegation can be revoked. Under the former law (art 80 of the version of Table A which applied before 1985) there was controversy as to the freedom of the directors to ignore directions of the General Meeting in certain cases, such as an instruction to commence legal proceedings in the name of the company. The case of *Shaw v John Shaw (Salford) Ltd* [1935] 2 KB 113, CA, though turning on the drafting of the special Articles of the company, rather than on any provision of Table A, appears to support a fairly strong judicial tendency to resist the giving of such direction by a majority of shareholders (though there was also authority – *Marshall's Valve Gear Co v Manning, Wardle & Co* [1903] 1 Ch 267 – that in these circumstances the majority could themselves commence proceedings in the name of the company). It is unclear whether a similar principle would apply under the new art 70. It is suggested that the change from ordinary resolution to special resolution as the basis for the giving of such instructions, deliberately made by the legislature in 1985, should carry with it the consequence that validly given instructions are not to be disregarded.

It should also be remembered that, at least in theory, there will always remain the more draconian option of dismissing the directors from office. This requires only an ordinary resolution (Companies Act 1985, s 303.), but various other difficulties may arise, including the possibility of a *Bushell v Faith* ([1970] AC 1099) clause, which Great Expectations Ltd does have (see **Appendix B**), and the risk of claims for wrongful and/or unfair dismissal (for the issues relevant to attempts to dismiss the directors, see **Chapter 11**), as well as the possibility that the unreasonable dismissal of a director might amount to unfairly prejudicial conduct under s 459 of the Companies Act 1985 (see **Chapter 14**). It is in any event a more extreme reaction, which may not be what the shareholders want to do in a given case.

Given that the directors have the management of the company, the next question is to identify the principles according to which that management is to be carried on.

9.2 Directors' duties

9.2.1 'Bona fide and in the best interests of the company'

In managing the business of the company the fundamental principle is that the directors must act *bona fide* and in the best interests of the company. This apparently simple statement of principle gives rise to many problems. These are explored in more detail in **Chapters 10** and **11**.

First, the standard of duty which is imposed is partly objective and partly subjective (*Norman v Theodore Goddard* [1992] BCC 14; *Re Barings plc* (No 5) [2000] 1 BCLC 523). It is ultimately for the court, should it prove necessary, to decide whether the actions taken were in fact in the best interests of the company, though at the same time it should be said that in practice the court will allow the directors a certain margin of appreciation, ie they will be prepared to accept that in many cases differing views could be taken about what the best interests of the company required, and will not seek to intervene so long as the directors have made a decision which appears reasonable and defensible in the cir-cumstances. An important aspect of this approach is that the court is reluctant to become drawn into the task of arbitrating on policy disputes within the company, which are better resolved by discussion among the participants, culminating if necessary in a vote accord-ing to the company law procedures.

The question of what is meant by the 'best interests of the company' is also a difficult one, since it often involves the directors in striking a balance between short term and long term, and between present shareholders and possible future shareholders.

9.2.2 Enforcing the directors' duties

Where there is a dispute within the company about the behaviour of the directors, the question naturally arises of how the directors' duties can be enforced. It is essential to understand that directors owe their duties to the company, not to the individual share-holders. Thus, as a general rule, it is not open to shareholders to sue the directors for breach of duty (*Percival v Wright* [1902] 2 Ch 421). Instead, this power lies exclusively with the company itself. This is potentially a source of difficulty for aggrieved shareholders, since the power to decide that the company will take legal action is a power which in the ordinary course of events is vested in the directors under art 70 of Table A, which was dis-cussed at **9.1** above. Naturally, it is not to be expected that the directors will be ready to cause the company to take action against themselves collectively, though presumably they might be prepared to take action against a minority of directors (or, more probably, ex-directors) who appeared to have breached their duties to the company.

In some cases it is possible for aggrieved shareholders to use the name of the company to bring a claim in the name of the company against the delinquent directors (see **Chapter 14**). Another possibility, which is also explored more fully in **Chapter 14**, is to use s 459 of the Companies Act 1985 and to bring a petition to the court under that section, alleging that the affairs of the company are being conducted in a manner unfairly prejudicial to the members or some part of the members (the Insolvency Act 1986, s 212 may also offer some prospect of success where the company is being wound up; see further **Chapter 23**). In a small number of situations, notably those involving takeovers, it may be possible to depart from the general principle that directors do not owe duties to shareholders (*Gething v Kilner* [1972] 1 All ER 1164; *Coleman v Myers* [1977] 2 NZLR 225).

9.3 The position of the shareholders

An important theme of this part of the book is that the power of the shareholders as such in a company is severely limited. Although they are the owners of the business, they do not have management rights (see **9.1** above) and their power to dismiss the directors is in practice often severely limited. In public companies this is rarely a problem, since the shareholders are often a disparate class having no interest in management. In small private companies the point is often irrelevant for a different reason, namely, that the shareholders and directors are often the same people. However, even in private companies the point can become an important and difficult one where, as in our scenario, the shareholders and the directors are an overlapping but not identical group. The obstacles placed in the way of shareholders who wish to manage the company provide a good illustration of the important differences between a partnership and a company. This aspect of the problem is considered in more detail in **Chapter 13**.

Another frequently encountered phenomenon is that of the minority shareholder who claims that the directors (or sometimes the other shareholders) are not treating him fairly. His views on company policy may be ignored, and in extreme cases the majority may even exclude him from attending meetings. If he is initially a director, he may find himself removed from the board. Disputes of this kind are one of the most difficult areas of company law, for the court is often called upon to intervene to override the majority decision-making process upon grounds which, according to interpretation of the facts, are either unfairly prejudicial, or the product of a dispute as to company policy or merely frivolous. **Chapter 14** examines the relevant legislation and case law.

9.4 Relationship with creditors

When Great Expectations was a partnership, the partners had a clear notion that they were personally liable to creditors for the firm's debts (see **Chapter 3**). Indeed, one of the major reasons for incorporating the firm was the desire to avoid this personal liability, and there is no doubt that as a general principle of company law, directors are not liable to creditors for the debts of the company – this follows from the doctrine of corporate personality (see **Chapter 8**), which implies that the company is a separate legal person and that the company alone is liable for its debts. In practice, however, matters are not nearly as simple as this.

The most important qualification on the principle that directors are not liable for the debts of the company arises from the fact that loan creditors of a private company – usually, as in the case of Great Expectations Ltd, the bank – will almost invariably require the directors of the company to give personal guarantees in respect of the loan which they have made to the company. These guarantees will be in addition to the charges (fixed and floating) which the creditor will have taken over the company's property. The practical consequence of this is that, at least so far as the bank is concerned, the liability of the directors is not limited except by the value of the personal assets available to the director and by any limit negotiated between the director and the bank. Edwina was obliged to give such a guarantee, though Arthur and Bill were able to escape on the ground that their assets were too insignificant to be of much value to the bank. In the case of Great Expectations Ltd, it should be noted that Duncan, as a major shareholder, has also given the company a loan (see **Appendix F**), but this is not secured by any personal guarantees from the directors.

At the same time there is effective protection against other creditors, a group which is likely to include virtually all the company's trade creditors who have supplied goods and/or services to the company on credit (this assumes that property in goods supplied has passed to the company; for the situation where there is a retention of title clause, see **Chapter 15**). As long as the company remains a going concern these creditors have no means to make the directors liable for its debts. The only situation in which directors are at risk of having to contribute personally to such liabilities arises where the company is in liquidation and the liquidator pursues the directors for fraudulent trading (Insolvency Act 1986, s 213) or wrongful trading (s 214), or the liquidator or other interested party brings proceedings for misfeasance (s 212). This area is dealt with in detail in **Chapter 23**, but it may be noted here that directors who have continued the business of the company when they knew, or should have known, that the collapse of the company was inevitable, or who have carried on the business of the company for a fraudulent purpose, or who have been guilty of any breach of duty towards the company, may, at the suit of the liquidator, be called upon to compensate the company (and thus, indirectly, the creditors) for any loss caused to the company by the decision to continue trading.

Thus, the directors need not be too concerned at the threats coming from suppliers. At the same time they would be unwise to disregard these threats completely, not least since unpaid creditors do have the option of applying to the court for the compulsory winding up of the company, provided that they are owed at least £750, which sum has not been paid to them within three weeks after the making of a statutory demand for it (Insolvency Act 1986, ss 122–125). Alternatively, such creditors could obtain judgment against the company for the sum outstanding. In practice this is likely to cause the bank to take a very unfavourable view of the company, and possibly to review its terms of lending. Many small companies which habitually delay payment of bills for the maximum possible time rely on the goodwill (or at least the forbearance) of creditors in not pursuing this remedy. Were the company to be confronted with a winding-up petition, it could no doubt rapidly satisfy the petitioning creditor's demands by reorganising its payments, but if all its trade creditors petitioned simultaneously, it would be in considerable difficulties. The role of trade credit in allowing small companies to survive from day to day (especially in difficult economic circumstances) should not be underestimated. The legal issues surrounding this method of doing business are explored more fully in **Chapter 15**.

An important point at which the shareholders and the creditors may find a conflict of interest is where it is proposed to distribute dividends to shareholders. Such dividends are of course the way in which shareholders obtain a return on their investment, but the distribution reduces the funds available to the company to meet its debts (on the other hand, shareholders cannot complain if the company reduces its apparent level of profit by making a substantial bad debt provision). Company law therefore insists that dividends are paid only out of profits of the company (see **Chapter 16**) and that the share capital of the company is not improperly returned to the shareholders (see **Chapter 17**).

9.5 Relationship with employees

The employees of a company may be regarded as forming the fourth of the major interest groups within the company. Clearly, the policies adopted by the company are likely to have an effect on the prosperity and job prospects of the employees. However, company law has not been very forthcoming in recognising employees as a legitimate interest group. It is only since 1980 that the directors have been under any obligation to take account of the interest of employees when making their decisions. The present rule is contained in s 309 of the Companies Act 1985, which provides that the matters to which the directors are to have regard in exercising their duties include the interests of the employees in general. However, s 309(2) then goes on to provide that this duty is owed to the company alone and is enforceable in the same way as any other fiduciary duty owed by the directors. It follows from this that it is not possible for the employees as such to enforce this duty, that power lying exclusively with the company (usually acting through the shareholders in General Meeting). Because of this it may well be suggested that the duty which s 309 imposes is of little practical significance. In the first place the duty is a very vague one. The directors are to have regard to the interests of the employees, but not to the exclusion of any other legitimate interests (principally the interests of the members), and the weighing of competing interests is, as indicated at **9.2** above, an area where the court will naturally allow the directors considerable latitude. It is therefore in most cases very unlikely that a court will be prepared to find that the directors have been in breach of their duty under this section. In the second place, even where there is the clearest imaginable breach of the duty, no action will be taken against the directors unless the shareholders so wish. Unfortunately, where the interests of the employees are disregarded, this will usually be for the purpose of furthering the interests of the shareholders (or, in cases of corporate sickness, the interests of the creditors through, for example, large-scale redundancies). Neither group is likely to be interested in proceeding against the directors for behaving in this way.

The truth appears to be that this section was introduced into the law for the purpose of overruling an earlier judicial decision (*Parke v Daily News* [1962] Ch 927), which held that it was not proper for the directors to take account of the interests of the employees even where conscience would have called upon them to do so. The effect of the section is that shareholders cannot legitimately complain when the directors do have regard to the interests of the employees, but that employees have no effective remedy where the directors ignore them. From the point of view of the employees, a possible solution would appear to be to acquire some shares in the company and then exploit the rights of shareholders to seek to bring a derivative action. Such a purchase of shares may be viable in a public company whose shares are quoted on the Stock Exchange, but in a company such as Great Expectations Ltd no shares are available for purchase (although there is a large amount of authorised capital available for issue, the directors have no plans to issue any of it, and would presumably not want to issue shares to employees anyway). Moreover, employee shareholders would have to show that they were being prejudiced in their capacity as members, which might well be difficult. However, the ease with which Charlotte is able to embarrass and inconvenience the directors by skilful use of her rights as a shareholder does serve to emphasise the value and importance of employees being shareholders (*Wallersteiner v Moir* [1974] 3 All ER 217, CA provides a good example of a case where this opportunity was adroitly employed to the great irritation of the directors). The present rule amounts to the recognition of employees as an interest group without any willingness to enforce recognition of their interests.

9.6 Advice to the parties

Much of the relevant advice is contained in the conclusions to **Chapters 10** to **17**, but some general points may be made here.

First, a company is significantly different from a partnership in terms of its managerial structure. Although shareholders own the company (just as partners own the partnership business), they do not manage it (unlike partners). The role of the directors is one which has no direct parallel in partnership law, for the directors need not be shareholders, yet the shareholders are required to make an effective delegation to them of much of the running of the business – although art 70 of Table A can be excluded, it is almost inevitable in anything but the very smallest company that the directors will be the managers, and a non-director shareholder is by definition in a relatively weak position.

Secondly, the directors owe no general duty to the creditors as long as the business is a going concern which can pay its debts. It is sometimes said that the company must be able to pay its debts as they fall due, but this is not really true. It would be more accurate to say that the company must be able to pay its debts when they become the subject of a statutory demand. The directors owe no duty to the creditors, and the only circumstances in which the trade creditors have any chance at all of pursuing the directors for any personal liability is where the company goes into insolvent liquidation (see **Chapter 23**).

The directors also find themselves in a strong position as against the employees, whose interests are poorly represented in English company law.

In the end, the only advice which can properly be given to Duncan is that he must either sack the directors, or let them get on with running the company. The directors, for their part, should concentrate on making the company profitable. Arthur and Bill should be advised that they are safe as long as the company survives, but that if it collapses they may be exposed to action by the liquidator. Charlotte wields very little influence within the company, having only 1.25% of the shares, and it is most unlikely that she can affect the management policies. She can remind the directors of their duties towards the employees, but there is no way in which she can enforce observance of these duties.

Edwina is in a fairly strong position. She has had to give personal guarantees for the company's borrowings, but, although she may be in some danger if the company collapses, there is little reason to think that the liquidator will pursue her for anything she has done so far. The practice of delaying payment on invoices may irritate creditors, but she does have a strong argument when she says that it aids the company's cash flow.

FURTHER READING

Goldberg, (1970) 33 MLR 177.
Wedderburn, (1976) 39 MLR 327.
Sullivan, (1977) 93 LQR 569.

10 Directors' Duties

LEARNING OUTCOMES

By the end of this chapter, you should understand the following:

- the duty of care owed by directors to the company;

- fiduciary duties owed by directors to the company;

- the duty of directors to act in the best interests of the company as a whole;

- the duty of care owed by directors to shareholders;

- the duty of care owed by directors to creditors;

- the duty of care owed by directors to employees;

- directors as individuals – substantial property transactions involving company property or transactions with the company – loans and credit transactions;

- the rule against profiting and relief from liability.

OVERVIEW

This chapter is concerned essentially with the relationship between directors and their company, and to a lesser extent with their relationship with other interested parties, though these latter relationships are explored more fully in later chapters. Directors are the agents of companies, and often (though not always) they are employees. They are also in practice the eyes, ears and mouth of the company. This is a complex relationship, which is extensively regulated through both statute and common law.

10.1 Duty of care

10.1.1 Standard of the duty of care

Directors owe their company a duty of care, and they will be liable to the company if they fall short of the relevant standard in carrying out their functions (*Henderson v Merrett Syndicates Ltd* [1995] 2 AC 145, HL). This duty is relatively light when compared with the onerous, if not draconian, fiduciary duties which are considered at **10.2** below.

The question of the extent of directors' duty is a complex one, where it may be suggested that standards have changed over the years. During the previous century attitudes hardened somewhat, not least because of greater awareness of the consequences to third parties of incompetence and laziness on the part of directors, and because of the trend towards small private companies, whose directors would normally be expected to adopt a hands-on approach to management. In *Dorchester Finance Co v Stebbing* [1989] BCLC 498, the court had little difficulty finding three directors negligent where no board meetings had ever been held and the usual practice was for two of the directors to leave all the affairs to one director, Stebbing, with the exception of signing blank cheques to assist him in his illegal actions. The fact that the two non-executive directors concerned also happened to be accountants appears to have at least influenced Foster J in his decision:

> For a chartered accountant and an experienced accountant to put forward the proposition that a non-executive director has no duties to perform I find quite alarming.

The wrongful trading provision introduced by s 214 of the Insolvency Act 1986, provides for an objective assessment of a director's behaviour for the purposes of determining whether such director caused his company to trade wrongfully. Nonetheless, the test has a subjective element in that a director's actual qualifications will be taken into account, not to lower the standard that might be expected from him but to tighten it up if he brings his own special qualities to his office (see **Chapter 23**).

Although the Insolvency Act provisions have no application to solvent companies, they do emphasise the modern trend towards expecting a higher standard of care from directors (this was a major concern behind the setting up of the Cork Committee, whose report led to the introduction of the Insolvency Act 1986), and there is some suggestion that this may in turn have led to the adoption of such standards by the court even where the company remains solvent. In *Norman v Theodore Goddard* [1991] BCLC 1028, Hoffman J said:

> The extent of the duty of care owed by a director has been discussed in a number of cases but I need mention only two principles which seem to me to emerge clearly from the authorities. First, a director performing active duties on behalf of the company need not exhibit a greater degree of skill than may reasonably be expected from a person undertaking those duties. A director who undertakes the management of the company's properties is expected to have reasonable skill in property management, but not in offshore tax avoidance. It may be that in considering what a director ought reasonably to have known or inferred, one should also take into account the knowledge, skill and experience which he actually had in addition to that which a person carrying out his functions should be expected to have. [Counsel for] Theodore Goddard submitted that the test was accurately stated in sec. 214(4) of the Insolvency Act 1986. ... I have not called for any argument on this point ... because I am willing to assume that the test is as [Counsel] submits.

(See also *Re D`Jan of London Ltd* [1994] 1 BCLC 561.)

The above may be contrasted with the leading older authority in this area, *Re City Equitable Fire Insurance Co Ltd* [1925] Ch 407, where Romer J suggested that the extent of a director's duty of skill and care was of a rather low standard and essentially to be determined on a subjective basis, having regard to the abilities of the director in question.

The subjective nature of the test propounded by Romer J had already been stated by Neville J in *Re Brazilian Rubber Plantations & Estates Ltd* [1911] 1 Ch 425:

A director's duty has been laid down as requiring him to act with such care as is reasonably expected from him, having regard to his knowledge and experience. He is, I think, not bound to bring any special qualifications to his office. He may undertake the management of a rubber company in complete ignorance of everything connected with rubber, without incurring responsibility for the mistakes which may result from such ignorance.

These propositions suggest a fairly low standard of care, and are in line with the attitude of the late 19th and early 20th centuries in this area. It is submitted that the preferred approach, at least for executive directors, is the more objective test approved by Hoffman J in *Norman v Theodore Goddard*. Support for this proposition can also be seen in the case of *Re Barings plc (No 5)* [2000] 1 BCLC 523, where the court held that the directors collectively and individually should have a continuing duty to acquire and maintain a sufficient knowledge and understanding of the company's business, so as to enable them to discharge their duties as directors (see also *Equitable Life Assurance Society v Bowley* [2004] 1 BCLC 180).

Directors' acts must therefore be assessed with regard to some objective analysis. The Law Commission, in *Company Directors: Regulating Conflicts of Interests and Formulating a Statement of Duties* (Report No 261), recommended (at para 5.15) that:

(1) *a director's duty of care, skill and diligence to his company should be set out in statute;*

(2) *the standard should be judged by a twofold objective /subjective test; and*

(3) *regard should be had to the functions of the particular director and the circumstances of the company.*

Although it must be clear that the entirely subjective test for determining the duty of care of a director propounded by Romer J has been discarded, It should also be observed that even Romer J, in *Re City Equitable*, accepted that attention must be paid to the size and nature of the company in determining the standard of care expected of a director. It is not clear that even his test would have allowed incompetence and lack of attention to detail on the part of Edwina and Bill, for Great Expectations Ltd is a very different company from City Equitable.

10.1.2 Provisions purporting to protect directors from liability

Section 309A of the Companies Act 1985 (inserted by the Companies (Audit, Investigations and Community Enterprise) Act 2004, and modelled on s 310 of the 1985 Act), provides that the section will apply in relation to any liability attaching to a director of a company in connection with any negligence, default, breach of duty, or breach of trust by him in relation to the company. It goes on to state that any provision (whether contained in the Articles or otherwise) which purports to exempt him to any extent from any liability within the terms of the section is void. Furthermore, any provision by which a company directly or indirectly provides for an indemnity for a director for any such breach of duty is also void. (The section does not, however, prevent the company from securing third party indemnity insurance in respect of any breach of duty on the part of a director.)

The directors therefore cannot by any provision, either in their contacts or in the Articles, seek to limit or exclude their liability to the company for any act of default on their part. The provision does not affect the power of the company in General Meeting to ratify, and therefore effectively to condone, conduct on the part of directors after full and frank disclosure of any breach of duty.

10.2 Fiduciary duties

The directors, as a body, must act *bona fide* for the benefit of the company as a whole and for a proper purpose (*Re Smith & Fawcett Ltd* [1942] Ch 304, CA, *per* Lord Greene MR: what constitutes the company as a whole is a difficult issue, see **10.3** below and *Regentcrest plc v Cohen* [2001] 2 BCLC 80; *JJ Harrison (Properties) Ltd v Harrison* [2002] 1 BCLC 162). The fiduciary nature of the directors' position in relation to the company makes it a breach of duty for a director to have any form of conflict between his own interests and the interests of the company. ('Fiduciary' refers to trust and confidence, and the duties are imposed by equity requiring a fiduciary not to abuse the trust and confidence implicit in his position.)

As this duty is owed by the directors to the company, neither the directors collectively nor the disinterested directors are competent to waive the duty, or to sanction any conflict of interest affecting one or more of their number. Only the company in General Meeting has this power. A strict application of this rule would mean that the directors would not be permitted to enter into any contractual arrangement with the company, including an arrangement for the payment of remuneration. For this reason provision is usually made in the company's Articles of Association (which may be regarded as an exercise by the General Meeting of its power to regulate the company's affairs) to prevent the duty from being breached in certain circumstances. For example, Table A, art 85 waives the rule against conflict, *provided* the director has disclosed the nature and extent of any material interest to the directors. The Companies Act 1985, s 317 goes further, in that it requires disclosure to the *directors* as a *board* of *any* interest (*Guiness v Saunders* [1990] 2 AC 663), though breach of this section involves only criminal sanctions and has no effect on the validity of any contract. It may be thought desirable to amend art 85 to include the same requirement of disclosure to the board as a whole. However, art 89 provides for a quorum of only two directors, whilst art 96 empowers the company by ordinary resolution to allow a director to vote on a matter in which he is interested. The combination of these two provisions may largely negate the apparent protection for shareholders provided by art 85 and s 317.

10.3 The company as a whole

It is very difficult to determine what the interests of the company as a whole comprise. The most straightforward approach would consider the company as merely the sum of its members; in satisfying their requirements the duty to the company would be discharged. However, a company is far more than a body of corporators: it is a separate legal entity which encompasses the interests of different groups of individuals – the directors, the employees, and the investors or members of the company (the creditors have been deliberately omitted from this list, since they have generally no right to intervene in the affairs of the company and company law protects their interests only to a very limited extent; see **10.3.2** below). For this reason the approach of this book is to examine how the directors discharge their duty to the company as a separate entity by having regard to these various, often competing interests. What is clear is that the directors do not owe a duty to an individual or to groups of individuals, except in so far as such interest has to be considered in discharging their duty to the company.

10.3.1 Shareholders

In *Percival v Wright* [1902] 2 Ch 421, the plaintiff shareholders offered to sell their shares to the defendant directors, who agreed to buy them at a certain price without disclosing that they were in fact negotiating separately with an outsider for a considerably higher figure. The plaintiffs claimed that the directors were in a fiduciary relationship to them and sought to avoid the transfer of the shares. The court, however, held that there was no fiduciary relationship between directors and shareholders individually.

This case is generally treated as the basis of the modern doctrine that directors owe no fiduciary duty to shareholders, but it can be seen that its true scope is somewhat problematic. First, it is not clear that in accepting the offer to sell the shares the directors were acting *as directors of the company* – it might equally be said that they acted in their personal capacity, in which case the fact that they were directors might be seen as irrelevant. Secondly, it might be said that there are good reasons for not requiring the disclosure of commercially sensitive information such as ongoing negotiations for the sale of the company; such an argument, however, would logically lead to the conclusion that the directors should have rejected the offer of sale, rather than that they were entitled to accept it without disclosing relevant facts. Thirdly, there is nothing in the decision which compels the conclusion that directors owe no duty which can be enforced by individual shareholders – the case decides that there is no *fiduciary* duty in relation to the making of profits and does not of itself preclude a finding that the shareholders can sue for breach of duties of skill and care. Despite these problems, there is no doubt that as a general rule (exceptions to this general rule are examined in **Chapter 13**), individual shareholders cannot at the present day sue directors for breach of the directors' duties to the company (the suggestion by Lord Bridge in *Caparo Industries plc v Dickman* [1990] 2 AC 605 that shareholders collectively might be able to sue is incomprehensible, unless it means that the company in General Meeting could institute proceedings).

On the other hand, if on the facts of a particular case it can be shown that the directors had undertaken to act on behalf of the shareholders as individuals then fiduciary duties will be owed to those shareholders. This is demonstrated in the case of *Allen v Hyatt* (1914) 30 TLR 444, where the directors in question had held themselves out as being prepared to act as agents of the shareholders in a particular transaction. The Privy Council had little difficulty finding that on the facts the individual shareholders were entitled to treat the directors as trustees for them. However, these duties arose from the agency relationship rather than from their position as directors. This is a line of reasoning which may well have relevance to a small private company like Great Expectations Ltd, where

Charlotte, and possibly Arthur, may be able to claim that because of the close relationship between the shareholders, the directors owe them similar duties (*Coleman v Myers* [1977] 2 NZLR 225).

There have also been a few cases where directors have been held to owe duties to individual shareholders. The best known of these are *Gething v Kilner* [1972] 1 All ER 1146 and the New Zealand case of *Coleman v Myers* (above), where it was held that directors making recommendations to shareholders about responding to takeover bids (especially contested takeover bids) owe a duty to avoid misleading those shareholders and to disclose any interest of their own in the proposed transaction. These cases differ from *Percival v Wright* in that, in them, at least one takeover bid had already been made, and it may be said that the situation where shareholders are preparing to sell their shares is a unique one, since they are considering realising their investment, and the advice which the directors give them goes beyond the ordinary managerial functions of the directors. Perhaps this is merely another way of saying that in giving such advice the directors do not really act as directors and the situation is therefore not within the principle that directors' duties are owed only to the company. The argument is by no means convincing, however, and it seems likely that these cases should properly be regarded as exceptions grafted on to a principle which looks increasingly uncomfortable, at least in the context of private companies.

10.3.2 Creditors

It is unlikely that directors owe a duty to creditors rather than a duty to consider the interests of the creditors in order to discharge their duty to the company, but much will depend upon the circumstances under consideration. The possibility that the directors might owe a duty to the creditors directly was suggested in *Winkworth v Edward Baron Development Co Ltd* [1986] 1 WLR 1512, at 1516, by Lord Templeman, who said:

> [A] company owes a duty to its creditors, present and future. The company is not bound to pay off every debt as soon as it is incurred, and the company is not obliged to avoid all ventures which involve an element of risk but the company owes a duty to its creditors to keep its property inviolate and available for the repayment of its debts. The conscience of the company, as well as its management, is confided to the directors. A duty is owed by the directors to the company and to the creditors of the company to ensure that the affairs of the company are properly administered and that its property is not dissipated or exploited for the benefit of the directors themselves to the prejudice of the creditors.

It is submitted that the better view (see **Further Reading**, below) is that the directors are bound to consider the interests of the creditors when (but only when) their actions would have a direct effect on the position of the creditors, as, for example, where the company has become insolvent or 'doubtfully solvent' (see *Brady v Brady* [1989] AC 755), when 'it is in a practical sense their assets and not the shareholders' assets that, through the medium of the company, are under the management of the directors pending either liquidation, return to solvency, or the imposition of some alternative administration' (*per* Street CJ, in *Kinsela v Russell Kinsela Pty Ltd* (1986) 10 ACLR 395, at 401). If the directors do decide to respect the interests of the creditors, as, for example, by taking a cautious view about declaration of dividends (see **Chapter 16**), it seems most unlikely that any court would be willing to intervene.

However, there is in any event no redress directly available to creditors who claim that their interests have been ignored by the directors (creditors may perhaps have a remedy where the directors have engaged in misrepresentation or other dishonest conduct towards them). The directors' duty remains to the company as a separate entity. If the company were to go into insolvent liquidation, the liquidator as agent of the company would be able to pursue the directors on behalf of the company for fraudulent or wrongful trading (Insolvency Act 1986, ss 213–214). Further, the directors could be pursued by a liquidator, administrator or any creditor for misfeasance, which would include breach of any duty owed to the company, though any contribution ordered would be paid to the company (Insolvency Act 1986, s 212, see **Chapter 23**).

10.3.3 Employees

Section 309 of the Companies Act 1985 provides that:

(1) The matters to which the directors of a company are to have regard in the performance of their functions include the interests of the company's employees in general as well as the interests of its members.

(2) Accordingly, the duty imposed by this section on the directors of a company is owed by them to the company (and the company alone) and is enforceable in the same way as any other fiduciary duty owed to a company by its directors.

This does not give the employees any standing to bring proceedings against directors who fail to consider their interests, since directors' fiduciary duties are enforceable only by the company (*Percival v Wright* [1902] 2 Ch 421, see **10.3.1** above). A shareholder who wished to restrain the directors from acting without regard to the interests of the employees would presumably face the same difficulty, unless it could be argued that this was bad management and thus conduct prejudicial to the members under the Companies Act 1985, s 459 (see **Chapter 14**), an argument which is not immediately attractive. On the other hand, where directors do take account of the interests of employees, s 309 of the 1985 Act appears to preclude a shareholder from challenging their actions, either as unfairly prejudicial conduct under s 459, or by any other means, such as alleging that the decision has been taken for an improper purpose.

10.4 Directors as individuals

A director as an individual is in a fiduciary position in relation to his company. This means that he must not put himself in a position where his duty to the company and his self-interest conflict, unless authorised to do so by the company (which means the General Meeting) after full disclosure of the circumstances, or, if permitted by the Articles, by his fellow directors (whether full disclosure is required in this situation – and to whom – will depend on the provisions of the Articles). Further, a director must not make any secret profit, or take advantage of a corporate opportunity which he might acquire by virtue of his status as a director of his company. There is obvious overlap between these two requirements, but it is possible to view them as distinct themes of the one rule that the director must not abuse the trust and confidence placed in him.

Article 85 of Table A requires full disclosure to the directors of any relevant interest in a proposed transaction (Companies Act 1985, s 232(1) and Sch 6 require disclosure in the form of notes to the accounts of details of the chairman's and directors' emoluments and other benefits; further details of loans, quasi loans and other dealings in favour of directors must be noted). If there is no disclosure then the transaction may be set aside; alternatively, the members may choose to ratify the agreement (*Movitex v Bulfield* (1986) 2 BCC 99,403, at 99,430), which will then be unimpugnable provided it does not amount to a fraud on the minority (see **Chapter 14**) or a fraud on creditors (*Re DKG Contractors* [1990] BCC 9030; as is usual in cases involving creditors, it is only on the liquidation of the company that there is any serious prospect of challenging the transaction). This equitable rule is strengthened by s 317 of the Companies Act 1985, which requires full disclosure to the board of directors. Failure to disclose under s 317 does not, however, mean that the transaction is invalid, though it provides for criminal sanctions for breach (s 317(7) and Sch 24). Further, disclosure under s 317 does not waive the rule against conflict. This can only be done by the company members by ordinary resolution, or in advance through the implementation of art 85 or a similar provision in the company's Articles of Association. It follows, therefore, that failure of a director to disclose to the other directors under art 85 renders the contract voidable at the instance of the company. It is more questionable whether any distinction can properly be drawn between disclosure to the directors informally or separately and disclosure to the board as a whole. Section 317 requires disclosure at a board meeting, and it is suggested that in any event there must be a clear disclosure; if this is not done at a board meeting, it should be made to all directors simultaneously, even if it is not in writing (*Guiness v Saunders* [1990] 2 AC 663; *Cowan de Groot Properties Ltd v Eagle Trust plc* [1991] BCLC 1045; *Lee Panavision Ltd v Lee Lighting Ltd* [1992] BCLC 22). Where, however, the company's Articles require disclosure to the board in the same way as s 317, failure to disclose to the board as a body will render the transaction voidable in addition to triggering the criminal sanctions under s 317 (see *Guinness v Saunders* [1990] 2 AC 663).

10.5 Substantial property transactions

Substantial property transactions are governed by s 320 of the Companies Act 1985. This is in fact a further control on directors who are in a position where their own self-interest and their duties to the company conflict. In addition to disclosure required under the Articles and s 317 (discussed at **10.4** above), s 320 provides for disclosure to and approval of the company in General Meeting, ie by ordinary resolution, where a director of the company or its holding company, or a person connected with such a director, wishes to acquire from or sell to the company one or more cash assets. The cash assets must be of the requisite value for s 320 to apply (not less than £2,000, but subject to that it exceeds £100,000 or 10% of the company's net asset value). This provision also applies to shadow directors (s 320(3)).

Failure to comply with s 320 makes the transaction voidable at the company's instance (s 322(1)), unless restitution is impossible or rights have been acquired *bona fide* for value and without actual notice by a third party, or if the transaction is affirmed by the company in General Meeting within a reasonable period (s 322(2)). Further, the director concerned will be liable to account to or indemnify the company along with any other director who authorised the transaction, unless he can show that he took all reasonable steps to secure the company's compliance with the section (s 322(5)), or, in the case of another director who was a party to the transaction, he can show that at the time the arrangement was entered into he did not know of the relevant circumstances (s 322(6)).

These provisions have not as yet proved relevant to the directors of Great Expectations Ltd, but should be borne in mind in later chapters (see **Chapters 19–21**) when the issue of further shares to directors is under consideration.

10.6 Loans and other credit transactions

It is prohibited for a company to lend money to one of its directors unless the amount of the loan, together with any other loans owed by him to the company, is not more than £5,000 (Companies Act 1985, ss 330(2)(a), 334, 339 and 341(1)). It is also prohibited for a company to give a guarantee or provide collateral security for a loan made by a third party to one of its directors (ss 330(2)(b), 341(1) and 331(2) (indemnity also prohibited)). These provisions apply to directors of the company, so a loan or collateral provided before a person becomes a director is not covered, and such loan or collateral does not have to be repaid on appointment. It will, of course, have to appear in the company's accounts (Sch 6; see **10.4** above). Section 330(5) provides that these provisions shall cover shadow directors. Exceptions are provided by the legislation:

(a) a subsidiary may make a loan, provide a guarantee or security where the director concerned is its own holding company (s 336(a));

(b) a money lending company will be permitted to provide a loan or security for one of its directors, provided the terms of such arrangement were the same as if granted to a person unconnected with the company and of the same financial status (s 338(1), (2) and (3))

(c) any transaction to provide a director with funds needed to perform his duties will be valid if approved by the company in General Meeting (s 337).

The civil remedies provided for contravention of s 330 are similar to those provided where s 320 has been contravened (see **10.5** above). Any transaction will be voidable at the company's instance unless:

(a) restitution is impossible; or

(b) a third party has acquired rights *bona fide* for value and without actual notice of the contravention (s 341(1)).

Further, the director concerned, and any other director who authorised the transaction, has a duty to account for any gain made and a duty to indemnify the company for any loss or damage resulting from the transaction. However, as with s 320, an authorising director will not be liable if he can show that at the time of the transaction he did not know the relevant circumstances constituting the transaction (s 341(5)).

10.7 The rule against profiting

10.7.1 Directors required to account for profits

The rule against profiting means that a director must account to his company for any profit acquired from transactions with the company (see **10.4** above) and also for any profit acquired by reason of the director's fiduciary position together with the opportunity and knowledge which result from it. For the rule to be applied, it is unimportant whether or not the company could itself have made the profit (*IDC v Cooley* [1972] 1 WLR 443). Further, as the rule is strict (*Regal (Hastings) Ltd v Gulliver* [1967] 2 AC 134), it in no way depends upon 'fraud or absence of bona fides' (at p144–5). The long-established severity of this rule may well be contrasted with the relative laxness of the duty of skill and care, which, even in its more modern form, sets a lower standard of conduct for directors (see **10.1.1** above).

10.7.2 Corporate opportunity doctrine

This aspect of the rule against profiting relates to a group of cases which deal with the directors benefiting personally out of an opportunity which had presented itself to their company. Many of the most important cases are Commonwealth decisions – indeed it is noticeable that there are very few reported English cases. A leading authority is *Cook v Deeks* [1916] 1 AC 554, where three of the four directors of Toronto Construction Co Ltd ('Toronto') negotiated a contract with a company client and formed a new company to carry it out. The three directors were also the holders of 75% of the shares in Toronto. The Privy Council held that they must account to Toronto for the profits made out of the contract. It was not possible for them to use their votes as shareholders to ratify the breach, as this would amount to a fraud on the minority (see further **Chapter 14**).

It should be noted that it is not possible for a director to relieve himself of his fiduciary obligation not to make a secret profit by resigning his position as a director if the benefit can be seen to accrue to him by virtue of the office he held. In *Industrial Developments v Cooley* [1972] 1 WLR 443, Cooley, an architect, was managing director of IDC, and as such he became involved in negotiations for a large contract with the Eastern Gas Board. IDC did not secure the contract because Eastern Gas Board preferred to deal with a private architect instead. Cooley thereupon staged his release from IDC and undertook performance of the contract for the Eastern Gas Board. The court held that he had to account for the profit he received. Roskill J said (at 446): 'There can be no doubt that the defendant got this Eastern Gas Board contract for himself as a result of work which he did whilst still the plaintiff's managing director.'

Similarly, in *Canadian Aero Service Ltd v O'Malley* (1973) 40 DLR (3d) 371, the defendants were the president and the executive vice-president of the plaintiff company. They negotiated on behalf of the company a large contract with the Government of Guyana. They subsequently resigned their positions with the plaintiff company and formed their own company, which secured the contract. The court ordered damages for breach of duty (it was unimportant for these purposes that their appointments as directors were defective).

The obvious problems here lie in deciding when a former director will cease to be liable for using the expertise and knowledge he has gained during his period in office. Clearly there has to be some limit on the scope of the doctrine, otherwise it would be in conflict with the policy behind the laws dealing with restraints on trade (*Island Export Finance Ltd v Umunna* [1986] BCLC 460). In *Canadian Aero Service Ltd v O'Malley* (above), the factors to be considered by the court in determining whether the former directors in question were in breach of their duty to that company would include:

> ... position or office held, the nature of the corporate opportunity, its ripeness, its specificness and the director's or managerial officer's relation to it, the amount of knowledge possessed, the circumstances in which it was obtained and whether it was special or indeed even private, the factor of time in the continuation of fiduciary duty where the alleged breach of duty occurs after termination of the relationship with the company, and the circumstances under which the relationship was terminated, that is whether by retirement or resignation or discharge. ((1973) 40 DLR (3d) 371, at 391)

An important and puzzling case is *Regal (Hastings) Ltd v Gulliver* [1942] 1 All ER 378, HL, where the defendants subscribed for shares in the subsidiary company of the company which they directed. When both companies were sold soon afterwards, the defendants were liable to account for the profit they had made on the shares in the subsidiary. This meant that the purchasing company was able to reclaim part of the purchase price. As Lord Porter said (at 394): 'That group will, I think, receive in one hand part of the sum which has been paid by the other.' Lord Russell stated that the duty to account in no way depended on fraud or absence of *bona fides*: 'The liability arose from the mere fact of a profit having, in the stated circumstances, been made.'

In that case it was held that the directors acquired their shares in the company by reason and in the course of their office as directors, and that this was decisive. The decision appears somewhat harsh. The duty to account could have been avoided if the parent company had, either prospectively or retrospectively, passed a resolution in General Meeting authorising the transaction. It also appears that there would have been no duty to account if the subsidiary company had sold all its property at a profit, leaving the defendants with shares whose value had increased – the liability seems to accrue only when the shares are sold. It is also to be observed that the whole transaction would have been impossible without the share capital subscribed by the defendants, and it is surprising that, having allowed other shareholders to make the same profit, they were prevented from keeping their own share of it. It is hard to avoid the conclusion that the decision is an over-technical application of a much older rule about the liability of trustees (*Keech v Sandford* (1726) Sel Cas t King 61), without regard to the fact that directors, though in a fiduciary position, are not trustees.

A further difficulty presents itself in the application of this doctrine, that is, the situation where the directors decide to reject an opportunity on behalf of the company and then proceed to take advantage of it for themselves. In *Peso Silver Mines Ltd v Cropper* (1966) 58 DLR (2d) 1, the board of directors of Peso decided after *bona fide* consideration to reject a proposal to purchase 126 prospecting claims. One of Peso's directors, Cropper, along with others incorporated a company, Cross Bow Mines Ltd, to purchase the claims. The Supreme Court of Canada decided that Cropper was not bound to account to Peso for his profit. Cropper and his co-directors acted in good faith, solely in the interests of Peso and with sound business reasons, in rejecting the offer. Moreover, there was no suggestion that the offer to the company was accompanied by any confidential information unavailable to any prospective purchaser, or that the respondent as director had access to any such information by reason of his office. More recently, in *Island Export Finance Co Ltd v Umunna* [1986] BCLC 460, the defendant resigned as director of the plaintiff company, which had won a contract to supply post boxes to the Cameroons but which was not actively seeking further orders. He subsequently set up a new company which did obtain further orders of the same kind. Hutchinson J held that he was not liable to account for profits he had made, since the plaintiff company had not been seeking repeat orders at the time and the defendant had not been influenced by any improper motive (it appeared that his resignation was for reasons unconnected with this contract).

It would seem that two essential matters must be established before the duty to account would arise in such circumstances:

(a) the profit must be derived from the director's position with his company; and

(b) the director must owe a fiduciary duty to his company (see **Further Reading**, below).

The latter can be avoided by the company's Articles or by ratification by the members in General Meeting, although it is important to keep in mind that any resolution of the company to this effect must not amount to a fraud on the minority (*per* Buckley J in *Hogg v Cramphorn Ltd* [1967] Ch 254).

10.8 Relief from liability

Where a director is in breach of duty to his company, he cannot rely on any provision in the company's Articles or in a contract with the company that he will escape liability or obtain an indemnity from the company for any liability he might incur (the Companies Act 1985, ss 309A and 310; see **10.1.2** above). Where a provision such as art 85 is concerned, which disapplies the rules against profiting and against conflict of interest and duty (see **10.2** above), it will not be construed as relieving a director of liability; rather it is seen as preventing a breach occurring in the first place (*Movitex v Bulfield* (1986) 2 BCC 99,403).

Section 727 of the Companies Act 1985 empowers the court to relieve a director of liability, wholly or partly, which has arisen in relation to any breach of duty, including a breach of the duty of care and breach of fiduciary duty, if, having regard to the circumstances of the case, the court finds that he has acted honestly and reasonably. However, the relief is not limited to cases of breach of specific statutory duty, since s 727 refers expressly to proceedings for 'negligence, default, breach of duty or breach of trust', terms which go much wider than mere breach of statutory duty. It is not clear when relief will be given in practice. It might be thought, for example, that *Regal (Hastings) Ltd v Gulliver* was an obvious case for the granting of such relief (see **10.7.2** above), yet the point does not even appear to have been argued. On the other hand, it is suggested in *Guinness v Saunders* (see **10.4** above) that relief will not be given where the director retains any property of the company, even if he has come by it honestly (relief under s 727 is not available where a director has incurred liability under s 214 of the Insolvency Act 1986 (wrongful trading); *Re Produce Marketing Consortium Ltd* [1989] 3 All ER 1).

10.9 Advice to the parties

The most practical advice which can be offered to Edwina and Bill, as the directors of the company, is that in relation to directors' duties company law is in effect very results-orientated. If the company prospers, it is most unlikely that there will be any challenge to what they do – there will be no liquidator and the creditors will have no right to intervene, whilst the shareholders are likely to be happy enough to take the profits; certainly Duncan will not complain, which will mean in effect that Edwina and Bill are safe as directors. Of course, all this will change if the company goes into liquidation, for the conduct of the directors will then come under much closer scrutiny by the liquidator.

Arthur, as Company Secretary (but not a director), is unlikely to be at risk of liability if the company does collapse, though his growing taste for lengthy holidays may give grounds for raising questions about his commitment to the business.

Charlotte, as an employee, has no effective power. As a shareholder she can obtain information about the company's activities and can ask awkward questions at General Meetings, but she has too few shares to wield any influence in a vote, and her only legal remedies would be those available in cases of abuse of power (these are dealt with in **Chapter 14**).

Duncan would do well to leave the directors to get on with running the company. The basic principle that management is in the hands of the directors should not be forgotten. It is ultimately the directors who bear the responsibility for company management, and for this reason the decision-making power is vested largely in them. If Duncan wants to be more actively involved in the management of the company, he can become a director – with 60% of the shares he can easily appoint himself to that position. If he does not want the responsibilities which such an appointment will entail, he should keep a proper distance. Edwina is probably justified in objecting to his irregular and ill-considered interventions. If Duncan has finally lost faith in the directors, he can remove Bill (but not Edwina, who is effectively protected by the weighted voting rights clause, see special art 2 – **Appendix B**). This, coupled with the appointment of himself to the board, ought to give him as much influence as he can legitimately expect.

FURTHER READING

V Finch, 'Directors' Duties Towards Creditors'(1989) 10 Co Law 23.

CA Riley, 'Directors' Duties and the Interests of Creditors' (1989) 10 Co Law 87.

Beck, 'The Saga of the Peso Silver Mines: corporate opportunity reconsidered' (1971) 49 Can Bar Rev 80.

Beck, 'The Quickening of the Fiduciary Obligation' (1975) 53 Can Bar Rev 771.

C Nakajima, 'Signing without reading' (1994) 15 Co Law 123.

A Walters, 'Directors' duties: the impact of the Company Directors Disqualification Act 1986' (2000) 21 Co Law 110.

11 Directors: Appointment, Removal and Role

LEARNING OUTCOMES

By the end of this chapter, you should understand:

- directors – the concept of directors – the minimum number of directors;

- shadow directors;

- executive and non-executive directors;

- appointment of directors – defective appointments;

- alternate and nominee directors;

- the board of directors – the Chairman – the Managing Director;

- remuneration of directors;

- termination of office – the *Bushell v Faith* clause.

OVERVIEW

This chapter is concerned with the problem of identifying who is a director, which requires an examination of how people become and cease to be directors.

The question will be simple enough in those cases where a person has been appointed to be a director, but there are other cases where a person exercises managerial functions in a company without holding any formal appointment. In such situations it may be important to know whether or not he is in fact a director, since the duties and liabilities of directors attach to all those who are in fact directors, irrespective of whether they have been formally appointed. Questions relating to the removal of directors are also addressed.

11.1 Minimum number of directors

Section 282 of the Companies Act 1985 requires every public company to have at least two directors and every private company to have at least one. However, because Table A, art 64 requires two directors unless the company authorises otherwise by ordinary resolution, a private company should amend art 64 if it wishes to appoint only one director (note there is no penalty for failure to maintain the statutory minimum number of directors). Great Expectations Ltd has made such an amendment (special art 3 – see **Appendix B**).

11.2 The concept of 'director'

Section 741(1) of the Companies Act 1985 provides that the term 'director' includes any person occupying the position of director, by whatever name called. For Charlotte this might well have implications if she were found to be occupying the position of director in covering for Arthur, even though Arthur himself did not have that title bestowed upon him. It is a question of function rather than label. In *Whitehouse v Carlton Hotel* (1987) 162 CLR 285, it was stated that a person would be a director if his permitted powers were over and above those that would be expected of a mere member or employee.

11.3 Shadow directors

A shadow director is defined as a person in accordance with whose directions or instructions the directors of the company are accustomed to act (Companies Act 1985, s 741(2)). A shadow director influences the directors in the exercise of their powers (*Re Unisoft Group Ltd (No 3)* [1994] 1 BCLC 609; *Secretary of State for Trade and Industry v Deverell* [2001] Ch 340). The degree of influence is crucial to a finding of shadow directorship (see Knox J, in *Re A Company (No 005009 of 1987)* [1989] BCLC 13 and *Re MC Bacon Ltd* [1990] BCLC 372). However, advice given in a professional capacity and acted upon by the directors does not make the professional adviser a shadow director; however, it is always possible for a professional adviser to be found to be a shadow director if, on the facts of the case, the nature and degree of influence oversteps the boundary (see **Chapter 23**).

The concept of shadow directorship appears to be important principally as between the director and the company. In situations where a director may incur liability to his company, a shadow director will normally be at risk of the same liability. The most common examples of this occur in relation to insolvency (see **Chapter 23**), but liability for breaches of duties of skill and care and fiduciary duties also provides useful examples (duties to disclose interests in transactions (s 317) and substantial property transactions (s 320) are other examples; see **Chapter 10**).

11.4 Executive and non-executive directors

It is important to begin by stating that the distinction between these two classes of director is not recognised by statute (although Table A does refer to executive directors). As a matter of law, a director is a director is a director. However, the expressions concerned have entered the accepted terminology of company law, and the following is an attempt to explain the distinction, as it is usually understood.

An executive director is one who devotes his working time to the management of his company. In private companies these are by far the more common type of director. Edwina and Bill are executive directors of Great Expectations Ltd. Non-executive directors, on the other hand, may have little or no real involvement with the management of the company, and will attend board meetings and generally oversee the direction of the company. They will be appointed to enhance the company and in recognition of their own particular qualities which they can bring to bear on company policy. They are commonly found on the boards of public companies and larger private companies, where their functions often relate principally to such matters as audit and directors' remuneration. Their value to the corporate structure has been recognised, for example, by the Cadbury Report (*Report of the Committee on the Financial Aspects of Corporate Governance* (London, 1992; see also the Combined Code for Listed Companies, 2003, FRC Code). Great Expectations Ltd has no non-executive directors.

11.5 Appointment of directors

Table A, art 78 provides for the *members* to appoint a person to the position of director by ordinary resolution; art 79 similarly provides for the *directors* to make an appointment, but such director holds office only until the next Annual General Meeting. The power of the majority to appoint the directors must 'be exercised for the benefit of the company as a whole and not to secure some ulterior advantage' (see *Re HR Harmer Ltd* [1959] 1 WLR 62, *per* Jenkins LJ, at 82).

Although Table A does not require directors to hold qualifying shares in a company, a company's Articles can make provision for a director to hold a minimum number of shares in the company (see **Chapter 4**). If this is the case, an appointee must acquire such shares as are necessary to comply with the relevant article within two months, unless the Articles provide for a shorter acquisition period. Failure to acquire or maintain a qualifying share holding will result in vacation of office (Companies Act 1985, s 291(1) and (3)).

11.6 Defective appointments

Although the notion of 'director' is based on substance not form, it is important that the intention to appoint a person to act as a director existed if his acts are to bind the company. Section 285 of the Companies Act 1985 provides:

> *The acts of a director or manager are valid notwithstanding any defect that may afterwards be discovered in his appointment or qualification; and this provision is not excluded by section 292(2) (void resolution to appoint).*

Further, Table A, art 92 provides:

> *All acts done by a meeting of directors, or of a committee of directors, or by a person acting as a director shall notwithstanding that it be afterwards discovered that there was defect in the appointment of any director or that any of them were disqualified from holding office, or had vacated office, or were not entitled to vote, be as valid as if every person had been duly appointed and was qualified and had continued to be a director and had been entitled to vote.*

The validation provisions require a person seeking to rely on them to have acted in good faith. The House of Lords decision in *Morris v Kanssen* [1946] AC 459 makes the distinction between a defective appointment and no appointment at all. Lord Simonds stated (at 471–2):

> *There is, as it appears to me, a vital distinction between (a) an appointment in which there is a defect or, in other words, a defective appointment, and (b) no appointment at all. In the first case it is implied that some act is done which purports to be an*

appointment but is by reason of some defect inadequate for the purpose; in the second case there is not a defect, there is no act at all. The section does not say that the acts of a person acting as director shall be valid notwithstanding that it is afterwards discovered that he was not appointed a director ... the section and the article, being designed as machinery to avoid questions being raised as to the validity of transactions where there has been a slip in the appointment of a director, cannot be utilised for the purpose of ignoring or overriding the substantive provisions relating to such appointment.

It may appear from this that the company cannot be bound by the acts of a person whom it has not even attempted to appoint. It is submitted that this notion is incorrect. If the person has been held out by the company as a director, even without any formal attempt to appoint, then ordinary agency principles (*Freeman & Lockyer v Buckhurst Park Properties (Mangal) Ltd* [1964] 2 QB 480) would surely mean that the company was bound by the acts of that person. These provisions might have been important in relation to Charlotte in our scenario, where she has been acting as a de facto Personnel Manager and covering for Arthur, if Arthur had himself been a director of the company. It may, however, be difficult to show that she was carrying out the activities of a director in performing either of these particular functions, given that Arthur is in fact the Company Secretary.

Section 285 and art 92 give rise to other problems. In s 285, it is not clear what is meant by 'afterwards' or by 'discovered'. The former expression should probably be regarded as requiring the state of knowledge to be determined at the time when the transaction is entered into, whilst the latter term ought to require discovery by the third party; given that the purpose of the provision is to protect innocent third parties, the vital question is surely as to their state of mind at the time of the transaction. (The 1989 revisions to s 35A of the 1985 Act may reduce the importance of this section, since they provide a very general and very generous protection for third parties dealing with a company.)

The apparent effect of art 92 is that a transaction entered into by an improperly constituted board, or without the necessary disclosure of interests by one or more directors, is not thereby rendered liable to challenge, though of course there would be a breach of duty by the director(s) concerned (see **Chapter 10**).

11.7 Alternate and nominee directors

Table A permits the appointment of alternate directors, that is a person who can take the place of an existing director who is absent. The appointee may be another member of the board, or, if approved by a resolution of the directors, an outsider (see art 65 and art 69). It would be somewhat unusual to appoint alternate directors in a small company such as Great Expectations Ltd.

Nominee directors will be appointed by a shareholder who has negotiated the right to appoint one or more directors to the board of a private company (see, eg, *Cumbrian Newspapers Group Ltd v Cumberland & Westmorland Herald Newspaper & Printing Co Ltd* [1987] Ch 1). Such a right will usually be a class right, in that it is conferred on the shareholder as member by creating a separate class of shares, the holders of which are given the right of appointment. If such a class of shares is created, the company's Articles will need to be amended; Table A envisages only one class of shares (although art 2 allows for the issue of different classes of shares, the rest of Table A deals only with a single class of shares), and any variation of such rights must be in accordance with s 125 of the Companies Act 1985 (see **Chapter 7**).

11.8 The board of directors

11.8.1 Delegation to and by the board

The shareholders have delegated their powers of management to the directors under art 70, which authorises the directors to act collectively as a 'board'. Article 72 then permits the board to delegate any of its powers to any committee consisting of one or more directors. It may also delegate to any Managing Director, or any director holding executive office, such of its powers as it considers desirable to be exercised by him.

Article 84 authorises the directors to appoint one or more of their number to the office of Managing Director (see further **11.8.3**, below), or to any other executive office. Great Expectations Ltd has appointed Edwina as Managing Director in recognition of her business experience and acumen. It is for the directors to determine the terms of any such agreement, including the remuneration of such executive, as they think fit. However, directors' remuneration apart from such executive payments must be decided upon by the members by ordinary resolution (art 82).

If the shareholders disagree with the activities of the board, it is possible to alter the company's Articles to restrict the powers of management bestowed by art 70 of Table A, and to reserve greater power to the General Meeting. However, an alteration requires a special resolution (Companies Act 1985, s 9), and is therefore impracticable in the case of Great Expectations Ltd, since Edwina alone holds enough shares to block such a resolution, and it cannot be imagined that she will vote for a restriction on her own powers. In any event, such restrictions are likely seriously to impair the ability of the directors to manage the company. Alternatively, as explained above, a special resolution would be effective to over-rule the directors in a particular case.

11.8.2 Chairman

Article 91 permits the directors to appoint one of their number to be Chairman of the board, and art 88 gives the Chairman a second or casting vote in the event of deadlock. It can be seen from **Appendix B** that Great Expectations Ltd has excluded this provision (special art 2). There is no Chairman of the board, so the question of a casting vote does not arise.

11.8.3 Managing Director

Article 84 provides for the appointment of a Managing Director, and allows the board to decide on the terms of this appointment, including the particular powers which are to be given to the Managing Director. This decision is binding as between the directors, but the position as regards third parties will depend on normal agency principles, especially the doctrine of ostensible or apparent authority (see **Chapter 3**). It is suggested that a third party is normally entitled to assume that a Managing Director has authority to exercise any of the powers of the company. The position in relation to other directors is less clear. Where a director has a title which indicates some limit on his authority, such as 'Finance Director' or 'Sales Director', it seems likely that this will operate as an effective restriction on his apparent authority.

The most difficult case is that of the person who is simply described as 'director'. It might seem that such a person has unlimited authority, but this involves the conclusion that there is no real difference, at least so far as outsiders are concerned, between a director and a Managing Director. In two older cases, *Houghton & Co v Nothard Lowe & Willis Ltd* [1927] 1 KB 246 and *Kreditbank Cassel GmbH v Schenkers Ltd* [1926] 2 KB 450, the Court of Appeal was reluctant to allow such authority to a director and to the manager of a branch of a bank. However, it is clear that this is an area where each case must turn on its facts, since it is necessary to ask what this third party would reasonably have thought in these circumstances. It should also be remembered that the practice of company law has moved on since 1927, with far more small, private companies. It is therefore suggested that these cases should be treated with some caution.

In a more recent case, *Panorama Developments Ltd v Fidelis Furnishings Ltd* [1971] 2 All ER 1028, Lord Denning MR was prepared to extend a broad authority to the Company Secretary, pointing out the changes in practice since the early days of company law (a further example of this trend may be found in the Companies Act 1985, s 35B). Reasoning applicable to the Company Secretary is clearly even more strongly applicable to a director. A final point in this area is that in modern companies a director may well have *actual* authority to enter into all manner of contracts on behalf of the company, so that the case can be resolved without reference to the question of apparent authority (see *Hely-Hutchinson v Brayhead* [1968] 1 QB 549).

The power of a managing director to bind the company externally can be obtained without the need for formal appointment. In *Freeman & Lockyer v Buckhurst Properties (Mangal) Ltd* [1964] 2 QB 480 the defendant company appointed four directors, and all four were needed to form a quorum. However, the day-to-day management was left to one of the directors, who entered into a contract with the plaintiffs, a firm of architects and surveyors, who were to apply for planning permission on the company's behalf. The company later refused to pay the plaintiffs' fees on the ground that the 'managing' director had not had authority to bind the company. The county court judge held that the company was bound because the director in question had 'apparent' authority to enter into contracts on behalf of the company, and this decision was affirmed in the Court of Appeal (see also *Hely-Hutchinson v Brayhead*, above).

11.9 Directors' remuneration

Table A, art 84 allows for the appointment of one or more directors to executive office. Although this term is not defined, it is usually understood to apply to individuals who are actively involved in the day-to-day running of the business. Edwina has been appointed Managing Director of Great Expectations Ltd. In larger companies such executive offices are likely to become more specialised, as discussed in **11.8.3** above. A major consequence of appointment to an executive office is that art 84 allows the directors to fix the remuneration for the holders of such offices, whereas the remuneration of a director who holds no executive office (or the remuneration of an executive director beyond that applicable to his executive office) must, under Table A, art 82, be fixed by an ordinary resolution of the General Meeting (in practice this is often excluded, as in *Guinness plc v Saunders*, see below).

If the company does not resolve to remunerate the directors, the directors will not be entitled to anything. That a director does not have a right to remuneration was stated quite emphatically by Bowen LJ in *Hutton v West Cork Railway* (1883) 23 ChD 654, at 672, in the following terms:

> A director is not a servant. He is a person who is doing business for the company, but not on ordinary terms. It is not implied from the mere fact that he is a director, that he is to have a right to be paid for it.

There can be no payment unless it is authorised by the Articles. Such authorisation is usually linked with a procedure for determining the amount. In the unlikely event that there is authorisation but no such procedure, it may be possible for the director to succeed in a claim for *quantum meruit*. Such a claim failed in *Guinness plc v Saunders* [1990] 2 AC 663 because a procedure for determining the amount of remuneration for the director in question was provided for in the company's Articles. If, however, the individual concerned is not a director of the company then a claim for *quantum meruit* may succeed (*Craven-Ellis v Canons Ltd* [1936] 2 KB 403).

11.10 Termination of office

11.10.1 Introduction

Table A, art 81 makes specific provision for the circumstances in which a director's office is vacated, as indeed does the Company Directors Disqualification Act 1986 (see **Chapter 24**). Table A, arts 73–75 also make provision for directors to retire by rotation, a provision which is usually excluded in small private companies. Great Expectations Ltd has indeed excluded this provision (special art 4; see **Appendix B**), which in any event does not apply to the holders of executive office (see Table A, art 84).

11.10.2 Dismissal

The shareholders may remove the directors from office. This is possible by ordinary resolution under s 303 of the Companies Act 1985, notwithstanding anything in the company's Articles or any agreement between the company and the directors. This is a valuable method for members who disagree with the actions of those in control. In the case of a quasi-partnership such as Great Expectations Ltd, it seems likely that any power to dismiss a director under s 303 should be exercised with caution, since there is always the possibility that the court would find in favour of the director being dismissed (albeit within the provisions of the Companies Acts) on grounds of inequitable behaviour (see *Ebrahimi v Westbourne Galleries Ltd* [1973] AC 360).

A director who is also a shareholder may be able to challenge an improperly motivated dismissal under s 459 of the Companies Act 1985 (see **Chapter 14**), but a director who has no shares cannot use this method and would have to rely on his rights under employment law, ie the rights not to be wrongfully or unfairly dismissed. Special notice is required of a resolution to dismiss a director and a copy must be sent to the director concerned, who is entitled to speak at the meeting even if not a shareholder (see Companies Act 1985, s 303(5)). Consequently it is not possible to dismiss a director by unanimous written resolution (s 381A(7) and Sch 15A, para 1(a)), unless provision to dismiss a director has been made elsewhere and provides for dismissal without permitting the director to make representations (see s 303(5) – 'This section is not to be taken as ... derogating from any power to remove a director which may exist apart from this section.') .

Giving the majority of the shareholders a right to dismiss the directors is logical enough, since they are the owners of the business and the power to appoint directors also resides in them. It is difficult to reconcile this with the decision in *Bushell v Faith* [1970] AC 1099, where the House of Lords upheld the validity of weighted voting rights which had been employed effectively to entrench the directors' position. In this case the directors' votes were increased to three from one vote per share, where a resolution relating to the removal of directors was proposed. The House of Lords, in interpreting s 303, was of the view that such rights or restrictions were not prevented under the legislation, since they did not purport to oust the efficacy of an ordinary resolution but merely made it more difficult to pass such a resolution. This was accordingly a matter for the members to agree upon in the company's Articles. The decisions in *Ebrahimi v Westbourne Galleries* [1973] AC 360 and *Re a Company (No 00477 of 1986)* [1986] BCLC 376 confirm this approach with regard to quasi-partnerships where a member has a legitimate expectation (although no express right) of being involved in the management of the company. A resolution to dismiss him under s 303 could amount to unfairly prejudicial conduct for the purposes of s 459 of the Companies Act 1985 (*Re a Company*), or inequitable conduct for the purposes of s 122(1)(g) of the Insolvency Act 1986 (*Ebrahimi*).

A more difficult question is whether *Bushell v Faith* would be followed if directors of a non quasi-partnership company were to seek to rely on multiple voting rights provided for in a company's Articles, given the policy reasons behind s 303. There is also the question whether unlimited weighting can be given to the votes of individual directors. In *Bushell v Faith*, the three directors were also the sole shareholders, and three votes per share were sufficient to give complete protection. In a case where an individual director held a much smaller proportion of the shares, a much heavier weighting might be required. In the case of Great Expectations Ltd, it should be noted that the weighted voting rights clause is apparently defective in that it does not give Bill complete protection against dismissal. It is sufficient to give him 150 votes on a resolution to remove him, but this can easily be outvoted by the others – indeed, Duncan alone can still remove him. In order to give him complete protection it would have been necessary to give him 40 votes per share, so that he would have 2,000 against a maximum of 1,950 in support of a resolution for dismissal. Although the logic of *Bushell v Faith* applies equally to all cases, it must be open to doubt whether the House of Lords would want to take quite so favourable a view of such a clause in the unlikely event that the matter is litigated again (as to this, see further **Chapter 7**).

11.11 **Advice to the parties**

The issues discussed in this chapter require relatively little in the way of advice to the parties. Perhaps the principal point to be made is that Charlotte should beware of covering for Arthur, lest she find herself becoming a *de facto* director.

Duncan should appreciate the workings of the *Bushell v Faith* clause, which restricts his power to dismiss the directors. It is open to question whether Duncan has been wise to allow Edwina to entrench her position in this way, though of course the Shareholder Agreement, which allows Duncan to require the other shareholders to buy him out, does give him considerable protection.

 Bill and Arthur should be aware that, albeit for different reasons, either can readily be dismissed by Duncan.

Edwina is strongly placed, being effectively irremovable as director and not having to retire by rotation.

FURTHER READING

PV Baker, (1970) 86 LQR 155.

12 The Role of the Bank

LEARNING OUTCOMES

By the end of this chapter, you should understand:

- the relationship between the bank and the members of the company;

- the means by which the bank provides finance to the company and secures its loans – inter alia by way of provisions in debentures – fixed and floating charges;

- the problem of the bank as a possible shadow director;

- the bank and the creditors of the company.

OVERVIEW

So far we have examined the relative position of the members and the directors of Great Expectations Ltd, and seen the effect of their different size holdings and their positions within the company on its activities. We have been concerned to see how the company's owners and directors each control its daily running and future development. Incorporation of the business, and the fact that Great Expectations Ltd is now a company separate and distinct from its members, considerably affected the relations of our characters both *inter se* and with outsiders. What has not yet been considered in any detail is the role of the company's bankers in the day-to-day life of the company. Although Bus Bank plc is not a shareholder, it is the company's major creditor, and, as is explained in this chapter, has in that capacity a very important and powerful influence on the company.

12.1 The bank and the members of the company

Bus Bank plc has been banker to the business ever since it was founded by George in the mid-1950s. It cannot be doubted that it has played a key role in the development and growth of the business, and without its continued support the business would not have reached its present position. One consequence of this long involvement is that the Bank sees itself essentially as a creditor of the *business*, and the fact that the business structure has changed from one of partnership to one of a private company has not affected its overall approach to the running of the account. Management accounts, including cash flow forecasts and forecast profit and loss accounts, have always been required, and one consequence of the creation of Great Expectations Ltd is that this requirement has now been established on a more formal footing, having become a term of the debenture between Great Expectations Ltd and Bus Bank.

The Bank also continues to require that the personal financial positions of the members of Great Expectations Ltd be made known to it, and 'groups' the company's account and its members' accounts together within the bank both for administration purposes and to ensure an overall picture of the financial position of the business. Such an approach is indicative of a relationship which is rather more than a debtor/creditor relationship with the company as a separate entity, and reflects the practical reality that the fortunes of the company cannot be disassociated from those of its members. Bus Bank has indeed taken a personal guarantee from Edwina to secure company borrowing, and this may be seen as justification for requiring information regarding her personal worth. Edwina was the only member from whom it was thought worthwhile taking a guarantee due to the lack of personal resources of the others, but this is a relatively unusual arrangement, for in most cases banks do take guarantees from all directors in an attempt to tie them into the fortunes of the company more closely; this is seen as an effective way of giving directors a strong incentive to do all in their power to make the company a success.

At the same time the Bank seems ambivalent about its relationship with the company. Despite its right to see management accounts and its effective power under the terms of the debenture to intervene in the company's affairs if it sees fit, it is always anxious to stress that it does not have the responsibilities of a director and is not competent in the field of interior design. Edwina has occasionally felt it necessary to remind the Bank of this elementary point when under particularly heavy pressure from the Bank in relation to management decisions.

On the other hand, the participants in the business are not entirely consistent in their attitudes and do not always insist that the Bank treat the company's members as distinct from itself. Much was made of the business acumen of Edwina in particular, and of the expertise and skill of Arthur and Bill when negotiations between Bus Bank and Great Expectations Ltd were taking place, and for this purpose they were happy to see the individuals equated with the company.

12.2 The bank and the activities of the company

'Financial planning' and 'business development' targeted at small businesses are services much marketed by banks, and are much used by companies such as Great Expectations Ltd. In practice many companies must, by virtue of the terms of the debenture contract, keep their bank furnished with detailed information concerning their activities on a regular basis. Quite apart from the security aspect of the debenture, it is under its terms that banks can formally insist on the production of periodic financial information and, if it is considered desirable, the maintenance of certain ratios, eg overdraft to stock levels and/or debtors. The debenture itself becomes the key which gives the bank access to the company's activities and its management decisions; the more dependent the company becomes on the bank's support, the more involved the bank becomes in the company's activities.

We have already considered the relative position of the members of the Great Expectations Ltd and its directors, and seen that Duncan, despite being the majority shareholder, cannot interfere with the directors' decisions concerning management. Moreover, Duncan is locked into the company to a significant extent, since it is only within the terms of the

Shareholder Agreement that Duncan can insist that the others buy him out, whereas both the loan from Bus Bank and the overdraft facility are expressed to be repayable on demand. This gives the Bank considerable leverage and provides for a real check on the activities of the directors, since failure to provide information required or to operate within agreed terms will necessitate fairly immediate explanation. For the most part this level of involvement of a bank in its company customers' activities is a reality of business life and one which does not necessarily hamper the company's legitimate activities. Edwina is familiar with such a degree of co-operation with banks and, for the most part, enjoys a good working relationship with Bus Bank in her capacity as Managing Director of Great Expectations Ltd. Bill and, to a lesser extent, Arthur have from time to time experienced considerable resentment regarding what they see as overactive bank involvement, particularly when the need for bank support for a lucrative but long-term contract needs to be ensured before the directors can make a decision. They believe the Bank to be overly technical in its approach to entrepreneurial decisions, which at times has caused Great Expectations Ltd to forgo potentially lucrative contracts.

Edwina's greatest concern with Bus Bank plc's involvement is centred on its attitude to the management accounts which she provides on a regular basis. The initial requirement was for information to be delivered to Bus Bank plc quarterly. Recently this has been amended to a requirement for monthly figures, the Bank claiming that this is normal business practice when a company operates close to its large overdraft facility over a considerable period of time. It is not so much the extra time and effort this involves that is the source of the problem, although Edwina believes that her time and energy would be more usefully spent on behalf of the company; rather, it is the Bank's interpretation of the information she produces and its, in her view, misguided 'advice' as to the company's business plans. For example, the figure in the management accounts for trade debtors includes a substantial sum owed to Great Expectations Ltd by a company called Bleak House Ltd (see **Chapter 3**, where Edwina secured this large contract). This is probably the largest client of Great Expectations Ltd, and it is viewed as a long-term contract. Initially payments were received on a monthly basis following the submission of an interim invoice. The payments were substantial and represented vital funds in the company's bank account. Recently, Bleak House Ltd has taken to sending part payments at irregular intervals, and has justified this to Edwina as being the result of restructuring within the company. Edwina is not unduly perturbed as Bleak House Ltd is a large, national company which has been established for more than 25 years. The incomplete payments have, however, increased Great Expectations Ltd's dependence on Bus Bank plc, in that the company's overdraft reflects the fact that smaller sums are being credited to its account. To make matters worse, Bus Bank plc is now refusing to accept 'aged' debtors (in which term Bus Bank plc includes all debts over 90 days old) in the figures provided by Edwina which, together with the other current assets, form the basis upon which the overdraft facility is reviewed. Aged debtors include a substantial sum owed by Bleak House Ltd – a sum which is a valuable asset in the books of Great Expectations Ltd. Bus Bank plc has suggested to Edwina that Great Expectations Ltd should refuse to undertake any more work for Bleak House Ltd until payments are brought up to date, and should seek to widen its client base as a matter of urgency. Great Expectations Ltd does not have the resources to seek new work unless it terminates its relationship with Bleak House Ltd and

Edwina resents this advice. She believes it to be further evidence that bank officials have no awareness of how the marketplace works. Nevertheless, Edwina has made fairly strong representations to Bleak House Ltd concerning unpaid invoices, only to back down when threatened with the possibility of the business, which provides a healthy profit margin for Great Expectations Ltd, being offered elsewhere.

Bus Bank plc officials have always operated on the premise that it is the interests of all parties if they get to know each other. Since the incorporation of Great Expectations Ltd, bank officials have presented themselves at the company's premises, usually with some advance warning and occasionally with a lunch invitation, and endeavoured to acquaint themselves with the company's activities. There is no doubt that while such behaviour by banks is not uncommon, it would be most unusual for any other creditor to act in this way. Indeed, it is unlikely that a trade creditor behaving in this way would be favourably (or even politely) received. Edwina considers herself fortunate that advice given on these visits tends to be general rather than relating to specific activities of the company. This is a very wise approach by Bus Bank plc, since overactive involvement in the affairs of a company customer is always in danger of being viewed as involvement as a shadow director (a shadow director is defined by the Companies Act 1985, s 741(2) as a person in accordance with whose directions or instructions the directors of the company are accustomed to act; see **11.3** above). A finding of shadow directorship could result in a bank incurring liability to the company in the event of insolvent liquidation (see further **Chapter 23**). Of course a finding of shadow directorship does not follow from the mere fact that the Bank is giving advice to its company customer (see *Secretary of State for Trade and Industry v Deverell* [2001] Ch 340). Generally, it would seem that, provided all professional advisers ensure that it is the directors who make any decisions and themselves believe in the wisdom of a business plan, such advisers will not have overstepped the boundary. In practice this can be difficult to achieve, especially since many companies are heavily dependent on the support of their bank; and although it may be possible to ignore some or all of the advice given if it is on a question of expansion or diversification, this is hardly the case where a policy decision has to be made as to whether or not to continue to trade while insolvent or doubtfully solvent. The importance of the banks' role in many crucial management decisions cannot be denied. There is no doubt that, due to their active involvement in many companies' affairs, banks are the most vulnerable of all professional advisers to a charge of shadow directorship. Knox J, on a preliminary point of law, found it to be arguable in *Re A Company (No 005009 of 1987)* [1989] BCLC 13. Unfortunately, from the point of legal clarity at least, in the resulting litigation (*Re MC Bacon Ltd* [1990] BCLC 372) after six days of oral evidence, this claim against the bank was not pursued (see **Further Reading**, below, and **11.3** above).

12.3 The bank and the creditors of the company

12.3.1 Personal guarantees from directors/members

Company borrowing is usually based on the company's ability to service the repayments together with a satisfactory level of available security, which, in a private company such as Great Expectations Ltd, will very often include personal guarantees from the company's directors. This latter point affects a company's other creditors, principally because the credit extended to the company is not based simply on its own worth. An extreme example serves to illustrate how this is so, although it is to be remembered that it is an extreme example and therefore unlikely to be a common occurrence.

Suppose Company X, which had a subscribed capital of £100, wished to persuade its bank that it should be given the benefit of a £100,000 loan. The bank would be unwilling to co-operate unless, first, Company X could service an acceptable repayment programme and, secondly, it could provide sufficient security. If the first requirement were satisfied, but the company had insufficient assets to provide the required level of security, a guarantee from a director of Company X, supported by a charge on his home (subject of course to a valuation and there being sufficient equity), might persuade the bank that the security position of Company X satisfied its requirements. The bank would undoubtedly insist on a debenture from the company expressed to cover its entire undertaking, not least because of the terms incorporated within it, but also because it would attach to stocks and debtors acquired by the expanding company. Company X is thus enabled to carry on business to a degree unmatched by its capital base; in other words, a company of little capital worth would be enabled to increase its activities in the marketplace. This necessarily involves the incurring of further credit from suppliers and provides the bank with further security as its floating charge is 'filled' with stocks and debtors, but it leaves the trade creditors extremely vulnerable as there is no effective cushion provided by the members which is available for all creditors, the members' involvement being kept outside the company and being available only for the bank under the guarantee, all other creditors being faced with an impenetrable corporate veil. In the absence of a minimum capital requirement for private companies aimed at providing a cushion for all creditors, variations on a scenario of this type are not uncommon.

12.3.2 Benefits of a floating charge

From the company's point of view a floating charge is a very convenient form of security, for it allows the company to borrow money on the basis of fluctuating assets, principally stock in trade and book debts (see *Re Spectrum Plus Ltd* [2004] EWCA Civ 670, on the application of floating charges on book debts). In many trading companies these assets are substantial, and the additional working capital which can be generated in this way is of considerable practical significance. From the bank's point of view, however, some care is needed to ensure that the security provided by a floating charge is as substantial as it appears. So far as stock in trade is concerned, it must be remembered that the security is valid only in so far as the stock really belongs to the company. Where the company has purchased stock under contracts containing retention of title clauses and has not paid for it (as is likely in cases where the company is in financial difficulty), that stock does not belong to the company (for more detail on this see **Chapter 15**). The value of the book debts will be greatly reduced in companies (of which Great Expectations Ltd is one) where the factoring of debts is practised (see **Chapter 15**). Furthermore, recent changes in the means by which a floating charge may be enforced by the creditor, introduced by Pt 10 of the Enterprise Act 2002, may reduce the effectiveness of this form of security (see **Chapter 22**).

12.3.3 Credit enquiries

It is established business practice for suppliers of goods on credit to businesses to initiate a credit enquiry of their prospective customer's bank. Equally, company customers would normally expect their bank to be asked to provide a status report to an enquiring supplier, both at the commencement of dealings between the parties and periodically thereafter. The bank would normally ensure that it had the express consent of its customer before responding to such a request (failure to obtain the consent of the customer might otherwise involve a breach of the duty of confidentiality owed by the bank – see *Tournier v National Provincial and Union Bank of England* [1924] 1 KB 461). However, replies to such credit enquiries tend to be far from informative and do not reflect the degree of knowledge possessed by the bank as to the true position of its company customer (knowledge which goes far beyond the conduct of the company in operating its bank accounts due to the company having to comply with requests for management accounts), and in many ways this is to be expected. Indeed in these circumstances customers would be unlikely to give their banks authority to make extensive disclosure as to their affairs.

The difficulties for banks arise in situations where they are themselves concerned with the company's exposure to credit and, indeed, are monitoring management accounts sufficiently closely to minimise risk to themselves. On the one hand they must avoid compromising their customer's position in respect of suppliers; on the other, they must endeavour not to give too misleading a picture to the enquirer (although the bankers' duty in tort to third parties is dependent on there being a special relationship between them – see *Hedley Byrne & Co Ltd v Heller & Partners* [1963] 2 All ER 575). As a rule of thumb, it has been suggested that a one word reply such as 'undoubted' is the most reliable, as the more words used tends to suggest that the bank is involved in a balancing act of trying to provide a favourable yet truthful response (see **Further Reading**, below).

12.4 Controlling the bank

It will be apparent from what has already been said in this chapter that banks' influence on small companies is very substantial. It is no exaggeration to say that most such companies rely on the continuing goodwill of their bank for their survival. Given that the overdraft is normally repayable on demand, and that few companies could comply with such a demand, the bank has the effective power to put the company into liquidation at any time. In these circumstances no sensible company director can afford to take a cavalier attitude to any 'suggestions' made by the bank about the management of the business. At the same time the bank has no real responsibility to the company, or to its creditors, for the way in which it exercises that power, save in the rare case where it becomes so involved in the management that it can be treated as a shadow director (there is no reported case in which this has happened). Its position as a secured creditor also gives it a considerable advantage over trade creditors when claiming in any liquidation.

This phenomenon of power without responsibility may well be thought undesirable, but it is by no means easy to see what can be done about it. The Cork Committee (*Report of the Committee on Insolvency* (1982)) refused to recommend the abolition of the floating charge (at para 1531), though it did recommend setting aside 10% of the proceeds of such charges as a fund for unsecured creditors (paras 1538–1550). A number of recommendations of the Committee have been implemented by Pt 10 of the Enterprise Act 2002 (see **Chapter 22**). An important practical consequence of the present rules is that banks have little incentive to scrutinise carefully the business plans put to them by prospective borrowers – if the company fails the bank is, despite the enactment of the Enterprise Act 2002, substantially protected by its security, and the losers will be the directors and the trade creditors. Banks would have more of a role in the company and would be exposed to greater risk if they took shares in it rather than being merely creditors, but a change of this kind is most unlikely to happen without legislation. Another possible way of limiting the bank's position would be to restrict or prohibit the taking of personal guarantees. Either of these would increase the bank's exposure, and might possibly lead to greater care by the banks in making loans to companies, though on the other side it might be argued that corporate lending would become almost impossible, to the detriment of both the banks and their prospective borrowers.

12.5 Advice to the parties

Bus Bank plc should take care that its active involvement in the affairs of Great Expectations Ltd does not lead to a suggestion that it is acting as a shadow director, especially as this could lead to liability for causing the company to trade wrongfully should it fail in the future. From a practical viewpoint, however, it should be pointed out that it would be a brave liquidator who pursued a bank on a charge of shadow directorship given the deep purse of a bank compared with that of a liquidator.

The directors of Great Expectations Ltd should be aware that they are ultimately at the mercy of the Bank, and that it is vital for them to preserve the bank manager's confidence in their ability to make a success of the company; it is not necessary to show that great profitability is imminent, but it is necessary to show that the financial trends are moving in the right direction and that the long-term prospects are good.

FURTHER READING

C Williams and A McGee, *A Company Director's Liability for Wrongful Trading*, ACCA Research Report 30 (1992).

13 Challenging the Controllers – Proper and Improper Conduct

LEARNING OUTCOMES

By the end of this chapter, you should understand the following:

- the delegation of powers of management to the directors of the company under art 70;

- the powers of the company and the powers of the directors;

- the proper purposes doctrine – management decisions;

- the effect of the Articles of Association.

SCENARIO

Edwina and Bill have been discussing at board meetings the idea of allotting more shares in Great Expectations Ltd. This will help the company to redress its 'horrendous gearing', about which their bank manager has repeatedly complained (see **Appendix F** for a note of the share capital and loan capital arrangements). Edwina is also aware that by issuing the shares to someone other than Duncan, it will be possible to alter the balance of power within the company and thus reduce Duncan's influence. They have already attempted to deal with the company's undercapitalisation by refusing to pay out large dividends, preferring instead to transfer profits to reserves. Although this has to some extent aided cash flow, it does not of itself increase the issued share capital. The idea of capitalising profits through the issue of bonus shares was discussed, but rejected on the ground that the company needed to keep the extra cash as reserves, which could be paid out as dividends in future years if the profit stream was not maintained.

Great Expectations Ltd must comply with s 80 of the Companies Act 1985 and ensure that an allotment of new shares is approved by the company by ordinary resolution, and this is proving difficult as Duncan is unwilling to see his control dissipated through the issue of new shares. He is unwilling to exercise his rights of pre-emption and take an appropriate proportion of the new shares himself. Edwina and Bill have therefore decided that the best way forward would be to allot shares to the employees under an employee share scheme, which avoids the need for an ordinary resolution under s 80. This can therefore be completed without reference to Duncan. Edwina and Bill would hope that when this is perfected, the employees will vote with the management and authorise a further issue of shares to an outside investor (another possibility in this context would be to create a voting trust, so that the directors retained effective control of the votes attaching to the shares in the scheme, though the employees would receive the dividends and the benefit of any increase in the capital value). Edwina already has in mind a former business associate of hers who might be willing to invest in Great Expectations Ltd. Because Duncan is proving to be something of an irritant at board meetings, and because they knew that he would object to the idea, Edwina and Bill refused to let Duncan attend the last board meeting when the proposal to issue new shares was discussed. They have decided to continue this practice in future, having read somewhere that Duncan's right to attend, although contained in the Articles, is an outsider right and is therefore unenforceable.

OVERVIEW

Great Expectations Ltd has chosen not to exclude art 70 of Table A, with the result that management matters have been delegated to the directors acting as a board. Article 70 is stated thus:

> Subject to the provisions of the Act, the memorandum and the articles and to any directions given by special resolution, the business of the company shall be managed by the directors who may exercise all the powers of the company. No alteration of the memorandum or articles and no such direction shall invalidate any prior act of the directors which would have been valid if that alteration had not been made or that direction had not been given. The powers given by this regulation shall not be limited by any special power given to the directors by the articles and a meeting of directors at which a quorum is present may exercise all powers exercisable by the directors.

Article 70 gives wide powers to the directors, and although these can be limited by different drafting of a company's own Articles, and directions can be given by the shareholders by special resolution, such limitation or directions cannot overrule a past act or decision of the directors. The courts have accepted the principle of division of powers between the shareholders and the directors, often described as the separation of ownership and control (see further **Chapter 11** and *Towcester Racecourse Co Ltd v Racecourse Association Ltd* [2003] 1 BCLC 260). The members cannot control the actions of the directors, although of course if they disapprove of the directors' behaviour they may curtail their management powers by amending the Articles (special resolution needed – Companies Act 1985, s 9) or by dismissing the directors (ordinary resolution needed – s 303).

As we saw in **Chapter 9**, Duncan is critical of a number of management decisions in particular he objected to the employee pay increases; payments to charity; the stricter and more expensive quality control system; and the large provision for bad debts. As we shall see, he will be unable to overrule the directors' decisions in his capacity as shareholder under any provision in the Articles; however, he may be able to challenge all or some of the decisions as not having been made *bona fide* in the best interests of the company as a whole or for a proper purpose. A more difficult issue is that Duncan is aware of the plan to issue more shares, and suspects that the true reason for this is to reduce his 60% share holding. He is not happy at this prospect, and may well want to challenge such a decision.

13.1 The directors' powers

It is necessary to distinguish here between the powers of the company and the powers of the directors. Historically, company law was very concerned to protect shareholders by insisting on a clear statement in the Memorandum of Association of the purposes for which the company was formed. Acts going beyond these purposes were then said to be *ultra vires* the company and the company was not bound by them (see further **Chapter 6**). The deficiencies of this rule became clear at an early stage, but it was only in 1989 that it was effectively reformed. The new s 35A of the Companies Act 1985, inserted by the Companies Act 1989 (s 108), makes the company bound by anything done by the directors, notwithstanding that this was beyond the powers of the company as laid down in the Memorandum of Association.

At the same time it is necessary to appreciate that a third party's entitlement to rely on the actions of the directors is affected by the ordinary principles of the law of agency. The directors are agents of the company (this is implicit in art 70 of Table A) and, in accordance with the rules of agency, the company will be bound by anything which the directors do on behalf of the company and which is within the actual or ostensible authority of the directors. The concept of actual authority considers the position from the point of view of what has in fact been agreed between the company and the directors, ie the contractual aspect of that relationship. Actual authority may therefore be expressly given – for example in a director's service contract – or arise by necessary implication from the director's position in the company (*Hely-Hutchinson v Brayhead* [1968] 1 QB 549, CA). Ostensible authority considers the position from the point of view of the third party who deals with the company. Where the third party would reasonably assume that the director had the necessary authority, the company will be bound, even if the director did not in fact have that authority (see **Chapter 11**).

Where a director acts beyond his actual and ostensible authority, the company will not be bound by his acts, but the director may incur personal liability if he has warranted to the third party that he was authorised to act in this way (*Collen v Wright* (1857) 8 E & B 647; the liability is not dependent on negligence by the agent, nor even on knowledge that the authority was being exceeded – *Yonge v Toynbee* [1910] 1 KB 215).

Where the act in question is beyond the directors' authority, it is possible for the company in General Meeting to ratify it (see Companies Act 1985, s 35A), unless the act complained of was in conflict with the company's constitution either because it was *ultra vires* the company (s 35), or because it was forbidden by the company's Articles (s 35A; see also *Boschoek Pty Co Ltd v Fuke* [1906] 1 Ch 148). The impossibility of ratification will mean that the company cannot sue on a contract entered into in these circumstances, but ss 35 and 35A of the Companies Act 1985 will protect third parties dealing with the company by allowing them to enforce the contract if they so choose.

The following discussion of managerial powers should be read in the light of this explanation of the rules of agency.

13.2 Powers of management

Where the general power of management has been vested in the directors, the shareholders are not permitted by ordinary resolution to give instructions to the directors, or to overrule their management decisions. In *Automatic Self- Cleansing Filter Syndicate Co Ltd v Cuninghame* [1906] 2 Ch 34, CA, the company's Articles had vested the powers of management in the board of directors in terms which were similar to art 70 of Table A. The members sought to pass an ordinary resolution directing the board to sell the company's undertaking to a new company, but the directors refused to co-operate. Collins MR stated the position thus:

> No doubt for some purposes directors are agents. For whom are they agents? You have, no doubt, in theory and law one entity, the company, which might be a principal, but you have to go behind that when you look to the particular position of the directors. It is by consensus of all the individuals of the company that these directors become agents and hold their rights as agents. It is not fair to say that a majority at a meeting is for the purposes of this case the principal so as to alter the mandate of the agent. The minority also must be taken into account. There are provisions by which the minority can be overborne, but that can only by done by special machinery in the shape of special resolutions. Short of that the mandate which must be obeyed is not that of the majority – it is that of the whole entity made up of all the shareholders. If the mandate of the directors is to be altered, it can only be under the machinery of the memorandum and articles themselves.

This was a case under a previous version of Table A, which purported to allow the giving of instructions by ordinary resolution. It may therefore be seen as strong evidence of the reluctance of the courts to allow interference with the managerial discretion of the directors. The current version of Table A allows directions to be given by special resolution, and it may be argued that this provision is more likely to be respected by the courts. An instruction backed by holders of 75% of the shares may be regarded as having more weight than one backed by only 51%, and the wording of art 70 suggests that a conscious decision has been made to give the directors substantial, but not unlimited, protection against interference by the shareholders.

At the same time it is important to keep in mind that the members can by ordinary resolution dismiss the directors under s 303, no matter what the Articles provide (though a *Bushell v Faith* clause may make this more difficult in practice – see **Chapter 11**), and no doubt this strengthens their position when seeking to persuade the directors in management matters. The exercise of membership rights is not generally subject to equitable considerations, though in quasi-partnership type companies such as Great Expectations Ltd this general principle may not apply (see, eg, *Ebrahimi v Westbourne Galleries* [1973] AC 360 (Insolvency Act 1986, s 122(i)(g) petition) and *Re A Company (No. 00477 of 1986)* [1986] BCLC 376 (Companies Act 1985, s 459 petition).

Article 70 applies specifically to provisions of the Memorandum and Articles. Where the Articles provide any limitation on the powers of the directors, this will be enforced. In *Quin & Axtens Ltd v Salmon* [1909] AC 442, HL, the company's Articles gave the two managing directors, Salmon and Axtens, a right of veto over certain management decisions.

Axtens sought to ignore Salmon's veto and gained the support of the General Meeting by ordinary resolution. The House of Lords held that the General Meeting had no standing to pass resolutions which were inconsistent with the company's Articles, and that Salmon's exercise of the veto must therefore be respected.

A particularly good illustration of the effect of this division of ownership and control is the case of *John Shaw & Sons (Salford) Ltd v Shaw* [1935] 2 KB 113, CA, where independent directors had been appointed as part of a settlement of an internal company dispute. The other directors, who were also the majority shareholders, sought to prevent the company instituting legal proceedings against them by passing a resolution to that effect in General Meeting. Greer LJ was very clear in his response (at 118):

> A company is an entity distinct alike from its shareholders and its directors. Some of its powers may, according to its articles, be exercised by directors, certain other powers may be reserved for the shareholders in general meeting. If powers of management are vested in the directors, they and they alone can exercise these powers. The only way in which the general body of the shareholders can control the exercise of the powers vested by the articles in the directors is by altering their articles, or, if the opportunity arises under the articles, by refusing to re-elect the directors of whose actions they disapprove. They cannot themselves usurp the powers which by the articles are vested in the directors any more than the directors can usurp the powers vested by the articles in the general body of shareholders ...

Although, as explained in **Chapter 9**, this case turns on a provision not found in Table A then or now, it does serve to emphasise the strong position of the directors.

The foregoing discussion assumes that the directors have authority from the company to act and, further, that they are able to reach a decision. If it is impossible to conduct board meetings because of the attitude of some or all of the directors, the General Meeting may appoint and remove directors, even if the power to appoint is under the Articles given solely to the board (Table A, art 79 allows the directors to appoint additional directors, though such appointment is valid only until the next Annual General Meeting) (*Barron v Potter* [1914] 1 Ch 895; under the Companies Act 1985, s 303, the power to remove directors cannot be taken away from the General Meeting). It is less clear that this result follows where board meetings are held but no consensus emerges. If a majority decision can be reached, that becomes the decision of the board. If the board is simply deadlocked, it seems that the *status quo* must continue until there is a change of directors or a change of opinion.

13.3 Proper purposes doctrine

Where directors exercise powers on behalf of their company they are bound to do so *bona fide* in the best interests of the company as a whole and for a proper purpose (see **10.2** above; *Re Smith & Fawcett Ltd* [1942] Ch 304; *Regentcrest plc v Cohen* [2001] 2 BCLC 80). Although the directors must act *bona fide* and for a proper purpose, their action may have more than one purpose. Further, directors who act for an improper purpose may nevertheless be acting *bona fide*. In *Hogg v Cramphorn* [1967] Ch 254, Buckley J stated that a director would be liable to his company if he acted either mala fide, or for an improper purpose.

The question of *bona fides* is to be decided with reference to a subjective test – did the director in question honestly believe he was acting in the best interests of the company? – which is discussed below. The question of whether the exercise of the power was for a proper purpose is to be decided objectively. This approach was approved by the Privy Council in *Howard Smith Ltd v Ampol Petroleum* [1974] AC 821, although, as Lord Wilberforce pointed out, it is impossible to 'define in advance exact limits beyond which directors must not pass'. The court must have regard to the power that has been exercised, examine the substantial purpose for which it was exercised and consider the *bona fides* of the directors in exercising the power. On matters of management the court will respect *bona fide* management decisions (see **13.4** below). In our scenario, for example, the issue of further shares which, if it happens, will effectively dilute Duncan's strength as majority shareholder, may have been prompted by mixed motives – both to raise additional capital and to weaken Duncan's position. Where mixed motives are involved, the court tries to discern what the main purpose or substantial purpose behind the directors' actions was. This is by no means an easy task and, although the question may not always be analysed by reference to a double test, ie *bona fide* and for a proper purpose, the subjective/objective approach will be employed. In the words of Lord Wilberforce in *Howard Smith* at 832:

> When a dispute arises whether directors of a company made a particular decision for one purpose or for another, or whether, there being more than one purpose, one or other purpose was the substantial or primary purpose, the court, in their Lordships' opinion, is entitled to look at the situation objectively in order to estimate how critical or pressing, or substantial or, per contra, insubstantial an alleged requirement may have been. If it finds that a particular requirement, though real, was not urgent, or critical, at the relevant time, it may have reason to doubt, or discount, the assertions of individuals that they acted solely in order to deal with it, particularly when the action they took was unusual or extreme.

In *Mills v Mills* (1938) 60 CLR 150 (High Court of Australia), the capitalisation of profits to the benefit of the ordinary shareholders and to the detriment of preference shareholders was recognised as benefiting the directors, although this was viewed as a corollary of benefit to the company. Often, in promoting the interests of the company, a director will also promote his own interests. Where the exercise of the power would adversely affect the interests of one class of shareholders to the benefit of another, directors must act fairly as between the different classes. *Mills v Mills* seems to suggest that the exercise of the power will be considered improper only where the power would not have been exercised but for the improper motive. In the case of *Punt v Symons* [1903] 2 Ch 506, Byrne J was of the opinion that shares issued by the directors had been issued with the immediate object of controlling a greater number of shares and thus the directors were not acting for a proper purpose.

The proper purposes doctrine has been considered mainly in cases where directors have exercised their powers to allot more shares to prevent a change in the control of the company. Section 80 of the Companies Act 1985 provides that directors must not allot shares, or grant options to subscribe for shares or issue securities convertible into shares without authority given by the members. Such authority may be provided in the company's Articles, or may be given by ordinary resolution (s 80(1) and (8)). The directors may of course exercise their votes as shareholders to authorise an allotment of shares, and the members collectively are entitled to ratify an otherwise improper act of the directors, though there is some authority that an oppressive exercise of voting rights by the majority may be set aside by the court (see further **Chapter 14** and especially *Clemens v Clemens Bros Ltd* [1976] 2 All ER 268).

The application of the proper purposes doctrine to the issue of shares causes particular problems when the share issue is made or proposed at a time when a takeover bid for the company is pending or expected. The rules in relation to takeovers are considered in **Chapter 21**.

13.4 Management decisions

The courts will not entertain an appeal from shareholders on the merits of a *bona fide* management decision. Lord Wilberforce said, in *Howard Smith Ltd v Ampol Petroleum Ltd* [1974] AC 821, at 832:

> There is no appeal on merits from management decisions to courts of law: nor will the courts of law assume to act as a kind of supervisory board over decisions within the powers of management honestly arrived at.

In order to determine whether a decision was a *bona fide* management decision, it is important to keep in mind that it is the interests of the company as a separate and distinct entity that must be considered. This is by no means an easy task (the concept of the company as an entity distinct from its shareholders has been discussed already in **Chapter 8**) and it is important to keep in mind the various, often competing, interests that make up the company as a whole when considering the *bona fides* of the directors, and also in order to determine whether they acted for a proper purpose. The importance of this approach is demonstrated by the case of *Parke v Daily News* [1962] Ch 927, where the directors, acting on the instructions of the majority shareholder who wished to avoid public criticism, made *ex gratia* payments to employees where the company was being wound up solvent. The act was successfully challenged by a minority shareholder as being an ultra vires act, in that it was not for the benefit of the company and further that it was for an improper purpose. The employees were not recognised in company law as a legitimate interest of the company at that time. In this particular respect, following the enactment of s 309, the directors of a company are now required to have regard in the performance of their functions to the interests of the company's employees, which effectively widens the proper purposes available to a company's directors. In other respects it is probably safe to say that the proper purposes doctrine does little to limit the activities of a company's directors where there is no allegation of bad faith.

The real difficulty lies in the balancing of competing claims, as in most cases decisions which adversely affect the employees, such as a pay freeze or even cut, will be to the benefit of the shareholders, who will as a result expect to see a corresponding increase in profit/reduction in losses, and vice versa where a benefit to employees will usually be at the expense of shareholders (see **Further Reading**, below). Another recognised interest of the company is the future shareholders, who may be disadvantaged by large profit distributions in that the capital growth of the company may be hampered – the position where the directors decide to capitalise profits, or a proportion of profits, at the expense of some existing shareholders who are looking for increased income is unclear (see further **Chapter 16**). In *Dawson International plc v Coats Patons plc* 1988 SLT 854, s 309 was interpreted to mean that directors should consider the interests of present and future members.

Another legitimate interest group is a company's creditors, who must be considered by the directors in the face of insolvency in order to discharge their duty to the company. It is less clear how much consideration they should receive where the directors of a company which is solvent, as in our scenario, seek to create a cushion to ensure further protection for the creditors by creating a large provision for bad debts in anticipation of defaulting debtors. The shareholders may feel aggrieved that much of a company's profit is dissipated when the directors behave in this way, or it may simply be the amounts that are the subject of dispute. Whichever it is, the question remains the same – can the directors be said to have acted in the best interests of the company and for a proper purpose? A duty to consider the interests of the creditors was acknowledged in *Lonrho Ltd v Shell Petroleum Co Ltd* [1980] 1 WLR 627 by Lord Diplock, and this duty would seem to arise where the company is solvent, although breaches of it are unlikely to lead to legal action against the directors if they can maintain the company's solvency. This is reflected by cases which would seem to support the statement that directors must keep the company's capital intact (*Re Halt Garage* [1982] 3 All ER 1016; see also **Chapter 17**), and further that they must ensure that 'the affairs of the company are properly administered and its property not dissipated or exploited' (*Winkworth v Edward Baron Development Co Ltd* [1986] 1 WLR 1512, at 1516). This would seem to strengthen the position of the directors where, in carrying out their management functions, they make provision for creditors which disadvantage the shareholders. It would be for the member(s) who challenged the management decision to show that the directors did not act honestly for what they regarded as the benefit of the company (*Richard Barady Franks Ltd v Price* (1937) 58 CLR 112).

More difficult perhaps is the issue of further shares which will affect the enjoyment by the majority shareholder of his position of relative strength. Would such an issue be made *bona fide* in the interests of the company as a whole? (See especially the case of *Clemens v Clemens Bros Ltd* [1976] 2 All ER 268.) The answer to this question must, it is submitted, depend upon a careful analysis of the reasons for the issue. If it is objectively justified in the interests of the company then the fact that it has the incidental effect of harming the position of a majority shareholder will not be a ground for attacking it. On the other hand, an issue made for the primary purpose of affecting the balance of power may be improper unless expressly accepted in advance by all shareholders, especially those who will be most adversely affected. This problem is of course seen very clearly in the case of Great Expectations Ltd, where Edwina wants to issue more shares in order to dilute Duncan's influence.

13.5 Effect of Articles of Association

In *Hickman v Kent or Romney Marsh Sheep-Breeders' Association* [1915] 1 Ch 881, it was held that the Articles of a company take effect as a contract between the company and its members (see further **Chapter 7**). It is important to keep in mind that it is only where the

Articles affect a person *qua* member that they can provide an enforceable contact (*Beattie v Beattie* [1938] Ch 708; *Eley v The Positive Government Security Life Assurance Co Ltd* (1876) 1 ExD 88). Where the complainant is seeking to enforce a right under the Articles it may be that the company has acted through its members (*Browne v La Trinidad* (1888) 37 ChD 1), or through its directors (*Eley v The Positive Government Security Life Assurance Co Ltd*, above). The contractual effect of the Articles is considered more fully at **7.3**.

13.6 Advice to the parties

As was foreshadowed in **Chapter 9**, the position of the directors against the shareholders is a strong one. Although they can be removed by ordinary resolution, the *Bushell v Faith* clause giving directors multiple votes per share on a resolution for their removal will make Edwina effectively irremovable, though Bill is still liable to be removed, even if Edwina votes with him (see **Appendix F** for the list of shareholdings).

Further, their ability to bind the company by their actions is extensive, and shareholders cannot effectively restrain them in advance, except where the proposed action is beyond the powers of the company and the shareholders find out about it in time to obtain an injunction – once the act is done the company will be bound.

This examination of the directors' powers and duties serves to reinforce the earlier view that the shareholders are obliged to leave the directors to get on with managing the company, or to go to the other extreme by seeking their removal from the board of directors.

FURTHER READING

'The Juridification of Industrial Relations through Company Law Reform' (1988) 51 MLR 156.

14 Challenging the Controllers – the Remedies

LEARNING OUTCOMES

By the end of this chapter, you should understand:

- remedies for shareholders;

- the rule in *Foss v Harbottle* – the derivative action – fraud on the minority by those in control of the company;

- s 459 petitions – unfairly prejudicial conduct;

- orders under s 461;

- the tactical use of s 459;

- the just and equitable winding up of companies – s 122(1)(g) of the Insolvency Act 1986.

OVERVIEW

The directors are faced with a number of problems as the business expands and more capital is needed. They have a strategy for dealing with these problems, but it is likely that their strategy will be challenged as not being in the best interests of the company and possibly as not being *bona fide* – Duncan will allege that the major reason for the proposed issue of shares is to dilute his share holding, and will no doubt rely on his exclusion from board meetings as evidence. The directors will argue that reducing Duncan's influence is not the primary motive; if that fails, they will fall back on the argument that it is in the company's best interests to reduce Duncan's share holding. Ultimately, the question will most probably be whether the conduct of the directors is unfairly prejudicial to Duncan's interests (Companies Act 1985, s 459), an imprecise phrase, the meaning of which will have to be explored. A crucial question in this chapter will be what remedies might be available to an aggrieved shareholder such as Duncan.

14.1 Possible remedies

The possible remedies for a dissatisfied shareholder are:

(a) at common law (fraud on the minority by those in control);

(b) under s 459 of the Companies Act 1985 (unfairly prejudicial conduct); and

(c) under s 122(1)(g) of the Insolvency Act 1986 (winding up on the just and equitable ground)

It is worth remembering ss 125–127 of the Companies Act 1985, which cover class rights, when considering the protection of minorities; see **Chapter 7**.)

It is probably true that s 459 of the Companies Act 1985 has rendered the other two remedies more or less redundant. Nevertheless, it is important to examine decisions of the courts relating to 'fraud on the minority by those in control' and the 'just and equitable ground for winding up' given that the test applied to the conduct complained of is markedly similar. It is difficult to predict what will amount to unfairly prejudicial conduct in the absence of a clear idea as to the size and nature of the business and the individuals who are involved with it. The authorities suggest a trend towards acknowledging what has become known as the quasi-partnership, a term with no precise meaning, although the most common characteristics of a quasi-partnership are the following:

(a) an association formed or continued on the basis of a personal relationship including mutual confidence;

(b) an agreement or understanding that all or some of the shareholders shall participate in the conduct of the business;

(c) restriction on the transfer of members' interest in the company *(Ebrahimi v Westbourne Galleries Ltd* [1973] AC 360).

It will be seen later in this chapter (at **14.4**) that it is the quasi-partnership which is most readily susceptible to the use of the protection afforded by s 459 of the Companies Act 1985 against unfairly prejudicial conduct.

14.2 The rule in *Foss v Harbottle*

The rule in *Foss v Harbottle* ((1843) 2 Hare 43) is used to describe the policy of the courts in refusing to hear a claim brought by a member of the company complaining about the actions of the majority or the controllers. If harm has been done to the company, as reflected by his interest, then it is the company that is the proper claimant in the proceedings and not the individual member.

In *Edwards v Halliwell* [1950] 2 All ER 1064, at 1067, Jenkins LJ listed situations where a member may be permitted to bring a claim. These may be summarised as follows:

(a) where what is complained of is an internal management matter, the courts are not willing to entertain a claim by a member unless it can be shown that his complaint warrants a derivative action (discussed at **14.3** below); or

(b) that the act complained of affronts a membership right, which would include a right to require the company to act *intra vires* (see s 35(2)), within its capacity limited in its Memorandum, and personal membership rights provided in the company's Articles (see further **Chapter 7**; note that these rights must be enjoyed *qua* member), and indeed the right every member has to require the company to act in accordance with its Articles, which may require that special resolutions be passed in order to act (s 35A(4)).

Where what is complained of are actions which have harmed the company then the only true exception is in fact the derivative action, so called because it is an action which is derived from the company itself, which does not initiate proceedings due to the wrongdoers or their supporters being in control. The basis for the derivative action is that there has been fraud on the minority by those in control.

14.3 The derivative claim – fraud on the minority by those in control

This is a claim brought by a member of the company to enforce a right of the company. It will be permitted where an alleged fraud has been committed against the company by those in control, the company itself being in the hands of the controllers and unable to bring the claim. The competent organ to instigate proceedings on behalf of the company will be the board of directors (Table A, art 70), and their reluctance may well be supported by the majority of the shareholders. In *Atwool v Merryweather* (1867) LR 5 Eq 464, Atwool brought an action on behalf of himself and other shareholders against Merryweather, Whitworth and the company, claiming that the contract between them should be rescinded because it included a concealed profit. Although the majority of the shareholders, including Merryweather and Whitworth, did not wish proceedings to be brought in the company's name, the court held that the minority were entitled to bring an action against them. Page Wood V-C said (at 468): 'The whole thing was obtained by fraud, and the persons who may possibly form a majority of the shareholders, could not in any way sanction a transaction of that kind.'

It appears that in recent years the courts have adopted a more restrictive attitude towards derivative claims (see *Cooke v Cooke* [1997] 2 BCLC 28). In particular, there is a reluctance in larger companies to permit the bringing of a derivative claim by a very small number of shareholders (see judgment of the Court of Appeal in *Prudential Assurance Co Ltd v Newman Industries (No 2)* [1982] 1 All ER 354). This trend appears sensible, for it is undesirable that a large company, especially a public company, should be held to ransom by the holders of only a very few shares. In such companies arguments about equity and legitimate shareholder expectations do not have the same force as in a small quasi-partnership (see, eg, the decision in *Re Blue Arrow plc* [1988] 3 BCC 618).

14.3.1 Meaning of 'fraud'

The point has already been made that a petition for relief on the grounds of unfairly prejudicial conduct under s 459 of the 1985 Act is likely to be the preferred remedy. The relevance of the authorities we will now examine is to assist with the interpretation of what amounts to unfairly prejudicial conduct, given that both the courts and Parliament seem to have converged in their understanding of what amounts to behaviour which can be challenged by minorities or those who are not in control.

The term 'fraud' in this context has developed over the years. Undoubtedly, fraud will be found where the majority of shareholders are appropriating to themselves property or interests of the company, as illustrated in the case of *Menier v Hooper's Telegraph Works* (1874) 9 Ch App 350, where Hooper's company, a substantial shareholder in the European Telegraph Co, diverted business to itself and caused the European Co to abandon proceedings against it. James LJ held that a derivative action (now claim) should be allowed. In *Alexander v Automatic Telephone Co* [1900] 2 Ch 56, a resolution passed by the company's directors required all subscribers to pay for an allotment of shares, with the exception of three of the directors. The Court of Appeal held that such a breach of duty by the directors, which was not known, or sanctioned by the other shareholders, meant that the only relief possible, given the control the three directors had over the company, was to permit a derivative action (now claim). Fraud for these purposes is not shown where the complaint is one of mere negligence (*Pavlides v Jensen* [1956] Ch 565), but if such negligence happens to result in a benefit to the wrongdoer at the expense of the company, this may amount to fraud for these purposes (*Daniels v Daniels* [1978] Ch 406).

Fraud in the sense of deceit could not be proved so readily, but fraud in equity is concerned not only with improper appropriation of company property but also with breaches of duty to the company, including situations where the directors are unaware of their breach, which result in some benefit being obtained by the directors in question.

Where the wrongdoers are in a position to ensure that the company does not pursue a claim against them, this may amount to fraud (*Prudential Assurance Co Ltd v Newman Industries Ltd (No 2)* [1981] Ch 257, *per* Vinelott J). The meaning of fraud for these purposes has been developed considerably, especially in recent years. In *Estmanco (Kilner House) Ltd v GLC* [1982] 1 WLR 2, a company had been created by a Conservative-controlled council to manage a block of flats. When the flats were sold to owner occupiers, they each received a share in the company, Estmanco. The council retained voting control of the company until all flats were sold, but covenanted to use its best endeavours to sell all the flats. A change in the political face of the council saw the flats being used to house the homeless, whereupon a flatowner, a non-voting shareholder, sought leave to pursue a derivative action (now claim) on the company's behalf against the Council to enforce the covenant, against the wishes of the Council. Megarry V-C held that the Council's behaviour amounted to fraud and permitted a derivative action, although he was clear in his view that injustice is not the correct test for fraud. He said:

> It does not seem to have yet become very clear exactly what the word 'fraud' means in this context; but I think it is plainly wider than fraud at common law, in the sense of Derry v Peek. On a valuable survey of the authorities, Templeman J recently came to the conclusion that this head permitted the minority to sue even though there had not been an allegation of fraud ... Apart from the benefits to themselves at the company's expense, the essence of the matter seems to be an abuse or misuse of power. 'Fraud' in the phrase 'fraud on the minority' seems to be used as comprising not only of fraud at common law but also fraud in the wider equitable sense of that term, as in the equitable concept of a fraud on a power.

14.3.2 Meaning of 'control'

The crucial point is whether the individuals concerned are in a position to prevent the company bringing a claim against the wrongdoers. Ordinarily this will mean control of the board of directors. It is in theory possible for the General Meeting to give the board directions on this by special resolution (art 70), but the wrongdoers could block this avenue if they have more than 25% of the shares. If the board choose to pursue the wrongdoers, such action could be prevented only by a special resolution to that effect, which requires the support of 75% of the votes (the effect of the ability to countermand the board of directors by special resolution has already been discussed in **Chapter 11**).

14.4 **Unfairly prejudicial conduct**

Section 459 of the Companies Act 1985 provides:

> *A member of a company may apply to the court by petition for an order under this part on the ground that the company's affairs are being conducted in a manner which is unfairly prejudicial to the interests of its members generally or some part of its members (including at least himself) or that any actual proposed act or omission of the company (including an act or omission on its behalf) is or would be so prejudicial.*

Section 459 was originally enacted as s 75 of the Companies Act 1980 to replace s 210 of the Companies Act 1948, which provided a remedy if the company's affairs were being carried out in a manner which was oppressive to some part of the membership. Drafting defects and a restricted interpretation of the term 'oppressive' meant that few cases were successful under that provision (the only reported successful applications were Re *HR Harmer Ltd* [1959] 1 WLR 62 and *Scottish Co-Operative Wholesale Society v Meyer* [1959] AC 324). However, it is important to know where s 459 came from, in order to determine whether it in fact provides a useful alternative for a minority shareholder who does not have control over the company, when compared with the derivative claim as an exception to the rule in *Foss v Harbottle* (see **14.2** and **14.3** above). It might certainly be more appropriate for a member of a quasi-partnership with a complaint against the controllers, as in our scenario, to petition under s 459 due to the wide powers granted to the court under s 461 (see **14.5** and **Further Reading** below; the critical view of the remedy in terms of time and expense expressed by Harman J in *In Re Unisoft Group Ltd* (No 3) [1994] 1 BCLC 609 should also be noted). Investors in a public company can, for example, simply sell their investment if their complaint about management practice is ignored, whereas in a private company this is not usually a realistic alternative (it is common in most private companies to see a share transfer restriction; quite apart from this, problems relating to valuation and availability of willing buyers make this an unrealistic option). Note, however, that the provisions of ss 459–461 do not apply just to quasi-partnership companies (*Re A Company (No 00314 of 1989)* [1991] BCLC 154).

In its original form, s 210 of the 1948 Act required a demonstration that the circumstances were such that it would be possible for the company to be wound up on the just and equitable ground, s 210 being seen as an alternative to this drastic remedy (discussed at **14.7** below); and although equitable considerations are brought to bear in order to decide what amounts to unfairly prejudicial conduct, restrictions such as 'he who comes to equity must come with clean hands' will not be a bar to relief, although they may affect the nature or extent of the remedy granted. In *Re London School of Electronics Ltd* [1986] Ch 211, LSE was a company running courses in electronics. Lytton, a teacher at LSE, held 25% of the company's shares, with the remainder being held by another company (CTC). The directors of LSE transferred most of LSE's students to another, CTC course, whereupon

Lytton set up a rival teaching institution taking some LSE students with him. Nourse J held that although Lytton's conduct was itself open to criticism, it did not prevent him seeking relief under s 459, although it could be taken into account when determining what relief, if any, he should receive.

Other cases decided under s 459 serve to illustrate the meaning of 'interests' and 'unfairly prejudicial'. The term 'interests' has been construed as wider than rights, although they must be interests *qua* member (*Re A Company (No 4475 of 1982)* [1983] Ch 178). Rights are something enjoyed by the members under the company's constitution, as we saw in **Chapter 7**, whereas interests will include legitimate expectations which may accrue to the individual concerned depending upon the facts of the particular case. For example, in *Re A Company (No 00477 of 1986)* [1986] BCLC 376, Hoffmann J said:

> In the case of a small private company in which two or three members have ventured their capital by subscribing for shares on the footing that dividends are unlikely but that each will earn his living by working for the company as a director ... the member's interests as a member may include a legitimate expectation that he will continue to be employed as a director and his dismissal from that office and exclusion from the management of the company may therefore be unfairly prejudicial to his interests as a member.

This approach had already been adopted where the court was considering whether exclusion from management might amount to a just and equitable ground for a petition to wind a company up (*Ebrahimi v Westbourne Galleries* [1973] AC 360). Another case which might well assist Duncan in formulating his complaint is *Re A & B C Chewing Gum Ltd* [1975] 1 WLR 579, where an investor who had contributed a large proportion of the company's capital was held to have a legitimate expectation that he would continue to have a say in the management of the business. Although this case was decided under s 122(1)(g) of the Insolvency Act 1986, it is suggested that at the present day the facts would be regarded as more appropriate for a s 459 remedy. In *Caratti Holding Co Pty Ltd v Zampatti PC* (1978) 52 ALJR 732, the court, although not able to rectify the company's Articles, was not prepared to enforce them if persuaded that they did not reflect accurately the intentions of the parties (see also *O'Neill v Phillips* [1999] 1 WLR 1092). However, where the Articles are not in conflict with other rights and expectations, and there is no suggestion of bad faith or impropriety, a member cannot complain that the Articles are unfair. In *Re Posgate & Denby (Agencies) Ltd* [1987] BCLC 8, it was held that the court would give full effect to the terms and understandings of the parties but such terms would not later be rewritten (see also *Re J E Cade & Son Ltd* [1991] BCC 360). Where the parties themselves seem to have provided in writing for all eventualities, it will be assumed that all rights and expectations are included in those documents (*Re Elgindata Ltd* [1991] BCLC 959). In the case of a public company the approach is far more strict. The expectations, rights and understandings of all parties must be available to outside investors and, as such, should be recorded in company documents (*Re Blue Arrow plc* [1987] BCLC 585).

The use of the term 'unfairly prejudicial' has been construed so as to confer a wide jurisdiction upon the courts (see *Re A Company (No 008699)* [1985] BCLC 382 *per* Hoffmann J; *In Re Saul D Harrison and Sons plc* [1995] 1 BCLC 14; *B S Holdings Ltd (No 2)* [1996] 1 BCLC 155). In *Diligenti v RWMD Operations Kelowna Ltd* (1976) 1 BCLR 36, Fulton J said: 'It is significant that the dictionary definitions support the instinctive reactions that what is unjust and inequitable is obviously also unfairly prejudicial.'

Another possibility which needs to be considered in s 459 cases is that the directors who are the target of the petition may wish to launch a petition of their own against a major shareholder. In the present case, Bill and Edwina are irritated and frustrated by Duncan's behaviour, and may well wish to see him cease to be a member of the company. One way to achieve this would be to ask the court to order a buyout of Duncan's shares on the ground that his behaviour is itself unfairly prejudicial. There are some difficulties in the way of this approach. It is not clear that Duncan can be said to be conducting the affairs of the company within the meaning of s 459. Although he wants to attend board meetings, the Articles give him no right to speak or vote at such meetings, and his attempts to telephone Edwina with instructions for the running of the company have been firmly rebuffed. He is able to be a nuisance, but he does not conduct the affairs of the company. Similarly, it is impossible for Bill and Edwina to bring themselves within the final words of s 459 by showing that some proposed act or omission of the *company* would be unfairly prejudicial (they may think that some of Duncan's actions meet this criterion, but that is not the test which the section lays down). Bill and Edwina may find themselves in the unenviable position of being on the receiving end of a s 459 petition without being able to retaliate in kind. This is a common situation where directors are in conflict with a major shareholder, since, as has already been demonstrated, a shareholder with fewer than 75% of the shares will not be able to overrule the directors and therefore cannot be said to be conducting the affairs of the company.

Since this provision was introduced in 1980 it is noticeable that the number of reported cases involving derivative claims and/or the rule in *Foss v Harbottle* has declined dramatically. This may be explained by the absence of technical restrictions on the bringing of a s 459 petition and greater discretion available to the court in making orders under s 461. That section allows the court to make whatever order it thinks fit, and in particular to order the majority to buy out the minority shareholders, to regulate the company's affairs in future, to authorise the bringing of proceedings on behalf of the company, or to require the company to do or refrain from doing any act. This list, though not exhaustive, contains most of the orders which are in practice likely to be made (see further **14.5** below). It should be noted that the power to authorise the bringing of proceedings in the company's name is in effect a power to permit a derivative claim, so that this kind of action may be regarded as being subsumed within s 459. In practice the most common order on a successful s 459 petition is for the buying out of the dissentient shareholder. This recognises the fact, often unwelcome to the dissentients, that they cannot be allowed to impose their will on the majority for any length of time – the best they can hope for is to get a fair price for their shares. In this context it should be noted that an order for the buying out of the minority should normally specify the date at which the minority share holding is to be valued, and this should normally be the date at which the petition is presented (see **Further Reading**, below). The point is likely to be of some importance, since ongoing disputes of the kind which lead to s 459 petitions frequently have a harmful effect on the company's performance, and the shares may well decline in value between the presentation of the petition and the hearing of the action. Orders regulating the conduct of the company's affairs in future are made only sparingly and reluctantly, for they threaten to involve the court in the ongoing supervision of company management, a thankless task which the court cannot hope to perform satisfactorily.

14.5 The remedies available

Where the court is satisfied that the circumstances for a s 459 petition exist, s 461 of the Companies Act 1985 gives power to make whatever order the court may think fit for remedying the situation. The unfettered nature of this power requires emphasis. However, s 461(2) goes on to list a number of examples of orders which the court might make. Although this list clearly cannot be exhaustive, it does include the most commonly made orders. Thus the court may:

> (a) regulate the conduct of the company's affairs for the future ...

This paragraph needs to be considered in conjunction with the one which follows it. Although the wording appears to allow for the granting of injunctions, this remedy, in the rare cases where it is granted at all, falls more naturally under para (b). Paragraph (a) is more likely to be applied to an order where some specific step is needed, such as a change in the Articles of Association, perhaps to remove a *Bushell v Faith* clause which is impeding the sensible management of the company. Alternatively, an order may be made forbidding a proposed change to the Articles or Memorandum.

> (b) require the company to refrain from doing or continuing an act complained of by the petitioner or to do an act which the petitioner has complained it has omitted to do ...

This paragraph allows the court to issue injunctions, either prohibitory or mandatory, to rectify the wrong of which the petitioner claims. The practical difficulty about this is that where intra-company disputes have become acrimonious (as is usually the case with a s 459 petition, since attempts to resolve matters amicably have presumably failed), judicial intervention is likely to be necessary on a regular basis. The courts are naturally reluctant to have any ongoing role in company management, a task for which they have neither the expertise nor the resources. Consequently, orders under this paragraph are rare.

> (c) authorise civil proceedings to be brought in the name and on behalf of the company by such person or persons and on such terms as the court may direct ...

This paragraph permits the court to authorise the bringing of a derivative claim of the type permitted at common law under the exceptions to the *Foss v Harbottle* principle, considered at **14.2** and **14.3** above. There are a number of reasons why a petitioner who wishes to bring such an action would be well advised to petition under s 459 rather than at common law. First, the test for eligibility for relief is more broadly expressed – there is no specific requirement of control by the wrongdoers, nor need the vexed question of the meaning of 'fraud' be broached. Secondly, the petition under s 459 can ask for different forms of relief, either alternatively or cumulatively. Thirdly, the court has a complete discretion as to the terms on which an order under this paragraph may be made; thus, it can also give directions as to costs and as to the conduct of the action, whereas there is some dispute whether this can properly be done at common law (see *Wallersteiner v Moir* [1974] 1 WLR 991). The existence of this paragraph has rendered the common law derivative claim largely obsolete.

> (d) provide for the purchase of the shares of the company by other members or by the company itself, and, in the case of a purchase by the company itself, for the reduction of the company's capital accordingly.

This is by far the most common order in successful s 459 petitions. Sometimes it is the remedy which the petitioner seeks. Where the Articles contain restrictions on share transfers, these may make it effectively impossible for a disaffected shareholder to sell his shares, since the directors may refuse to recognise any attempted transfer of them. In such circumstances a s 459 petition may be the only way to force a sale. In other cases the buying out of the petitioner may not be at all what he wants. He may wish to see the court make an order under para (a) or para (b) above. The difficulties already discussed surrounding orders under these paragraphs may prevent him from achieving this objective, and the court may not be prepared to offer anything more than a compulsory buy out. This will at least have the effect of getting the petitioner the value of his shares. It will also put an end to this source of friction within the company, though not in the way the petitioner would prefer. A shareholder contemplating a s 459 petition would therefore do well to appreciate that the result may be the end of his participation in the company.

An alternative solution under para (d) is for the petitioner to seek to buy out the shares of one or more of the other shareholders. In reality this is unlikely where the petitioner is a minority shareholder, partly because of the probable expense and partly because the principle of majority rule means that the dissentient minority is always likely to be seen as the problem rather than the solution (but see *Re Brenfield Squash Racquets Club Ltd* [1996] 2 BCLC 184).

Paragraph (d) also contemplates the possibility of ordering the company to purchase its own shares. This can be done only where there is sufficient distributable profit within the company to support such a purchase, since it would otherwise involve an unlawful return of capital (see **Chapter 17**). This will be an appropriate solution where the company has surplus funds but the individual shareholders do not, or where it is not desired to transfer the shares to other shareholders because of possible disruptive effects on the balance of power within the company.

Where a buyout order is made, the question of the date at which the shares should be valued will inevitably arise. The existence of the s 459 petition is likely to result in a decline in the value of the shares because of the uncertainty which it creates, whilst the underlying dispute which leads to the presentation of the petition is also likely to exert its own debilitating influence on the company's profitability. It follows that the petitioner would generally prefer to have the shares valued at the earliest possible date, whereas the respondents who must buy the shares would prefer a later date. The statute gives no help in answering the question, and the case law is conflicting and unhelpful (see **Further Reading**, below). It is submitted that as a matter of principle the court ought to seek to put the petitioner in the position in which he would have been if the wrongful conduct had not taken place. In general this points to a date no later than the date of presentation of the petition. In some cases it might even be arguable that an earlier date should be chosen, since the dispute will no doubt have gone on for some time before the petition is presented. It must be admitted, however, that there is no reported case in which a date earlier than the date of the petition has been chosen, and that there are some in which the date of the making of the order has been preferred.

14.6 Tactical use of s 459 petitions

The imprecise nature of the requirement of 'unfairly prejudicial' conduct in s 459 tends to encourage dissatisfied shareholders to resort to the section very readily – it is by no means easy to say with confidence that the complaints of such a shareholder will necessarily be dismissed by the court. This in turn creates an opening for the tactical use of such proceedings (and for the threat of the use of such proceedings). In any dispute within a company it is possible for the minority to raise the question of s 459 as a means of putting pressure on the majority to accommodate their views, and the disruptive effect on the company of such a petition, even if unjustified and ultimately unsuccessful, is so great that the threat must often be taken seriously. Even where proceedings are issued, it by no means follows that the petition will ever come to trial, nor that either side really wants it to come to trial – the issue of the petition may be only another step in the ongoing tactical manoeuvres of the parties (see In *Re A Company (No 00836 of 1995)* [1996] 2 BCLC 192, where the court considered the possibility of striking out petitions where, inter alia, they were being pursued in pursuit of a family feud and not for commercial reasons; see also *Re Rotodata Ltd* [2000] 1 BCLC 122).

A further tactical question which may be raised concerns the choice between a s 459 petition and a s 122 winding-up petition, as discussed at **14.7** below. Although it might at first sight appear that most petitioners would prefer a s 459 petition, since this will normally result in the survival of the company (save in exceptional cases such as *Jesner v Jarrad Properties* [1993] BCLC 1032), it may occasionally be advantageous to seek a winding up, partly because the threat of this more drastic solution may be more effective in securing concessions from the majority, and partly because a winding-up order, if made, would offer the possibility of being able to buy the company more cheaply from the liquidator than would be possible if the shares had to be sold on a going-concern basis. It should be said, however, that there would seem to be some risk that the court would see through such a stratagem, and that there is a risk that the failure of the s 122 petition will leave the minority with no remedy at all, whereas a s 459 petition might at least have secured some relief.

14.7 Just and equitable winding up of companies

Section 122(1)(g) of the Insolvency Act 1986 allows the court to order the winding up of a company on the ground that it is just and equitable that the company should be wound up. In the past this provision was used in cases of deadlock (see *Re Yenidje Tobacco Co Ltd* [1916] 2 Ch 426) and fundamental breakdown in quasi-partnerships (see *Ebrahimi v Westbourne Galleries Ltd* [1973] AC 360), but it is important to note that the cases similar to those decided under this provision may now be suitable candidates for a s 459 petition. Cases such as *Re Yenidje Tobacco Co* and *Re Zinotty Properties Ltd* [1984] 1 WLR 1249 would seem to be suitable for a buy-out order under s 461(2)(d) (see **14.5** above), though in the former case it is not obvious who should buy out whom. Failure of substratum is also a standard reason for a winding up, the classic example being *Re German Date Coffee Co* (1882) 20 ChD 169, but it is to be observed that this is a case of a 19th-century public company in an era where objects clauses were strictly construed and the doctrine of *ultra vires* was given full effect. In the context of an early 21st century private company after the abolition of ultra vires, it cannot be imagined that the facts of this case would produce a winding up. At most the situation calls for the compulsory buy out of the petitioners, perhaps by the company itself, since their real complaint was that they subscribed for their shares under a misapprehension.

The third commonly cited ground is collapse of trust and confidence, the leading example being *Ebrahimi v Westbourne Galleries Ltd* [1973] AC 360. It is again submitted that at the present day a winding-up order would be inappropriate – the company was very profitable, and the petitioner's legitimate grievances could have been perfectly well resolved if he had been allowed to sell his shares to the respondents at a fair market valuation. Indeed in that case the petition did ask in the alternative for relief under s 210 of the Companies Act 1948 (see **14.4** above), and it was only the technical deficiencies of that section which prevented the granting of such relief.

Attention is also drawn to s 125(2) of the Insolvency Act 1986, which precludes a petition for winding up on the just and equitable ground where there is any other suitable remedy. Certainly, since 1980 there have been relatively few reported cases of successful petitions on this ground.

14.8 DTI investigations

Sections 431–432 of the Companies Act 1985 empower the Secretary of State for Trade and Industry to appoint inspectors to report on the affairs of a company where he sees fit to do so. Although as a matter of law these powers are exercisable in relation to both private and public companies, there are no known cases of the appointment of inspectors in the case of a private company, the exercise of the power being in practice confined to listed companies whose affairs are of more general interest. The participants in Great Expectations Ltd would therefore be unwise to look to these provisions as a way of dealing with any of their internal disputes.

14.9 Advice to the parties

Duncan is in a strong position as he is able to exercise pre-emption rights under s 89 of the Companies Act 1985. Edwina and Bill can circumvent this by entering into the employee share scheme, preferably protecting their own position by setting up a voting trust. However, in doing this they do risk a challenge from other shareholders, who may want to know why this tactic is being used. Edwina and Bill should be able to justify their actions by pointing to the need for increased share capital and the impossibility of using other methods to obtain it. Duncan will no doubt become increasingly dissatisfied with the performance of the directors, but it is important to remember that the *Bushell v Faith* clause in the Articles does prevent Duncan alone from removing them from the board (though of course it does not give them complete protection against shareholder dissatisfaction). Duncan may be minded to try a s 459 petition, but it is unlikely that this will succeed, partly because the directors have a rational justification for what they are doing, partly because it is Duncan's own conduct which has driven them to their current tactics.

FURTHER READING

KW Wedderburn, 'Shareholders' rights and the rule in Foss v Harbottle' [1957] CLJ 194, [1958] CLJ 93.

B Hannigan, 'Section 459 of The Companies Act 1985 – a code of conduct for the quasi partnership?' [1988] LMCLQ 60.

DD Prentice, 'Minority shareholder oppression: valuation of shares' (1986) 102 LQR 179.

The Law Commission, *Shareholder Remedies*, Consultation Paper No 142.

15 Holding the Balance between Creditors

LEARNING OUTCOMES

By the end of this chapter, you should understand:

- the nature of securities – fixed and floating charges;

- the concept of crystallisation;

- registration requirements of charges on the company's assets;

- negative pledge clauses;

- priority between fixed and floating charges;

- goods supplied to a company – the effect of retention of title clauses in sale of goods contracts;

- deposits;

- factoring of debts.

SCENARIO

Edwina has introduced the company to a range of sophisticated financial control techniques. Clients are always asked to pay a non-returnable deposit of 10% before the work is commenced. Where goods are supplied to clients as part of the contract, they are always subject to a retention of title clause until paid for in full. Great Expectations Ltd always buys goods on credit (terms 30, 60 or 90 days) and usually subject to a retention of title clause (the clause used when buying antiques from YOCS is reprinted in full at **15.3.2** below, and always delays as long as possible before paying. In many cases this means not paying on the due date. Wherever possible the company's book debts are factored in order to improve the cash flow.

It will also be remembered that part of the company's financing comes from Bus Bank, which has a debenture from the company secured by a fixed and floating charge (see **Chapter 4**).

OVERVIEW

This chapter looks at a number of issues which lie on the fringes of company law, and the law relating to sale and supply of goods and services. These issues have given rise to a series of quite complex cases.

15.1 Fixed and floating charges and unsecured debt

As was explained in **Chapter 4**, company debt financing is frequently arranged through a mixture of secured and unsecured debt. The most important unsecured debts will be the sums due to trade creditors. The problems which may arise for this group, and possible strategies available to them, are considered at **15.2** and **15.3** below. Secured debts will be secured by either a fixed charge or a floating charge

15.1.1 Fixed charges

One form of security is the fixed charge, which is in effect a mortgage of a fixed asset such as land or buildings. In this area the rules of company law overlap with those of land law. Where property subject to a mortgage is sold by its owner, the mortgage must be repaid out of the proceeds of sale. This fact imposes a substantial practical restriction on the mortgagor's freedom to deal with the property. In the case of a debenture creating a fixed charge over a company's assets, it is usual to go further by including a provision that the company is forbidden to sell the asset without the mortgagee's consent. The registration requirements for fixed charges are also affected by their character as interests in land. Where the land is unregistered a legal mortgage does not require to be registered as a land charge (indeed there is no provision for registering it). A puisne mortgage, ie one not protected by deposit of title deeds, should be registered as a Class C(i) land charge. However, mortgages of this class will normally be second mortgages, since a first mortgagee will normally require the title deeds. An unregistered land charge is void against a purchaser for value of the land (Land Charges Act 1972, s 4), though it is only the security which is affected, not the debt itself. A legal mortgage, being a legal interest in land, is good against all the world irrespective of notice. As between themselves, successive legal mortgages normally rank in the order of their creation. Legal mortgages take priority over equitable mortgages.

A mortgage granted by a company should also be registered in the company's own Register of Charges and at Companies House. The rules in relation to this, and the consequences of non-registration, are the same as in the case of floating charges, and are set out at **15.1.2** below.

15.1.2 Floating charges

At any given time most companies will also have assets other than land, and they may wish to use these as the basis for further financing. For many companies two major classes of asset are the stock-in-trade, ie those goods which the company is intending to supply to its own customers and which it is holding pending sale and delivery, and the book debts, ie those debts owed by customers to whom goods have been supplied or for whom work has been done. Two important characteristics of both these classes of asset are that they will normally have some content but that the content will change on a fairly regular basis, as goods are bought and sold and as debts are paid and incurred. The former characteristic makes these classes of asset suitable for use as security, whilst the latter characteristic makes it inappropriate to use fixed charges, since the debt secured on a fixed charge becomes payable immediately on the sale of the asset which is subject to the charge. In the case of book debts and stock-in-trade it is intended that the company should be able to deal with these freely, the charge being enforced only if the company goes into liquidation or receivership (see *Re Spectrum Plus Ltd* [2004] EWCA Civ 670). A charge which achieves these objectives is known as a floating charge, and is commonly used as a way of securing indebtedness on these classes of assets.

A number of legal issues arise in relation to floating charges, and it is convenient to begin with questions of definition. The classic definition of the incidents of a floating charge is found in *Re Yorkshire Woolcombers Association Ltd* [1903] 2 Ch 284, as follows:

(a) the charge must be on a class of assets, present and future, of the company;

(b) the class must be one which in the ordinary course of business is expected to change;

(c) the company is free to deal with the assets as it sees fit until the happening of some specified future event.

It may be added that when that event happens, the charge ceases to float over the class of assets for the time being and attaches itself instead to the assets which are in the class at that moment (together with any assets which are subsequently added to the class). This process is referred to as crystallisation and the event which brings it about is said to be a crystallising event. The most common crystallising event is the liquidation or receivership of the company, though the question of exactly which events bring about crystallisation is itself an important and difficult one (see **15.1.2.1** below).

15.1.2.1 Crystallising events

There is no statutory list of crystallising events. In the case of floating charges created before 15 September 2003 (the date on which Pt 10 of the Enterprise Act 2002 came into force, see **Chapter 22**), the appointment of an administrative receiver, a power which was always included in the charge contract prior to the above date, caused a floating charge to crystallise. In respect of any floating charge created after the above date, the powers of the chargee to appoint an administrative receiver are severely restricted. Nevertheless, the appointment of an administrative receiver, a receiver or an administrator will cause the charge to crystallise.

Subject to the above, it is for the charge contract to specify the exact circumstances in which the charge will cystallise. The appointment of a liquidator to the company operates as a crystallising event since the company is no longer able to deal with its assets in the ordinary course of business (see further **Chapter 22**). It has also been suggested that a floating charge may crystallise either when the company ceases to be a going concern, or when it ceases to carry on business (*William Gaskell Group Ltd v Highley* [1994] 1 BCLC 197; *Re Woodroffes (Musical Instruments) Ltd* [1986] Ch 366). Unfortunately, both these tests give rise to some difficulties. The concept of a going concern is normally used only in relation to certain accounting questions (this aspect of the phrase is dealt with in **Chapter 18**), and the test is not easy to apply on a day-to-day basis, since it requires careful study of the current position of the accounts. It is in principle desirable that the crystallisation of a charge should be fairly easily established, since serious consequences flow from it, and this may be seen as a powerful argument against accepting that charges crystallise on this event. Cessation of business is more easily recognised, so this particular argument does not apply in relation to the second test. However, a more serious difficulty may be perceived if one considers what purpose the concept of crystallisation is intended to serve in relation to floating charges. Given that assets subject to a floating charge may normally be dealt with freely so that the company can obtain money in order to meet its debts (including those secured by the floating charge), it may be suggested that crystallisation is intended to preserve and protect the position of the chargee in those situations where the company's position has deteriorated so seriously that the prospects of raising further significant sums towards the meeting of the debt are remote, and it is necessary to give the chargee the security of knowing that at least the assets currently included in the class of assets charged are available as security. This would explain why receivership and liquidation are treated as crystallising events, but it would leave the cessation of business as a borderline case. A closing-down sale, for example, may be held even after business has ceased, which shows that significant assets may be realised. On the other hand, the cessation of business presumably means that no new assets will be added to the class; the subsequent sale of assets within the class will therefore reduce the security available to the chargee. From this point of view it may be said that a cessation of business which is intended to be permanent ought to be treated as a crystallising event.

The question whether automatic crystallisation clauses ought to be regarded as effective is discussed at **15.1.2.3** below.

15.1.2.2 Multiple floating charges

Another significant problem which occurs in relation to floating charges is that companies may create more than one floating charge over the same class of assets. There is nothing inherently impossible about charging the same class of asset twice, though a common result of doing so is that the charge exceeds the total value of the assets in the class. In this case, however, the question of priority between the two charges will arise if the charge crystallises. At first sight it would seem logical that the charge which came first in time should prevail, but two significant complicating factors intervene here. The first is the requirement of registration in relation to company charges.

Registration requirements

The detailed rules are set out in ss 395–411 of the Companies Act 1985. Section 395 creates the requirement of registration, and s 396 lists those charges which must be registered. The most important types of charge requiring registration are:

(a) a charge on land or any interest in it (but not a charge for rent);

(b) a charge on book debts of the company;

(c) a floating charge on the company's undertaking or property.

It will be appreciated that the last of these is a residual category which, if broadly interpreted, is capable of including all the others. In practice, it should be interpreted as covering only those charges which are not specifically dealt with elsewhere. It should be noted that this category will include the kind of charge over goods which has been held to have been created in some of the cases relating to purported retention of title clauses (as to this see **15.3** below).

A floating charge must be registered against the company in its Register of Charges at Companies House. The purpose of this requirement is to enable anyone dealing with the company (and in particular anyone who is subsequently contemplating lending it money) to see the existence of the charge. It also serves to establish the date from which the charge is to be considered as having priority.

In addition, the company must keep its own Register of Charges at its own registered office, and charges must also be registered there (Companies Act 1985, s 407). This requirement includes every kind of charge and is not restricted to the list of transactions required by s 396 to be registered with the Registrar. This means that in order to obtain reliably complete information about the state of a company's borrowings, it is necessary to search both registers. This is obviously an undesirable state of affairs, but its potentially awkward consequences are at least mitigated by the relative unimportance of the classes of charge which are registered only in the company's own register.

A charge is required to be registered within 21 days of the date on which it is effected (Companies Act 1985, s 395(1)). The company is under an obligation to deliver the pre-scribed particulars to the Registrar of Companies, and in the case of default its officers are liable to a fine (s 399(3)). However, the adverse consequences of non-registration are more serious for the creditor, and the Companies Act 1985 therefore allows the creditor to deliver the particulars (s 399(1)). It is suggested that the creditor would be well-advised to take this option.

Registration is required by the Companies Act, but although the date of registration is important it is not the sole factor in determining priority – the charge must be registered within 21 days of creation – in these circumstances it is then the date of creation which determines the priorities between *properly* registered charges.

Where the charge is not registered within the 21 days it is still possible to register it out of time. However, in this event it takes effect for priority purposes on the date of registration, and is therefore subject to any other charges which have been registered in the meantime or to any other events which have affected the company's property, including the crystalli-sation of charges and the appointment of a receiver or liquidator (s 400).

New rules contained in the Companies Act 1989 which would have revised the system for registration of company charges have never been brought into force, and it now seems possible that they may never come into force, as the whole subject of company charges may be reviewed yet again.

It should be noted that where there are two floating charges created at different times by the company over its assets, and the second crystallises before the first, then that fixed charge has priority over the first charge, even after the first charge itself crystallises (see *Griffiths v Yorkshire Bank plc* [1994] 1 WLR 1427; the opposite conclusion has been drawn in Canada, see *Re Household Products Co Ltd and Federal Business Development Bank* (1981) 124 DLR (3d) 325).

Negative pledge clauses

Even where all competing charges are duly registered, the second complicating factor must be taken into account. Sometimes the second charge may expressly state that it is to rank in priority to all other charges on the same class of asset, or, less ambitiously, that it is to rank equally with such other charges. In principle this appears to be possible, despite being a clear example of defeating an existing vested right. In order to prevent it, first charges on a class of asset very frequently include clauses forbidding the creation of further charges ranking equally with or in priority to the first charge. These clauses are commonly referred to as negative pledge clauses. The question then arises whether they are capable of achieving their objective.

Given that the first charge has been duly registered, it is possible for the second chargee to discover its existence, though not to discover the detailed terms of the charge except by insisting that the company supply a copy of the first charge as a pre-condition to the granting of the second charge. This follows from the fact that the form for registering particulars of charges at Companies House does not include any provision for disclosing the existence of a negative pledge clause. In practice, though, asking to see the first charge would almost certainly be an unwise course of action. This conclusion follows from the fact that the courts have consistently held that the second charge is effective in its own terms unless the second chargee has actual knowledge not only of the existence of the first charge but also of its terms, and in particular of the negative pledge clause (see *G & T Earle Ltd v Hemsworth Rural District Council* (1928) 44 TLR 605 and *Chisholm Textiles Ltd v Griffiths* [1994] 2 BCLC 291). From this point of view the second chargee would therefore be well advised not to investigate too closely the terms of the first charge.

15.1.2.3 Automatic crystallisation clauses

The position may change somewhat when a further commonly-encountered clause is considered. This is an extension of the idea behind the negative pledge clause, and it provides that the subsequent creation of any charge ranking equally with or in priority to the charge in which the clause is contained will result in the automatic crystallisation of that charge. This clause, commonly known as an automatic crystallisation clause, seeks to address the apparent deficiencies of the negative pledge clause by ensuring that the crystallisation of the first charge does not depend on the state of knowledge of the second chargee in relation to the contents of the first charge.

There has been considerable academic and judicial discussion about the validity of automatic crystallisation clauses (see Nourse J (obiter), in *Re Woodroffes (Musical Instruments) Ltd* [1986] Ch 366; Hoffmann J, in *Re Brightlife* [1987] Ch 200, at 214–5; and The Cork Committee (1982, Cmnd 8558, paras 1578–9)). The difficulty with such clauses arises largely from the fact, discussed at **15.1.2.1** above, that there is no definitive list of what can and cannot be a crystallising event. In principle there is no obvious reason why the parties in any given case should not agree between themselves the events on which the charge is to crystallise, and if this view is accepted, then automatic crystallisation clauses appear to be effective. However, there is a severe practical difficulty here. Where the first charge contains an automatic crystallisation clause, the company may cause it to crystallise without appreciating that it has done so (since the directors may well not read the fine print of the first charge, and may not understand it if they do read it). This may lead the company to go on dealing with the assets charged, notwithstanding that the charge has crystallised. The proceeds of these sales ought to be set aside for the creditor, but in practice this will almost certainly not happen, and the money will be lost. When the company subsequently goes into liquidation, the automatic crystallisation clause will therefore be found to be useless, even if effective as a matter of legal theory.

Another difficulty in this area is that the right to charge assets is arguably one of the basic rights of a company so long as it is a going concern. On this basis there would appear to be public policy objections to allowing automatic crystallisation clauses. The fundamental problem is that of holding the balance between successive creditors whilst simultaneously allowing the company a reasonable opportunity to secure finance for itself, and respecting so far as possible the parties' freedom to make their own contracts. This rather delicate exercise may explain why courts in different jurisdictions have taken different approaches to the problem of automatic crystallisation clauses.

Possibly the best available compromise would be to say that such clauses are in principle capable of being valid, but that a court will examine them closely and will construe them strictly.

15.1.3 Priorities as between fixed and floating charges

This is a subject of some complexity. The question arises only where the same asset is subject to both a fixed and a floating charge. The usual rule is that the date of registration is important, as explained at **15.1.2.2** above. However, the holder of a subsequent legal charge may rank ahead of the holder of an earlier equitable charge, provided that the legal chargee acted in good faith and without notice. In practice there will be few cases where this will be relevant, since the purchaser of an interest in land has constructive knowledge of duly registered land charges (see the Land Registration Act 2002) and of equitable charges duly registered at Companies House (*Wilson v Kelland* [1910] 2 Ch 306). Where an earlier charge contains a restrictive clause of some kind the position is further complicated in the ways described at **15.1.2**.

15.1.4 Distinguishing between fixed and floating charges

Given that different rules apply to the two types of charges, it is obviously important to be able to tell them apart. The definition of a floating charge given in *Re Yorkshire Woolcombers Association* Ltd [1903] 2 Ch 284 (see **15.1.2** above; the judgment of the members of the House of Lords in this case is reported sub nom *Illingworth v Houldsworth* [1904] AC 355) may appear to make this task relatively straightforward, but occasional difficulties do arise. In *Re Atlantic Medical Ltd* [1993] BCLC 386, the company was in the business of leasing medical equipment under operating leases and under hire-purchase contracts. It charged the operating leases and the sums receivable under hire-purchase contracts in favour of the banks which financed it. The charges were expressed to apply to future sums as well as to sums already due. Vinelott J held that this was a fixed charge over the assets in question, notwithstanding that it appeared to satisfy all the requirements of the *Yorkshire Woolcombers* test. The decision is by no means easy to understand.

In *Re New Bullas Trading Ltd* [1993] BCLC 1389, the charge was on the book debts of the company, but was described as a fixed charge, in an apparent attempt to give the creditor a more favourable position in the event of a winding up. Knox J held that the description used by the parties could not be sustained: this was in substance a floating charge because it fell squarely within the *Yorkshire Woolcombers Test*, and priorities would be determined accordingly (see *Re Spectrum Plus Ltd* [2004] EWCA Civ 670). Unfortunately the Court of Appeal in the *Re New Bullas* case held that the charge contract, at the time when receivers were appointed, created fixed charges over the book debts. The approach of Knox J at first instance in *Re New Bullas*, in determining the nature and effects of a charge contract, was, however, reaffirmed by the Privy Council in *Agnew v Commissioner of Inland Revenue* [2001] 2 AC 710 (doubt was also cast upon the Court of Appeal decision in *Re New Bullas* by Lord Phillips MR in *Re Spectrum Plus*, the Court preferring the approach to this question taken in *Agnew*; it is expected that the House of Lords in *Re Spectrum* will overrule *Re New Bullas*). In *Agnew*, the Privy Council endorsed the principle that in determining the nature of a charge contract, the court must discover not whether the parties intended to create a fixed or floating charge and then give effect to that intention, but rather the rights the parties intended to create, and then, as a matter of law, determine whether those rights constitute a fixed or floating charge. This is an admirably commonsense approach to the problem, and contrasts very favourably with the decision in *Re Atlantic Medical Ltd* and that of the Court of Appeal in *Re New Bullas*.

15.2 Trade creditors

15.2.1 Introduction

The problems of trade creditors, ie those who have supplied goods and/or services to the company on credit terms, will now be examined. In order to understand this area of the law it is necessary first to be familiar with some provisions of the Sale of Goods Act 1979.

15.2.2 The Sale of Goods Act 1979

This Act regulates contracts for the sale of goods, ie contracts under which the seller transfers or agrees to transfer property in goods to the buyer in return for a money consideration (Sale of Goods Act 1979, s 2). For the purposes of the law relating to sale of goods it is important to know at what point the property in the goods passes from the seller to the buyer, and the relevant sections of the 1979 Act for these purposes are ss 17–19. Section 17 provides that in a contract for the sale of specific goods property passes when the parties intend it to pass. Section 18 provides a number of rules for determining, in the absence of evidence of contrary intention, when property passes in cases of both specific and generic goods. The most important of these are Rules 1 and 5. Rule 1 provides that in a contract for the sale of specific goods, property passes at the time when the contract is made; whilst Rule 5(1) provides that in the case of contracts for the sale of unascertained goods, property passes when goods of the contract description are unconditionally appropriated to the contract by one party with the assent of the other. This would normally be not later than the time when goods are delivered to the buyer.

However, s 19 expressly contemplates that the seller may reserve the right of disposal beyond the time when property would otherwise pass, whilst s 17 allows the parties to make their own agreement about when property in specific goods should pass.

The distinction between specific and unascertained goods is also important here. Goods are specific only where the contract provides that a particular item shall be provided. It is not enough that a make or type of goods is selected. Thus, a contract for the sale of a copy of this book is not initially a contract for the sale of specific goods, since any copy of the book will presumably do perfectly well, and property will not pass until one particular copy is appropriated to the contract. On the other hand, a contract for the sale of one person's copy of the book, perhaps made more valuable by the underlinings and annotations in it, is from the outset a contract for the sale of specific goods – no other copy of the book will do.

It will be appreciated that Great Expectations Ltd normally buys goods in bulk, and therefore makes contracts for the sale of unascertained goods. Where the company supplies goods to clients this will not normally take place under a contract for the sale of goods, but rather under a contract for the sale and supply of work and materials. These are regulated by the Supply of Goods and Services Act 1982, which does not contain provisions determining when property passes, though it is suggested that principles similar to those contained in the Sale of Goods Act 1979 should and would be applied to determining the passage of property in such cases (see the rules of presumed intention laid down by s 18 of the 1979 Act). This point may come to be of some practical significance if the company goes into liquidation at a time when clients have, for example, ordered particular wallpaper or paint, but these materials have not yet been applied to the walls of the client's house.

Where goods are in the possession of the buyer but have not yet become his property because of a clause in the contract under which he bought them, problems arise if he sells them on to a third party (the more complex problems which occur where the goods are processed, either by the original buyer or by a third party, are considered below). It is a general principle of English law that a person cannot give a better title to property than he himself has, and in relation to contracts for the sale of goods this principle is implemented in s 21 of the Sale of Goods Act 1979. However, the principle is also subject to certain limited exceptions, and the exception which is of interest in the present context is that contained in s 25 of the same Act. This applies where a buyer of goods is in possession of them and sells them on to a third party. It provides that in such circumstances the sale is treated as if it were a sale by the true owner of the goods. In other words, the third party gets a good title to the goods. The apparent breach of the principle that a person cannot give a better title than he has himself is neatly avoided by deeming the sale to be made by the true owner, though there is no doubt that the effect of the section is to allow a non-owner who is in possession of the goods to make an effective disposition of them.

These rules, coupled with the risk that a buyer of goods will become insolvent without paying for them, have led to the development of retention of title clauses, which are considered at **15.3.2** below.

15.3 Financing devices in small companies

15.3.1 Introduction

Retention of title clauses (see **15.3.2** below) are commonly used in commercial sales where goods are supplied on credit (and this includes most commercial sales). They are designed to protect the position of the unpaid seller in the event that he is unable to obtain payment, especially where the purchaser goes into insolvent liquidation. In the absence of such a clause it is very likely that ownership of the goods will have passed to the buyer, so that the seller's only remedy is to sue for the agreed price, a remedy which will be of no practical value if the buyer is insolvent. However, legal complexities arise where the goods have been processed or disposed of by the buyer and where the buyer is a limited company.

The practice of asking for deposits (see **15.3.3** below) is a very common one, designed to encourage clients not to rescind orders already given and to protect the company against costs already incurred where orders are cancelled. The difficulties in this area arise if the company does not do the work to an adequate standard, or if the company goes into liquidation leaving work outstanding. The company will wish to argue that deposits are not in any circumstances refundable, but this argument is problematic in both of the situations mentioned above. Where the work is not done properly, the client may at least be able to claim a set-off against the contract price, and in more serious cases this may be more than the total price so that in effect the deposit would have to be returned. The same result might be achieved where the company goes into liquidation. However, in the latter case the company will not have the money to refund deposits, and disappointed clients will not be able to make any priority claim on the company's inadequate funds unless the deposits have been kept in a separate trust account, a practice which is adopted by some companies, but not by Great Expectations Ltd.

Factoring of debts (see **15.3.4** below) is the process of selling those debts to a third party at a cost somewhat less than the full value of the debt in return for immediate payment. The advantage to the company is that it receives the money immediately, thus aiding cash flow, and does not have the trouble of collecting payment. In effect the factoring company takes on the cash flow disadvantage and the risk of non-payment in return for an initial fee.

15.3.2 Retention of title clauses

In order to understand retention of title clauses it is necessary to be aware, in outline, of the rules governing the distribution of the assets of an insolvent company. These are covered in detail in **Chapter 23**. It is sufficient here to note that the rights of the holders of fixed and floating charges, as well as the expenses of the liquidators and the claims of preferential creditors, all rank ahead of the rights of unsecured creditors such as those who have supplied goods to the company on credit. The practical result of this is that in most insolvent liquidations the unsecured creditors receive little or nothing in respect of their claims, since the inadequate assets of the company are swallowed up by the claims of those higher in the chain.

These rules can, however, be circumvented if the goods which have been supplied to the company still belong to the seller. This is because the seller's claim is then not a contractual claim for the agreed price, but a proprietary claim for goods which are his property. Great Expectations Ltd frequently enters into contracts with YOCS plc for the purchase of antiques, and YOCS's standard terms and conditions of sale include the following clause:

> *Risk in the goods passes to the buyer immediately on delivery, but legal and equitable title to the goods remains vested in YOCS until the goods have been paid for in full. The purchaser acknowledges that until that time it holds the goods as bailee for YOCS. The purchaser agrees to allow YOCS access to its premises at any reasonable time for the purpose of inspecting and/or repossessing goods supplied under this contract which are still the property of YOCS. If the goods are sold to a sub-purchaser before payment in full has been made the purchaser holds the proceeds of sale in trust for YOCS and must pay them into a separate designated bank account clearly identifiable as a trust account for the benefit of YOCS. Where sale proceeds are paid into such an account the obligation to pay the purchase price for the goods is discharged to the extent of such payment.*

Under ss 17 and 18 of the Sale of Goods Act 1979 (see **15.2.2** above), property in specific goods normally passes to the buyer when the contract is made, whilst property in unascertained goods (as where the goods have to be selected from a bulk) will occur when such goods are unconditionally appropriated to the contract. Most often this will occur on delivery of the goods to the buyer (*Carlos Federspiel v Charles Twigg* [1957] 1 Lloyd's Rep 240). There is, however, a large body of case law on attempts by sellers to reserve title to themselves even after delivery, and these cases require careful examination.

The first such case was *Aluminium Industrie Vaassen BV v Romalpa Aluminium Ltd* [1976] 2 All ER 552, where the contract had been translated into English from a Dutch original. That case concerned the supply of strips of aluminium. Title was not to pass until the goods had been paid for in full. If the buyers used the strips in the creation of anything else, ie if they processed them into other objects consisting partly of aluminium and partly of other things, then the ownership of the new objects was to be transferred to the buyers as security for payment of the purchase price, the buyers holding the mixed goods as 'fiduciary owners' for the sellers. The buyers were given an express right to sell the mixed goods, but so long as they had not fully discharged their indebtedness to the plaintiffs they were required, on request, to assign to the sellers the benefit of any claim which they might have against the persons to whom they had sold them. At the time when a receiver was appointed to the company, quantities of unprocessed aluminium strips were held by the company. There was also £35,000 held in a separate account and representing the proceeds of sale of mixed goods. The sellers claimed both the strips and the £35,000. The claim for the strips does not appear to have been disputed, and it is hard to see how it could have been, for these strips fulfilled all the practical requirements of an effective retention of title – they were in their original condition, they were readily identifiable and they could easily be repossessed. The question of the £35,000 was much more difficult. There is no general principle that a purchaser of goods who has not paid for them holds them as agent or bailee for the vendor, but in this case the Court of Appeal was able to fix on the fact that the contract expressly required the purchaser to hold the goods as 'fiduciary owner'. This phrase, apparently a translation from the Dutch, is not familiar to English lawyers, but the Court of Appeal held that it must be construed as creating a relationship of agency and bailment between the parties. As one of the fiduciary duties of an agent is to account to his principal for the proceeds of sale of goods sold under the agency, it followed that those proceeds were the property of the sellers, who could trace them and recover them in priority to other creditors of the buyers.

Romalpa was a case of immense importance, but it is necessary to be clear what was not in issue in it. The question of recovering goods after they had been mixed with others did not arise, neither did the question of tracing proceeds of sale into mixed funds or the question of claiming goods purchased with the proceeds of sale of the original goods. The subsequent cases in this area have addressed some of these issues.

The second case was *Re Bond Worth Ltd* [1979] 3 All ER 919. This concerned synthetic fibre supplied to the buyers, who used it in the manufacture of carpets. Under the contract of sale the risk in the property passed to the buyers on delivery, but equitable and beneficial ownership of the goods was to remain with the sellers until full payment had been made for all fibre supplied to date, or until prior resale of the fibre. In the event of resale the sellers' beneficial entitlement was to attach to the proceeds of sale; in addition, if the fibre was converted into, or became a constituent of, other products, the sellers were to have equitable and beneficial ownership of the proceeds of sale of those other products (though there was no attempt to give the sellers any title to the products themselves).

The buyers processed the fibre (with other fibres) into yarn, which was in turn processed and woven into carpets. The buyers became insolvent, owing the sellers some £587,000. The buyers were then in possession of yarn made from fibre, some, but not all, of which had been paid for, and of fibre and yarn from elsewhere. The sellers claimed to trace their title into the stocks of yarn held by the buyers and into the proceeds of sale of the carpets into which it had been incorporated. It was, of course, quite impossible to separate the fibre from the yarn and carpets in which it was now contained. The attempt to claim title over the yarn was therefore bound to fail, since a finding that the title remained in the sellers would have led to insuperable problems of enforcement. However, Slade J rejected the sellers' contentions altogether on a more broadly-based ground. It is to be observed that the sellers in this case did not purport to reserve the legal title to the goods – an important factual distinction between this case and *Romalpa*. Thus, it was clear that the legal title did pass. Although the contract purported to reserve equitable title, there was no doubt that the buyers were entitled to sell and/or process the fibre which they had bought. When they subsequently sold it they did so as principals, keeping any surplus over the purchase price and having to make good any deficit. Thus, again unlike *Romalpa*, they could not be said to be selling the goods as agents or bailees for the sellers. Consequently, Slade J held that the only possible interpretation of the contract between the parties was that the buyers were required to grant to the sellers a charge over the goods which had been transferred to them. This was a charge over a floating class of assets, since the charge did not prevent the buyers from dealing with the assets in the course of their business. However, floating charges over the assets of a limited company are void against a receiver or liquidator if not duly registered. This charge had not been registered, of course, since the sellers were quite unaware that it was in fact a charge. Accordingly the sellers' claim failed.

The third case in this area was *Borden (UK) Ltd v Scottish Timber Products Ltd* [1979] 3 All ER 961 CA. Here, the subject matter of the contract of sale was resin, which the buyers then incorporated into chipboard. In practice, resin supplied under this contract was normally processed in this way within two days of its receipt. The contract of sale contained a simple reservation of title clause, without any attempt to deal with the proceeds of sale or the ownership of goods into which the resin was incorporated. When the buyers went into insolvent liquidation the sellers claimed the proceeds of sale of the chipboard (there being no separate resin left) on the basis that the chipboard was subject to a charge in their favour and that they could therefore trace into the proceeds of sale (at first instance they also claimed ownership of the chipboard, but this claim was decided against them by the judge and they did not pursue it in the Court of Appeal – see *per* Buckley LJ at 964f). The Court of Appeal rejected the sellers' claim. It was held that the resin remained the property of the sellers so long as it existed in a separate identifiable form, but no longer. In other words, the reservation of title ceased to be effective when the resin was incorporated into the chipboard. There was nothing in the contract between the parties to justify the conclusion, reached by the judge of first instance, that the buyers were required to provide substituted security in the form of a charge over the chipboard, neither was there any relationship of agency or bailment between the parties such as would justify the imposition of a fiduciary duty on the buyers to account to the sellers for the proceeds of sale of the chipboard. This conclusion could be reached by looking at the arrangement between the parties. It was never contemplated that the resin would be returned to the sellers, so the relationship was obviously not one of bailment, and any sale or processing of the resin by the buyers was for the buyers' own account, since they took any profit and bore any loss. The Court also observed (though this was not a necessary part of the decision) that any charge which had been created over the chipboard would have been subject to the Companies Act rules on registration, and would therefore have been void against the receiver. The Court also queried the possibility of tracing into mixed goods where the original goods have lost their character as a result of being incorporated into something new.

The next case to come before the courts in this area was *Re Peachdart* [1983] 3 All ER 204. This concerned the sale of leather to be used in the manufacture of handbags. Under the retention of title clause, payment became due on delivery and the sellers had the right to resell the goods as soon as payment was overdue. In addition, the contract purported to reserve title in any finished products made from the leather until payment in full, and to create a fiduciary relationship between the parties allowing the sellers to trace the proceeds of sale of such items in the hands of the buyers. When the buyers went into insolvent liquidation they had some unused leather, some partially completed handbags, some finished handbags and the proceeds of sale of some others. The sellers claimed title to all these. Vinelott J reached the conclusion that the buyers were not bailees and that title to the leather could not remain with the sellers after the time when the buyers began the process of turning the leather into handbags. Instead the sellers merely had a charge on the goods (and subsequently the proceeds of sale) after that point. The inevitable consequence of this was that the charge was void for want of registration. This result is at first sight surprising, since, as the judge admitted, it disregards the express provision of the contract that the title was to 'remain' with the seller. There is an obvious difficulty in applying the purported retention of title clause to cases where the goods have entirely changed their identity, but it may well be argued that this does not happen where leather is processed into a handbag, the only additions being a minimal amount of thread and a few metal accessories. It is hard to avoid the conclusion that the judge was unduly influenced by the arguments as to the practical difficulties of giving effect to the contract, especially in relation to the proceeds of sale, where the express creation of a fiduciary relationship appears to have been ignored.

In *Hendy Lennox (Industrial Engines) Ltd v Grahame Puttick Ltd* [1984] 2 All ER 152 the sellers supplied diesel engines to the buyers, who incorporated them into diesel generating sets and sold them on. The engines remained at all times identifiable by their serial number and were capable of being removed from the generating sets. There was a retention of title clause under which the sellers were entitled to repossess the goods if payment was overdue, but, in contrast with *Re Peachdart Ltd*, payment was not due until the end of the month following the month of supply. When they went into receivership the buyers had three such engines on their premises, two of which had been incorporated into generating sets. After the commencement of the receivership all three engines were delivered to sub-buyers as part of generating sets. The sellers claimed part of the proceeds of sale of the generating sets on the basis that, immediately before the delivery of the generating sets to the sub-buyers, they had been entitled to assert a proprietary right to the engines. Staughton J held that the sellers were not entitled to possession of engines delivered to the buyers until the expiry of the credit period (although the engines remained their property). Property in the two engines already incorporated into generating sets passed to the sub-buyers before the sellers were ever entitled to retake possession, and the sellers could not maintain a claim for the proceeds of sale. However, the sellers did have a valid claim to the proceeds of sale of the third engine, since they had had a valid claim to possession of it immediately before it was delivered to the sub-buyers.

A separate question then arose whether the buyers were obliged to keep the proceeds of sale of this engine in a separate account for the benefit of the sellers. This turned on a question considered in some of the cases discussed above, namely, whether there was a fiduciary relationship between the parties. Staughton J held that bailment relationships do not automatically give rise to fiduciary obligations (though it may well be accurate to say that they normally do so). In the present case the determining factor was that the contract of sale provided an alternative remedy for the sellers, namely, repossessing the goods. This must be considered as excluding any fiduciary obligation in respect of the proceeds of sale. In this way the case could be regarded as materially different from *Romalpa*. It is difficult to see why this conclusion necessarily follows from the availability of the right to possession. There are in cases of this kind various ways in which the buyers might default on their obligations. One is by not paying for the goods while retaining them, whilst another is selling the goods without having paid for them. The simplest and best argument for having two different remedies is that these two situations require different remedies in order to protect the position of the seller.

In *Re Andrabell Ltd* [1984] 3 All ER 407, the sellers supplied travel bags to the buyers, who resold them to consumers. Payment was due 45 days after delivery, and property was not to pass until payment had been made. The buyers resold the bags, paid the proceeds into their general bank account, and went into liquidation without paying the sellers for the bags. As the buyers no longer had the bags, the only question before the court was whether the buyers were accountable to the sellers for the proceeds of sale. The sellers sought to rely on the fiduciary relationship which, they said, normally arose in cases of bailment and agency. Peter Gibson J rejected the sellers' claim, holding that no fiduciary obligation existed. The buyers were not agents for the sellers, since they resold the bags for their own account and the contract contained no provision requiring the bags to be stored separately or the proceeds of sale to be kept separately. It was to be implied from the 45-day credit period that the buyers were entitled to use the proceeds of sale as they saw fit during that time. This case is of some considerable importance, for the kind of contract which was in issue in it is a very common one – probably much more common than some of the elaborately drafted contracts encountered in the other cases discussed in this section. What the case shows is that in a simple sale of goods contract of this kind, the retention of title clause is for all practical purposes useless once the goods have been resold, for the goods cannot be reclaimed from the sub-buyer (Sale of Goods Act 1979, s 25) and there is no proprietary claim to the proceeds of sale.

In *Clough Mill Ltd v Martin* [1984] 3 All ER 982, CA, the substance in question was yarn, and there was an elaborately drafted retention of title clause which purported to give the sellers ownership of any mixed goods in which the yarn came to be incorporated. When the buyers went into receivership, a dispute arose about unused yarn still in their possession. It is to be noted that the sellers made no attempt to exert rights over yarn which had been incorporated into other products (despite the wording of the clause), and indeed it is difficult to see how they could have done so in the light of the decision in *Borden*, discussed above, for any rights over the mixed goods would surely have been a charge. The Court of Appeal held that their retention of title over the unused yarn was effective as between sellers and buyers, and did not amount to the creation of a charge. The buyers could not be considered to have granted a charge over the goods since they had never had title to them. A further point in this case concerned the exercise by an unpaid seller of a right to possession of the goods under the contract of sale. The Court of Appeal said that in such circumstances the seller may only sell enough of the goods to discharge the unpaid purchase price; if he sells more, he is accountable to the buyer for any surplus.

The next case in this group is *Armour v Thyssen Edelstahlwerke AG* [1990] 3 All ER 481, HL (In the interim there had been a few other cases of lesser importance: see *Pfeiffer v Arbuthnot* (1987) 3 BCC 608; *Tatung v Galex Telesure Ltd* (1989) 5 BCC 325; *Specialist Plant Services Ltd v Braithwaite* (1987) 3 BCC 119.) The *Armour* case holds remarkable echoes of *Romalpa*, for it too concerned steel strips, which the sellers supplied under a contract containing a retention of title clause. The case concerned only the unused steel in the hands of the buyers. The House of Lords held that the retention of title clause was effective to make this steel the property of the sellers. The case may at first sight appear straightforward, but its significance for English law is greatly obscured by the fact that it is a Scottish case, where the decision turned on the principle of Scots law (but not English law) that it is impossible to create a charge over a chattel without giving possession of that chattel to the chargee. The House of Lords was able to hold that the principle had no application in the present case because no charge had been created, the property never having been transferred to the buyer.

Two more recent cases, which may conveniently be taken together, have added a further twist to this area of the law. The cases are *Modelboard Ltd v Outer Box Ltd* [1993] BCLC 623 (Nicholas Hart QC) and *Compaq Computer Ltd v Abercorn Group Ltd* [1993] BCLC 602 (Millett J). In both cases there was a retention of title clause, a clause under which the purchaser acknowledged that it held goods as bailee for the seller until they were paid for, a clause making goods produced by the application of any process to the contract goods also the property of the seller and a clause requiring the purchaser to hold the proceeds of sale on trust for the seller. There was also a separate clause requiring the purchaser to pay for the goods within 30 days of the end of the month in which they were supplied to the purchaser. This particular combination of clauses had not appeared in any of the previous cases, and the result reached in these two cases is perhaps surprising. In both it was held that the clauses created charges on the goods, which charges were void for non-registration. The reason for this conclusion lies in the clause requiring payment of the purchase price. It was necessary to consider the relationship between this clause and the retention of title provisions, especially the requirement that the proceeds of sale be held in trust. It was rightly pointed out that the seller could not expect to receive both the purchase price and the proceeds of sale; consequently, the trust of the proceeds of sale must be capable of being defeated by payment of the purchase price. On this basis the true relationship was that there was merely a charge on the proceeds of sale, rather than a trust, and the charge was of course registrable. It should be observed that these arguments do not apply to the actual retention of title in goods still held by the purchaser in their original state. So far as these were concerned, the retention of title was still effective.

These 10 cases taken together present a somewhat confusing picture of the law in this area. However, it is submitted that a number of simple propositions may be derived from them, as follows:

(a) A clause reserving legal and equitable ownership to the seller until payment of the purchase price (whether for this consignment or for all consignments) is effective as between seller and buyer. Consequently, an unpaid seller remains the owner of the goods and can assert his ownership against the buyer and, in the event of the receivership or liquidation of the buyer, against the buyer's other creditors. In practice this right can be enforced only if the goods are clearly identifiable as being the seller's goods and are in their original condition.

(b) A claim by the seller to the proceeds of sale of goods which have been sold without being paid for faces formidable difficulties. In the absence of a clause imposing a fiduciary obligation or an obligation to keep the proceeds of sale in a separate account, it is unlikely that the court will be prepared to find the existence of such an obligation – the buyer cannot normally be regarded as bailee of the goods since there is no intention that he should redeliver them to his seller, neither is he usually the seller's agent since any resale will be for the buyer's account not the seller's account. The difficulties inherent in the bailment and agency analysis mean that courts will be reluctant to give full effect to fiduciary obligation clauses even where they are encountered. The presence of a trust clause is likely to be insufficient where there is also an express obligation to pay the purchase price within a specified time. Indeed, it might be argued that trust clauses will always be ineffective, since payment of the purchase price will always be at least an implied obligation.

(c) The seller will almost never be entitled to assert his title to the goods, even if they are in their original form, against a sub-buyer. This follows from s 25 of the Sale of Goods Act 1979, which allows a buyer in possession to give a good title to a sub-buyer notwithstanding that he himself has no title to the goods. The only exception to this occurs where the sub-buyer does not act in good faith, or where he has reason to be aware that his seller has no title to the goods.

(d) Once the buyer has begun processing the goods into something else or incorporating them into mixed goods, the seller's reservation of title is for all practical purposes ineffective, even though the manufacturing process has not been completed.

(e) Any attempt to make a claim on the finished goods, or on the proceeds of sale thereof, is likely to be treated as creating a charge on the goods. This will be a floating charge and will be void against the liquidator or receiver of the company unless registered at Companies House. Since in practice such charges are never registered, the seller will have no effective protection in these circumstances.

In applying these principles to the clause used by YOCS in its standard contract of sale, it can be seen that a further refinement has been introduced in an effort to deal with the point identified in *Modelboard Ltd v Outer Box Ltd*. The clause does now specifically remove the obligation to pay the purchase price once the proceeds of sale have been paid into a trust account, and it may be that this will be effective to allow the clause to operate as a reservation of title rather than as a charge. There should in any event be no difficulty in cases where Great Expectations Ltd is still in possession of the original goods – YOCS will be entitled to repossess them, and it can be seen that an express right to enter Great Expectations Ltd's premises for the purpose has been included (though Great Expectations Ltd might be able to render this useless by storing the goods on someone else's premises). It may be noted that this clause says nothing about what happens where goods supplied under the contract are incorporated or processed into other goods. Although such a clause is often encountered, it would be inappropriate in the present case, given that the goods supplied are antiques, which will be neither processed nor incorporated.

15.3.3 Deposits

Where advance deposits are taken from customers, problems can arise where there is a delay in doing the work, where the work is not done to a satisfactory standard, or where the company taking the deposits goes into receivership or liquidation without doing the work. These situations require to be treated separately.

Where there is delay in doing the work, the client may seek to cancel the contract and to recover the deposit. In such cases the first question is whether the company is in breach of any legal obligation. Section 14 of the Supply of Goods and Services Act 1982 implies into a contract for services an obligation to carry out the work within a reasonable time. Since Great Expectations Ltd clearly does provide services under its contracts with clients, this section is in principle applicable. However, it is to be noted that it applies only where the contract contains no provision for determining the time at or by which the service is to be provided. It is unlikely that a company such as Great Expectations Ltd would wish to tie itself down to a specific date for completing work, not least since this might in some cases be dependent on its ability to obtain materials from its own suppliers. Consequently, it is first necessary to ask whether Great Expectations Ltd is guilty of not completing the work within a reasonable time. The notion of reasonable time is not further defined within the Act, and the application of the section in any case must therefore be a question of fact.

If it is determined that there has been unreasonable delay, the next question is as to the consequence of that delay. The Supply of Goods and Services Act 1982 merely states that the obligation to do the work within a reasonable time is a term of the contract; it gives no guidance as to whether it is to be treated as a condition or a warranty. Although there is no authority on the point, it is submitted that the proper way of dealing with this section is to treat the obligation which it imposes as an innominate term, ie a term the breach of which may or may not give rise to a right to terminate the contract according to the effects of the breach (see *Hong Kong Fir Shipping Co Ltd v Kawasaki Kisen Kaisha Ltd* [1962] 2 QB 26). This approach prevents clients from terminating for relatively minor delay (though it would still entitle them to damages) but allows termination where the delay is very lengthy. In the event of a relatively minor breach, the effect would be that the client would be entitled to deduct an appropriate amount from the final cost, but would not be entitled immediately to claim the return of his deposit. In the event of a breach serious enough to be treated as a breach of condition, the client would be entitled to terminate the contract and thereupon to reclaim the deposit, as well as suing for damages for any further loss caused by the breach.

Similar considerations apply when the work is done but not to a satisfactory standard. Here the relevant statutory provision is s 13 of the Supply of Goods and Services Act 1982, which implies an obligation to do the work to a reasonable standard. This section applies only where the contract contains no provision for determining the appropriate standard. Again, the obligation is merely defined as a term, but it is again submitted that the appropriate approach is to treat it as an innominate term. On this basis the consequences of breach would be the same as those applicable to a breach of the obligation to do the work within a reasonable time.

Where the company goes into liquidation or receivership without doing the work, the position is more complicated. Clients will no doubt wish to claim that the money they have deposited with the company remains their property, so that they are entitled to assert a proprietary right to it in priority to unsecured creditors. An argument of this kind may succeed where the money has been kept in a separate, designated account, but the more usual situation will be that the company has simply mixed the deposits with its ordinary funds, probably paying them into its general bank account (which is likely to be overdrawn anyway). This is strong evidence that the deposits were not intended to remain the property of the clients, who will therefore not be able to recover them. In theory of course they would have a contractual right to recover the deposit once it became apparent that the work would not be done, but they will be merely unsecured creditors of the company and will therefore have no realistic prospect of enforcing that right.

15.3.4 Factoring

Factoring involves assigning the debts owed to the company by clients to a third party in return for an immediate payment of an amount less than the full amount of the debt. The discount in effect represents the fee which the factoring house charges for the service of providing immediate payment and taking on the responsibility of debt collection. Factoring can have substantial beneficial effects on a company's cash flow. Most small companies such as Great Expectations Ltd have an overdraft in addition to the bank loan which originally finances the business, and in view of the high cost of overdrafts, together with the degree of influence this gives to a bank over a company's affairs, schemes for reducing the level of the overdraft are attractive to many small companies.

English law recognises the right to recover on a debt as a species of property, usually referred to as a *chose in action*. Being property, it can readily be assigned to another, and the process of assignment is now regularised and regulated by s 136 of the Judicature Act 1925. This allows the assignee of a written assignment of a debt to sue the debtor directly, provided that notice of the assignment has been given to the debtor. In practice it is possible to give such notice at the same time as making a formal demand for payment of the debt.

15.4 Advice to the parties

This chapter has considered some of the ways in which the interests of different creditors in a company may be protected. A fundamental distinction which emerges from it is that between loan creditors, ie those who have explicitly lent money to the company and have been able to obtain security for that loan, and trade creditors, who have supplied goods and/or services to the company on credit, who have not yet been paid, and who have no effective security unless, in the case of suppliers of goods, they have been able to incorporate effective retention of title clauses into their contracts with the company. Generally speaking, loan creditors are likely to be in a much stronger position than trade creditors. Indeed, it is fair to say that trade creditors generally have no control over the way in which the company is managed, whereas loan creditors often have rights in the loan contract which entitle them to receive regular accounts of the company.

Lastly, it is important to be aware of the relationship between the different techniques of creditor protection discussed in this chapter. It has been seen that Great Expectations Ltd frequently buys goods under contracts which contain retention of title clauses. This is likely to mean that at any given time much of its stock-in-trade does not belong to it. A consequence of this ought to be that the bank is unwilling to make a loan backed by a floating charge on the stock-in-trade, since such a charge can obviously not apply to goods which do not belong to the company. In practice, however, this does not appear to be treated as a serious problem by banks.

A similar problem ought to arise in relation to floating charges on the book debts. It will be recalled that the company makes extensive use of factoring, and the natural consequence of this is to reduce significantly the level of book debts. Again, this should make it more difficult to obtain a floating charge secured on those debts.

In an ideal world it would be possible to advise the company to deal with these various problems by paying for goods more rapidly and, perhaps, by persuading debtors to pay more rapidly, thereby reducing the need for factoring. Unfortunately, this advice would be wholly unrealistic for the great majority of small companies, and Great Expectations Ltd is no exception.

FURTHER READING

A Walters, 'Priority of the floating charge in corporate insolvency: *Griffiths v Yorkshire Bank plc*' (1995) 16 Co Law 291.

DM Hare and D Milman, 'Debenture holders and judgment creditors – problems of priority' [1982] LMCLQ 57.

A Hicks, '*Romalpa* is dead' (1992) 13 Co Law 217.

16 Profit Distribution

LEARNING OUTCOMES

By the end of this chapter, you should understand:

- the issue of dividend payment;

- the concept of distributable profits;

- the concept of prudence;

- breaches of the distribution rules;

- circumventing the distribution rules.

SCENARIO

Great Expectations Ltd has become moderately profitable. The audited accounts for the year ending 31 December 2002 show a profit of £80,000. The accounts are reproduced as **Appendix E**. The question arises, what is to be done with this profit? The directors have proposed that the entire amount should be distributed by way of dividend.

As usual, the suggestion is proving controversial. Duncan would like to see the company making more profit, because he relies on the dividends to finance his involvement with steam trains, but he retains enough business acumen to believe that it would be better to retain some profit within the company to invest for the future. He is also aware that the figure of £80,000 includes a significant item for work-in-progress, for which the company has not yet been paid, and that the high level of stocks held by the company means that there is nothing like enough cash within the company to finance a dividend of these proportions. This point has also been forcibly made by the company's auditors, in discussion with the directors.

Edwina, on the other hand, is short of cash, and wants to take the maximum amount of profit from the company without delay. She is disappointed that only £80,000 is available for distribution. She proposes that the company, which has been able to reduce its reliance on its overdraft (though the debentures in favour of the bank and of Duncan remain), should ask the bank for a fresh loan in order to pay twice this amount. If this is considered unacceptable, Edwina has an alternative scheme. She points out that the company holds considerable stocks of design and decoration materials. She proposes that these be sold to Great Expectations (Ideas) Ltd at a substantial profit. Interim accounts for the period January–March 2003 will then be prepared, showing this profit, which will immediately be distributed to shareholders.

OVERVIEW

This chapter deals primarily with problems relating to dividend payments. Dividends are an essential part of the mechanism of company law. They are the means by which shareholders obtain a return on the money which they have invested in the company. Dividends are declared on the company's shares at the rate of so much per share. In this way the return received by shareholders is proportionate to their original investment. However, a company does not have complete freedom in deciding how much to distribute by way of dividend.

The first point is that there are legal restrictions on a company's freedom to make distributions of its assets. In particular, only realised profits may be distributed. It is therefore necessary to decide in each case how much profit the company has in fact made. The rules on this topic are contained in Pt VIII of the Companies Act 1985. In the present situation the matter is made more complicated because schemes have been proposed which are aimed at artificially increasing the amount of profit.

A second difficulty is that the directors of a company must also consider how much profit can prudently be distributed. A distribution which is not forbidden by the Companies Act may still be imprudent, and it is part of the directors' duties to act in the best interests of the company in this matter, as in all others.

A third point arises from the debentures held by the bank and by Duncan. It is usual to insert in such debentures provisions restricting the company's freedom to distribute profits. Often the drafting of these restrictions merely mirrors the legal restrictions under the Companies Act, but in some cases more severe limitations are found.

If the shareholders do decide that a dividend should be declared, it will be necessary to ensure that the correct procedures are complied with to make the declaration a lawful one.

From a procedural point of view various other questions arise as to how any breaches of the company law rules here can be restrained or redressed.

16.1 Distributable profits

16.1.1 History

The rules relating to the distributability of profits are contained in Pt VIII of the Companies Act 1985. Historically, these rules originated in a concern to prevent the return of the company's capital to shareholders, a process which was thought to prejudice creditors and to be inconsistent with the notion of the company as an ongoing entity (though it may be noted that the lack of minimum capital requirements for private companies significantly reduces the practical value of this point; see also **Chapter 4**). This rationale underlies many of the 19th-century decisions in this area (*Guinness v Land Corporation of Ireland* (1882) 22 ChD 349, CA; *In Re Oxford Benefit, Building and Investment Society* (1887) 35 ChD 502, Kay J; *In Re Alexandra Palace Company* (1882) 21 ChD 149, Fry J).

Such returns of capital are now permitted, subject to the rules in ss 135–137 of the Companies Act 1985, but the Pt VIII rules still serve as a means of preventing evasions of those requirements. The Companies Act 1980 strengthened the restrictions. Before that time the only prohibition was on making distributions out of capital, but the 1980 Act required that distributions be made only out of profits available for the purpose. This represents an important additional restriction on a company's freedom to distribute its assets. Under the old rules the only requirement was to keep in the company a sum representing the paid-up capital. In many companies this is a very small amount – Great Expectations Ltd has a paid-up capital of only £4,000, and the retention of this sum would do little or nothing to protect creditors. The new requirements go further by requiring distributions to be based on properly prepared accounts, and thus to take note of whether profits have been realised or not, as well as of future and contingent liabilities. Any distribution of a company's assets will be a distribution for these purposes, unless it is an issue of bonus shares, a purchase of the company's own shares out of capital, a reduction of capital under s 135 of the Companies Act 1985 or a distribution in the course of a winding up (s 263(2)). These matters are excluded from Pt VIII because they are subject to their own special rules, contained elsewhere in the Companies Act. The most common case of a distribution is of course the payment of a dividend, but the above definition shows that many other events may be distributions, including transactions at an undervalue. Where such transactions involve directors, they may be subject to s 320 of the Companies Act 1985 (see **Chapter 10**). However, the Pt VIII rules apply only to distributions to shareholders (s 263(1)). Improper distributions to non-shareholders may give rise to a constructive trust (*Re Aveling Barford Ltd* [1989] BCLC 626).

16.1.2 Profits available for the purpose

Part VIII of the 1985 Act also gives a somewhat restrictive definition of 'profits available for the purpose'. It is therefore necessary to examine this definition in some detail. Section 263(3) of the Companies Act 1985 provides that:

> A company's profits available for distribution are its accumulated, realised profits, so far as not previously utilised by distribution or capitalisation, less its accumulated realised losses, so far as not previously written off in a reduction or reorganisation of capital duly made.

The first point to be noted is that this definition is seriously defective, in that it does not define 'profit' (or 'loss') at all. The distributable profits are defined by reference to a concept of realisation of profits and losses, but no guidance is given on what is meant by profit or loss. This is a very difficult issue, for the matter is one on which there is no general agreement among either lawyers or accountants. A much quoted definition of profit is that given by Fletcher Moulton LJ in *Re Spanish Prospecting Co Ltd* [1911] 1 Ch 92, CA.

> 'Profits' implies a comparison between the state of the business at two specific dates usually separated by an interval of a year. The fundamental meaning is the amount of gain made by the business during the year. This can only be assessed by a comparison of the assets of the business at the two dates... If the total assets of the business at the two dates be compared, the increase which they show at the later date as compared with the earlier date (due allowance of course being made for any capital introduced into or taken out of the business in the meanwhile) represents in strictness the profits of the business during the period in question.

It is to be noted that at the present day the comparison implied in this passage is not always done on an annual basis. Although companies are required to prepare accounts only once a year, it is common to prepare them more often as an aid to managerial decision making. References in the passage to profits may be taken as applying equally to losses, if the assets at the later date happen to be less then those at the earlier date. Similarly, references to assets must include references to outstanding liabilities of the business.

Although this definition is in many ways a helpful one, it still glosses over all the important and difficult questions which are encountered when trying to calculate the profit made by a business. These questions concern the valuation of the assets and liabilities which are being compared. There are difficult questions about, for example, the valuation which should be placed on any stock which the company holds, the valuation of any work-in-progress, the value to be attributed to any land or buildings which the company owns. The 2002 accounts of Great Expectations Ltd include items for stock and work-in-progress and (though not for land and buildings, since the company merely leases its business premises and owns no other real property). It is normal to value stock at the lower of cost and market value at the accounting date. Whilst cost can readily be ascertained, market value is less easy to establish. It may also fluctuate according to market conditions, so that the figure shown in the accounts may rapidly come to be out of date. Similar problems arise in relation to liabilities. Where contractual liabilities have already been incurred, the matter is relatively easy, though even here problems can arise, but in other cases the extent (and even the existence) of future liabilities may be in doubt. The 2002 accounts of Great Expectations Ltd include a provision of £25,000, which was originally set aside in 2001. This arises from legal proceedings in which the company is being sued by a former client who claims that the company negligently executed a contract for the design and decoration of the interior of his office. Although the litigation is still proceeding, the directors of Great Expectations Ltd believe that the company will ultimately have to pay compensation, and their best estimate of the total amount of compensation and legal costs is £25,000. However, this is necessarily an estimate and may prove to be either too large or too small. This item is included in the accounts because the directors are satisfied that the amount involved can be ascertained with reasonable accuracy. If the amount could not be estimated because of uncertainty over either liability or quantum, the correct course would be to classify the liability as a contingency and to include a note in the accounts to that effect, but not to include any item in the profit and loss account or in the balance sheet. It is clear that liabilities must be included when calculating the profit, and the figure at which they are estimated will obviously have an impact on the eventual profit or loss. These various difficulties in valuation of assets are all the subject of considerable discussion and controversy among accountants, though in a number of cases accounting rules have been devised which provide at least a clear answer, if not necessarily always a very satisfactory one.

In relation to these questions of ongoing valuation, it should also be noted that in practice the financial creditors (ie the bank) will often insist on receiving regular management accounts, which will enable them to monitor the level of stock-in-trade and/or book debts (for other aspects of the bank's role, see **Chapter 12**).

16.1.3 Profits and realised profits

The statement in s 263(3), that only realised profits may be distributed implies that there is a difference between 'profits' and 'realised profits'. The nature of this difference is far from clear. One situation dealt with in the Companies Act is that of a profit generated by a revaluation of the company's fixed assets. Accountants regard such a profit as one which can properly be included in the accounts, but the Companies Act provides that such a profit is not normally distributable (s 275(1), subject to the exception in s 275(2)). If any more general meaning is to be given to the word 'realised' in the present context, it must be that a profit is realised when it is convertible into money, or into an asset convertible into money at a price which can be ascertained with reasonable certainty. This is a much narrower definition than that commonly used by accountants, and would largely rule out the inclusion of any work-in-progress, which clearly conflicts with established accounting principles (Financial Reporting Standards, FRS 18 and FRS 5; see also **Chapter 14**). It is also relevant to note that the 1980 and 1981 Companies Acts were intended to bring the accounting definitions of profit more or less into line with the legal definitions, and this narrow view of realised profit is certainly inconsistent with that aim. Perhaps the best view, in a very uncertain area, is that, save where the statute otherwise provides – as in s 275 – profit is recognised for distributability purposes when it is realised, realisation being determined according to accounting principles, which are discussed below.

16.1.4 Generally accepted accounting principles

The rule that only realised profits may be counted when calculating the amount available for distribution gives rise to many difficulties. The question whether a profit is realised for these purposes depends upon whether it is treated as realised according to 'generally accepted accounting principles' (Companies Act 1985, Sch 4, para 90). Unfortunately, it is often difficult to establish what those principles are, or how they operate in a given case. This results from the curious fact that there is no generally accepted definition of 'realised profit' in use among accountants. Indeed, the concept of realisation has provoked substantial debate among accountants (see **Further Reading**, below). The uncertainty is particularly acute in relation to the artificial profit creation schemes which Edwina is suggesting in the present case, and which are considered below.

16.1.5 The accruals basis

As a general rule it may be said that the realisation of profit is dealt with according to what accountants call the 'accruals' basis. This means that a sum is treated as received, and any resulting profit as realised, once the company is legally entitled to it. It is partly for this reason (and partly for reasons connected with taxation) that work-in-progress must be recognised in the annual accounts and is counted towards the year's profit (this rule does not apply to traders who are allowed to prepare their accounts on the cash basis, ie treating money as received only when they actually get the cash, but a company providing services, such as Great Expectations Ltd, would not in practice be allowed to use the cash basis). Obviously, one consequence of this is that profit may be treated as earned, and thus available for distribution, before the company has received the cash involved. This helps to explain why, in some cases, including the present one, the company's profit for accounting purposes may exceed the amount of cash available to it. This point must of course be borne in mind when considering how much can prudently be distributed. Another oddity of the use of the accruals concept is that Sch 4 to the Companies Act 1985 requires accounts to be prepared on the basis of 'prudent' assumptions. Treating money as received when it is only owing is a practice which might well be regarded as less than prudent (money which is substantially overdue may well have to be written off in whole or in part as a bad debt), but the accruals concept is well established in accounting theory and practice.

In calculating the amount of distributable profit it is necessary to deduct any accumulated realised losses. This rule, which also dates from 1980, means that losses made in previous years must be made good before any profit can be distributed In this respect the 1980 Act overruled *Verner v General and Commercial Investment Trust* [1894] 2 Ch 239, CA. The amount of profit is to be determined according to the accounts of the company. All companies are required to prepare and file annual accounts, albeit that private companies may file abbreviated accounts (Companies Act 1985, s 235, as substituted by Companies Act 1989). The rules in relation to accounts generally are dealt within **Chapter 18**, and the most recent annual accounts are the starting point for the determination of distributable profits. If these accounts show profits, and those profits have not been fully distributed, then the balance may lawfully be distributed. This includes profits from previous years which have not already been distributed. This is the significance of the word 'accumulated' in the phrase 'accumulated realised profits'. If the most recent accounts do not show any profit, or if all the profit which they show has since been distributed, then the company may not make a distribution unless interim accounts are prepared. These accounts must relate to the period since the date of the last annual accounts, and any profit which they show will normally be available for distribution.

However, the relationship between profit as declared in the accounts and profit available for distribution under Pt VIII of the Companies Act 1985 is a problematic one. The present rules are derived in part from an EEC Directive, the Second Directive on Company Law (79/91/EEC), and it is generally thought that they were intended to make accounting profit and distributable profit the same thing (see **Further Reading**, below) . For the most part this has been done, but there are a number of respects in which the technicalities of the accounting rules may produce a different result. These areas include gains and losses on foreign currency transactions and depreciation of investment property.

In the present case two schemes have been proposed for the purpose of increasing the profits. Edwina's scheme is to borrow money. In some circumstances it is permissible to borrow money in order to pay a dividend (see **Further Reading**, below). This will be so where profits shown in the accounts are invested in assets, so that the company is short of cash. There is an element of that in this case. The company has only some £64,000 in the bank, though the profit figure is somewhat greater. It would therefore be permissible to borrow the other £16,000 to distribute as a dividend, assuming that the bank was prepared to make such a loan. It is another question entirely whether such a course of action would be prudent. The company, which is already heavily indebted, would acquire a very substantial overdraft, as well as depriving itself of all its cash, and it is most unlikely that this is in the best interests of the company, whether this is construed as meaning the existing or future shareholders, the employees or the creditors, or some mix of these groups. Edwina's scheme, however, goes even further than this. She wants to borrow enough to pay £160,000. This means a loan of £100,000. Even in the unlikely event of the bank agreeing to this, it is clear that the loan would not increase the distributable profits.

If the money is borrowed, the company will of course have extra cash, but this cash cannot properly be recorded in the accounts as a profit. Whilst the balance sheet will show an increase in the company's cash in hand, it will also be necessary to show that there is an increased debt in the amount of the loan. These items would be included in the balance sheet, the asset appearing under 'cash at bank' and the liability forming a new category of 'creditors due after more than one year', but there would be no impact on the profit and loss account. Thus, there will be no net increase in the profit, and it will not become possible to pay an enhanced dividend.

Edwina's alternative scheme is more complex. It seeks to take advantage of uncertainties over the concept of realisation in relation to profits. The most obvious case of a realised profit occurs where an asset is sold at a profit to a person unconnected with the company and cash is received in return. Under this scheme the sale would be to a subsidiary company of Great Expectations Ltd, so that the asset would remain within the group. It is to be remembered that the accounts which determine the amount of distributable profit are those of the individual company rather than those of the group of companies. This rule may be seen as an example of the strict application of the doctrine of corporate personality. It is unclear whether the veil might be pierced in order to prevent an apparently inappropriate reliance on the doctrine in these circumstances, in accordance with principles suggested in *DHN v Tower Hamlets* [1976] 1 WLR 852 (see **Chapter 8**). Auditors seem generally to assume that this is not a realistic possibility (see **Further Reading**, below), and it may therefore be suggested that this scheme is effective to increase the distributable profits of the parent company. There may, though, be a difficulty. If the assets are sold at more than their market price, this will effectively reduce the value of the net assets of the subsidiary company. The shares of the subsidiary company are of course owned by the parent company, and the value of those shares will be reduced in line with the reduction in the value of the net assets. This diminution in value should be reflected in the accounts of the parent company, where the shares of the subsidiary are shown as an asset. The diminution should then offset the profit gained by selling the assets in the first place, so that there will be no increase in the net profits. Clearly, this difficulty does not arise if the assets are sold for a fair market price. Curiously, the sale for fair market price is effective to increase the net profits even if the consideration does not immediately pass, since, as explained above at **16.1.5**, the accounting rules recognise the profit as realised once the company has a legal right to the money. This would create a situation in which it might be lawful for the company to borrow to finance the dividend. It is this version of the scheme which will have to be used in the present case. Unfortunately, this gives rise to a further difficulty. Although the subsidiary company appears to be marginally profitable, it does not have enough cash to buy more than a very small proportion of the parent company's stocks.

This scheme must also be considered against the background that the directors must act with prudence. If it appeared that the purchase price was never going to be paid, then it is most unlikely that the directors could justify using the realisation of this profit as the basis of a dividend. There is also the position of the subsidiary company to consider. This has the same directors as the parent company, but in their capacity as directors of the subsidiary Bill and Edwina must consider whether the scheme is in the best interest of that company. The proposal is in effect that the subsidiary should enter into a contractual commitment to buy the assets, knowing that it has no use for them and has no prospect of being able to acquire the funds to pay for them. It is submitted that they clearly cannot properly approve anything of the kind – to pay a dividend based on an asset whose value is at best doubtful cannot possibly be regarded as prudent. It may be noted in passing that this situation provides an example of another problem commonly encountered in groups of companies, namely, that individuals are directors of more than one company in the group, and may find themselves facing a conflict of interest between two or more companies. In the present case, as often happens, the point may be of only theoretical importance. As directors of the subsidiary company Bill and Edwina owe duties to that company, but only the shareholders can cause action to be taken to enforce those duties. The only shareholder is of course the parent company, which will not take action if Bill and Edwina act in accordance with its interests. The other group to be considered is made up of the creditors of the subsidiary company who might lose if these companies went into insolvent liquidation. A glance at the accounts shows, however, that this company has only negligible outstanding liabilities, so this too can be ignored for all practical purposes.

More elaborate versions of the scheme under discussion here are sometimes encountered, in which the purchase price does not actually pass between the two companies involved in the deal, or where the money is first lent by the seller to the purchaser. There is considerable controversy over the effectiveness of these schemes, but it is suggested that all are effective for distributable profits purposes (see **Further Reading**, below), subject to dealing properly in the accounts with the value of any interest in subsidiary companies, though in every case it would of course be for the directors to consider the questions examined at **16.2** below, namely, whether the schemes were in the best interests of the company and whether it would be prudent to distribute profit generated in this way.

16.2 The concept of prudence

The duty of the directors is to act *bona fide* in the best interests of the company (*Re Smith and Fawcett* [1942] Ch 304, *per* Lord Greene MR). Consequently, they will have to consider how much of the £160,000 can sensibly be distributed. Clearly, money which is retained within the company can be reinvested to produce further growth. If too much money is paid out, the company may begin to experience cash flow difficulties which, in an extreme case, could even push it into liquidation. Here the directors are under a certain amount of pressure from the shareholders. This creates a difficult dilemma for them. Although the *Bushell v Faith* clause in the Articles of Great Expectations Ltd is effective to protect at least Edwina from removal (see **Chapter 7**), they are naturally concerned to retain the goodwill of the members. At the same time, the duty to act prudently is imposed partly for the benefit of creditors of the company, and the directors must always remember that they may be personally liable if their incompetent or imprudent management causes the company to fail (Insolvency Act 1986, ss 212–214; see **Chapter 23**). In these circumstances it is no defence to say that they acted as instructed by the members, for the point will have been reached some time previously, where the company's financial difficulties make the interests of the creditors a significant factor in the balancing exercise which company directors must constantly perform.

16.3 Procedure

In the first instance it is for the directors to recommend how much should be distributed. This proposal must then be considered by the General Meeting, which may decide to distribute less than the directors have recommended, but may not decide to distribute a larger amount than that recommended (Table A, art 102). Once the General Meeting has resolved to pay a dividend, the sums concerned become a debt due from the company to the members (*Re Severn & Wye & Severn Bridge Railway Co* [1896] 1 Ch 559).

16.4 Breaches of the distribution rules

In the present case there is some danger that Great Expectations Ltd is going to pay more than the law allows. In this event a number of problems arise. Section 277 of the Companies Act 1985 allows the company to reclaim the dividend (or that part of it which was unlawful) from any shareholder who knew, or should have known, that the distribution was unlawful. This may result in all the excess payment being recovered, but depends upon the exact circumstances, since in some cases some or all of the shareholders may be able to plead that they had no reason to suspect that the dividend was improper. There is a further difficulty about the position where a shareholder has no reason to be aware of the unlawful nature of the distribution. Section 277 does not say that in such cases the shareholder comes under no duty to repay the dividend. Indeed, s 277(2) expressly provides that s 277(1) is without prejudice to any other rule of law which might require the repayment of the money. Thus, where the directors are aware of the unlawful character of the payment, but the shareholders are not (it is suggested that this will be a very rare situation, at least in the case of small private companies such as Great Expectations Ltd), the money will not be recoverable. Where the company declares the dividend under the influence of some misapprehension, the position will depend upon the nature of that misapprehension. If the misapprehension is as to a matter of law then the money will not be recoverable (*Bilbie v Lumley* (1802) 2 East 469); whereas if the money is paid under the influence of a mistake of fact, it will be recoverable (*Kelly v Solari* (1841) GM & W 54). Where the dividend is not fully recoverable, it may be necessary to investigate how the impropriety came about. It is possible that the accounts contain some error which the auditors should have detected. Although the company is in principle entitled to rely on the audited accounts, this applies only where those accounts have been properly prepared and show a true and fair view (Companies Act 1985, s 271). Alternatively, the accounts may be properly prepared but the directors may have misunderstood them, or, in extreme cases, may have wilfully decided to ignore them.

Where the unlawful dividend arises from the directors' error, it would appear that the directors may be personally liable to compensate the company, since they will have recommended a dividend which was not lawfully payable. This assumes that the directors have acted negligently. The directors' liability is of course more clearly established should they take the drastic step of ignoring the accounts. In those cases where the accounts are themselves defective, the directors may say that they relied upon the company's auditors in concluding that the dividend was payable. It is unclear whether this will avail them as a defence against the company: in principle they must take responsibility for the recommendation which they make, but a director's duty is only to act honestly, and to exercise such reasonable care and skill as is expected of a director in the particular situation and circumstances, and it may be that a court would not hold them liable if they had on this basis reasonably relied upon expert advice.

The more difficult issue here is whether the company can properly be said to have suffered a loss. It seems a strange use of language to say that a company which pays a lawful dividend thereby suffers a loss, although clearly it pays out money for no tangible return (there is perhaps an intangible return in the form of shareholder satisfaction). It is a matter of some controversy whether the same argument applies to the payment of an unlawful dividend. The element of shareholder satisfaction is likely to be the same, assuming that no action is taken to recover the dividend (and if the dividend is recovered, then any loss is thereby reversed), and the 'loss' to the company is the same in both cases. Of course, accepting this argument involves saying that the company cannot proceed against anyone other than the shareholders because it suffers no loss, and this seems a rather surprising conclusion. There is no authority on the point. It is unclear whether directors who were held liable in these circumstances (assuming such to be possible) could then proceed against the auditors on whom they had relied. Such a claim would have to be brought in tort, since the auditors are engaged by the company, to whom they owe their primary duty, and the directors do not have a contract with them; further, the decision of the House of Lords in *Caparo v Dickman* [1990] 1 All ER 568 would present a serious obstacle to such recovery – if the auditors are not liable to individual shareholders, to whom they do report, it is hard to see how they can be liable to directors, to whom they do not report. The matter has been further considered by the Court of Appeal in *McNaughton v Hicks* [1991] 1 All ER 134 and *Morgan Crucible Co plc v Hill Samuel Bank Ltd* [1991] 1 All ER 148. Although these cases impose some qualifications on the rule stated in *Caparo v Dickman*, the basic principle that the auditors owe their duties to the company is unaffected. It suggests that the auditors owe a duty only to the shareholders as a class, and thus not to the directors. Again, it seems unfair that auditors who have made mistakes in the accounts should escape liability, but it is argued on behalf of the auditors that the accounts are not their accounts but the directors' accounts, and it may be that this argument will prevail. The company's right to bring a claim against the auditors depends in any event upon deciding that a loss has been suffered. Even if this point can be met, there is still the question of who bears the responsibility for any errors in the accounts. The liability of the directors and the liability of the auditors ought to be considered together. Otherwise there is some danger of holding that the directors are not liable because they reasonably relied upon the auditors, but that the auditors are not liable to the company because the matter is not their responsibility.

A final point in this area is that a breach of duty by the directors is one which should not be regarded as capable of being ratified by the General Meeting. The main purpose of the distribution rules is creditor protection, and allowing ratification by the General Meeting would have the effect of enabling the directors to escape any sanction for a breach of duty at the instance of the principal beneficiaries of that breach, since an unlawful distribution is not in any event criminal, so that the only possible sanction is a claim on behalf of the company.

16.5 Circumventing the distribution rules

As has been shown, there are many uncertainties about the lawfulness of the proposed dividend. Indeed, there are many cases where it is by no means clear that a dividend can lawfully be declared, and others where it is clear that no dividend is possible because there is no profit. In such cases it may still be possible to take money out of the company. The payment of salaries to employees does not depend upon the existence of profits, and is therefore an alternative means of rewarding those involved with a company. In many small companies, where the shareholders are also the employees and the managers, this approach works well. In the present case, though, there are other problems. First, salaries can only be paid to employees in return for work done by them. Not all the shareholders of Great Expectations Ltd are employees of the company. Even if they were employees, it is usual to pay salaries in proportion to the work done by an individual, and this is of course not necessarily the same as payment in proportion to the shareholding, which is the result of declaring a dividend. So the payment of salaries will not in this case produce the desired result. A further problem is that the payment of salaries may be more expensive for the company. This is because employers who pay salaries must pay National Insurance Contributions on those salaries. Employees also pay National Insurance Contributions on the sums which they receive. No National Insurance Contributions are payable on dividends. This is naturally a strong incentive to small companies to distribute assets by way of dividend rather than by way of salary wherever possible. The dividend route is especially appropriate in the present case since Duncan is not employed by the company, though he is the principal shareholder.

16.6 Advice to the parties

Duncan has a majority shareholding, but he is not a director. The board of directors can recommend the declaration of a total dividend of £80,000, and the General Meeting can approve this by an ordinary resolution. Duncan is of course in a position to defeat this resolution by voting against it, and it seems unlikely that any other shareholder will be able to treat this as unfairly prejudicial conduct to the minority for the purposes of a petition under s 459. This concept is dealt with in **Chapter 14**. Duncan's strongest argument is that the distribution is imprudent, and that there is a substantial risk that the company will become insolvent if the money is distributed. He can point to the fact that the directors risk personal liability if their actions cause the company to go into liquidation.

Edwina's first scheme does not appear to work. If the accounts show a certain amount of profit, but some of this is tied up in assets, it is lawful to borrow money in order to improve the cash flow position, though it may not always be prudent to do so. However, Edwina appears to be proposing the borrowing as a means of increasing the total amount of profit, and this is not permitted. If this scheme is adopted, the resulting distribution will be unlawful and the excess over £80,000 will be recoverable from shareholders in proportion to the amounts which they have received. The directors would surely be in breach of duty to the company, since the scheme is obviously both unlawful and imprudent.

Edwina's second scheme is possibly lawful, though undeniably contrived. The principal check on it is again the fact that it may be unwise to burden the group of companies with debt in this way. If Duncan were to change his mind and vote for the scheme, the directors would be placed in a very difficult position. Although Edwina is effectively irremovable, it is suggested that the duty the directors owe to the shareholders generally, and possibly to creditors, is incompatible with acquiescing in the scheme. The logic of this is that the directors should not have proposed it in the first place, and at this late stage they should resign rather than incur the risk of personal liability by implementing the arrangement.

FURTHER READING

RD Morris 'Distributable Profit in Britain since 1980: A Critical Appraisal' (1991) 27 Abacus 15.
C Noke, 'Realised profits: unrealistic conclusions' [1989] JBL 37.
JP Carty, 'Borrowing to Pay Dividends' *Certified Accountant*, January 1986.
A McGee and D Mumford, *Distributable Profits – The Auditor's Role* (1991).

17 Shareholders v Creditors – Capital Maintenance and Capital Reduction

LEARNING OUTCOMES

By the end of this chapter, you should understand:

- capital maintenance;
- capital reduction – power to do so in the Articles of Association;
- approval by the court;
- the position of the creditors of the company;
- bonus shares;
- unlawful asset transactions.

SCENARIO

Duncan is becoming rather disgruntled at the lack of returns from the company. Although there is little in the way of profit, Edwina is receiving a very substantial salary with considerable benefits in kind. The others are puzzled rather than unhappy – they cannot understand why it is that the company is apparently fairly successful, yet there is no money available for them. Arthur and Bill also believe that it ought to be possible for them to get their money out of the company any time they choose to do so. Edwina has tried to explain that company law does not permit this, but Arthur and Bill are having some difficulty in understanding this.

OVERVIEW

The general principle of company law is that the share capital must not normally be returned to the shareholders, being intended as a permanent fund which is available for the benefit of creditors. However, there are a number of exceptions to this principle, not all of which fit well into any logically coherent scheme. These include distributions of bonus shares and reductions of capital authorised by the court, as well as company purchases of its own shares (dealt with in **Chapter 20**).

17.1 The general principle

The share capital of the company is intended to be a permanent fund available to creditors to meet the company's debts. This is implicit in the notion that the share capital is the money which the shareholders put at risk when establishing the company. As the shareholders incur no personal liability for the company's debts beyond the amount, if any, unpaid on their shares, it is obviously important that the share capital be maintained so that there is at least some fund against which the creditors can have recourse. At the same time the share capital is intended to be used as part of the company's working capital (a bank overdraft is often the other major source of this), and there is thus always a risk that it may be lost through imprudent or unfortunate transactions. In addition, it may at any given time be represented by assets of the company which are not readily realisable. There is no rule that the company must have cash in hand to the amount of the share capital – indeed many companies operate more or less permanently on the basis of an overdraft – but the creditors are entitled to expect that in the event of a winding up of the company it will be possible to realise assets at least to the value of the issued share capital. Given that in many small companies the issued share capital forms only a small part of the total working capital, this is not a very onerous requirement.

The general principles in this area were established in a number of 19th-century cases, of which the most important was *Trevor v Whitworth* (1888) 12 App Cas 409. The so-called 'capital maintenance doctrine' may be stated as being that the company is not entitled to return to shareholders the capital which they have paid on their shares. Unlawful repayments of this kind may happen either:

(a) expressly by means of a capital repayment, or by means of the company purchasing its own shares from shareholders (as to this see **Chapter 20**); or

(b) indirectly by an unlawful distribution of profit (as to this see **Chapter 16**), or an unlawful asset transaction between the company and a shareholder, or by the payment of obviously excessive salaries in relation to the amount of work being done by a person.

Edwina is receiving a substantial salary and may be at some risk under (b) above, but the principal risk here lies with Arthur, whose growing taste for lengthy holidays brings the value of his contribution to the company into serious question.

The present law is derived from the 19th-century cases, but is in some respects more restrictive than the rules developed by those cases, especially in relation to the declaration of dividends. This chapter concentrates on returns of capital and unlawful asset transactions.

17.2 Reductions of capital

17.2.1 Introduction

A company may sometimes desire to reduce its issued capital, either because it has surplus funds which it wishes to return to shareholders, or, more commonly, because it has suffered losses. In the latter case the rationale for the restatement of the company's capital base is that the sums represented by the issued capital no longer in fact exist for the benefit of creditors, and that it is wrong in principle to allow creditors to believe that they do exist. However, such reductions may not be made without the permission of the court, for there is an obvious opportunity here for companies to reduce their capital so as to prejudice their creditors when there is no real need to do so. This would obviously be incompatible with the objective of creditor protection which lies behind the capital maintenance doctrine. The relevant rules are contained in ss 135-141 of the Companies Act 1985, which aim to strike an appropriate balance between the interests of shareholders and the interests of creditors. In this context it is right to recognise the interests of creditors even when the company is solvent, and ss 135-141 aim to do that.

17.2.2 Methods of reduction

Section 135 allows a company to reduce its share capital if it is authorised to do so by its Articles of Association. A special resolution is required to effect the reduction, which is then subject to confirmation by the court (see **17.2.3** below). The reduction may take any form, but in particular s 135(2) lists a number of things which may be done:

(a) the outstanding liability on shares which are not fully paid-up may be extinguished; or

(b) any paid-up share capital which is lost or unrepresented by available assets may be cancelled (with or without extinguishing or reducing liability on any of its shares); or

(c) paid-up share capital which is in excess of the company's requirements may be paid off (again with or without extinguishing liability on any of its shares).

Where necessary the Memorandum of Association may be altered to reflect these changes.

These three possibilities raise somewhat different issues. The first of them, the extinction of liability on partly-paid shares, does not involve any return of capital to shareholders, since all that happens is that the company's right to make a call for payment on those shares disappears. It should be noted, however, that this solution will not always achieve equality of treatment between different shareholders. Where some shares are fully paid, but others, perhaps issued later, are only partly paid, this scheme benefits the holders of the partly-paid shares rather than affecting all shareholders equally. The second solution, cancelling paid-up share capital, does not suffer from this objection, since the cancellation will be done on a pro rata basis. Neither does it involve repayments to shareholders, since it is only to be used where the share capital is no longer represented by assets. One of the arguments which may be made in favour of reducing the share capital in these circumstances is that the nominal share capital is in fact no longer available to creditors, and that it is desirable to acknowledge this fact by reducing the nominal capital to the level which is really available. The third solution, paying off unnecessary capital, is unlike the other two in that it does involve an actual return of capital to shareholders. In most developing companies this justification is unlikely to be available, since few companies can really say that they have no need of any shareholders' funds which they hold – at the very least they can be used to reduce borrowings.

17.2.3 Approval by the court

Once the necessary special resolution has been passed, the company must apply to court for confirmation of the reduction. If there is to be no diminution of liability in respect of unpaid shares and no return of capital to any existing shareholder, then the obtaining of the consent should be more or less a formality, but in any other case the provisions of s 136 apply. By s 136(3) of the 1985 Act, any creditor who has a claim against the company is entitled to object to the confirmation of the resolution. The reason for this is plain enough. The reduction of the share capital is also a reduction in the amount of the fund to which the creditor is entitled to look for settlement of his debt, and it therefore prejudices the creditor's position. The court is therefore required to establish who are the creditors of the company and for what amounts, and shall offer all such creditors the opportunity to object to the proposed reduction. To this end the company prepares a list of the creditors of which it is aware, and advertises for any others to come forward. If a creditor is not prepared to consent to the proposed reduction, then the court has discretion to dispense with his consent if the company agrees to make suitable provision for paying off the debt in question, ie by creating a fund out of which such creditors can be paid. Alternatively the court may direct, if special circumstances exist, that these provisions of s 136 shall not apply, either generally or in relation to any class or classes of creditors.

Once the court is satisfied that the necessary steps have been taken in relation to any possible creditors, it may make an order confirming the reduction of capital (Companies Act 1985, s 137(1)). This order may be made subject to whatever terms and conditions the court thinks fit. In particular the court may require the company to publish the reasons for the reduction, or such other information about the reduction as the court thinks fit for the purpose of giving proper information to the public. The court may also require the company to include in its name for a specified period after the making of the order the words 'and reduced' (Companies Act 1985, s 137(2)).

Where a company's share capital is reduced, the liability of the members in respect of partly-paid shares is also reduced, so that the outstanding liability is limited to the difference between the amount of the share as fixed by the order of the court and the amount which the shareholder has already paid on the share. This rule is important where the company opts to reduce capital generally, rather than merely to reduce liability on partly-paid shares, ie where it takes the second of the three options listed in s 135(2), rather than the first (see **17.2.2** above).

17.2.4 Registration

Once a reduction of capital has been authorised by the court, it must be registered with the Registrar of Companies, and it takes effect on the date of that registration (Companies Act 1985, s 138(2)).

17.2.5 Further protection of creditiors

Section 140 of the Companies Act 1985 has further significant provisions for the protection of creditors who, through no fault of their own, are not entered on the list of creditors. These people are prejudiced by the loss of their right to object to the reduction;

in most cases this loss will be purely theoretical, since their claim will not be extinguished by not being included in the official list, and the company will still be able to pay it. In exceptional cases, however, the exclusion of the debt may lead to a situation where the company is unable to pay the debt after the reduction of capital (this is most likely to happen where the company pays off apparently unwanted capital, since in other cases the company's assets are not in fact reduced). In this situation s 140(3) provides that contributories – ie, the holders (or former holders) of partly-paid shares – will be liable to the creditor in the same way as if on the date of registration the company had been wound up, ie the creditor can ignore the reduction of capital when claiming against these contributories. Section 141 also imposes criminal liability on any officer of the company who is party to the wilful concealment of the identity of a creditor.

17.3 Acquisition by a company of its own shares

Sections 142–150 of the Companies Act 1985 deal with the acquisition by a company of its own shares. Such acquisition is clearly a breach of the principle that the company's share capital should not be used in refunding sums paid by shareholders, and it is therefore not normally allowed, though an important exception arises under ss 159–171 of the Act, which is explained in detail in **Chapter 20**. Another exception mentioned in s 143(2) occurs where shares are forfeited for failure to pay any sum due in respect of them. The general prohibition applies both to the redemption of shares by acquiring them from the holder on terms that they are to be cancelled, and to the acquisition of the shares from the holder in such a way that they remain in issue but are considered to be owned by the company. However, there is no prohibition on the company acquiring its own shares otherwise than for valuable consideration (Companies Act 1985, s143(1)). This rule follows from the fact that the objection to companies acquiring their own shares is that the acquisition involves a return of capital to the shareholders. Where the company gives no consideration, ie the shares are simply transferred or surrendered, the objection clearly does not apply.

A possible way to circumvent these rules is offered by s 144 of the 1985 Act. This allows shares in a company to be issued to a person who is a nominee for that company. This scheme does not contravene the principle that a company cannot hold shares in itself, since the shares are held in the name of the nominee, and companies are not normally concerned with the beneficial holding which lies behind the name on the share register. However, s 144 goes on to provide that where this scheme is used the shares are to be treated as being owned by the nominee on his own account, and the company is to be treated as having no beneficial interest in them. Section 144(2) further provides for what is to happen where the nominee is called upon to pay sums outstanding on the shares and is unable to do so within 21 days of the call. If the shares were issued to him as a subscriber to the Memorandum, the other subscribers to the Memorandum become liable to pay for the shares, whilst in any other case the directors of the company at the time of the issue of the shares to him or of his acquisition of them become liable to pay for the shares. The effect of this is that the shares will remain in issue – an important point since it ensures the maintenance of the share capital – but the company will not be obliged to pay for them.

17.4 Bonus shares

As was mentioned in **Chapter 16**, a company may use accumulated profits to issue bonus shares. This is an alternative way of dealing with unwanted profits, as an alternative to a reduction of capital as discussed at **17.2** above. The effect of this is that shareholders receive further shares without having to pay for them out of their own resources. This is on the face of it good news for the shareholders, but it must be understood that the effect of doing this is to convert the accumulated profits, which would otherwise have been available for distribution by way of dividend, into part of the company's share capital, which is of course not so available.

A common use for the device of bonus shares is where it is proposed to accept investment from new participants in the company and it is desired to allocate the benefit of profits to date to the existing shareholders, but without taking that capital out of the company. This allows the acceptance of a larger external investment without undue dilution of the holding of the existing members. This scheme might well be attractive to Duncan, since it would allow him to preserve his 60% shareholding.

17.5 Unlawful asset transactions

Another way in which capital may effectively be returned to shareholders is through asset transactions between members and the company. If the company buys an asset from a shareholder at an overvalue, or sells an asset to a shareholder at an undervalue, then this is in effect a distribution of the company's capital. If the shareholder is a director, specific statutory rules apply to regulate the lawfulness of the transaction (Companies Act 1985, s 320; see **Chapter 10**), irrespective of whether proper value is given and received. Where the transaction is with a shareholder it is also necessary to look at the question of value, and this will be so even if the shareholder is also a director and the rules relating to transactions with directors have been fully complied with.

There is a shortage of authority on the problems arising from asset transactions with shareholders, but it seems clear that such a transaction in which the company does not receive full value is effectively a distribution of the company's assets, which can be lawful only to the extent that the company has profits available for distribution (for the rules relating to distributable profits, see **Chapter 16**). Where there are no such profits (or where the profits are insufficient to support the effective distribution of assets which has taken place), there is an unlawful return of capital. It seems likely that the directors would incur personal liability to make good the loss, unless they can show that they did not act negligently, whilst s 277 of the Companies Act 1985 may make the shareholder who receives such a distribution liable to repay it to the company if he knew, or ought to have known, that the transaction was unlawful (for more detail on this subject, see **Chapter 16**).

Whether a criminal offence is committed in these circumstances is far from clear. A director who knowingly is a party to a decision by the company to enter into an unlawful transaction with him may possibly be guilty of the theft of the company's property (this possibility has been increased since the decisions of the higher courts in *R v Gomez* [1993]

AC 442, HL and *R v Phillipou* (1989) 89 Cr App R 290, CA, although when appropriation of the company's property takes place in these circumstances is not still entirely free from doubt). In any event it would be necessary to prove dishonesty on the part of the director, and this may be difficult in many cases. Where the shareholder who is party to the transaction is not also a director, the prospects of criminal liability become even more remote, since that shareholder will not have been a party to the decision to authorise the transaction in the first place. Section 458 of the 1985 Act imposes criminal liability on those responsible for carrying on the company's affairs fraudulently or with intent to defraud creditors, but it will be relatively rare that the necessary intention can be established against directors in such cases – at worst their intention is likely to have been to benefit shareholders, without thinking particularly about the effect on creditors.

Another possibility which requires consideration is that individual shareholders might be able to proceed against directors in these circumstances, either on the basis of a fraud on the minority or under s 459 of the 1985 Act. The former option would require proof of fraud against shareholders, which is unlikely since the shareholders are more likely to be the beneficiaries of this conduct. The latter option is more plausible, since the weakening of the company's financial base may well have detrimental effects on shareholders and thus amount to unfairly prejudicial conduct (as to these possibilities, see further **Chapter 14**).

17.6 Advice to the parties

The attitudes displayed by the shareholders in this chapter reveal that they are suffering from some fundamental misconceptions about the nature of a company, and in particular about the ways in which a company differs from a partnership. If the business were still a partnership, it would be possible to allow partners to withdraw their capital; indeed, it would be possible to pay off all the partnership's capital in this way. Such conduct can be permitted in a partnership because the partners retain unlimited liability for the debts of the business, and this liability is unaffected by the transfer of capital from the partnership accounts to the pocket of individual partners (though the position of the partners inter se may be affected if only some of the partners withdraw capital in this way – as to this, see **Chapter 2**). In a company the position is quite different. The creditors are not entitled to look to the directors or the shareholders personally for payment of the company's debts, and it is therefore necessary to restrain the dissipation of the company's assets in this way.

Three pieces of advice may helpfully be offered to the shareholders in this case. The first is that a look at the company's accounts may well reveal that it is possible to pay at least some money to the shareholders without violating any of the relevant legal principles. Those who work in the business can properly be rewarded by salaries commensurate with their contribution, whilst there may be enough working capital which is not share capital to allow other payments. On the other hand these payments may be most unwise if the company receives nothing in return. The second is that if they really want to distribute more money from the business, they may have to give serious consideration to the idea of disincorporating, ie returning to partnership status. The third is that in any event their wish to take money out of the business is ill-informed and ill-advised. No business can hope to prosper if it has insufficient working capital, and it is not generally a good idea

18 Company Accounts

LEARNING OUTCOMES

By the end of this chapter, you should understand:

- accounting requirements for companies;

- directors' responsibilities and the role and duties of auditors – the directors' and auditors' reports;

- small and medium sized companies and groups – accounting procedures;

- dispensing with the laying of accounts in the case of small companies;

- the Companies (Audit, Investigations and Community Enterprise) Act 2004.

SCENARIO

The 2003 accounts of Great Expectations Ltd were approved by the General Meeting in March 2004. These accounts are reproduced at **Appendix E**. A comparison of these accounts with the 2002 accounts (also **Appendix E**) shows that the company's financial position has deteriorated markedly during 2003. Two major factors contributing to the decline are the large salary paid to Edwina, the £25,000 provision for contingent liabilities in the 2002 accounts which has now increased to £100,000 with the need to make a substantial provision for bad debts arising out of the expected insolvency of Bleak House Ltd. It can be seen that matters are so bad that the auditors have qualified the accounts.

None of the participants is happy about these accounts. Bill and Edwina are embarrassed because the company has made a loss after seeming at one stage to be prospering. They are trying to persuade the others that the accounts should not be taken too seriously, as they are produced only to comply with statutory requirements and do not really explain the true picture properly – it is the management accounts (see further **Chapter 12**), produced more frequently and intended to provide usual information for decision-making, which show something much closer to the true situation. Duncan is convinced that his forebodings about the distribution of £80,000 in early 2003 were justified. Although he does not really understand the technicalities of the accounts, he can see that the company has made a loss, and is alarmed at the apparent diminution in the value of his investment, as well as cross at the decision to exclude him from any participation in the decision-making process. Charlotte has seen the qualification on the accounts as to the value of stock; the combination of this and the loss made in 2003 has led her to conclude that the company will not survive. She is therefore worried about her employment prospects. The only point which is clear in all this disagreement is that the statutory accounts are by no means easy to interpret, and that no two people in the company can agree on their purpose or significance.

OVERVIEW

This chapter deals with the rules governing the preparation and presentation of accounts by a company. These rules are of a somewhat technical character, and are often regarded by law students as being of little interest or importance. This chapter aims to show that this view is misplaced. The rules relating to accounts are intended as an essential part of the process by which the managers of a company explain to the shareholders (and perhaps others) how they have managed the company over the past year and how well they have done. In the case of large public companies the accounts can have a major bearing on the company's financial standing and future prospects. In a small company their role is likely to be less prominent, not least because the shareholders and the managers are often very largely the same people. In Great Expectations Ltd, though, there are shareholders who are not managers (Charlotte and Duncan), and each of these in his/her own way places great weight on the accounts. One of the questions to be addressed in this chapter is whether they are right to do so. Just what do the accounts really reveal? This is a question which involves problems of accounting theory and practice, as well as purely legal issues. A related question is who the statutory accounts are for. Technically they are a report by the directors to the shareholders, but in practice they may to some extent also be relied upon by the creditors, though the major creditor in most private companies, ie the bank, will want to see regular management accounts as well as the statutory accounts (see further **Chapter 12**), and will insert a clause to this effect in the loan agreement.

18.1 Accounting requirements

The statutory requirements are set out in Pt VII of the Companies Act 1985, as amended by the Companies Act 1989. These rules deal both with the keeping of accounts by the company and with the auditing of accounts by independent auditors. Part VII of the Act divides the detailed provisions into a number of smaller headings, and for convenience these headings are largely followed in this chapter.

18.1.1 Accounting records

Every company is required to keep proper accounts (Companies Act, 1985 s 221(1)) which are sufficient to show with reasonable accuracy the financial position of the company at any given time and to enable the directors to prepare the statutory accounts required under other provisions of Pt VII of the Act. A private company must keep accounts for three years from the date on which they are made (Companies Act 1985, s 222(5)). The accounting records are normally kept at the company's registered office, though they may alternatively be kept in such other place as the directors think fit (Companies Act, 1985 s 222(5)).

18.1.2 Financial years and accounting reference periods

Companies are allowed to choose the date on which their financial year ends (Companies Act 1985 s 224(2)). This date is known as the 'accounting reference date' (Companies Act 1985, s 224(3A)). If the company does not make a choice as to its accounting reference date then that date falls on the last day of the month in which the anniversary of the company's incorporation falls, for companies incorporated after 1 April 1996. Great Expectations Ltd, having been incorporated in 2001, has in fact opted for a year-end which corresponds with the end of the calendar year. It is for this reason that the accounts reproduced in **Appendix E** are in each case made up to the end of a calendar year.

A particular difficulty arises when a company is first formed if it wants to choose an accounting reference date which would give it an initial accounting reference period of more or less than one year. Section 224(4) requires that the initial accounting reference period must be at least six months and no more than 18 months long. Subsequent accounting reference periods are always exactly 12 months long, unless the company exercises its option under s 225 of the 1985 Act to alter an established accounting reference date. In such a case the company must give notice of the change to the Registrar of Companies, and must state whether it wishes to extend its current accounting reference period to the second occasion on which the new accounting reference date falls after the change, or to shorten it so that it expires on the first occasion when that date falls after the change (Companies Act 1985, s 225(3)). A change involving an extension of the accounting reference period cannot be made more than once in any five-year period (Companies Act 1985, s 225(4)).

The accounting reference period is important, because it is to this date that the accounts must be made up.

18.1.3 Annual accounts

It is the duty of the directors of the company to prepare annual accounts. These accounts consist principally of two documents: the profit and loss account; and the balance sheet. The former shows the profit or loss of the company for the accounting reference period, whereas the latter shows the financial position of the company as at the end of the accounting reference period. Schedule 4 to the 1985 Act contains detailed requirements as to the form in which these documents must be presented. However, the most important single provision about the accounts is to be found in s 226(2), which requires that the profit and loss account shall give a true and fair view of the of the profit or loss of the company for the financial year, and that the balance sheet shall give a true and fair view of the state of affairs of the company as at the balance sheet date. The section also provides that compliance with the provisions of Sch 4 to the Act, and with the other provisions of the Act, is not sufficient if it does not result in compliance with the true and fair view requirement. The company is required to give whatever additional information is necessary, or to depart from the requirements of the Act in whatever other way is necessary, in order to produce a true and fair view. The expression 'true and fair view ' is not defined anywhere in the legislation, and its meaning is a matter of some considerable dispute (see **Further Reading**, below).

The accountancy profession, through the Accounting Standards Board, has developed a series of guidelines (known as 'accounting standards') to deal with some of the more commonly encountered problems in relation to the preparation of accounts, and these standards are more or less universally adopted. The latest form of these standards is the Financial Reporting Standards (FRS). It is sometimes argued that compliance with the standards is of itself sufficient to give a true and fair view. Unfortunately, this simple view of the matter cannot be sustained, for Sch 4 to the 1985 Act provides (in para 36A) that the accounts shall include particulars of any departure from accounting standards, together with an explanation of the reasons for them. Although this provision emphasises the weight given to accounting standards, it also makes clear that in some cases it will not be appropriate to follow them (for how else could there ever be a case where a company consciously chose not to follow them and was able to justify this decision?). It follows that the concept of true and fair view must involve something more than mere compliance with accounting standards. The question what more it involves is linked with the complex question of the purpose of the accounts, which is also explored at **18.4** below.

18.1.4 Company groups

Sections 227–230 of the 1985 Act deal with another problem which is of concern to Great Expectations Ltd, namely, the operation of the accounting rules in relation to groups of companies. It will be recalled that the company has a wholly-owned subsidiary, Great Expectations (Ideas) Ltd. This is not a trading company, being used largely as a holding vehicle for the company's stocks of material. It charges its parent a management fee, but has no other income. Section 227 requires the directors of the parent company to prepare group accounts as well as the individual accounts for the parent company. Group accounts consist of a consolidated profit and loss account and a consolidated balance sheet for the group as a whole. **Appendix E** includes the accounts of the Great Expectations Group for the relevant years in addition to the accounts of Great Expectations Ltd itself.

The true and fair view requirement (see **18.1.3** above) applies to the group accounts in the same way as it applies to the individual accounts of the parent company, though obviously it is the position of the group which must be fairly described. The normal rule is that all subsidiaries of the parent company must be included in the consolidation, though s 229 allows certain limited exceptions to this principle. The most important exception in relation to groups of small companies such as the Great Expectations group is that contained in s 229(4), which states that subsidiaries must be excluded from the consolidation where their activities are so different from those of the parent company that to include them in the consolidation would be incompatible with the requirement to give a true and fair view. This is merely a specific application of the general principle that the requirement to give a true and fair view overrides all other rules and requirements of the Companies Acts relating to the form and content of accounts. However, it is to be noted that it is not open to the directors of a company to invoke this exception merely because the activities of the subsidiary companies involve different goods or services than those of the parent company. This is of relevance when dealing with the Great Expectations Group, where exactly such differences are found. It is nevertheless suggested that the directors of Great Expectations Ltd are obliged to produce consolidated accounts for both companies, since the inclusion of the subsidiaries is not incompatible with the giving of a true and fair view of the position of the group.

18.1.5 Notes to the accounts

It has been seen already that a company may be required to add notes to its accounts in order to provide fuller explanation of the numerical information given by those accounts (see **18.1.3** above). Sections 231 and 232 of the Companies Act 1985 impose specific requirements to disclose certain information in notes to the accounts (see **18.1.3** above). Section 231 (together with Sch 5, to which that section gives effect) deals with related undertakings. The identity of each of the company's subsidiaries must be stated, as must certain details about the share holdings in the subsidiary and the location of its registered office. It may be noted that more limited information would be required in relation to any subsidiary which formed part of the group but which was excluded from the consolidated accounts under the provisions of s 229.

Section 232 (and Sch 6, to which that section gives effect) imposes requirements of disclosure in relation to the emoluments and other benefits of directors and certain other persons. The purpose of these provisions is to bring to the attention of the members of the company the level of emoluments and compensation for loss of office (if any) paid to the directors.

18.1.6 Approval and signing of accounts

Section 233 of the Companies Act 1985 is a very important provision. It imposes a requirement that the accounts be signed by one director on behalf of the board as a whole. The significance of this is that in signing the accounts the directors take responsibility for their accuracy. Under s 235(5), it is an offence for directors knowingly to approve accounts which do not comply with the requirements of the Companies Acts as to form or content, or as to the giving of a true and fair view (prosecutions under this section are, however, very rare; the only known instance is that of the prosecution of the directors of the Argyll Group in 1979).

18.1.7 Directors' report

Under s 234 of the Companies Act 1985 (as amended by Pt I of the Companies (Audit, Investigations and Community Enterprise) Act 2004), the directors of a company are required to prepare for each financial year of the company a report containing a fair review of the development of the business of the company and its subsidiary undertakings during the financial year and of their position at the end of it, and stating the amount (if any) which the directors propose should be declared as dividend and the amount (if any which they propose to carry to reserves. As was explained in **Chapter 16**, the amount recommended by the directors as dividend is the maximum amount which may be paid, since it is not open to the General Meeting to decide upon a dividend larger than that recommended by the directors (though the General Meeting may decide upon a lower amount than recommended). The report must also give the names of all persons who have been directors during the year in question and must give certain other factual information about the company.

Section 234A requires the directors' report to be signed on their behalf by a director, or by the Company Secretary. As with the accounts, it is an offence knowingly to be party to the signing of an inaccurate directors' report.

18.1.8 Auditors' report

When the directors have prepared the accounts, it is then necessary for them to be audited by an independent and suitably qualified outsider (Companies Act 1985, s 235). The right to act as auditor of a company's accounts is regulated by the Companies Act 1989 (Pt II, as amended by the Companies (Audit, Investigations and Community Enterprise) Act 2004, see **18.1.11** below). Section 19 of the 1989 Act replaced s 256 of the Companies Act 1985 with a new provision. Section 256(3) has itself been replaced by provisions in Part I – Chapter 2 of the Companies (Audit, Investigations and Community Enterprise) Act 2004), which empower the Secretary of State to make grants in respect of a wide range of activities relating to financial reporting and administration, in addition to or for the purposes of bodies concerned with issuing accounting standards, overseeing such standards and/or investigating departures from such standards.

In practice the audit function is normally carried out by persons who are qualified as accountants. In many small companies the auditors also act as general financial advisers to the company, a situation which may be seen as causing undesirable conflicts of interest between their position as advisers and their position as independent auditors, but which is not in any way illegal. Section 235(2) requires the auditors to state in their report in the accounts whether in their view the accounts have been properly prepared in accordance with the Companies Acts, and in particular whether they comply with the requirement to give a true and fair view. A number of important points need to be understood in relation to the auditors' report.

First, s 235(1) describes this report as being a report to the members of the company, rather than to the company itself or to the directors, and this wording appears to represent the original idea behind the statutory audit requirement, namely, that the accounts are the major means by which the directors keep the shareholders informed of the progress of the company, and the role of the auditors is to provide an independent check on the legitimacy of those accounts. Unfortunately, there are at the present day a number of significant difficulties with this theory. The first is that the auditors are not liable to the members at large for any errors in the accounts. This important principle was established by the decision of the House of Lords in *Caparo v Dickman* [1990] 1 All ER 568, HL, where an action was brought against the auditors by shareholders in the company, who had relied on the audited accounts in buying enough shares in the company to acquire control of it, but who alleged that after taking control they had discovered that the accounts were inaccurate and misleading. The House of Lords held that the auditors owed no duty of care to prospective shareholders who bought shares on the faith of the accounts, since the purpose of the accounts is to allow shareholders to exercise informed control over the company and not to provide information to possible speculative investors. At the same time there is no duty to individual shareholders, since the duty is owed to the shareholders as a whole rather than to individuals.

It is not clear from this decision whether it would be possible for the shareholders to bring a claim if they all agreed to participate in it. Although this would seem a logical possibility, it should be remembered that English law does not normally recognise the concept of a class action such as this. It is of course open to the company to bring a contractual claim against the auditors, but in such proceedings the damages recoverable would be limited to the loss suffered by the company as a result of the faults in the accounts. In most cases this damage will be negligible or non-existent, and the claim will not enable the recovery of any losses suffered by individual shareholders who have relied on the accounts.

Even if these difficulties can be overcome in an individual case, there are further problems in bringing a claim against the auditors because of defects in the accounts. Section 235 requires the auditors to express an opinion as to whether the accounts have been properly prepared. It is not correct to say that the auditors certify the accuracy of the accounts – their function is a much more limited one than that. The accounts are essentially the directors' accounts, and it is the directors who must take responsibility for their accuracy. On the other side of the case it may be argued that s 237 of the 1985 Act requires the auditors to take such steps as are necessary to enable them to form an opinion as to whether the accounts have been properly prepared, and whether they show the necessary true and fair view. In some cases this will no doubt expose the auditors to liability, but their liability is not established merely by showing that there are defects in the accounts, since these defects may exist despite the taking of all reasonable steps by them – it has been said judicially that the task of the auditor is to be a watchdog, not a bloodhound (*Re Kingston Cotton Mill (No 2)* [1896] 2 Ch 279, at 288, *per* Lopes LJ), and this means that the auditor is not required actively to look for irregularities, though he must of course draw attention to them if he sees any. It might justly be added that another duty of a watchdog is not to let his attention wander while on duty, thereby missing evidence of wrongdoing when it passes before him.

18.1.9 Publication of accounts and reports

The accounts and the directors' report must be sent to every member of the company and every debenture holder (the relevance of this in relation to retention of title clauses is explored in **Chapter 15**) at least 21 days before the General Meeting at which copies of the accounts are to be presented. Section 241 requires the accounts and report, together with the auditors' report, to be laid before the company in general meeting. These documents must also be sent to the Registrar of Companies within 10 months of the end of the accounting period to which they relate (seven months in the case of a public company; Companies Act 1985, s 244). These requirements form an essential element in the disclosure rules in company law, which aim to ensure that significant information about limited companies is in the public domain (see also **Chapter 1**), though it may be noted that the vigour with which they have been enforced has varied from time to time.

18.1.10 Revision of defective accounts and reports

The 1989 Act introduced some new provisions into the 1985 Act relating to the revision of accounts and reports which are subsequently shown to have been defective in some respect. Prior to this Act there was no provision for amending accounts once they had been audited and approved by the General Meeting. Section 245 of the Companies Act 1985 empowers the directors of the company to prepare revised accounts or a revised report if they see fit. The detailed rules on this subject are contained in the Companies (Revision of Defective Accounts and Report) Regulations 1990 (SI 1990/2570). These require that the revised accounts (or, where appropriate, the supplementary note) be prepared as at the date of the original accounts, and that they give a true and fair view at that date. Thus, matters arising between the date of the original accounts and the date when the revision is in fact prepared are to be ignored. The auditors must report on the revision in the same way as they reported on the individual accounts, and must also state whether in their view the original accounts failed to comply with the Act in the respects identified by the directors and relied on by them as the reason for preparing the revision. This is of course a source of potential embarrassment for auditors, who may have reported on the original accounts and expressed the opinion that those accounts did in fact give a true and fair view. When commenting on the revision, they will no doubt be asked to state that the original accounts did not give a true and fair view, the obvious implication of which is that they were mistaken in their first opinion. For this reason it is likely that in most cases different auditors will be asked to report on the revised accounts.

Under s 245A of the Companies Act 1985 the Secretary of State is empowered to call upon the directors of a company for an explanation of any matters relating to the accounts or report which raise a question as to whether the accounts have been prepared in accordance with the Act. If he is not satisfied with the explanation given by the directors, he may apply to court for an order under s 245B requiring the directors to prepare revised accounts, and, where appropriate, to have them properly audited. Section 245C (as amended by the Companies (Audit, Investigations and Community Enterprise) Act 2004) allows the Secretary of State to authorise other persons to make application to the court for the same purpose. This power has been exercised in the Companies (Defective Accounts) (Authorised Persons) Order 1991 (SI 1991/13). This Order confers the power to make such applications on the Accounting Standards Board, which is a subsidiary organ of the Financial Reporting Council. This power has already been exercised in a small number of cases, all of them relating to public listed companies, and it is inevitable that the cases which attract sufficient controversy and interest to warrant the expense of making an application will relate almost exclusively to such companies, which tend to have a large number of shareholders and whose accounts are subject to considerable critical expert scrutiny in a way which does not happen to private companies.

18.1.11 The Companies (Audit, Investigations and Community Enterprise) Act 2004

Part I of this Act is intended to strengthen the independence of the system of supervising auditors, the enforcement of accounting and reporting requirements, the rights of the auditors to information and the company investigations regime, which has been noted above. Many of these provisions relate to the auditing of listed companies. Even the provisions which could relate to a private company are extremely unlikely to apply to the companies which form the subject matter of this book, which for accounting purposes are regarded as small companies (the significance of which is considered at **18.2** below); they are therefore not considered further.

18.2 Small and medium-sized companies and groups

18.2.1 Exemption from certain accounting requirements

The detailed accounting requirements of the Companies Acts are somewhat relaxed in relation to smaller companies and groups. The provisions relating to these are contained in ss 246–249 of the 1985 Act. The concepts of small and medium-sized are defined by reference to three tests, namely:

(a) aggregate turnover;

(b) aggregate balance sheet total; and

(c) aggregate number of employees.

In order to qualify for the exemption, a company or group of companies must satisfy any two of the three tests in the year for which it wishes to claim the exemption. The table below shows the limits under each of the three headings for the exemption (Companies Act 1985, ss 246 and 249).

Small and medium-sized companies: limits for accounting purposes

	Turnover	Balance Sheet	Employees
Small company	Not more than £5.6 million	Not more than £2.8. million	Weekly average not more than 50
Medium-sized company	Not more than £22.8 million	Not more than £11.4 million	Weekly average not more than 250
Small group	Not more than £5.6 million net or £6.72 million gross	Not more than £2.8 million net or £3.36 million gross	Not more than 50
Medium-sized group	Not more than £22.8 million net or £27.36 million gross	Not more than £11.4 million net or £13.6 million gross	Not more than 250

These exemptions are not available to public companies (Companies Act 1985, s 246(3)), even if they qualify according to the above table, nor to any group of companies which includes a public company (Companies Act 1985, s 248(2)). In determining whether the group includes a public company, the question is whether such a company is included within the group accounts for which the exemption is being claimed.

Schedule 8 to the 1985 Act sets out the details of the exemptions granted to small and medium-sized companies. For a small company such as Great Expectations Ltd these are quite substantial; there is no need to disclose whether accounting standards have been complied with in the preparation of the accounts; a much abbreviated version of the balance sheet may be delivered to the Registrar, and the profit and loss account and directors' report need not be delivered to the Registrar at all. However, this does not excuse the directors from the obligation to prepare these documents, to submit them to the auditors and to lay them before the company in General Meeting (but see **18.2.2** below). In the case of medium-sized companies, the exemption with respect to accounting standards is again applicable and an abbreviated balance sheet may be delivered to the Registrar, but the profit and loss account and the directors' report must be delivered.

The value of these exemptions is somewhat questionable. Small and medium-sized companies and groups are given limited protection from the disclosure requirements imposed on larger companies, but there is unlikely to be any significant saving in time or cost, since full versions of the accounts are still required for internal purposes, and will of course be demanded by loan creditors under the terms of any debenture. Indeed, it is arguable that taking advantage of the exemptions may involve greater cost, since it will then be necessary to produce an additional abbreviated version of the balance sheet which would not otherwise have been required. **Appendix E** contains such balance sheets for Great Expectations Ltd and the Great Expectations Group for 2002 and 2003, and it can be seen from these that the advantages to the company of producing them are very limited. Indeed, these documents are included for information only, Edward and Bill having decided that there was no significant benefit to the company in taking advantage of the small companies exemption.

It should also be noted that for financial years ending before 30 March 2004, audit exemption was available only to what were defined informally as 'very small companies'. These were companies with a turnover of not more than £1 million and a balance sheet total of not more than £1.4 million. The extension of this exemption to virtually all small companies (see SI 2004/16) has not affected the position of any of the companies that form the subject matter of this book, since they qualified for this exemption both before and after 30 March 2004.

18.2.2 Dispensing with laying of accounts

One of the effects of the Companies Act 1989 has been to relax the requirements in relation to General Meetings for small companies. This policy has been carried over into the rules relating to the laying of accounts and reports before the General Meeting. Section 252 of the Companies Act 1985, which was substituted by the Companies Act 1989, allows a private company to pass a resolution dispensing with the requirement to lay the accounts and the directors' report before the General Meeting. Where this is done, the requirement to communicate these documents to the members is met by sending copies of them (together with the auditors' report on them) to every member of the company. However, s 253 of the same Act allows any shareholder to require that accounts be laid before a General Meeting, and it then becomes the duty of the directors to convene a General Meeting for the purpose of considering the accounts and directors' report.

18.3 Qualifications to the accounts

It was mentioned in the **Scenario** above that the 2003 accounts have been qualified by the auditors, and a glance at **Appendix E** will show that the qualification relates to the value of stocks held at the accounting reference date. Qualifications of this kind do not prevent the accounts from complying with the statutory requirements, since it is normally understood that the qualification, when taken in conjunction with the accounts themselves, is sufficient to allow the accounts to give a true and fair view.

18.4 Advice to the parties

It is easy to understand why the shareholders in Great Expectations Ltd are confused about the accounts. The unfortunate fact is that the statutory audited accounts tell the reader relatively little of the information he might wish to know about the state of the company and about trends within it. These accounts operate within a number of highly artificial constraints (especially in relation to the balance sheet) and they have to be considered within the terms of those constraints. Thus, the balance sheet does not state the value of the company at any given date. Rather, it states the assets and liabilities as calculated and expressed in accordance with accounting conventions. The profit and loss account is rather less artificial, though the calculation of profit is again done in accordance with specific accounting conventions, especially in relation to such items as depreciation and the treatment of work-in-progress. The profit and loss account can only give an overall result for the last accounting year: it cannot identify trends within that year. The reality is that the accounts are a poor basis for evaluating the company. Any shareholder who is seriously interested in financial questions, as well as any potential investor in the company, whether in the form of equity or of debt, should not rely on them, but should insist instead on seeing the company's management accounts, which the directors will prepare regularly (if only to satisfy the requirements of the bank), including particularly the cash-flow analysis and projections. Perhaps the best practical advice which can be given to the shareholders in Great Expectations Ltd is therefore to accept that the company must comply with the statutory accounting and auditing requirements, but not to become too concerned about the results of that compliance.

FURTHER READING

A McGee, 'The true and fair view debate: a study in the legal regulation of accounting' (1991) 54 MLR 874.
K P E Lasok and E Grace, 'The true and fair view' (1989) 10 Co Lawyer 13.
H Evans, 'True and fair revisited' [1990] LMCLQ 255.

19 Company Expansion

LEARNING OUTCOMES

By the end of this chapter, you should understand:

- the procedure for issuing new shares – the concepts of authorised and issued capital;

- the directors' authority to allot;

- pre-emption rights;

- the proper purposes doctrine;

- issue of shares at a premium;

- the corporate opportunity doctrine.

SCENARIO

The bank has persuaded the directors of Great Expectations that there is at present too little share capital and too much debt finance. The directors want to expand, but the bank has made it clear that there can be no question of further loan capital unless there is a substantial injection of equity first. Edwina has been considering bringing in new blood, and money, for some time (see **Chapter 13**). She is friendly with Frederick, a director of Ye Olde Curiosity Shoppe plc ('YOCS'), a company which, as mentioned in **Chapter 15**, is a major supplier of Great Expectations Ltd. YOCS is Frederick's family company – his father is Chairman and his brother is Managing Director. Frederick, influenced partly by the accounts and partly by Edwina, has been able to use his family connections to persuade the board of YOCS to subscribe for new shares in Great Expectations Ltd. He has also privately promised Edwina that he will subscribe personally for any shares not taken up by YOCS. Bill and Edwina are now considering how best to give effect to this scheme. It has also dawned on Edwina that a reorganisation of the share structure will have the incidental benefit of reducing Duncan's influence.

19.1 Procedure for issuing new shares

If Great Expectations Ltd wishes to issue further shares to YOCS or Frederick, it will be necessary to ensure that three different sets of legal rules are complied with:

(a) the authorised capital of the company;

(b) the directors' authority to allot; and

(c) pre-emptious rights.

These are examined in detail below.

19.1.1 Authorised capital

The Memorandum of Association of the company is required to state the authorised capital of the company. This rule appears to have been introduced to protect shareholders in the typical 19th-century public company, who would have wanted to know the maximum extent to which new shareholders could be introduced, thereby diluting their holding in the equity of the company. Rather like the ultra vires rule, this doctrine may well be seen as having outlived its usefulness.

Great Expectations Ltd currently has an authorised capital of £5,000, divided into 5,000 shares of £1 each: 2,000 shares have been issued. It seems likely that the company will want to issue a significant number of shares to a prospective new shareholder, since a substantial injection of capital appears called for. It will therefore be necessary to increase the authorised capital. Fortunately, this is not a difficult process. It requires only an ordinary resolution of the company (Companies Act 1985, s 121), though, uniquely among ordinary resolutions, this one needs to be filed with the Registrar of Companies (s 123). The Company duly filed a resolution to increase its authorised capital to £1 million £1 shares (see **Appendix F**).

An oddity of the Companies Acts is that there is no provision stating expressly what consequences follow if shares are issued beyond the authorised capital. In principle the answer ought to be that the allotment is void, since the shares which the company has purported to issue do not and cannot exist. However, it is to be observed that this consequence does not apply to shares issued without authority by the directors, as explained at **19.1.2** below, and it is by no means clear that it applies where the authorised capital is exceeded. If it were to be held that shares issued in excess of authorised capital were void, some very difficult problems could arise. The matter is simple enough where all the shares are issued to a single person, but where they are issued to a number of people, the correct solution is not so obvious. Suppose that Great Expectations Ltd, which has 3,000 unissued shares, were to issue 2,000 shares to Frederick and 10,000 to YOCS. It is clear that 9,000 of these 12,000 shares are unauthorised, but which 9,000? Possible solutions include deciding that each of them has received 1,500 shares, or apportioning the 3,000 valid shares in the ratios in which the purported allocation was carried out (here 500:2,500) or determining the validity of the allotments according to the order in which they are carried out. This last solution would be available only where the allotments are not done simultaneously, but appears to be correct in those cases.

There is no guidance in the Companies Acts as to which of these solutions, if any, is the correct one, and the difficulties of resolving the problem may point in the direction of deciding that the allotment is valid notwithstanding the lack of authority. Some arguments may be presented in favour of this conclusion. First, it is possible to see an analogy with the rules relating to ultra vires transactions, where the modern law inclines strongly in the direction of protecting third parties who enter into transactions with companies. On the other hand, it is possible to view such an allotment as an attempt to do something which is logically impossible (since it is a purported allotment of something which does not exist) rather than just legally impossible – if Great Expectations Ltd enters into a contract to sell the company's Rolls-Royce at a time when it does not own such a vehicle, it is surely absurd to suggest that the abolition of the ultra vires doctrine validates the contract; the difficulty with the contract is not that it is ultra vires, but that it is impossible in a practical sense.

Secondly, it might be argued that the company should be estopped from denying the title of the allottees of the shares, though this argument can work only where the allottees have no knowledge of the irregularity. The best practical way of dealing with this problem is of course to ensure that the authorised capital is adequate to support the proposed allotment. It should be a simple matter to pass the necessary ordinary resolution. Indeed, it may be suggested that the resolution should increase the authorised capital well beyond what is immediately contemplated as likely to be required – there is no good reason why it should not be increased to, say, one million shares of one pound each, as has been done in the case of Great Expectations Ltd. It must be remembered that an increase in the *authorised* capital does not of itself bring about the issue of more shares – there is no reason why a company should not have shares which are authorised but not issued.

19.1.2 Directors' authority to allot

Once it is established that the authorised capital is adequate, the next point is to check that the directors have authority to allot the shares. This authority is not automatic. Section 80 of the Companies Act 1985 requires that it be conferred expressly on the directors, either by the Articles of Association or by special resolution of the company. The authority may be general, ie applying to all the unissued share capital of the company, or may be limited to particular amounts of share capital. It is even possible to confine the authority to a specified allotment to named individuals. The purpose of this rule is to allow existing shareholders some control over the issue of new shares by the directors, and a major concern underlying this is the danger that directors will, by issuing new shares to persons of their choice, significantly affect the balance of power within the company.

If the authority to allot shares is conferred by the Articles of Association, it can be of indefinite duration (and normally will be). Special art 7 of the Articles of Great Expectations Ltd confers such authority on Bill and Edwina (see **Appendix B**). Where such authority is conferred by special resolution, it must be for a defined period not exceeding five years (Companies Act 1985, s 80(4)). It is usual to confer that authority for the full five-year period, and in many small companies a standard item on the agenda for the AGM is to extend the authority for a further year, so that the unexpired period is always between four and five years.

The existence of the requirement for authorisation of the directors makes the rules relating to authorised capital, discussed at **19.1.1** above, largely obsolete. If it is possible to pass a special resolution authorising the directors to make an allotment, then it is surely possible to pass an ordinary resolution increasing the authorised capital. If the power is in the Articles, there is no need to ask the General Meeting for approval, so that the question of shareholder objections does not arise. The rules as to authorised capital pre-date those as to the authority of the directors, and the two sets of rules now co-exist.

If an allotment is made without the necessary authority, the directors of the company and anyone else who is knowingly concerned in that allotment commit a criminal offence punishable with an unlimited fine (s 80(9)). Curiously, though, this illegality does not affect the validity of the allotment (Companies Act 1985, s 80(10); for the possibility of a challenge based on improper exercise of discretion, see **19.2** below).

19.1.3 Pre-emption rights

The third set of rules which must be heeded when making an issue of new shares is that which relates to pre-emption rights. These rules are found in ss 89–95 of the Companies Act 1985. Pre-emption rights are the rights of existing members of the company to be offered any new shares before these are allotted to outsiders. Section 89 of the Companies Act 1985 provides that wherever it is proposed to allot new shares in a private company, these shares must first be offered to the existing shareholders in proportion to their shareholdings. The offer must be made on the same terms as, or on more favourable terms than, the terms on which it is proposed to offer the shares to any outsider, and the proposed allotment to the outsider may not proceed unless and until the time for acceptance of the offer by existing shareholders has elapsed without that offer being taken up. Where some, but not all, of the pre-emption rights are exercised, it is of course open to the directors to allot to outsiders those shares which were offered to existing shareholders but not accepted by them.

The requirements of s 89 do not apply to allotments made wholly or partly for non-cash consideration (s 89(4)). This exclusion does offer certain opportunities for circumventing the purpose of the legislation. It is not necessary that the allotment shall be wholly for non-cash consideration – any such consideration will exclude s 89. Bill and Edwina could make use of this provision, for example by allotting shares to YOCS in return for antiques of the kind which YOCS normally supplies to the company. In such a case the question of whether the company had received full value for the shares might well arise. (It is possible that the qualification of the accounts in relation to stock valuation, mentioned in **Chapter 18**, could arise from the injudicious use of such a scheme.)

Section 91 allows a private company (but not a public company) to include in its Memorandum or Articles a provision excluding s 89 generally or in relation to allotments of a particular description. Separately from this, s 95 allows the pre-emption rights to be disapplied in the case of a specific proposed allotment (or to be applied with such modifications as may be desired) by means of a special resolution of the company. Sections 91 and 95 should be read together, for they adopt the general principle in this area that a provision which could have been included in the Articles – by means of a special resolution (Companies Act 1985, s 9 – see **Chapter 7**) – may alternatively be adopted in a particular case, also by means of a special resolution.

Section 92 of the Act deals with the consequences of an allotment in disregard of the pre-emption provisions. It provides that the company and every officer of it who knowingly authorised or permitted the contravention are jointly and severally liable to compensate any person to whom an offer of shares should have been made for any loss, damage, costs or expenses which the person has sustained or incurred by reason of the contravention. In analysing this provision it is first necessary to ask what loss such a person could suffer. Obviously, he has not received the shares, but neither has he paid for them. If the shares were being offered to him at a fair market value, it may seem that he has suffered no loss. The loss is more readily identifiable where the shares were being offered at less than the net asset value of shares in the company at that time (it is assumed that the shares are not being offered at a discount to their par value, since this would contravene s 100 of the Companies Act 1985). In such a case the immediate profit which the shareholder would have made had he accepted the offer is a ready measure of his loss. Even where the shares are offered at a fair value, it may be possible to argue that there is some loss if it appears that there were reasonable prospects of growth in value, though on the other side it will no doubt be said that these prospects are to some extent incorporated in the notion of fair current value.

In many cases it will be possible to identify another way in which the disregard of the pre-emption rights has caused loss to the existing shareholders. A natural effect of this disregard will be to reduce the proportion of the company's shares held by the previous shareholders. There will be loss of dividend entitlement, assuming the company to be profitable (if it is not profitable then it is much less likely that the disregard of pre-emption rights will be controversial), and there may also be loss of control of the company's affairs – either a loss of a majority shareholding, or possibly a loss of negative control if a particular shareholder or group of shareholders see their holding reduced below 25%. Few shareholders would doubt that either of these events was a significant loss to them, but valuing that loss may be a difficult task. A further general difficulty in this area is that of causation. Where it appears that the shareholder concerned would not have taken up the pre-emption rights anyway (perhaps because he could not afford to do so), it is suggested that s 92 does not provide any remedy, since the shareholder's losses are not properly to be regarded as having been incurred by reason of the contravention of s 89.

What is not clear from s 92 is whether an aggrieved shareholder whose pre-emption rights have been disregarded can make any claim to have the missing shares transferred to him. This would obviously have to be a proprietary claim against the allottee of the shares, rather than against the company or its directors. Section 92 confers no such right, but neither does it state that the right does not exist. The question therefore appears to be one which depends upon ordinary notions of proprietary rights. Applying these principles, it seems unlikely that any claim can be made. Although the shareholder was no doubt entitled to be offered those shares, they never in any sense belonged to him, and it is hard to see how he can make any proprietary claim to them. There would in any event be quite serious difficulties in applying in practice the notion that he was entitled to claim them. Where shares have been wrongfully allotted to a number of persons, it would be necessary to decide which of these shares belonged to the individual shareholder who complained, and there is no procedure by which this decision can be made. It therefore seems necessary to conclude that no claim to the shares can be pursued.

19.2 The proper purposes doctrine

Even where the directors are able to comply with all the statutory requirements in relation to the issue of new shares (see **19.1** above), the question of proper purposes will still arise. The power to issue shares, like every other power of the directors, must be exercised *bona fide* in the best interests of the company (see **Chapter 13**). A purported allotment may be set aside where this requirement is not observed (*Howard Smith Ltd v Ampol Petroleum Ltd* [1974] AC 821, PC), and if a shareholder challenges a purported allotment, the court may refer the matter to a General Meeting on terms that the shares purportedly issued may not be voted in deciding the question (*Hogg v Cramphorn* [1967] Ch 254, Buckley J).

The General Meeting may ratify an allotment made *mala fide* (*Bamford v Bamford* [1970] Ch 212, CA), though such ratification would presumably not preclude the possibility of a derivative claim or a s 459 petition (see **Chapter 13**).

In the present case Duncan will no doubt realise that the proposed allotment will dilute his shareholding, and may well seek to challenge it on that ground. Bill and Edwina will reply, with some justification, that the primary purpose of the allotment is to strengthen the company's capital base and to open up the possibility of further finance from the bank. At the same time it cannot be denied that Edwina is aware of the effect on Duncan and is by no means unhappy about it. If Duncan does litigate this question, he will have to choose between a direct challenge to the allotment and a s 459 petition. If he chooses the former route, attention is likely to focus on the narrow question of the purposes for which the allotment is to be made (*Howard Smith Ltd v Ampol Petroleum Ltd*, above), whereas a s 459 petition would open up the broader questions of unfair prejudice and Duncan's legitimate expectations in the company (*Re Cumana Ltd* [1986] BCLC 430, CA).

19.3 Issue of shares at a premium

It will sometimes happen that shares are issued at a premium, ie at a price which exceeds their nominal value. In these circumstances, s 130 of the Companies Act 1985 applies, and the company is obliged to create within its accounts a 'share premium account' to which it must transfer the amount of the premium paid on the shares. The practical effect of this is that the premium must be treated as being part of the company's share capital and is not available to use for the ordinary purposes of the company.

Section 130 allows premium to be used for a limited number of purposes. One is to support the issue of fully paid-up bonus shares to existing members of the company (see s 130(2), in which case these funds simply become part of the ordinary share capital again). Other purposes are to write off the company's preliminary expenses (not relevant on an issue of further shares, though it may occur where the initial shares are issued at a premium), to pay the commission associated with the issue of shares or debentures, and to provide for any premium payable on the redemption of debentures.

Sections 131 and 132 of the Companies Act 1985 provide relief from the restrictions of s 130 in certain cases of mergers between two companies and in cases of group reconstructions. Merger relief under s 131 is covered in **Chapter 21**. In relation to group reconstructions the following points should be noted. Section 132 applies where the issuing company is a subsidiary of another company (here referred to as the 'holding company') and issues shares to the holding company, or to another wholly-owned subsidiary of the holding company, in return for non-cash assets transferred from any company which is in the same group as the issuing company and the holding company. This need not be the same company as the one to which the shares are issued.

Where s 132 applies, the effect is that the issuing company is not obliged to transfer to its share premium account any amount in excess of what the Act calls the minimum premium value. This is defined by s 132(3) as the amount by which the base value of the consideration for the shares allotted exceeds the aggregate nominal value of those shares. Section

132(4) then defines the base value of the consideration as the amount by which the base value of the assets transferred exceeds the base value of any liabilities of the transferor company assumed by the issuing company as part of the consideration for the assets transferred. The base value of assets is the lesser of book value and historic cost, whilst the base value of liabilities is book value. The effect of these rather complex definitions may be summarised as follows: the amount to be transferred to share premium account is only the net addition to the assets of the issuing company which arises because the issuing company receives more in total for the shares issued than the nominal value of those shares.

Although the requirement of a share premium account is sometimes seen as a disincentive to the issue of shares at a premium, it is in fact merely a relatively unimportant accounting requirement which should not cause undue difficulty to any company. It arises from the rule, discussed in **Chapter 17**, that the share capital of a company must be maintained as a fund available to creditors. Thus, all the money received for the issue of the shares must be treated as part of the share capital, either under the heading of nominal capital or as part of the share premium account. Without s 130 it would be possible to circumvent this rule by issuing shares of very low nominal value at an apparent premium, and to use that premium for distributing dividends to existing shareholders.

19.4 Corporate opportunity doctrine

Even if the statutory procedures can be complied with, Frederick, as a director of YOCS, may still be in some difficulty. His knowledge of the possibility of subscribing for the shares came to him because of his position as a director of YOCS, and the doctrine of corporate opportunity, already discussed in **Chapter 10**, would seem to prevent him from taking advantage of the opportunity for himself without the agreement of YOCS.

19.5 Advice to the parties

From the point of view of the company there should be no great difficulty about issuing new shares to YOCS and Frederick. The correct procedures will have to be followed, but it seems likely that the necessary shareholder consents can be obtained. It is of course desirable to take into account the effect on the balance of power within the company of issuing these new shares.

YOCS has already agreed to subscribe for the shares, but has stipulated for certain changes in the Articles – YOCS is to have the right to appoint two non-executive directors to the board, as well as the right to require existing shareholders to buy its shares within three years of the allotment (a 'put option', see **21.1**) and enhanced pre-emption rights for further share issues. Despite these clauses, Edwina will retain the managing directorship and will thus have substantial day-to-day power to bind the company. The problem for YOCS is lack of information and lack of direct involvement in management. It would be possible to add further clauses entitling YOCS to see management accounts, but even this will not prevent the taking of unwise decisions. Regular board Meetings could be required, with reports from Edwina of her activities. This would no doubt cramp her style somewhat, but the meetings would still take place after decisions had been made. The only way to exercise effective control over Edwina is to require that her actions be approved in advance by the non-executive directors. Even this has drawbacks. The non-executive directors would rapidly become executive directors; if Edwina did take actions without seeking approval, the company would almost certainly still be bound, unless clients and suppliers were given notice of the restriction; most seriously, Edwina would argue, quite rightly, that this rule made her job impossible – a duly appointed Managing Director must be entrusted with the job of management and left to get on with it.

From Frederick's point of view the position is more difficult. He is already a director of YOCS, and it seems unlikely that that company will approve of his actions in taking the balance of the shares for himself. Any action taken against him by YOCS is of course only indirectly the concern of Great Expectations Ltd, but the prospect of such action may in the end be sufficient to dissuade him from buying the shares, and this would very definitely be a problem for Great Expectations Ltd. The best advice to give Frederick must be that he should not go ahead with this scheme without making full disclosure to YOCS and obtaining its prior consent. Unfortunately, this advice may well fall on deaf ears.

Duncan faces some tricky tactical problems. His reluctance to allow the dilution of his shareholding is entirely natural, but he will not find the proposed allotment easy to challenge. If he tries to use the proper purposes doctrine, Bill and Edwina will point to the undoubted need for more capital, though they may be in rather more difficulty when asked to explain why they have chosen to make a non-cash allotment to YOCS rather than a cash offer to existing shareholders. Despite this, they may be able to show that the injection of new capital was their primary motive. In view of this Duncan may well conclude that his best hope of success lies in petitioning under s 459 of the Companies Act 1985 on the basis that this is a quasi-partnership in which he has a legitimate expectation of being a majority shareholder, so that the introduction of YOCS is unfairly prejudicial to him. Although this argument is attractive at first sight, it too has its difficulties. For one thing the possibility of alterations in share ratios does follow from the Companies Act rules on the issue of new shares, and it cannot automatically be assumed that the original majority shareholder is entitled to retain that status forever. A second point is that s 459 petitions are inherently dangerous, in that the court has unlimited discretion as to the remedy to be granted (s 461), and Duncan may find himself compulsorily bought out, when his intention was to restrain the allotment (*Re A Company (No 003096 of 1987)* (1987) 4 BCC 80; *Re A Company (No 006834 of 1988)* [1989] BCLC 365). Given that there is a shareholders' agreement, under which he is entitled to insist on this anyway (see **Appendix D**), he would obviously be unwise to resort to litigation which is likely to have the same result in addition to being extremely expensive and disruptive.

It can be seen that Bill and Edwina face something of a dilemma. The need for more capital is urgent, but they would be well-advised to restrain the impulse simply to ignore the rights of existing shareholders. In any event, they presumably do not want to see YOCS become a majority shareholder, since this would amount to a takeover, which is likely to be rapidly followed by the dismissal of Bill as a director (Edwina is of course protected by the *Bushell v Faith* clause). A better idea would be to persuade YOCS to take a substantial shareholding, but at the same time to negotiate the issue of further shares to the existing shareholders. This will inevitably dilute Duncan's shareholding, since there will be a major new shareholder, but by issuing him at least some shares the directors may be able to avoid litigation. Other shareholders in the company may not be able to afford to subscribe for large numbers of shares, and a way of dealing with this problem would be to issue the new shares partly paid. In this way everyone can have some shares, thus preserving a reasonable power balance while also obtaining sufficient capital. **Appendix F** shows a possible scheme along these lines, and in the following chapters it is assumed that this scheme has been implemented.

20 Corporate Reconstruction

LEARNING OUTCOMES

By the end of this chapter, you should understand:

- the transfer of shares in a private limited company;

- the repurchase by a company of its shares;

- financial assistance by a company for purchase of its shares.

SCENARIO

Duncan has had to face the reality that the courts are unlikely to be willing to protect the status quo within the company and that no matter which form of relief he may petition for under s 459, the likely outcome is that the others will buy him out. His solicitor pointed out that this result could be achieved without the need for litigation, by exercising the option included in the shareholder agreement (see **Appendix D**). Duncan had been minded to fight his corner in an attempt to resist what in his mind amounted to an abuse of power. His only interest in litigation had been to prevent Edwina having her way over the issue of further shares. As the realisation dawned on him that this was to be an unlikely outcome, together with the fact that the company is no longer particularly profitable, he has now decided to exercise the option for the others to buy him out.

This decision will inevitably cause considerable difficulties for the other shareholders, who are now called upon to find the cash to purchase the shares. The agreement calls for the shares to be valued as at the date when Duncan formally gives notice of the exercise of the option, and it is expected that this will result in a valuation substantially in excess of the par value. One possible solution which has been mooted is that the company itself should buy Duncan's shares. Alternatively, Frederick has expressed an interest in taking on some or all of Duncan's shares.

This extra financial pressure on the shareholders has come at a time when the company is looking to them to pay for their further shares, which were issued to them only partly paid (see **Chapter 19**). A demand for payment for both Duncan's shares and for the amounts outstanding on their own shares would most likely bankrupt all three of them. One scheme which Edwina believes will assist them in this predicament is for the company to waive its right to any further sums due for the partly-paid shares and to treat them as fully paid up. Surely, she argues, the company can do this.

OVERVIEW

This chapter is concerned primarily with various ways in which shares in a company may change hands (the procedure for issuing new shares was examined in **Chapter 19**). Existing shares may be sold by their holders, either to persons who are already shareholders or to outsiders who thereby become members. Restrictions contained in the Articles of Association may make the issue of new shares easier than the transfer of existing shares. The company may in certain circumstances be able to purchase its own shares, or to give financial assistance for others to do so.

20.1 Transfer of shares

In the scenario Duncan wants to dispose of his shares. This makes it necessary to consider the rules relating to transferability of shares in companies. The starting point is that shares are assumed to be freely transferable. Table A contains no restrictions on the transfer of fully-paid shares, though art 24 does give the directors a discretion to refuse to register the transfer of a share which is not fully paid, and most of the shares in Great Expectations Ltd are not fully paid. In private companies this state of affairs is often regarded as somewhat unsatisfactory. Many such companies, including Great Expectations Ltd, have emerged from former partnerships, and are for this reason sometimes referred to as 'quasi-partnerships' (this concept is of particular importance in relation to minority protection, which is the subject of **Chapter 14**). In a partnership it is not possible for a partner to assign his share of the business to an outsider without the consent of the remaining partners, and in small companies it is often desired to reproduce the effect of this rule. The usual method of doing so is to include in the Articles of Association some form of restriction on share transfers (before 1980 private companies were required to include in their Articles some provision restricting share transfers; although this rule no longer exists, many private companies do still have such restrictions). The exact details of these restrictions admit of almost infinite variation, but a number of common themes may be identified. Most share transfer provisions follow more or less along the lines of one of these themes.

The most draconian approach is to allow the directors absolute discretion to refuse to register transfers of shares to a person of whom they do not approve. This has been adopted by Great Expectations Ltd (see **Appendix B**, special art 5). In theory such a provision could allow the directors to refuse to register a transfer to a person who already holds shares in the company. They may wish that he was not a shareholder at all, or they may take the view that it is undesirable that his shareholding should be increased. The only restriction on the exercise of this discretion by the directors would be the usual overriding requirement that the powers of the directors must be exercised bona fide in the best interests of the company (for the details of this rule see **Chapter 13**).

If this approach is considered too restrictive, an alternative is to allow shareholders to transfer shares freely to members of their immediate family (a phrase which needs to be defined carefully if this approach is to be adopted) whilst requiring directors' consent for other transfers. This system is most commonly used where a company has been set up by two or more families. Although there may be several individual shareholders, it is likely that the participants conceive of the company of being divided among a number of families in specified proportions. On this basis there is no reason why a readjustment of the shareholdings within one of the families concerned should be of interest to the directors, but a change which brings in a shareholder from outside the existing families, or which shifts the balance of power between the families, is a matter of some concern to the directors.

Where the company is not divided between families in this way, another possible approach is to include a pre-emption clause in favour of other existing shareholders, or in favour of the directors themselves. The shareholders of Great Expectations Ltd have provided for this in the Shareholder Agreement (see **Appendix D**). Under this system a shareholder wishing to sell his shares must first offer them to other shareholders or to the directors. In our scenario Duncan must first offer his shares to Arthur, Bill and Edwina. If a clause of this kind is used, it is necessary to include clear and appropriate provisions about valuation of the shares. Merely requiring the sale to be at a 'fair value' is too vague to work satisfactorily, whilst a provision allowing the directors to fix the value is almost certain to lead to difficulties, since the directors are unlikely to be indifferent as to who gets the shares, and are always vulnerable to allegations of bad faith in the valuation. The only satisfactory approach here is to provide for some independent valuation. Some differences of detail arise according to who has the pre-emption rights under the Articles, or shareholder agreement, and who is the intending purchaser of the shares. Where the pre-emption rights are in favour of other shareholders, it is usual to provide that they apply only where it is proposed to sell to someone who is not already a shareholder. Where the rights are in favour of the directors, they often apply even to sales to existing shareholders. One possible defect with a transfer article giving pre-emption rights to directors is that the rights can be invoked only if the directors have the cash to pay for the shares at the time when the offer is made. If they do not, then the transferor is effectively freed from any restriction on the transfer.

As the shareholders in Great Expectations Ltd are not related to each other, the company has a transfer article of the first kind mentioned above. It is therefore open to Bill and Edwina to veto any transfer of shares if they do not approve of it, provided of course that they can justify their refusal as being in the best interests of the company.

Where directors do exercise a power to veto a share transfer (whatever the details of the provision giving them that power), the effect is that the transfer will not be recorded in the company's Register of Shareholders and the intended transferee will not therefore become the legal owner of the shares. However, if a share transfer form is executed, this will be an effective assignment of the equitable interest in the shares. The resulting separation of the legal and equitable interests in the shares will create a trust, in which the transferor becomes the trustee, whilst the transferee becomes the beneficiary. The shares are thus held for the benefit of the beneficiary on a bare trust. The transferor must exercise his membership rights in the company for the benefit of the transferee and in accordance with any instructions given by the transferee. The transferee is also entitled to any dividends which may be declared on the shares. However, the company is not obliged to deal with the transferee; indeed, it cannot properly do so, since the transferee does not become a member of the company. The transferor is still a member of the company, and is therefore the person entitled to receive information about the company and to attend its meetings (though he could appoint the transferee as his proxy). The company will pay the dividends to the transferor, though he will of course be obliged to hand them over to the transferee. This is obviously an untidy and unsatisfactory state of affairs, and it is no doubt for this reason that few purchasers will accept a transfer of the shares unless they are first assured that they will be recognised and registered by the directors.

20.2 Company repurchase of own shares

20.2.1 Requirements to be fulfilled

As Great Expectations Ltd is a private company, it is possible for it to buy back its own shares, provided that certain initial requirements are fulfilled. First, it is necessary to check that the company's Articles of Association confer power to repurchase shares (Table A, art 35). A look at the Articles as reproduced in **Appendix A** will show that in their original form they did not contain such a power. It will therefore be necessary to amend them to confer this power by passing a special resolution (see **Chapter 7**). Next, it must be remembered that the effect of the purchase must not be to leave the company with only redeemable shares (Companies Act 1985, s 162(3)). Fortunately, this is not a problem in the present case.

Section 162 of the Companies Act 1985 allows a company to purchase its own shares. Section 159 of the same Act allows a company to issue redeemable shares, but the power under s 162 to purchase the company's own shares is not limited to redeemable shares. Redeemable shares are shares which are issued on terms that the company and/or the shareholder may require them to be redeemed in specified circumstances. Great Expectations Ltd has no redeemable shares, but the rules relating to purchase of own shares for the most part apply equally to purchases of redeemable shares and purchases of non-redeemable shares. The exception to this general principle is that non-redeemable shares may in some cases be purchased out of capital under s 171 of the 1985 Act, which is discussed later.

Section 160 of the Companies Act 1985 allows the purchase of the company's own shares only out of the distributable profits of the company (but see **20.2.2** below), and 'distributable profits' are for this purpose defined in the same way as in Pt VIII of the 1985 Act, which relates to distributions of the company's assets (for Pt VIII, see **Chapter 16**). Sections 163–166 of the Act deal with market purchases and off-market purchases of the shares. As Great Expectations Ltd is not a listed company, any purchase of its shares will necessarily be off-market. Section 164 requires that the terms of the proposed purchase be approved by special resolution of the company in advance of the making of the contract. In passing the special resolution, s 164(5) prohibits the counting of the votes attached to the shares which it is proposed to purchase.

Where a company makes a purchase of its own shares, s 169 of the Companies Act 1985 requires it to make a return to the Registrar of Companies within 28 days, giving details of the number and nominal value of shares purchased and the date on which they were delivered to the company.

20.2.2 Purchase out of capital

Private companies (but not public companies) may in some circumstances purchase their own shares otherwise than out of distributable profits or out of the proceeds of a fresh share issue, ie the purchase may be made out of capital. This possibility constitutes a major exception to the general prohibition on returning the company's capital to its shareholders. This may be done only where the available distributable profits and the proceeds of any fresh issue of shares are together insufficient to fund the purchase of the company's shares, and it is only the difference between the purchase price and the total available from profits and proceeds of issue which may be paid out of capital.

Section 172 provides that the question whether the company has profits available for distribution and the amount of such profits is determined for the purposes of purchasing shares out of capital according to the rules set out in s 171, rather than in accordance with the rules in ss 270–275, which apply for the purposes of distributions within Pt VIII of the 1985 Act.

20.3 Financial assistance for purchase of own shares

The major rules relating to this subject are contained in Pt V, Ch VI of the Companies Act 1985 (ss 151–158). Such assistance is generally prohibited whether the assistance is given before the acquisition (s 151), at the time of the acquisition (s 151), or subsequently through the release of liabilities already incurred (s 152). It is to be noted that this last rule shows why Edwina is quite wrong to suggest that it would be possible for the company to write off the sums still outstanding on the partly-paid shares.

The concept of financial assistance is broadly defined (s 152) and includes:

(a) financial assistance given by way of gift, guarantee, security or indemnity, other than an indemnity in respect of the indemnifier's own neglect or default, or by way of release or waiver;

(b) financial assistance given by way of loan or any other agreement under which any of the obligations of the person giving the assistance are to be fulfilled at a time when, in accordance with the agreement, any obligation on another party to the agreement remains unfulfilled, or by way of the novation of, or the assignment of rights arising under, a loan or such other agreement; or

(c) any other financial assistance given by a company the net assets of which are thereby reduced to a material extent, or which has no net assets. The net assets are the aggregates of assets less liabilities. However, these terms must be restricted to their technical legal meaning (*British and Commonwealth Holdings plc v Barclays Bank plc* [1996] 1 WLR 1).

Section 151 prohibits a wide range of devices, including the following:

(a) a loan made by a company to finance the borrower's purchase of shares in the company (*Selangor United Rubber Estates Ltd v Craddock (No 3)* [1968] 1 WLR 1555);

(b) a purchaser undertaking a liability (to a third party) as part of the consideration for the shares, but failing to discharge that liability, or causing the company to discharge it (*Wallersteiner v Moir (No 1)* [1974] 1 WLR 991);

(c) a purchase by a company of assets at an inflated price to enable the vendor of the assets to buy shares in the company (*Belmont Finance Corporation Ltd v Williams Furniture Ltd (No 2)* [1980] 1 All ER 393).

Where assistance is given in contravention of s 151, the company is liable to a fine, and every officer of it who is in default is liable to imprisonment or a fine, or both. In addition the transaction is void and unenforceable (*Selangor United Rubber Estates Ltd v Craddock (No 3)*, above). Moreover, the directors responsible can be sued for breach of trust (*Steen v Law* [1964] AC 287). There may also be a claim in the tort of conspiracy (*Belmont Finance Corporation v Williams Furniture Ltd (No 2)*, above). It is unclear whether any claim lies against any third parties who might be involved.

It is possible to escape the operation of s 151 by showing that the company's principal purpose in giving the assistance is not to give it for the purpose of that acquisition, or where the giving of assistance for that purpose is merely an incidental part of some larger purpose of the company and the assistance is given in good faith in the interests of the company (s 153). The test is in large measure a subjective one, since it depends upon the company's perception of the purpose of giving the assistance. Moreover, deciding whether there is some larger purpose also involves a considerable element of judgment.

Other exceptions are available for: a distribution by way of lawful dividend, or in the course of a winding up, the allotment of bonus shares, a reduction of capital confirmed by order of the court under s 137 of the 1985 Act, a redemption or purchase of redeemable shares, made in accordance with ss 159–181 of the 1985 Act, anything done in pursuance of an order of the court under s 425 of the 1985 Act (compromises and arrangements with members and creditors), anything done under an arrangement made in pursuance of s 110 of the Insolvency Act 1986 (acceptance of shares by liquidator in winding up as consideration for sale of property), anything done under an arrangement made between a company and its creditors which is binding on the creditors by virtue of Pt I of the Insolvency Act; where the lending of money is part of the ordinary business of the company, the lending of money by the company in the ordinary course of its business, the provision by a company, in good faith in the interests of the company, of financial assistance for the purposes of an employees' share scheme, the provision of financial assistance in connection with steps taken to facilitate share transactions between present or past employees and/or their spouses or minor children, the making by a company of loans to persons other than directors employed in good faith by the company with a view to enabling those persons to acquire fully paid shares in the company or its holding company to be held by them by way of beneficial ownership.

Sections 155–158 then deal with the circumstances in which private companies may give financial assistance in connection with the purchase of shares in the company notwithstanding the prohibition in s 151. Either the company must have net assets, which are not reduced by the giving of the assistance, or the funds must be provided from distributable profits (s 155(2)). Section 155 does not permit the giving of assistance by a subsidiary for the acquisition of shares in the holding company if the company is also the subsidiary of a plc, which is itself the subsidiary of the holding company.

Consider the group structures set out below:

A Ltd

B plc

C Ltd

C Ltd may not give assistance for the purchase
of shares in A Ltd

A plc

B Ltd

C Ltd

C Ltd may give assistance for the purchase of shares in B Ltd. Section 155 does not prohibit it from giving assistance for the purchase of shares in A plc, though s 153 may do so.

Unless the company which is to give the assistance is a wholly-owned subsidiary, the
giving of assistance must be approved by a special resolution of the company in General
Meeting (s 155(4)). Where the assistance is given by a subsidiary for the acquisition of
shares in its holding company, the assistance must be approved by the company giving it,
the holding company and any intermediate holding company. Thus, in the second example
above, A plc, B Ltd and C Ltd must all give the approval. However, the above rule does not
apply to wholly-owned subsidiaries. Thus, if either B Ltd or C Ltd is wholly owned, no special resolution is needed. The special resolution is needed if either is not wholly owned. It
must be passed on or within one week after the date on which the directors make the special resolution required by s 155 (s 157(1)). In most cases the meeting will be an
Extraordinary General Meeting, which will require 14 days' notice. The content of the resolution must be shown in the notice, together with the fact that it is being proposed as a
special resolution. Short notice procedure is available, provided that the necessary majority
of members consent.

Persons holding at least 10% of the shares (10% of the members in a company not limited by shares) may petition the court for the cancellation of the resolution, provided that
they have not voted for the resolution or consented to it (s 157(2)). The procedures and
powers of the court when such an application is made are the same as those for an
objection to the re-registration of a public company as private under ss 53 and 54 of the
1985 Act (s 157(3)). The statutory declaration made by the directors, together with the
auditors' report annexed to it, must be available for the inspection of members at the
meeting where the resolution is passed. Failure to comply with this requirement renders
the resolution ineffective (s 157(4)).

The directors of the company giving the assistance are required to make a statutory declaration in respect of that assistance. Where the assistance is given in connection with the
purchase of shares in the company's holding company, a similar declaration must be made
by the directors of the holding company and of any intermediate holding company (s
155(6)). The statutory declaration must give particulars of the assistance to be given, and

of the nature of the company's business, and must identify the person to whom the assistance is to be given (s 156(1)). The declaration must also state that in the directors' opinion the company will be able to pay its debts immediately after the assistance is given, and that the company will be able to pay its debts as they fall due during the year immediately following the giving of the assistance. In the rare case where it is proposed to commence the winding up of the company within the next 12 months, the requirement is that the company will be able to pay its debts within 12 months of the commencement of the winding up (s 156(2)). In forming their opinion the directors must take account of the same liabilities (including contingent and prospective liabilities) as would be relevant under s 122 of the Insolvency Act 1986 to the question whether the company is able to pay its debts (s 156(3)). These factors are set out in s 123 of the Insolvency Act (see **Chapter 23**).

A report from the company's auditors must be annexed to the statutory declaration. This must state that the auditors have enquired into the company's affairs and are not aware of anything to indicate that the opinion expressed by the directors as to the above matters is unreasonable (s 156(4)). The statutory declaration and auditors' report must be delivered to the Registrar together with the special resolution. If no special resolution is required (because the company providing the assistance is a wholly-owned subsidiary) then the declaration and report must be delivered within 15 days of the making of the declaration (s 156(5)). A contravention of s 156(5) renders the company and every officer of it who is in default liable to a fine and, for continued contravention, a daily default fine (s 156(6)). A director who makes the statutory declaration without having reasonable grounds for the opinions expressed in it is liable to imprisonment or a fine, or both (s 157(7)).

Where a special resolution is required, the assistance shall not be given before the expiry of four weeks from the date when the resolution is passed (or the last of them in group situations where more than one special resolution is required). This allows time for dissentient shareholders to petition the court under s 157 (s 158(2)).

The only exception to the above rule is found where every member of the company (or all the companies, if more than one) who was entitled to vote on the resolution voted in favour of it. In this event, the four-week waiting period does not apply. If there is a petition by dissentient shareholders then the giving of the assistance is postponed until the final determination of the petition, unless the court orders otherwise (s 158(3)). The latest time for the giving of the assistance is eight weeks from the making of the statutory declaration (or, if more than one, from the making of the earliest of the statutory declarations, see s 158(4)). One odd point here is that the earliest available time is measured from the passing of the resolutions, whereas the latest possible time is measured from the making of the declarations. Also, the relevant declaration is the earliest one, whereas the relevant resolution is the latest one. In cases involving several companies, careful attention to timing is needed, or it is possible to get into a situation where compliance with all the rules is impossible.

20.4 Advice to the parties

Repurchase of the company's own shares is not a matter to be undertaken lightly. As a commercial matter it is necessary to ask whether this is genuinely in the best interests of the company. Where a company is prospering, the redemption of some of its shares may seem an appropriate way of rewarding shareholders and reducing their risk (though it is also desirable to take account of the effect of the proposals on the balance of power within the company and on future dividend returns for shareholders whose shares are being repurchased). Where the company is not prospering – as is certainly the case here – the idea of reducing the share capital available to meet the legitimate demands of creditors seems a very odd one. The only other proper reason for redeeming shares is that it is desirable to buy out a shareholder – perhaps because he is causing trouble within the company and it seems appropriate to get rid of him. The directors must always remember that in recommending and approving a scheme for the repurchase of shares (as in everything else) they are required to act in the best interests of the company. In the great majority of cases those interests will be better served by finding a purchaser for the shares of anyone who is desperate to leave the company than by agreeing to a repurchase of the shares by the company. In the present case it is hard to believe that buying out a shareholder is the appropriate way to proceed.

Fortunately for the company, the Shareholder Agreement does not require the company to buy back Duncan's shares – indeed, it would be difficult to draft such an agreement effectively, since there would always be the possibility that the company did not have the funds to make such a purchase lawful, in which event the contract would clearly be unenforceable for illegality. There are also difficulties in the way of any suggestion that the company should give someone else financial assistance to purchase Duncan's shares. None of the exceptions to s 151 seems to apply here; the only possibility would be the larger purpose exception, and that is unlikely because the purpose is without doubt the restructuring of the share capital. If Arthur, Bill and Edwina are unwilling to buy Duncan's shares (or cannot afford to do so, as seems quite likely) then the best option must be to find someone who is willing to take those shares and who has the resources to pay for them personally. There is of course such a person on the scene – Frederick – and it seems that he will have to be allowed to become a shareholder.

FURTHER READING

M J Sterling, 'Financial assistance by a company for the purchase of its shares' (1987) 8 Co Law 99.

21 Takeovers and Mergers

LEARNING OUTCOMES

By the end of this chapter, you should understand:

- the nature of takeovers and mergers in respect of private companies;

- the put option;

- takeovers and mergers – merger relief;

- group reconstructions;

- directors' duties in relation to a proposed takeover/veto clauses;

- the takeover process and its aftermath.

SCENARIO

The board of directors of Ye Olde Curiosity Shoppe plc ('YOCS') is not at all pleased at Frederick's behaviour in secretly buying shares in Great Expectations Ltd from Duncan. It is positively alarmed to discover that the other shareholders have not been able to take up all Duncan's shares and that the company itself has had to buy some of them. The board views this as evidence that the other shareholders have little faith in the company, and it is worried that the company did not really have the spare cash to buy these shares. It has have now decided that YOCS too must terminate its ill-fated involvement with Great Expectations Ltd, and therefore proposes to invoke the put option contained in the agreement under which YOCS invested in the company (see **Chapter 19**). It will be remembered that this gave YOCS the right to require the other shareholders to buy it out at the original allotment price at any time within three years of the allotment. The board also give Frederick the choice between resigning from the board of YOCS and being sued by YOCS for breach of his duty to the company by making a secret purchase of the shares. Frederick wisely chooses the former option.

It will be obvious that the remaining shareholders are in no position to honour their agreement – they have recently exhausted their reserves of cash buying out Duncan, but the contract is clearly drafted and there is no doubt that YOCS is acting entirely within its rights in making this demand.

Frederick's father is understandably embarrassed by the turn which events have taken, and in a final gesture of family solidarity he makes one further attempt to help. He introduces Frederick to a company called Hard Times plc, which specialises in rescue operations for ailing private companies.

At the start of this chapter the position is that Hard Times and Great Expectations Ltd are in discussion about the possibility of a rescue scheme under which Hard Times will buy the shares presently held by YOCS, as well as injecting further capital in the form of either additional shares or a new loan.

OVERVIEW

This chapter is concerned with the process by which the control of a company's affairs is transferred from one party to another. It is necessary at the outset to make two distinctions. The first is between takeovers and mergers. In a takeover, control of a company (commonly referred to as the target company) is acquired by a third party. In a merger, two companies (sometimes more than two, but not often) transfer their shares or assets to a third company, which thereafter takes the place of the merging companies. It can readily be seen that a merger implies a relationship approaching equality between the parties, whereas a takeover implies a relationship of inequality.

The second distinction is that between share-based transactions and asset-based transactions. In the former the restructuring is effected by a transfer of the shares of the target company to the new parent company, or by a transfer of the shares of all the merging companies to the new merged company, with shares in the new merged company being issued in exchange. In an asset-based transaction the original entities may continue to exist (and even to retain their original shareholders) but the assets of the companies concerned are transferred to the new parent company, or merged company, as the case may be. As will be seen below, each of these schemes may have its own advantages and disadvantages.

21.1 The put option

It is convenient to deal first with the put option held by YOCS. It will be remembered that YOCS negotiated this as part of its original investment in the company (see **19.5**; it will be recalled that the option could be exercised within three years of the allotment). The disadvantage of a put option from the point of view of the remaining shareholders is that they cannot control when it will be exercised, and if it is exercised they may be required to pay money which they do not readily have, as has happened here. On the other hand, the events which have happened demonstrate clearly enough the wisdom of YOCS in stipulating for this option.

We are told that Arthur, Bill, Charlotte, Edwina and Frederick do not have the cash to honour the put option, and this creates a very serious situation for them, since they have apparently no defence to a claim by YOCS claiming specific performance of the contract and/or damages for breach of contract. Ultimately, they face personal bankruptcy if YOCS should choose to pursue such a claim to judgment and enforcement.

Frederick is of course the immediate cause of this dilemma, since it is his secret purchase of some of Duncan's shares that has precipitated the crisis. However, it is unlikely that the others have any remedy against him, since he does not appear to have committed any breach of a duty owed to Great Expectations Ltd. He was clearly in breach of his duties to YOCS (as to directors' duties in this situation, see further **Chapter 10**), for which he has paid through the loss of his seat on the board of YOCS.

In these circumstances the shareholders have no alternative but to look to rescue from outside, and it is in this context that Frederick's father introduces them to Hard Times plc.

21.2 Takeovers

It is fairly clear that what is being contemplated in the present case is effectively a takeover. Hard Times plc will take a majority equity stake in the company, ie its investment will take the form of shares rather than the purchase of assets. An important consequence of this is that the company will be able to appoint directors to the board of Great Expectations Ltd and may be able to remove the existing directors (though, as is explained in **Chapter 11**, getting rid of the existing directors may be more difficult). Any attempt to remove the existing directors will no doubt run into problems in relation to the *Bushell v Faith* clause in the Articles (these clauses are discussed in detail in **Chapter 7**), though, as has been seen, the clause presently contained in the Articles may not be properly drafted to give full protection to all directors.

Other important consequences follow from a takeover. The target company becomes a subsidiary of the acquiring company. This has implications for the preparation of accounts (as to these matters, see **Chapter 18**), taxation (in respect of the group taxation regime) and the distribution of profits. There is considerable doubt about the freedom of the acquiring company to cause the subsidiary to distribute its profits after a takeover.

21.2.1 Directors' duties in relation to a proposed takeover

Where a takeover of a company is proposed, the directors of the target company may find themselves in a difficult position. They are of course obliged to act in the best interests of the company, and they will have to consider two questions in particular. The first is whether they should advise shareholders generally to accept the bid, and the second is whether they should accept the offer in respect of any shares which they themselves hold.

An important general point to be made at this stage is that most of the issues discussed here are relevant only in those cases where the directors do not hold a majority stake in the company. If they do hold more than half the shares then it is effectively up to them as shareholders, rather than as directors, whether the bid succeeds. Some of the defensive tactics discussed below will therefore become irrelevant. However, even where the directors do hold the majority of the shares, there is still a risk that they will recommend a bid which undervalues the company because it is made by a company with which they are associated, and they see the bid as a means of gaining effective control of all the shares.

So far as the first question is concerned, the directors may face a conflict of interest. A frequent consequence of a takeover is that the directors are removed and replaced by the nominees of the acquiring company. Directors who recommend a takeover bid must therefore know that they are recommending a course of action which is likely to cost them their own jobs. There is thus a natural temptation to resist any takeover bid, and the first step in such resistance may well be a recommendation to the shareholders that they should not sell their shares. Although directors do not generally owe duties to shareholders (see **Chapter 10**), this situation provides an exception to the general rule. In *Gething v Kilner*

[1972] 1 WLR 337, it was held that directors making a recommendation to shareholders in connection with a takeover bid must do so honestly and carefully. This means that the directors must consider carefully whether or not to make any recommendation in relation to the bid. If they do decide to make a recommendation, they must then look carefully at the merits and demerits of the bid, and must come to a conclusion without being influenced by the effect of the recommendation on their own personal position. Directors may incur personal liability to shareholders who rely on a recommendation which has been reached in disregard of these principles. Usually, this will be a recommendation to reject the bid, though there may occasionally be cases where the bid is made by associates of the directors (or even by a company controlled by the directors for the purpose of removing troublesome shareholders), and in these circumstances the directors may be tempted to recommend a bid which rather undervalues the shares. It is submitted that aggrieved ex-shareholders should also have a right of action against the directors in such a case.

A more extreme version of the same problem arises where the directors wish to take positive steps to fight the bid. A common response to a bid to acquire the existing shares is to seek to issue more shares, preferably to opponents of the bid (perhaps the directors themselves) so as to deter the acquiring company. Other defensive tactics include burdening the company with large amounts of debt (sometimes known as the 'poison-pill defence'), or voting the directors lucrative long-term service contracts which the acquiring company will find very expensive to buy out (sometimes known as a 'golden parachute'). Such clauses do not require the shareholders' approval unless the contract is for more than five years without the possibility of termination by the company (Companies Act 1985, s 319). In some instances these tactics may work in the sense that the takeover bid is successfully resisted, but directors should remember that their duty to the company does not permit them to engage in any of these tactics except for the benefit of the company, and all these devices are, for varying reasons, very difficult to justify from that point of view.

As a general point it may be observed that it is for the shareholders collectively to decide whether or not to accept the bid. If the directors genuinely believe that the bid is not in the best interests of the company, they should put their case rationally to the shareholders. The adoption of other devices to frustrate the bid tends to suggest that the directors are not really convinced of the merits of their case, or that they are concerned with questions other than the merits of the argument – such as their own position in the company. It must also be remembered that shareholders considering a bid are not required to act in the best interests of the company – they have made a speculative investment in the company and they are entitled to consider whether their own interests would be best served by realising that investment. It is in principle improper for the directors to seek to influence that choice by adversely affecting the company's position.

Further points may be made in relation to each of the devices alluded to above. The issue of new shares is problematic both in principle and from the point of view of procedure. As a matter of principle, shares should be issued when the company needs new capital and when the directors conclude for good reasons that additional share capital would be more appropriate than debt financing, or when it is desired to bring additional shareholders into the company for the company's benefit. The idea that shares must not be issued for other reasons is sometimes known as the 'proper purposes' doctrine (see **Chapter 13**). An issue made for the purpose of frustrating a takeover bid is unlikely to satisfy this doctrine. In terms of procedure the directors will need to have authority to issue new shares (Companies Act 1985, s 80; see **Chapters 13** and **19**) and will need to obey (or validly disapply) the pre-emption rights created by s 89 of the Companies Act 1985 before they can issue shares to people of their own choosing. If they attempt to do this in the course of a takeover battle, alert shareholders may well appreciate what is happening and prevent them from doing so.

The poison-pill defence raises different issues. Questions of internal company procedure will rarely arise, since borrowing is normally in the hands of the directors. However, a small private company which is heavily in debt to the bank may find that the bank is decidedly unhappy about the sudden creation of large additional debts for no good commercial reason. Even if the bank's debenture does not require the bank's approval for such a step, the company is likely also to have an overdraft which the bank can call in at any time. A threat from the bank to do this if unjustified debts are created is likely to be sufficient to stop the directors in their tracks. As a matter of principle the creation of new borrowings is obviously something which should not be done without good cause. It is also a two-edged weapon; if it succeeds in deterring the prospective bidder, the directors will be left with a company burdened with excessive debt, which will make their job more difficult and which is likely in time to make the shareholders dissatisfied with them.

The golden parachute device is perhaps the most blatantly improper of those considered here. It does nothing to protect the interests of existing shareholders, being more in the nature of an insurance policy for the directors. Contracts of this kind entered into in apparent contemplation of a takeover bid will be very hard to justify. Indeed, it is suggested that an acquiring company which discovers the existence of such contracts should simply ignore them. The directors may seek to sue for wrongful dismissal or to claim the amounts allegedly due under the parachute clause, but the acquiring company should counterclaim against the directors for breach of duty in granting themselves these clauses. This may be more difficult if the clause is for more than five years and the directors have managed to persuade the shareholders to approve it in a General Meeting.

21.2.2 Directors' veto clauses

Where the company's Articles of Association include a clause allowing directors to refuse to register a transfer of shares (see **20.1** above), this may appear an alternative way for the directors to block a takeover of which they do not approve (for whatever reason). Problems of procedure and principle again arise. Procedurally, it will be necessary to examine the veto clause carefully. There is no single standard form for such clauses, and it must be a matter of construction to decide whether in the circumstances of the particular case it is possible for the directors to invoke it. As a matter of principle, this power of the directors must again be exercised in the best interests of the company, and an unreasonable refusal to register a transfer may be challenged, either as unfairly prejudicial conduct under s 459 of the Companies Act 1985 or by means of an application to court to rectify the share register.

21.2.3 The takeover process

Much depends on the extent to which the takeover is an agreed process between the directors of the target company and the directors of the acquiring company. In the case of an agreed takeover, the directors of the target company may recommend the bid to their own shareholders. If the latter accept it, the shares can be transferred to the acquiring company without difficulty. Where the takeover is opposed by the directors of the target company, it becomes a question of the acquiring company's ability to persuade enough of the target company's shareholders to sell their shares. In public companies this may lead to well-publicised battles between the rival factions, but this is partly a consequence of the much larger number of shareholders normally found in public companies. In private companies the opposition of the directors is often fatal, since they often control a majority of the shares. Even where their shareholding is less than this, the other shareholders are likely to be strongly influenced by their recommendation. Hostile takeovers of private companies are therefore something of a rarity, though it must be admitted that the target company's directors are sometimes persuaded to agree only because they see that agreement as the company's last chance to avoid complete collapse. It may be supposed that the directors of Great Expectations Ltd feel something of that sort in the present case.

21.2.4 The aftermath of a takeover

Although there are no legal rules which require any particular consequences to follow after a takeover, there are at least two common consequences which do have important legal implications. The first is that the directors are likely to be dismissed. The new owners of the company will normally have the power to pass an ordinary resolution to that effect. In some instances this may be affected by the existence of a *Bushell v Faith* type weighted voting rights clause (clauses of this kind are considered more fully in **Chapter 7**), which purports to protect the directors from dismissal. However, it is to be expected that a prudent acquirer of the company will insist on the removal of these from the Articles as a pre-condition of the acquisition, or alternatively will require the directors to undertake to resign on completion of the takeover. Arthur, Bill and Edwina therefore need to take great care in negotiating with Hard Times plc if they have any aspiration to save their own positions, and it must be admitted in the present case that Great Expectations's record does not make a strong argument for retaining any of the three of them on the board, though no doubt Arthur and Bill have skills which are useful to the company, so that they might reasonably expect to be retained as employees.

The second common consequence of a takeover is that the acquiring company will wish to review the operations of the acquired company in order to decide what steps need to be taken for its future development. Many takeovers result from the underperformance of the target company, and it is thus not surprising that reviews of this kind very often result in a significant restructuring of the company involving a reduction in the workforce. This is also all too likely to occur in the present case. Although statutory regulations prevent the automatic dismissal of employees when a business is taken over in an asset takeover (such a dismissal would happen otherwise because the identity of the employer would have changed); the point does not arise in a takeover by shares, since the employing company is the same one, which is merely under new ownership. There is nothing to prevent a subsequent round of redundancies following on from the review of the business.

21.3 Merger relief

Mergers, in the sense described in the **Overview** above, give rise to other problems.

21.3.1 Companies Act 1985, ss 130 and 131

The general problems relating to share premium accounts required under s 130 of the Companies Act 1985, and the accounting problems to which they give rise, are covered at **19.3**. The particular aspect of share premium accounts which must be examined here is that which arises when in a merger or takeover shareholders of the target company receive shares in the acquiring company as consideration for their shares in the target company. This is a very common way of structuring deals of this kind. The question of a share premium account will arise if the shares in the acquiring company are issued at a premium to their face value.

21.3.1.1 Determining whether there is a premium

In a cash transaction this is of course a simple matter of comparing the cash price of the allotment with the face value of the shares, but the situation presently being considered is that where the consideration for the issues of shares in the acquiring company is shares in the target company. It is therefore necessary to value those shares in order to establish whether the value received by the acquiring company exceeds the nominal value of the shares in the acquiring company which are issued in exchange.

This will commonly happen, since most successful companies which have been in business for some time will have a net asset value per share which exceeds the nominal value of the shares. If s 130 applies to the transaction then any premium on the issue of the shares for the purposes of the takeover must of course be put into the share premium account, and is subject to the rules applying to that account (for the details of this see **Chapter 18**). In these circumstances s 131 of the Companies Act 1985 may apply (see **21.3.2** below). The further requirement which must be satisfied for the application of s 131 is that the acquiring company must have acquired in pursuance of this share exchange arrangement a holding of at least 90% of the equity of the target company. Section 131(4) makes clear that it is not necessary for all these shares to have been acquired in exchange for shares of the target company; it is sufficient that after the exchange the acquiring company holds at least 90% of the shares. Thus, s 131 may be available in the very common situation where the acquiring company has a substantial shareholding in the target company before making a full takeover bid and then reaches a 90% holding in consequence of that bid.

Two further important refinements on the s 131 rules may be noted. The first is found where the share capital of the target company is divided into classes. Section 131(5) then requires that the 90% holding must exist in relation to each of the classes of shares taken separately. It is not enough to have 90% of the ordinary shares if only 75% of the preference shares are held. The second refinement is relevant where some of the 90% holding of shares is held by the holding company of the acquiring company (ie the company which is intending to claim the relief offered by s 131), or by a subsidiary of the acquiring company. The shares held by the holding company or subsidiary are to be treated as being held by the acquiring company for the purposes of determining eligibility for s 131 relief.

21.3.2 The nature of the relief

Where s 131 applies, the effect is that s 130 does not apply. Thus, none of the consideration for the issue of the shares in the acquiring company need be transferred to the share premium account.

If for any reason the transaction in question does not qualify for s 131 relief, then the ordinary share premium rules will apply. This will often cause problems, since a cash sum will have to be transferred to the share premium account even though the company will not have received any cash. It is therefore clearly desirable to take advantage of merger relief whenever it is possible to do so.

21.4 Group reconstructions

Another issue which arises for Great Expectations Ltd in the present case is that the company has a subsidiary – Great Expectations Ideas Ltd. This has been in existence for some time. It is likely that any acquiring company (which would effectively acquire the whole group, since the subsidiary is 100% controlled) would want to review the group structure. It must be admitted that the present structure makes very little sense. There was never any need to have a separate company for the public relations work, of which there was never a great deal (and at present there is virtually none). The review of the group structure would therefore probably conclude that the subsidiary should be wound up, all its assets and liabilities being transferred to the parent company. A glance at the 2002 accounts (**Appendix E**) will show that this should not be too difficult a task, as the subsidiary does not have much in the way of assets or profits.

21.5 Advice to the parties

Great Expectations Ltd is clearly in some considerable financial difficulty; indeed, its very survival must be in question. In these circumstances the appearance on the scene of Hard Times plc must seem to the hard-pressed shareholders a welcome relief. This is a rather misleading impression for various reasons. First, because of the likely effect on the directors and the employees, discussed at **21.2.4** above. Secondly, because Hard Times plc, as a company experienced in rescues of this kind, will want to see very definite action taken to reverse Great Expectations's decline. Those employees whose jobs are saved (including Arthur and Bill) must expect to come under much closer scrutiny from the new owners of the business. Arthur's fondness for going on holiday is likely to attract unfavourable attention, for example. It may be said that the arrival of Hard Times plc represents the last chance for Great Expectations Ltd, whose directors must hope that Hard Times plc is prepared to take them on.

21.6 Subsequent developments

Negotiations between the two companies continued for some time, and reasonable progress was made. Unfortunately, at the same time the 2003 accounts of Great Expectations Ltd were being prepared. The company tried very hard to persuade its auditors to give an unqualified audit report, but was in the end unable to do so. The company's financial situation was so serious that the auditors felt obliged to issue a going concern qualification (for the details of such qualifications see **Chapter 18**), and Hard Times plc, alerted by this, ultimately broke off the negotiations, concluding that even that company's expertise in rescuing struggling companies would not be enough to save Great Expectations Ltd.

22 Company Sickness

LEARNING OUTCOMES

By the end of this chapter, you should understand:

- company voluntary arrangements;
- administration;
- the appointment of an administrative receiver – the Enterprise Act 2002, Pt 10.

SCENARIO

The break down in the takeover talks with Hard Times plc brought Great Expectations Ltd to crisis point. The management had to act with expediency in order to avoid panic amongst its creditors which could have led to an untimely end for the company if a creditor were to have petitioned for its winding up. The directors decided to present the company's dilemma in the most favourable light in order to persuade the creditors to allow them sufficient time to turn the company around, which in their view would have been to the advantage of all interested groups (ie, creditors, employees, shareholders). Meetings with the shareholders and the creditors were arranged, at the creditors' convenience, for the following week, and the company's accountants were instructed to prepare cash flow forecasts and profit predictions in readiness for those meetings. The objective had been to persuade both the shareholders and the creditors as to the wisdom of agreeing to a voluntary arrangement. This in turn would have given the directors the voluntary moratorium they had hoped for. Unfortunately, YOCS had lost patience with Great Expectations Ltd and indicated its unwillingness to co-operate any further; indeed YOCS reclaimed a number of items sold to Great Expectations Ltd (but not paid for), relying on the retention of title clause in the contracts of sale. This action gave the directors little option but to apply to the court for an administration order, having recognised the gravity of the position they faced. To concede loss of management powers seemed a worthwhile price to pay for a general moratorium on future creditors' claims. Bus Bank plc, horrified at the depletion of Great Expectations Ltd's stocks, was unwilling to comply and, on the instructions of its Head Office, appointed a receiver under its debenture. The debenture was created before 15 September 2003, and therefore the power to appoint a receiver remains unaffected by the coming into force of Pt 10 of the Enterprise Act 2002 (ss 248–250), which restricts the power to appoint a receiver in respect of floating charges created after the above date.

OVERVIEW

This chapter is not intended to be an exhaustive account of the various regimes available to a company in financial difficulty; for such a discussion students are referred to the many specialist texts which have been written (eg, Fletcher, *The Law of Insolvency* (Sweet

& Maxwell), Goode, *Principles of Corporate Insolvency Law* (Sweet & Maxwell)). We have, however, given an outline of company voluntary arrangements, the administration procedure and administrative receivership, in order to facilitate a basic understanding of their respective roles.

22.1 Company voluntary arrangements

22.1.1 Proposal to enter into a voluntary arrangement

Sections 1–7 of the Insolvency Act 1986 provide for a company, including one that is in administration or which is being wound up, to enter into a voluntary arrangement with its creditors. The procedure is initiated by the making of a proposal to the company and to its creditors for a composition in satisfaction of its debts, or a scheme of arrangement of its affairs. The proposal must provide for a 'nominee' to act in the voluntary arrangement, either as trustee or in some other capacity for the purpose of supervising its implementation.

Section 1 imposes limitations on the persons permitted to make the proposal and the persons eligible to be appointed as nominee. The proposal will be made by the company's directors acting collectively, unless the company is in administration or liquidation (if the company is in winding up then it is the liquidator who must make the proposal, and if it is in administration then the proposer will be the administrator), and it is not necessary that the company be insolvent. For this reason it is a useful route where the directors take the view that it is better for all concerned that the company avoid winding up or administration despite having financial difficulties which they may believe relate mainly to cash flow problems. An advantage for the directors is that while the arrangement is in place the directors retain their powers of management, unlike the administration procedure (see **22.2** below), and although the company does not benefit from any general moratorium, whereby creditors are prevented from suing for their debts, the creditors who agree to the arrangement are bound by it once it has been duly approved, and this effectively prevents them taking an independent course of action for the recovery of their debt.

The terms of the proposal must follow the requirements of s 1, although that section provides for only the barest essentials of the agreement with the details being left to the contracting parties themselves. As with any other contract, the consensus between all parties must be apparent from the terms of the arrangement, and if this is so then the contract will be binding on all concerned. Although the position of secured and preferential creditors is protected by s 1(3) and (4), such creditors could choose to take the unusual step of modifying their rights through an arrangement. Any such modification requires their positive consent. Unsecured creditors are also free to adopt any arrangement they see fit. They may agree to a rateable return on amounts outstanding, for example 75p in the pound, or perhaps accept a proposition that different rates of return should be made for different types of creditor, for example small creditors to receive a higher return than large creditors.

22.1.2 The role of the nominee

The nominee, who is required by statute to be a person who is qualified to act as an insolvency practitioner, becomes a supervisor of the arrangement when it is in place. His first task for the company is to prepare a report, based on his personal assessment of the business, as to the soundness and fairness of the voluntary arrangement proposed. This report must be submitted to the court within 28 days (Insolvency Act 1986, s 2). In order to prepare this report the nominee must have submitted to him by the proposer:

(a) a document setting out the terms of the proposed voluntary arrangement; and

(b) a statement of the company's affairs, together with other information, in correspondence with the requirements imposed by the Insolvency Rules 1986 (SI 1986/1925).

Once these are in place the nominee will call meetings of both the company and its creditors (Insolvency Act 1986, s 3). The Insolvency Rules stipulate the timing and notice requirements of these meetings, the general requirement being that parties to be summoned to the meetings be given at least 14 days' notice of them. At this stage in a company's life the interests of the creditors are of greater importance than those of other recognised groups (see the discussion of the various interests of a company in **Chapter 9**), and this is acknowledged in r 1.13, which provides that the convenor has a duty to have regard primarily to the convenience of the creditors when fixing the venue for the meetings, and the meeting of creditors must be held in advance of the meeting of members (*Commissioners of Inland Revenue v Adams & Partners Ltd* [2001] 1 BCLC 222).

22.1.3 Voting on the proposal

At their respective meetings the creditors and the members may vote, by proxy if they so wish. The number of votes ascribed to each creditor is in proportion to his debt; members' votes are determined by the company's Articles. At the creditors' meeting the proposal to adopt the arrangement must be passed by a majority of more than three-quarters of the value of the creditors present or voting by proxy; at the members' meeting, unless otherwise stated in the Articles, the resolution to adopt the arrangement must be a simple majority of those voting in person or by proxy. If the arrangement is adopted by both meetings the result must be notified to the court and to all who were notified of the meeting (s 4(6); r 1.24(1)–(4)).

Once approved, the voluntary arrangement is binding on all those who were entitled to be present at the meeting, whether or not they attended and voted (s 5(2)). Section 6 of the Insolvency Act 1986 does provide a right to challenge either the approved arrangement itself or the manner in which the approval was obtained, although such challenge must be made within 28 days from the date that notice of the results of the meetings was given to the court.

22.1.4 Implementation of the voluntary arrangement

When the voluntary arrangement has taken effect, the responsibility for its implementation rests with the nominee or his representative, who becomes known as the 'supervisor of the voluntary arrangement' (Insolvency Act 1986, s 7(2)). If the supervisor is required to continue the business, or to trade on behalf of the company or to realise assets of the company, he must keep records and accounts which detail his dealings and record all receipts and payments. Both the supervisor's role and that of the company's directors are defined by the terms of the arrangement and under it the management may remain in place.

Once the voluntary arrangement has been completed the supervisor must within 28 days send notice of the fact to all creditors and members of the company, who are bound by the arrangement, and the notice must be accompanied by a copy of the supervisor's report summarising all receipts and payments made by him, and explaining any difference between the original proposal and its actual implementation. This notice must also be sent to the Registrar of Companies and to the court within the same 28-day period.

22.1.5 Small companies

By virtue of s 1A of the Insolvency Act 1986 and Sch A1, an eligible or small company (see **Chapter 18** for a definition of this concept) may obtain a moratorium on any creditor action while a proposal for a voluntary arrangement is considered, without having to go into administration.

22.2 Administration

22.2.1 Objectives of and consequences of administration

The administration procedure, the major innovation of the insolvency reforms of 1985–6, was implemented following a strong recommendation by the Cork Committee (*Report of the Review Committee on Insolvency Law and Practice* (1982), Cmnd 8558). The procedure has since been amended by Pt 10 of the Enterprise Act 2002. The objective behind administration is to facilitate corporate rescue by providing for an ailing company to be run by rescue specialists, who would attempt either to rehabilitate it or to secure a better return on the realisation of its assets than would be possible under winding up. Previously a successful rescue operation depended on the existence of a suitably drafted debenture contract which conferred sufficient powers on the receiver appointed under it to act on behalf of the company. Administration, on the other hand, is available to all companies experiencing financial difficulties, including those subject to floating charges which have crystallised (see **Chapter 15**).

The objectives of an administration order may be set out as follows (see s 1A of and Sch B1 to the Insolvency Act 1986):

(a) rescuing a company as a going concern;

(b) achieving better results for the company's creditors as a whole than would be likely if the company were wound up;

(c) realising property in order to make a distribution to one or more secured or preferential creditors. (It should be noted that the range of preferential creditors has been considerably reduced by s 251 of the Enterprise Act 2002.)

Objective (a) must be given priority by the administrator unless it is, inter alia, not reasonably practicable to secure this objective.

An administrator may be appointed by the court making an administration order (s 7(4)(b) and Sch B1, paras 10 and 12), by the holder of a floating charge (Sch B1, para 14), by the company or its directors (Sch B1, para 22).

It is worth noting that an administration order may not be made after the company has gone into liquidation.

It will be recalled that Bus Bank plc managed to prevent Great Expectations Ltd obtaining an administration order (see **Scenario**, above). This is due to that fact that by virtue of Sch B1, para 26 to the Insolvency Act 1986, where a petition for an administration order is proposed, notice of it must be given immediately to any person who has appointed, or who is or may be entitled to appoint, an administrative receiver. This means that the holder of a floating charge who is entitled to appoint a receiver (or administrator, see **22.3** below) is given the opportunity to do so, an opportunity which was taken by Bus Bank plc, thus preventing the granting of an administration order.

For floating charges created after 15 September 2003, known as 'qualifying charges', the power to appoint a receiver is considerably restricted (see s 72A of the Insolvency Act 1986 and SI 2003/2095). The only option available is the appointment on the part of the charge holder or the court of an administrator. This is not the situation for Bus Bank plc because the creation of the floating charge pre-dates 15 September 2003.

While a company is in administration the following consequences arise by virtue of Sch B1, para 43 to the Insolvency Act 1986. By this provision creditors cannot, without the consent of the administrator or permission of the court, enforce any charge on or security over the company's property, or take any steps to repossess goods in the company's possession under any hire purchase agreement, conditional sale agreement, chattel leasing agreement or retention of title agreement. This is precisely the advantage the directors of Great Expectations Ltd were looking to when they decided to apply to the court for an administration order. Furthermore, in our scenario, YOCS had begun to retrieve goods supplied under its retention of title clause, an activity which would have had to stop if a petition had been presented.

22.2.2 The powers of the administrator

The directors of Great Expectations Ltd had wanted to retain their position during the company's crisis, hence the desire for a voluntary arrangement; however, they could not have remained as managers if the company had been placed into administration. They would not have been dismissed automatically from their directorships, but they would not have had any powers for as long as the order endured. An administrator takes over the management of the company in this situation, displacing the directors as the competent organ of the company in this respect, although the directors must continue to fulfil their other duties such as the filing of annual returns. In practice the directors may find themselves ousted as a result of the administration order, because the administrator acting in the interests of the company is empowered to alter the management team as he sees fit if he believes it will enhance what he is trying to achieve. This might lead to the dismissal of the directors and the appointment of new or additional ones (Insolvency Act 1986, Sch B1, para 61). It should be noted here that the Company Directors Disqualification Act 1986 is available against directors of companies which have 'at any time become insolvent' and so includes companies in administration. Indeed the administrator is obliged to report to the Secretary of State immediately he becomes aware of anything which might constitute a *prima facie* case for the making of an order under s 6(1) of the Company Directors Disqualification Act 1986 (unfitness). The directors of Great Expectations Ltd are without doubt mindful of their own potential personal liability both under the guarantee outstanding (Edwina) and under ss 213 and 214 of the Insolvency Act 1986. To avoid liquidation would be of benefit to them in this respect (see further **Chapter 23**).

The administrator acts as an agent of the company, thus the company is bound by all acts performed validly by the administrator. Even if there is some defect with the appointment, nomination or qualification of the administrator, his acts will be valid in law (Insolvency Act 1986, s 232). Consequently, the position is the same as for other agents of the company, ie directors (see **Chapter 10**). A further aspect of the administrator's ability to bind the company is provided by Sch B1, para 69 to the Insolvency Act 1986, which states that where a person deals in good faith and for value he need not concern himself as to whether the administrator is acting intra vires. However, this protection for third parties places the onus firmly on them to show good faith and value. A further provision in favour of the administrator under Sch B1, para 64 provides that any power conferred on the company or its officers by the Insolvency Act 1986, the Companies Act 1985 or by the company's own Memorandum and Articles, which could be exercised in such a way as to interfere with the exercise by the administrator of his powers, shall not be valid except to the extent that consent is given by the administrator himself.

Schedule B1, para 59(1) to the Insolvency Act 1986 confers wide powers upon the administrator, who is empowered to do 'anything necessary or expedient for the management of the affairs, business and property of the company'. It has already been noted that the administrator may remove any director and appoint any person to a directorship, whether to fill a vacancy or otherwise, as he sees fit. His aim will be to acquire a management team which he believes will benefit the company's return to prosperity by the time the order expires or is discharged. He can at any time call meetings of interested parties, ie creditors and members, in order to consult directly with them on matters of importance, so, for example, he might look for a vote of confidence from them before making a decision to hand back the reins to the management team.

Section 234 assists the administrator in that it permits him to apply for an order from the court to require a person who has in his control or possession any property, books, papers or records to which the company appears to be entitled, to pay, deliver, convey, surrender or transfer such items to him. Section 235 imposes a duty to co-operate with the administrator on persons presently or formerly connected with the company, and this involves an obligation to give full information to the administrator concerning all aspects of the company. There is also a requirement that such persons attend for private examination at any time reasonably required.

The administrator has power to deal with company property which has been charged, including property subject to a floating charge. This means that encumbered property can be disposed of and dealt with, subject to the requirement that any substitute property or proceeds should go first in paying the obligations owed to the chargee (Sch B1, para 71).

22.2.3 Avoidance of prior transactions

This subject is dealt with in **Chapter 23**, but for completeness it is worth mentioning here that as an 'office holder' within the meaning of the Insolvency Act 1986, an administrator is enabled to look at earlier concluded transactions of the company in order to determine if any of them can be reopened and funds or property returned to the company for the benefit of the company as a whole. For example, if the company has with intent preferred one creditor over others, or disposed of company property at an undervalue, such transactions could be reversed (see further **Chapter 23**).

22.2.4 Duties of an administrator

The primary duty of the administrator is to devise his proposals for rescuing the company. These proposals must be complete within eight weeks of the company entering into administration and then sent to the Registrar, creditors and members of the company (Insolvency Act 1986, Sch B1, para 49). A copy of the administrator's report must be laid before a meeting of the creditors of which not less than 14 days' notice has been given, and either copies should be sent to all members or advertisements placed which indicate the address from which copies can be obtained. The proposals are considered by the meeting which then votes on them (Sch B1, para 53). The proposals can be modified before approval, provided the administrator is in agreement. The result of the meeting is reported to the court and to the Registrar of Companies. Where the creditors' meeting has declined to support the proposals the court has a wide discretion as to how to respond, although in practice, unless there were overwhelming evidence to suggest that the purposes of the order could still be attained, the court would be most likely to assist the company in moving onto the next phase of insolvency, liquidation.

22.3 Administrative receivership

It should be noted here that the following discussion of administrative receivers is subject to a qualification. By virtue of ss 248–250 of the Enterprise Act 2002 (see s 8 of and Sch B1 to the Insolvency Act 1986), the power to appoint administrative receivers under floating charges created after 15 September 2003 is severely restricted, and the holders of floating charges created after that date will under such charges only have the power to appoint an administrator to enforce their security. The power to appoint a receiver is maintained in respect of floating charges created before the above date, as was the case in respect of the floating charge created in favour of Bus Bank plc.

22.3.1 What is an 'administrative receiver'?

The term 'administrative receiver' appeared for the first time in the Insolvency Act 1986, and it identifies the individual who is both receiver and manager for a company. The role is usually taken on by a member of the accountancy profession who, with a suitably qualified team, will take over the running of the business from the directors with a view to selling off its assets as a going concern, or, more rarely, devising a plan to trade the company out of its difficulties. The latter course may well involve substantial restructuring and rationalisation.

An administrative receiver is defined in the Insolvency Act 1986, s 29(2), which provides for him to be:

(a) receiver or manager of the whole (or substantially the whole) of a company's property;

(b) appointed by or on behalf of the holders of any debentures of the company;

(c) secured by a charge which, as created, was a floating charge, or by such a charge and one or more other securities (s 29(2)(a)); or

(d) a person who would be such a receiver or manager but for the appointment of some other person as the receiver of part of the company's property (s 29(2)(b)).

There are many similarities between the role of administrative receiver and that of an administrator, which is hardly surprising given that the administration procedure was based largely on that of receivers and managers. Similarities include the following:

(a) Both are deemed the agent of the company unless liquidation begins.

(b) Both are 'office holders' within the definition in the Insolvency Act, which means that both enjoy extra powers, duties and privileges.

(c) Both can dispose of property charged to another creditor, although, unlike an administrator, the receiver must first obtain permission from the court under s 43.

(d) Both must prepare a statement of affairs, copies of which must be submitted to both the creditors and to the Registrar of Companies.

(e) The acts of both an administrative receiver and an administrator are valid notwithstanding any defect in their appointment (s 232).

22.3.2 Appointment of an administrative receiver

In order to be appointed an administrative receiver a person must be a qualified insolvency practitioner. An administrative receiver is appointed by or on behalf of the debenture holder. It is for the debenture contract to list exhaustively the situations in which a receiver is to be appointed, as the courts are not willing to imply a power into a debenture if it is not expressly provided for. For example, in *Cryne v Barclays Bank plc* [1987] BCLC 548, the court refused to imply a power to appoint simply because the security was in jeopardy.

22.3.2.1 Situations usually provided for in the debenture

The power to appoint a receiver will be exercisable on the occurrence of a specified event provided for in the debenture (but only in respect of floating charges created before 15 September 2003, see above). It is normal for these specified events to be indicators that the company is in financial difficulty. The most common ground for appointment is non-compliance with a demand for payment. The demand for payment need not specify the exact amount being claimed, as this may hinder a creditor in his recovery if he has to produce exact figures (see *Bunbury Foods Pty Ltd v National Bank of Australasia Ltd* (1984) 51 ALR 509, at p 619–20). In any event, the amount due may be disputed. If the demand is for more than is actually due, this will not invalidate the demand, but payment by the debtor of the correct amount due would invalidate a subsequent appointment of an administrative receiver since there would have been no breach of the debenture terms. Although the debtor is allowed a reasonable amount of time in order to meet the demand, this does not stretch to sufficient time to enable the debtor to raise finance elsewhere (*Cripps (Pharmaceuticals) Ltd v Wickenden* [1973] 2 All ER 606). Provided the debenture holder acts in good faith, he is entitled to consider his own interests first and need not be concerned as to the fate of the debtor company (*Shamji v Johnson Matthey Bankers Ltd* (1986) 2 BCC 98,910).

22.3.2.2 Other events commonly specified

Other events commonly specified as warranting the appointment of an administrative receiver are as follows:

(a) the company being wound up, either voluntarily or by the court (if the liquidator is already in control of the company's assets then the receiver must seek the leave of the court before he can take possession of the assets secured under the debenture);

(b) execution being levied against the company's property by a judgment creditor;

(c) the company being in breach of one of its obligations included in the debenture, for example the production of management accounts or the maintenance of acceptable liquidity ratios;

(d) the company ceasing to trade, or there being a real threat that trade will cease;

(e) the enforcement by another creditor of his debt or security.

22.4 Effect of appointment of administrative receiver

Section 44(1) of the Insolvency Act 1986 provides:

The administrative receiver of a company—

(a) *is deemed to be the company's agent, unless and until the company goes into liquidation;*

(b) *is personally liable on any contract entered into by him in the carrying out of his functions (except in so far as the contract otherwise provides) and on any contract of employment adopted by him in the carrying out of those functions; and*

(c) *is entitled in respect of that liability to an indemnity out of the assets of the company.*

From this we can see that there is a presumption that the receiver is an agent of the company and not of the debenture holder. This is in many ways beneficial for the debenture holder, who appoints the receiver without becoming a principal. For example, the appointing debenture holder cannot be made liable if the receiver commits a wrong during the course of his appointment (*Re Simms* [1934] Ch 1), neither will he be liable for debts incurred by the receiver (*Cully v Parsons* [1923] 2 Ch 512), nor will the receiver's remuneration have to be met by him, being payable by the company before payment of preferential debts (s 60(1), see further **Chapter 23**). On the other hand there are disadvantages for the debenture holder, as illustrated by the case of *Cretanor Maritime Co Ltd v Irish Marine Management Ltd* [1978] 1 WLR 966, where the receiver appointed to an Irish company which was subject to a *Mareva* injunction, could not transfer the company's money to Ireland for the benefit of the debenture holder because the obligation imposed upon the company was also imposed upon the receiver as agent of the company.

22.4.1 Company management under administrative receivership

If the floating charge has not already crystallised by the time the receiver is appointed, his appointment will result in its crystallisation. The charge becomes a fixed equitable charge and the company's management can no longer deal with those assets. The directors and officers lose all of their powers of management, although they retain their statutory obligations, for example to file returns, etc. An important right which the directors (and probably the shareholders) do not lose, is the right to instigate proceedings in the company's name where the controller, here the receiver, is unwilling to pursue litigation which may be beneficial to the company and may be described quite properly as an asset of the company. This is illustrated by the case of *Newhart Developments Ltd v Co-operative Commercial Bank Ltd* [1978] 2 WLR 636, where the receiver refused to sue his appointer, the bank, for breach of contract on behalf of the company. The directors issued a writ without his approval and the Court of Appeal refused to set it aside (see also *Watts v Midland Bank plc* [1986] BCLC 15). This is not surprising in the light of the approach taken by the courts when any controllers refuse to instigate proceedings against themselves in a situation which might amount to a fraud on the minority by those in control (see **Chapter 14**). It is hardly for the benefit of the company as a distinct entity to refuse to consider litigation which might swell the pool available for the entire body of creditors.

22.4.2 Powers of a receiver

These are usually found in the debenture itself, although a statutory list, which reflects the standard set of terms usually included in a debenture (see the comments of the Cork Committee (Cmnd 8558, para 494)), is provided by s 42 of and Sch 1 of the Insolvency Act 1986.

22.4.3 Duties of a receiver

These are relatively light, although more recently the courts and the Insolvency Act 1986 have tightened up the rules as to the accountability of receivers. At common law, the receiver's position as agent of the company is not accompanied by the onerous duties that apply to an agent's position. See the decision of the Court of Appeal in *Standard Chartered Bank Ltd v Walker* [1982] 1 WLR 1410, where it was held that a receiver must, in addition to acting bona fide, ensure that he is not negligent in the exercise of his powers. This represents a departure from the previous position, whereby a receiver was required merely to act bona fide, but there is no overriding duty to the company as a distinct entity and the receiver must have paramount regard to the debenture holder's interests, even if this is in conflict with the interests of the unsecured creditors (*Re Northern Developments (Holdings) Ltd* (1978) 128 NLJ 86). It is worth noting however that ss 46–49 of the Insolvency Act 1986 does now require the receiver to keep unsecured creditors informed about the progress of the receivership.

Various statutory duties are imposed upon receivers by both the Companies Act 1985 and the Insolvency Act 1986, and a full discussion can be found in one of the specialist texts on the subject.

Edwina, who had at this stage been feeling tremendously burdened by the trials she had experienced in the final months of Great Expectations Ltd's fight for survival, had been further frustrated by her perception of the continued treachery of her business associates. She had believed Bill to be inept but honest, but Arthur became to her a justifiable target for her frustration, as she believed him to be guilty of culpable inactivity. In the midst of the company's downfall, Arthur had been away on yet another holiday. In her anger, Edwina focused on Charlotte and Frederick, who she believed were as much to blame. Edwina and Frederick had parted on unpleasant terms, and Frederick and Charlotte had become allied in the process. Charlotte's crusades could no longer be said to have no effect on the running of the company, since Frederick had indicated his willingness to use his voting power to dismiss the directors, in particular Edwina. Edwina believed that the company had been undermined by incompetents. The catalogue of disputes which culminated in the company's collapse included one over the issue of a cheque payable to 'The Working Women's Association', a registered charity, issued by Bill at Frederick's (and Charlotte's) insistence. In Edwina's opinion, this had contributed to the company's intolerable cash flow position. Her reaction, although to prove disastrous for the future survival of the company, had seemed to her at the time to be in the best interests of the company. The employees, who, in her opinion, had been the backbone of the company, deserved at least as much as this 'charity cheque'. Consequently, Edwina had used her power to give the workforce (including herself) a bonus payment equivalent to one year's salary.

An immediate and predominant concern of Edwina had been the personal guarantee she had executed in favour of Bus Bank plc to secure the company overdraft up to £50,000. This was, in turn, supported by a second charge on her flat. As soon as the full implication of this 'error' had become horribly apparent, she had devised a scheme designed to salvage what she could out of the mess. Edwina had honestly believed that she could turn the company around, *given time*, and it was this that would have been her major goal; however, she could no longer be sure that she would remain in office long enough to see through the necessary restructuring of the company. Her scheme therefore had had two objectives: the first was to embark on a long-term salvage operation – Edwina had never considered this to be otherwise than legitimate, believing that creditors need not be informed of the crisis. The second, and overriding, objective had been to take positive steps to reduce her own personal exposure. Consequently, reducing the company's indebtedness to the bank had been given priority. Keeping the bank happy had long been recognised by Edwina as being of paramount importance because, in her experience, once a company's bank has taken an 'attitude' towards a company, ensuing difficulties become inevitable. She had also wanted to keep all creditors firmly behind the 'corporate veil', and as the bank was the only creditor to have recourse to her personal assets, any reduction in the bank borrowing had become crucial. To achieve this Edwina had tightened credit control, and at the same time deferred payment to creditors. In addition further credit from new suppliers had been obtained, thus giving Edwina more breathing space, and she had closed a separate bank account, originally opened to comply with the retention of title clause included in the contract of sale between Great Expectations Ltd and YOCS, and had those funds placed into Great Expectations Ltd's account.

Edwina had worked days that began with the dawn chorus and sometimes lasted well into the night. At times it had looked as though she might have saved the day, like the true heroine she was; but alas, as we saw, Great Expectations Ltd went into receivership despite last-ditch efforts to secure a creditors' voluntary arrangement or, in the alternative, an administration order. Bus Bank plc and YOCS are now involved in a dispute as to the entitlement to the company's stock and the proceeds of sale, Bus Bank plc claiming all current assets under the floating charge and YOCS seeking to rely on the terms of their retention of title clause in the contracts of sale. A liquidator has now been appointed following a resolution to wind the company up as a creditors' voluntary winding up; however, unless he can manage to re-open certain concluded transactions and succeed in pursuing the company officers for a contribution order, there will be no funds available for the unsecured creditors.

OVERVIEW

We are concerned in this chapter with both an examination of the transactions entered into by a company during the 'twilight' period and the role of a company's directors when it is insolvent or doubtfully solvent. In many situations the directors will strive until the bitter end to bring their company back from the brink, not least because of the tremendous personal, not to mention financial, commitment they will have made to the company, but also because it will in all likelihood be their major, if not only, source of income. However, it is immediately apparent that the greatest potential conflict between the directors' personal interests and the interests of the company as a distinct entity presents itself when insolvency threatens. There is evidence of such a conflict in the scenario at the beginning of this chapter between Edwina and Great Expectations Ltd. It would be naive to imagine that a director in Edwina's position would accept the loss of her home gracefully as a result of a guarantee given when the company's future looked decidedly rosy, especially where she believes herself to be in a position at least to reduce her personal exposure by trading on. It must also be remembered that very often a director believes himself to be doing his utmost to secure the survival of the company rather than bringing down the shutters immediately a serious financial crisis is encountered. The loss to creditors may be exacerbated by reacting in either way, but the law provides that to continue to trade fraudulently, with intent to defraud creditors or wrongfully, when a director knew or ought to have known that there was no reasonable prospect of the company being able to meet its debts as and when they fall due, is unacceptable unless the directors took every step to minimise the loss to creditors (Insolvency Act 1986, s 214). What is legally acceptable and what is morally acceptable may well mesh in the application of the law. This is a matter which is explored in this chapter and in **Chapter 24**, where we look at the disqualification of directors for unfitness.

Whatever the legality and the morality of continuing to trade, it is not always easy to determine the dominant purpose or motive behind the decision to continue to trade. It is surely a fine line between trading on in the hope that the company will recover and trading on in order to reduce the indebtedness to the bank so as to reduce personal liability under a contract of guarantee. The timing of a director's activities too can be a major factor, for example for a retailer to wait until after the Christmas boom when a the bank account will often be at its healthiest, or when a large consignment of goods supplied on credit is delivered so as to 'fill' the floating charge, will undoubtedly influence the directors' behaviour. From the scenario we know what motivated Edwina into her course of action, but it will be very difficult for a liquidator to substantiate such a finding from the facts. Gathering evidence requires time, and – for lawyers and accountants at least – time means money. We are not concerned in this chapter with the difficulties of collating evidence, but this factor must be borne in mind when discussing the way in which the law can deal with a situation such as this.

Having recognised the potential conflict facing a director of an ailing company, it then becomes important to examine the remedies offered by the law to a company's creditors who may have been prejudiced as a result of a director's conduct.

For the purposes of this chapter, the first issue we can detect from the scenario is that Edwina has knowledge that at best the company is facing a serious financial crisis and at worst it is insolvent. This would suggest that her behaviour after this point would be scrutinised by the liquidator. However, the accounts show the company to be solvent, therefore much depends upon the weight of any contrary evidence which may indicate that Edwina was, or ought to have been, in a position to know better. A second issue is the possible breach of duty to the company by Bill. The duty of care at common law that is owed by a director to his company in conducting its affairs may become more stringent when a company becomes insolvent and/or where the director is an executive director with specialist expertise or knowledge (see **Chapter 10**). Another related issue is that of Frederick's position, and possibly Charlotte's also, in regard to the management of the company. Possible liability as shadow director will have to be explored.

While the company continues to trade the directors will have the powers of management vested in them by the shareholders; however, the importance of recognising that the directors owe their duties to the company as a separate and distinct entity is crucial. The shareholders' power to ratify any action of the directors which is in excess of their powers is limited when the company no longer has its capital intact, or where there is an act to commit a fraud on the company (*Aveling Barford Ltd v Perion Ltd* [1989] BCLC 262). When Edwina made the bonus payment to the employees and Bill signed the cheque in favour of the 'Working Women's Charity', they may have been acting outside the scope of their powers if the payment was not *bona fide* in the best interests of the company and for a proper purpose (see **Chapter 13**).

Exactly what is meant by the phrase 'best interests of the company' needs to be explored. We have already identified various groups within a company who may be said to have an interest in the company, namely, the shareholders, the employees and the creditors (discussed in outline in **Chapter 9**). The difficulty is in deciding how to prioritise these interests, especially in times of conflict or potential conflict. If a director gets his priorities wrong he may wind up in breach of his duty to the company (on this see **Chapter 10**). In an insolvency situation the most obvious conflict will be between the shareholders and the creditors, a conflict which is accentuated when it is a company such as Great Expectations Ltd, where the major shareholders are also in position as management, thus controlling the company's activities. From the scenario it is evident that there is also a conflict between the employees and the creditors, where the bonus payment can probably be said to have been made largely at the expense of the creditors. The conflict between the various groups of creditors also becomes evident; the most obvious instance is that between the floating charge holder and the supplier of goods under a retention of title clause. This has been discussed in **Chapter 15**. The availability of any contribution from the directors following any order under ss 212–214 of the Insolvency Act 1986 would probably be restricted to the unsecured creditors, although this itself may yet be challenged by the holder of a floating charge.

23.1 Risk capital or supply of credit?

The obvious interest creditors have in a company is that the shareholders' 'stake' should remain intact. It is the fortune of the owners of the company that should swing with the success or failure of the business. After all, YOCS would not be enamoured with the notion that its role has changed from that of supplier to that of chief investor in an interior design business of which it has little or no experience. Similarly, Bus Bank plc, when seeking to justify its strict adherence to lending formulas, will explain that it is merely a supplier of finance to the company rather than an investor in Great Expectations Ltd, and will point to the comparatively low return it receives when compared with the returns previously enjoyed by the entrepreneurs themselves.

The rules regarding maintenance of capital, which have already been dealt with (see **Chapter 17**), recognise the importance of the distinction between risk capital and the supply of credit. These rules seek to protect creditors from acts that would result in company assets being removed for the benefit of a shareholder or shareholders at the expense of creditors, and are strengthened in the case of small private companies by s 238 of the Insolvency Act 1986 (transactions at an undervalue, discussed at **23.3** below). This is because in many small companies – indeed in many medium-sized companies – the members and the directors will often be one and the same, with the result that company assets can be removed by way of remuneration or fees (*Re Halt Garage Ltd* [1982] 3 All ER 1016; see **Chapters 16** and **17**). The liquidator of Great Expectations Ltd may try to recover the charity payment and the bonus wages under this provision. Unfortunately, this may not be a practical solution, as shall be seen, therefore the liquidator may wish to consider pursuing the directors themselves for breach of duty and recoup the loss to the company from them (Insolvency Act 1986, s 212, discussed at **23.7.2.1** below). He may of course choose to do both.

23.2 Examination of prior transactions

When the winding up or administration of a company commences, any of its obligations which remain unperformed cannot be enforced unless, of course, the administrator or liquidator decides to comply, which would only be in circumstances where it is believed to be the best course of action for the company. Similarly, transactions which were concluded before administration or liquidation commenced cannot be disputed. This cut-off date is good for all purposes and is a necessary feature of both procedures. In certain limited circumstances, however, a liquidator or administrator, described as an 'office holder' for the purposes of the Insolvency Act 1986, can re-open concluded transactions where an unfair advantage has been conferred by the company on a particular creditor or other person to the detriment of the general body of creditors. To some extent this assists the office holder to observe the *pari passu* rule which is fundamental in this area of law (Insolvency Act 1986, s 107 (voluntary winding up) Insolvency Rules 1986, r 4.181(1) (compulsory winding up)). In simple terms it means that creditors are to be treated equally in the distribution of a company's assets, receiving a rateable return on moneys owing to them. To treat one creditor or group of creditors in a more favourable way than the general body of creditors offends the spirit of this rule, and such activities are vulnerable to attack by an office holder under one of the provisions of the Insolvency Act 1986, a discussion of which follows. Of course the principle of *pari passu* is rarely achieved in practice, it being perfectly legitimate for creditors to gain an advantage in advance of winding up by becoming a secured creditor. The granting by the company of security to the advantage of one creditor is itself vulnerable where it impinges upon the notion of fairness between creditors acknowledged to exist in insolvency law, and this will be where the security is granted during what is known as 'the twilight period' if, during that period, the company was unable to pay its debts (see **23.3** below).

Further inroads into the *pari passu* principle are made by the special position of preferential creditors. This group must be paid in full before payments can be made to the holder of a floating charge and to the unsecured creditors (although the number of preferential creditors has been significantly reduced under s 251 of the Enterprise Act 2002).

As between the unsecured creditors, a supplier of goods may have successfully included a retention of title clause in the sale agreement which puts him in a better position than another supplier of goods who has failed, whether by design or default, to do so. It should be noted that a supplier of services cannot reserve title to anything, unless of course he supplies goods as well as services to the same company (retention of title clauses are discussed more fully in **Chapter 15**).

Despite these difficulties with the *pari passu* principle, as a principle of equity it is protected to some considerable extent by the various provisions of the Insolvency Act 1986 which are discussed below.

23.3 Transactions at an undervalue

Section 238 of the Insolvency Act 1986 makes it possible for an office holder to apply to the court for an order to reverse a transaction at an undervalue. The term itself includes a gift to a person made by the company, or a transaction entered into for which the company receives either no consideration or consideration the value of which is significantly less than the value, in money or money's worth, of the consideration provided by the company. Both the charity payment made by Great Expectations Ltd and the bonus payments made to its employees are obvious candidates for scrutiny by the liquidator in our scenario. The payment to charity is, quite clearly, a gratuitous one, but the bonus payments to the employees present more difficulties in this regard, although much depends upon their rights contained in their contracts of employment. If no provision is made for the payment of bonuses, it is likely that these payments could be seen as gratuitous, the company being under no legal obligation to make such a payment. The amounts concerned will probably be substantial enough to warrant action being taken by the liquidator given that they amount to an extra year's salary, but in a practical sense recovery may prove very difficult, especially if the money has already been spent, or if the employees have unalterably altered their position as a result of receiving it. On the other hand, Edwina's individual payment may be substantial enough to make it worthwhile for the liquidator to pursue that particular transaction. There are, however, a number of conditions which must be met if an application to the court is to succeed under s 238:

(a) *The company must be in liquidation or administration. This is clearly satisfied in the scenario.*

(b) *The company must have entered into the transaction at an undervalue at a relevant time, ie either two years ending with the onset of insolvency, or, in the case of administration, between the time of presentation of a petition for an administration order and the making of an order on that petition.* This condition reflects the requirement that for such transactions to be re-opened they must have occurred during the twilight period, which for s238 is two years. Again this condition is met by the facts of our scenario.

(c) *The company was unable to pay its debts within the meaning of s 123 of the Insolvency Act 1986 either at the time of entering into the transaction, or in consequence of entering into it.* This condition is the one most likely to present the liquidator with evidential difficulties. If the company appears to be capable of paying its debts as and when they fall due at the time of the disputed transactions, the creditors have no cause for complaint because no unfair advantage is being conferred upon the recipient. Great Expectations Ltd probably appeared from its management accounts to be solvent for longer than it actually was, and may have succeeded in meeting its then current liabilities only by incurring fresh obligations to the same or new parties. The presence of a doubtful debtor in the current assets of Great Expectations Ltd emphasises the difficulties of establishing just how solvent a company is at any given time.

(d) *The defence under s 238(5) of the Act is not available.* This defence exemplifies the notion of acting in the best interests of the company. Certain payments which might otherwise be seen as transactions at an undervalue may be justifiable on the grounds that they are *bona fide* payments made in carrying on the company's business to its benefit. It would be much harder to justify the charity payment in this way, as it is difficult to see what gain an ailing company could make as a result of such a gesture; however, the payment to the employees might be acceptable if evidence were adduced indicating the desirability of such positive steps of encouragement designed to persuade key personnel either to remain loyal to the company, or to become more diligent and productive. Edwina's bonus may be more difficult to justify on these grounds.

(e) *The court must not be debarred by s 241(2) from making the order.* This restricts the orders which can be made by the court in favour of *bona fide* transferees and recipients in good faith, for value and without notice. This defence will not avail the 'Working Women's Association' as it has not provided any value. On the other hand, the employees who received the bonus payments may well seek to justify them as having been received for value, although the payment of an amount equivalent to a year's salary may raise serious questions as to bona fides and notice of any impropriety.

(f) *Application for the order is made by the office holder.* In other words, by the administrator or liquidator.

23.4 Preferences

The fact that a creditor has been preferred over other creditors immediately before the onset of insolvency does not prevent him from retaining what is, after all, his money. This in itself is not an affront to the *pari passu* rule (see discussion in *The Report of the Review Committee on Insolvency Law and Practice* (The Cork Committee) (1982) Cmnd 8558, para 1254). Section 239 of the Insolvency Act 1986 is concerned with impropriety on the part of the *company*, therefore it is not the fact that a creditor has been preferred that is important but the desire of the company to produce such an effect (s 239(4)). Once the requisite desire can be shown on the part of the company then, provided the court is satisfied that the other conditions of the section are fulfilled, an order requiring the restoration of the status quo will be made.

The conditions to be satisfied under s 239 follow to a large extent those mentioned in **23.3** above in the discussion of transactions at an undervalue. Thus:

(a) the company must be in liquidation or administration;

(b) the preference must have been given at a relevant time (six months, unless given to a person connected with the company when it is extended to two years);

(c) the company was unable to pay its debts either at the time of the transaction, or as a result of making it;

(d) the court is not debarred by s 241(2) from making the order; and

(e) the application is made by the office holder.

To give a preference means in effect that the preferred creditor is put in a more favourable position than the other creditors. However, new credit advanced to the company in exchange for security, or terms which put that creditor in a better position than the other creditors, do not amount to a preference to the extent that it is represented by new value provided by him. It is only the putting in a better position of an existing creditor for existing debts that can amount to a preference. In the scenario, Edwina had adopted a positive plan to reduce Great Expectations Ltd's borrowing from the Bus Bank plc. She did this in order to reduce her own future liability under the guarantee she had given to the Bank, which would have required her to make up any shortfall following the Bank's realisation of the company's assets by the receiver under its debenture. There is nothing in the scenario to suggest that Bus Bank plc was pursuing the company for the repayment of the overdraft; indeed the company may well have been working within its facility due to Edwina's strategy. If the Bank had been demanding repayment this would have destroyed the notion of free will on the part of the company, which is crucial if the company is to be shown to have been influenced by a desire to produce such an effect. In the scenario it is clear that Edwina was seeking to prefer herself as a surety. The fact that there was no desire to prefer the Bank is overridden by evidence of a desire to prefer the surety, Edwina. This in itself is sufficient to amount to a preference under s 239. It may be that on a given set of facts the company could be seen to be preferring both the principal creditor and the surety, although in this scenario the Bank does not seem to be included.

23.5 Extortionate credit transactions

Extortionate credit transactions can be set aside or varied by the court under s 244 of the Insolvency Act 1986, where the transaction was entered into by the company within three years of its going into liquidation or administration. Obviously the company must then be in liquidation or administration, and it must have been a party to the transaction.

'Extortionate' is a somewhat difficult term to define, but some assistance may be derived from ss 138(1), 139(1) and 171(7) of the Consumer Protection Act 1974. The transaction must be shown to have been oppressive rather than simply unfair, reflecting the inequality of the bargaining power of the parties. In this situation the court is likely to find that the transaction is indeed extortionate, and so exercise its power either to vary its terms or to set it aside.

23.6 Floating charges for past value

The giving of security to an existing creditor at a time when a company is facing liquidation has long been recognised as being unfair, amounting to the conferment of an advantage on that particular creditor over the general body of creditors. For the most part, claims under s 245 of the 1986 Act, which is concerned with floating charges for past value, are more likely to be brought under s 238, transactions at an undervalue (see **23.3** above), given that it reaches back further in time – two years in all cases compared with 12 months under s 245, although this period is itself extended to two years where the charge is given in favour of a person connected with the company. A big advantage of bringing a claim under s 245 is that for a charge given in favour of a connected person it is not necessary that the company shall have been insolvent at the time of giving the charge or as a consequence of giving it. Clearly someone involved with the day-to-day running of the company will have advance warning of problems ahead, and is certainly in a good position to set about putting himself in a better position than other creditors. Creditors generally are not in a position to know when a company is doubtfully solvent, especially when it can meet its debts as and when they fall due.

23.7 Examination of officers

23.7.1 Breach of duty by the directors

The directors can discharge their duty to the company only by considering the various interests it comprises. This is by no means an easy task, and deciding what weight they should give to the various competing groups is fraught with difficulty. In extreme situations a contrast can be shown: for example, a company which is a financial success needs to consider the creditors only in so far as debts should be met as and when they fall due; whereas a company that is hopelessly insolvent has its creditors as its primary interest group in all matters. What is less clear is the situation where a company is in the twilight period and the directors are taking management decisions which will promote only one group at the expense of other groups.

If the shareholders feel that the management are giving insufficient weight to their position then, in theory at least, they have some recourse (see further **Chapter 14**). However, the first difficulty a creditor will encounter if he tries to enforce the duty to consider his interests against the company, is the lack of machinery available to seek redress. Technically we are concerned with a breach of duty to the company, and it is therefore for the appropriate organ to initiate proceedings on behalf of the company (*Foss v Harbottle* (1843) 2 Hare 461, 67 ER 189). Unless the company is in receivership (see **Chapter 22**) or liquidation, creditors have no recourse if the directors fail to consider their interests, even in a situation which involves a possible breach of the directors' duty to the company. Where the company is in liquidation the authority lies with the liquidator, creditors having no standing to bring proceedings on their own behalf (discussed below). Despite there being some support for the argument that directors also owe a duty to the creditors directly, it is unlikely that this is more than a duty to consider their interests. In *Winkworth v Edward Baron Development Co Ltd* [1986] 1 WLR 1512, at 1516, the Law Lords agreed with Lord Templeman when he said that:

> *A duty is owed by the directors to the company and to the creditors of the company to ensure that the affairs of the company are properly administered and that its property is not dissipated or exploited for the benefit of the directors themselves to the prejudice of the creditors. (emphasis added)*

A creditor who sought redress for breach of this duty would presumably be suing in tort (see **Further Reading**, below), although there is no unambiguous English authority on this point and Lord Templeman's dictum was *obiter*. The Commonwealth cases seem to support the view that the directors' duty is to the company alone but that it can be discharged only by considering positively the various interests of the competing groups (*Walker v Wimborne* (1976) 137 CLR 1, at 7; *Nicholson v Permakraft (NZ) Ltd* [1985] 1 NZLR 242, at 249), and it is submitted that this view is probably correct as it is in keeping with such bastions as the *Salomon* principle (see **Chapter 8**) and the rule in *Foss v Harbottle* (see **Chapter 14**). The crucial point, though, is to decide what is meant by consideration in this context. If we turn to the situation Great Expectations Ltd finds itself in, for example, presumably it would be open to Edwina and Bill to say that they had considered all legitimate interests of the company but still decided that, in their view, the company was best served by drawing the charity cheque (to keep the shareholders happy) and by making the bonus payments (to keep the employees happy); the creditors, although considered before making these decisions, were no more than one factor (see **Further Reading**, below).

The ability of the company, through a liquidator or an administrator, to scrutinise and possibly re-open concluded transactions such as these, emphasises the point that the creditors must not be prejudiced by activities which are concluded in the run-up to liquidation. When faced with such conflicting interests, it is more likely that the court would decide questions of prominence in the light of the particular circumstances of each individual case, which would include the financial position of the company.

In *West Mercia Safetywear Ltd v Dodd* (1988) 4 BCC 30, at 33, the Court of Appeal decided that a director had breached his duty to the company when he had failed to consider the interests of the creditors at a time when a company was undeniably insolvent.

Dillon LJ approved the following dicta from *Kinsela & Anor v Russell Kinsela Pty Ltd (in liq)* [1986] 4 NSWLR 722, at 730:

> In a solvent company the proprietary interests of the shareholders entitle them as a general body to be regarded as the company when questions of the duty of directors arise. If, as a general body, they authorise or ratify a particular action of the directors, there can be no challenge to the validity of what the directors have done. But where a company is insolvent the interests of the creditors intrude. They become prospectively entitled, through the mechanism of liquidation, to displace the power of the shareholders and directors to deal with the company's assets. It is in a practical sense their assets and not the shareholders' assets that, though under the medium of the company, are under the management of the directors pending either liquidation, return to solvency, or the imposition of some alternative administration.

The real difficulty, and one that has already been alluded to, is where the company is hovering over the brink, so to speak, yet fails to give considerable weight to the interests of the creditors. If this is found to amount to breach of duty to the company, it will be recognised only if the company subsequently fails, and then the very difficult question that arises is as to when the breach of duty first occurred.

23.7.2 Statute

Part IV, Ch X of the Insolvency Act 1986 is headed 'Malpractice before and during Liquidation; Penalisation of Companies and Company Officers; Investigations and Prosecutions', and it is this Part of the Act which concerns us in part of this chapter.

Sections 206 to 211 inclusive come under the title 'Offences of Fraud, Deception etc', and are concerned with criminal offences that are committed through malpractice on the part of past or present officers of the company. Although there are many situations where the liquidator need only prove the *actus reus* on the part of the accused, the onus being placed on the accused to show that he had no intent to defraud (ss 206(4)(a), (b); 207(2); 208(4); 210(4)), these sections are concerned with criminal sanctions against delinquent directors, therefore dishonesty, as it appears from all the circumstances envisaged in these sections, is a prerequisite.

Sections 212 to 217 are included under the heading 'Penalisation of Directors and Officers', and offer a civil remedy for creditors against directors and officers who are found to have been involved in malpractice. Sections 212–214 are those which may impose liability on directors or officers, so an understanding of these provisions is a very important requirement for every company director and his adviser(s) (s 215 is concerned with proceedings under ss 213 and 214, and ss 216 and 217 restrict the re-use of company names). There is considerable overlap between these three sections and, in practice, a liquidator may well pursue the director under all three; but there are also significant differences between the sections, as will become apparent when we apply them to our scenario and the events surrounding the demise of Great Expectations Ltd.

23.7.2.1 Misfeasance – s 212

This is a summary remedy against a person who has either been an officer, a liquidator, an administrator or an administrative receiver, or who has in some other way been involved in the management, promotion or formation of a company, and who has misapplied or retained, or become accountable for any money or other property of the company, or been guilty of any misfeasance or breach of any fiduciary or other duty in relation to the company. The effect of this provision is to empower the court in the appropriate circumstances to order a person to repay, restore or account for money or property, or any part of it, with interest at such rate as the court thinks just, or to contribute such sum to the assets of the company by way of compensation in respect of the misfeasance, or breach of fiduciary or other duty as the court thinks just. The right to make an application is conferred upon a liquidator, an official receiver, any *creditor* (a creditor has no standing to apply under ss 213 and 214) or contributory who has first obtained leave of the court. Where a company is insolvent a contributory is unlikely to benefit from an order under s 212, but such a person will be a suitable applicant under s 212. Note that s 212 does not apply unless the company is in the course of winding up. Therefore if the company is placed in the hands of a receiver, for example acting on behalf of the bank as debenture holder, then s 212 is not available.

The scope of s 212 seems to be very wide. Not only does it provide a method of recovering money and property that has been misapplied, it also provides liability for breach of any fiduciary or other duty. The duties themselves are to be found in the well-established rules of the common law and equity – eg, the duty not to make a secret profit (see **Chapter 10**) and the duty to act bona fide in the best interests of the company – and are to some extent now embodied in specific statutory provisions (see the Companies Act 1985, ss 309, 317, 459; Insolvency Act 1986, s 214), but such breaches would be actionable under s 212 even though it is likely that this would not be used alone.

There will often be many complaints against a director – eg, transactions at an undervalue, preferences, the improper exercise of the power to manage the company resulting in payments being made that are not in the best interests of the company as a whole, and perhaps some suggestion of fraudulent or wrongful trading (discussed at **23.7.2.2** and **23.7.2.3** below) – and clearly s 212 is wide enough to cover them all. If we look at the conduct of Edwina, Bill, Charlotte and Frederick in the present scenario, Edwina and Bill as directors assume potential liability, and, further, Frederick and possibly Charlotte may be shown to be involved in the management of the company (although this may be difficult to prove in Charlotte's case). Section 212 would seem to be capable of covering all the acts of malpractice of our players. In addition, it is open to any creditor or contributory, with the leave of the court, to apply to the court for an examination of their conduct. It is certainly possible that YOCS, or those creditors of the company duped into providing credit during Edwina's final scheme, might feel sufficiently aggrieved to request the court to examine her conduct during the twilight period. And we must not forget Duncan, who, despite being unable to gain anything financially, may feel that the behaviour of his business associates should be scrutinised, especially as they had cost him his investment while at the same time managing to emerge with sizeable directors' emoluments.

If an application under s 212 was being brought by the liquidator then it would in all probability be alongside other provisions which deal with specific acts of malpractice. In *West Mercia Safetywear Ltd v Dodd* (1988) 4 BCC 30, Dodd was held to be liable for misfeasance when he transferred £4,000 to a company creditor with the intention of paying off a valid debt but without regard to the interests of the general body of creditors. This payment was solely to reduce his potential guarantee liability to that creditor. This was undoubtedly a preference (see **23.4** above), and indeed there was clear fraud in this case, but it will be remembered (see above) that this was where the notion of negligence was introduced into English law. It seems that a director will be guilty under s 212 if he is in breach of his duty to consider the interests of the creditors at a time when the company is insolvent, and this could be useful if, for example, Bus Bank plc or YOCS felt sufficiently motivated to apply to the court for an examination of the conduct of the directors or officers.

It must be noted that while a creditor can apply under this provision, any contribution order or recovery of property or money will still have to paid to the liquidator. Consequently there may be little incentive for a creditor to fund such an application.

23.7.2.2 Fraudulent trading – s 213

Section 213 deals specifically with situations where a company has continued business with intent to defraud creditors, which means that the test will be subjective. Liability may be incurred by *any person* (s 212 was concerned with officers of a company) if, in the course of the winding up of a company, it appears that any business has been carried on with intent to defraud creditors of the company or creditors of any other person, or for any fraudulent purpose. The court may declare any parties who were knowingly a party to such activities liable to contribute to the assets of the company as the court thinks proper. Section 213 is dependent upon the company being in the process of winding up, a restriction which is not applicable under s 458 of the Companies Act 1985 which imposes criminal penalties for fraudulent trading.

Fraud requires actual dishonesty (*Re Patrick & Lyon Ltd* [1933] Ch 786). In order to determine whether a person has been dishonest, it used to be thought that the standard was to be judged by 'current notions of fair trading among commercial men, real moral blame'. However, this needs to be reconsidered in the light of the Court of Appeal's ruling in *R v Lockwood* (1985) 2 BCC 99, 333, where the notion of 'one standard of dishonesty for criminal cases in general and a separate and more restricted standard of dishonesty for cases involving commercial fraud' was not accepted. It would seem safer to determine fraud on the standard expected by ordinary honest people rather than by business or commercial men.

The objective of this provision, it would seem, is to protect creditors from being exposed to unacceptable risk when they deal with limited companies. It is not enough that the person, usually the director, continued trading in times of financial difficulty because he felt that the company could trade it out or that there was 'light at the end of the tunnel'. Edwina's behaviour immediately before the collapse of Great Expectations Ltd is hardly unique; certainly it is not uncommon for the directors of a sinking company to delude themselves into thinking that the crisis can be salvaged by one more lucrative contract. There was a suggestion, however, that this might be acceptable business practice, in the much cited but unreported case of *White & Osmond (Parkstone) Ltd* (unreported but referred to in *R v Grantham* [1984] 2 All ER 166), and it became known as the 'sunshine test' on the basis of Buckley LJ's dicta. He said that:

> ... there is nothing to say that directors who genuinely believe that the clouds will roll away and the sunshine of prosperity will shine upon them again and disperse the fog of their depression are not entitled to incur credit to help them get over the bad time.

In *R v Grantham* this approach was disapproved by the Court of Appeal, which felt that the test was simply whether the company could pay its debts as and when they fell due or shortly thereafter. If it could not, then to continue to trade may expose the directors to criminal and personal liability for fraudulent trading.

Fraudulent trading can be shown even if there is only one transaction (*R v Lockwood* (1986) 2 BCC 99,333, at 99,431; *Re Sarflax* [1979] Ch 592), although it is more likely that a series of transactions will together indicate fraud.

It will be remembered that s 213 provides for a civil remedy for fraudulent trading, whereas s 458 of the Companies Act 1985 provides for a criminal conviction, if proved. The penalty under s 458 is imprisonment, a fine or both. Section 213, on the other hand, can result in the court requiring a contribution from the perpetrators as the court thinks fit. The liquidator in the case of Great Expectations Ltd will be faced with a very difficult task if he attempts to show fraud on the part of Edwina because he will need to show that she was dishonest. The difficulty would be even greater in respect of Arthur, Bill, Frederick and Charlotte.

23.7.2.3 Wrongful Trading – s 214

Liability imposed on directors and shadow directors

Section 214 imposes liability on *directors* (note s 212 is concerned with directors and officers, and s 213 with any person), including shadow directors, where a company has gone into insolvent liquidation and at some stage before the commencement of the winding up the directors knew, or ought to have known, that the company could not avoid going into insolvent liquidation. Liability under this section can be avoided if the directors concerned can bring themselves within the statutory defence, which excuses them from liability if they can show that they took every step in order to protect creditors at the stage when the impending insolvency was or should have been anticipated (s 214(3)).

At first sight this section looks very promising, at least to the liquidator of Great Expectations Ltd. Section 214 deals only with the conduct of a company's directors, compared with the much wider range of individuals targeted by ss 212 and 213. However, s 214 does include the behaviour of shadow directors. The uncertainty created by the definition of a shadow director, contained in s 251 of the Insolvency Act 1986, is in part to blame for the initial panic in 1986 when this provision became law (see McGee and Williams, 'A Company Director's Liability for Wrongful Trading', ACCA Research Report 30). The Act defines a shadow director as 'a person in accordance with whose directions or instructions the directors of the company are accustomed to act'. It is as result of this section that Frederick, and indeed Charlotte, may face liability in respect of wrongful trading in relation to Great Expectations Ltd. However, a person is not a shadow director solely because he advises the company in a professional capacity, for example as solicitor, accountant or banker. The requirement is for one party clearly to be controlling the actions of another, and would include, for example, the situation where a bankrupt installs his or her spouse as sole director while claiming himself to be a mere employee or consultant, or where a controller, wishing to remain anonymous, installs and instructs others. The position is more complex for those who are acting in a professional capacity, because although this of itself is insufficient to come within the definition of a shadow director, if they become involved in the running of a company, particularly when that company is having financial difficulties, to the extent that the directors are taking instructions from them, they are at risk of being found to be shadow directors.

There is undoubtedly a very fine line between acting professionally and becoming 'involved' in a company's affairs. A company in financial difficulty is more likely to need close monitoring and advice on financial matters, especially on proposed courses of action. For advisers involved in such 'intensive care' arrangements, great care will need to be exercised to ensure that the directors themselves believe in the wisdom of a given proposal and adopt it as their own. Obvious examples are the corporate rescue departments of banks and accountancy firms, instructed by banks to monitor companies which may have a moderate to good chance of survival provided a major *supervised* restructuring programme is undertaken. These so-called 'company doctors' are not immune from the threat of shadow director status. On a preliminary point of law, Knox J found that a bank could be held liable as a shadow director in an appropriate case (*Re A Company (No 005009 of 1987)* [1989] BCLC 13). However, this particular claim was dropped at the trial in this case, and consequently no guiding judgment emerged (*Re M C Bacon Ltd* [1990] BCLC 324).

If the practical realities are allowed to intrude for a moment, it has to be said that it would be a brave liquidator who would pursue a bank or major firm of accountants on this issue. The legal costs alone would in most cases render such a course uncommercial; indeed the likelihood of an appeal would render any victory rather hollow! (See further McGee and Williams, above.). In any event, input from a bank into the decision-making process of a company, for example advice as to the make up of the board or on a proposed business plan, could be couched in such a way as to appear as conditions of lending or of continued support.

The aims of s 214
A recognised need for minimum standards for company directors
It has been suggested that this provision is reflective of the trend towards a requirement that directors be more 'professional' (see **Chapter 10**). Indeed, the concept behind the wrongful trading provision, which emerges from the report of the Cork Committee (*Report of the Insolvency Review Committee, Insolvency Law and Practice* (1982), Cmnd 8558), indicated a need for an effective machinery which would to make it possible for those who have suffered loss as result of wrongful trading to be compensated. The test applied to the directors' conduct would be an objective one (s 214(7)), which would ensure that satisfactory minimum standards were attained (s 214(4)(a); for an application of this see *Re DKG Contractors Ltd* (1990) 6 BCC 903). For those directors who are 'overqualified' for their particular tasks (for example, a retired accountant directing a small, unsophisticated business), to satisfy such minimum standards would not be enough to avoid liability. The subjective element of the test would take into account their greater knowledge or skill (s 214(4)(b)). The objective standard of care would be imposed where the company was unfortunate enough to go into insolvent liquidation, and was in contrast to the rather low standard of care that was acceptable where the company remained solvent (*Re City Equitable Fire Insurance Co Ltd* [1925] Ch 407, although recent case law now suggests that the test for determining the standard of care of directors of a solvent company may be more stringent than previously thought, see further **Chapter 10**).

From the scenario it might be suggested that there was no reasonable prospect of Great Expectations Ltd recovering the bad debt included in the debtors' figure, and that this fact was known to Edwina. Of course, if a director in Edwina's position should have known of the threat, the objective test will be satisfied and Edwina could face liability from that point on; but on the other hand, it may be difficult to show what a reasonable director in Edwina's position ought to have known. It becomes apparent how difficult a task it is for a liquidator to adduce evidence of special knowledge if attempting to show that a director should have known better. The objective test requires that a director reaches a minimum standard, and will accord to him the degree of knowledge of the company's affairs he ought to have had. This means that Bill cannot plead ignorance if the only reason he was in the dark was because he failed to understand the business side of the operation. An extreme view is that it should, in theory, be possible for a court to find that a company has traded wrongfully from the date of incorporation if from that time it was undercapitalised and remained so, especially where the nature of the business itself meant that it had no prospect, on an objective assessment, of avoiding insolvent liquidation (*Re Fairmont Tours Ltd* (unreported, 1990) was a case that illustrated the fact that the court might be willing to go that far; indeed the Cork Committee envisaged just such a situation, see para 1785).

The provisions that deal with fraud aim to deter and punish those with fraudulent intent, whether the company is solvent or otherwise. In contrast, it would seem that reckless and negligent behaviour can be challenged only when a company is insolvent. This is hardly in keeping with the notion of a 'professional' director. It has been suggested that this objective assessment is a very effective deterrent (see McGee and Williams, above), yet the only inducement to a director to behave is the threat of personal liability. Quite apart from the fact that this threat is very often present in any event due to the widespread use of director guarantees (discussed below), it is becoming clear that the unwillingness of liquidators to pursue directors for wrongful trading will see this threat retreat quite considerably in the future. Failing to pursue negligent directors will eventually erode any inducement to behave professionally as s 214 is perceived as amounting to no more than an empty threat. If Edwina and Bill see their own bad debtors out of their reach, for the purposes of obtaining compensation, despite having caused considerable loss to Great Expectations Ltd through bad management, they are more likely to feel out of reach themselves when they consider their own potential liability to the liquidator of Great Expectations Ltd.

Compensation for those who suffer loss
Another aim of s 214 is undoubtedly to compensate those who suffer loss as a result of wrongful trading. Indeed, the Cork Committee stated quite clearly that: 'Compensation ought, in our view to be available to those who suffer foreseeable loss as a result, not only of fraudulent, but also of unreasonable, behaviour.'

This compensatory aim of s 214 was acknowledged by Knox J in *Re Produce Marketing Consortium Ltd* (1989) 5 BCC 569, who felt that jurisdiction under this provision was primarily compensatory. The difficulty is that it is the company as a distinct entity that is being compensated, not the creditors. Although the court is given some flexibility by s 214, this is related to the amount of the contribution order and not to its application. The amount will reflect the loss to the company as a result of the directors' conduct, but the court will not be competent to look at the identity of the creditors to ensure that the order does indeed compensate those who have suffered loss. However, note the approach taken by Knox J in *Re Produce Marketing Consortium Ltd*, where he chose not to ignore the culpability of the directors when determining the amount of the contribution order. It is submitted that His Lordship's approach was wrong. If the section is compensatory then the culpability of the directors should not be a factor.

The recommendation of the Cork Committee was that the court should be given far more flexibility with regard to the beneficiaries of any award. The situations in which this would enhance the compensatory aim of the provision were recognised as being too many to list, but the Committee did give some helpful examples to illustrate their reasoning (para 1797). One type of creditor identified by them was the one who gives credit at a time when the company is insolvent, in other words a creditor who is faced with unacceptable risk from the moment he enters into the contract from which the credit stems. It is unfortunate that this kind of flexibility was not incorporated into the legislation, because the court has no alternative but to direct that any order be paid direct to the liquidator, who must apply it in the order prescribed by law (Insolvency Act 1986, s 107 (voluntary winding up); Insolvency Rules 1986, r 4.181(1)). We know from the scenario that Edwina set about a deliberate policy of seeking out new credit when she knew that the company was ailing. These creditors will not be treated any differently in the subsequent distribution of any compensation order.

The section also fails to address the difficulties presented with the idea of loss to creditors. Obviously all creditors are prejudiced when a director causes a company to trade wrongfully, but this does not mean that all suffer loss. For example, a bank which has managed through contracts of guarantee to circumvent the corporate veil (see **Chapter 8**) in respect of company borrowing can hardly be said to have suffered loss if it is able to pursue the surety for the loan.

Closely connected with this inability on the part of the court to consider individual creditors in the application of any contribution order is perhaps the biggest obstacle of all to the success of s 214, legal costs. If a liquidator is to bring a claim under s 214, he must be prepared for an expensive fight. The investigation and compilation of evidence alone would make a sizeable dent in any 'pool' available for distribution. He may find that creditors would prefer to receive more 'pence in the pound' rather than risk the pool of assets in the preparation of a case. If the company has been milked dry before liquidation, the liquidator will have no fighting fund with which to pursue directors, and it seems that few liquidators would accept an indemnity of a creditor, save where the creditor in question happens to be a bank or of similar financial standing. The fact that a liquidator must apply any proceeds from a successful s 214 claim *pari passu* is a major disincentive to an individual creditor who might otherwise have considered funding a claim. In our scenario we can see that there is no fighting fund to speak of, unless the liquidator is successful in reopening certain concluded transactions. Bus Bank plc may, of course, consider funding the liquidator, but it is able to access the personal assets of Edwina without needing to do more than demand performance of the contract of guarantee. YOCS is equally unlikely to fund a claim, as it would not see any recognition of this risk in the distribution of any order made against the directors.

Defence to a charge of wrongful trading

Section 214 itself provides a defence to a charge of wrongful trading. Where a director, who knew or ought to have known that the company had no reasonable prospect of avoiding insolvent liquidation, can show that he took *every* step to minimise the potential loss to the company's creditors, he will escape personal liability. The Act itself gives no assistance as to the way in which the word 'every' is to be construed, except to say that the steps that should have been taken should have minimised loss to creditors. Exactly what action is required will be unique to each individual company. The level of sophistication and experience will vary considerably with each individual director, with little commonality even where the businesses pursued are of a similar size or kind. One possible solution might be to determine what steps should have been taken as a bare minimum given the facts of the case, before determining whether further steps were called for.

The effect of this defence, in practical terms, can only be guessed at, but it seems at least suggestible that it may be working as a filter for liquidators in determining whether or not to pursue a wrongful trading claim on commercial grounds. The more steps taken by a director, the less-clear cut the case. However, in many situations the steps taken by directors of ailing companies will not be those envisaged by this defence, and may themselves amount to wrongful trading. For example, trying to minimise the loss to old creditors at the expense of new ones, even if the amount of the company's indebtedness to the creditors as a whole is reduced. If a director were really concerned to minimise loss to creditors then those creditors should receive the benefit of full, frank disclosure before extending further credit to the stricken company. No matter how meritorious the directors' actions, to put existing creditors at further risk with a *chance* of minimising the total loss is not a decision that should be theirs.

The culpability of the directors may figure largely in the minds of liquidators when deciding whether or not to pursue a claim. From the comparatively few cases reported so far it would seem that thin capitalisation is a common feature of the companies that have produced the wrongful trading claims (indeed the Cork Committee felt that this provision would go some way to appeasing those who advocated a minimum capital requirement (para 1785)).

Directors' personal guarantees and lack of culpability

It has already been mentioned that some creditors do not need to look to s 214 of the Insolvency Act 1986 to avoid the corporate veil. They seek to protect themselves against loss by tying the directors into the fortunes of the company from the outset. This is achieved by requiring the directors to give personal guarantees in support of their companies, usually backed up by a charge over the director's chief asset, his home. This is a practice favoured particularly by banks (see McGee and Williams, at **23.7.2.3** above). If the company does fail due to the inadequacies of the management, the bulk of a director's personal assets may already be earmarked, with the result that the director becomes in effect a 'man of straw' and ultimately not worth pursuing by a liquidator.

Another factor is that the liquidator may not regard the directors as really culpable, and although the section is not designed to act as a penal sanction (it is worthy of note that ss 212–217 come under the heading 'Penalisation of Directors and Officers'), this may influence his decision as to whether or not to pursue a director (in *Re Produce Marketing*

Consortium Ltd (1989) 5 BCC 569, Knox J took into account the degree of the directors' culpability when exercising his discretion as to the amount of the contribution from the two directors).

23.8 Advice to the parties

Advising Arthur, Bill, Charlotte, Edwina and Frederick at this stage of events is rather like shutting the stable door after the horse has bolted. It is far too late for them to adjust their conduct in respect of the company when the threat of proceedings being pursued by the liquidator is a live one. In many ways this emphasises a failing of the wrongful trading provision of the Insolvency Act in its objective of improving standards of competence amongst company directors generally (see **23.7.2.3** above). In practice they are unlikely to be pursued by the liquidator for misfeasance, fraudulent or wrongful trading, although much depends upon the fighting spirit of the committee of creditors, which, if prepared to fund the liquidator in civil claims against them, might be able to persuade him that sufficient evidence is available to warrant him pursuing the matter further. Unfortunately the liquidator's task is hindered considerably where company accounts and other records are poorly maintained, although curiously enough this is itself evidence of wrongful trading!

Edwina is likely to emerge with the greatest loss of all the participants in Great Expectations Ltd due to the fact that she has personally guaranteed the company's bank accounts. The Bank will not hesitate to act upon this guarantee. Her large salary payment is the most vulnerable of all the pre-liquidation payments, and it is likely that the liquidator would seek to re-open this and reclaim that money for the general body of creditors. It is less likely that the smaller and more numerous payments made to the other employees would be worthwhile re-opening as this would probably prove too costly to pursue, rendering such an action uncommercial.

FURTHER READING

CA Riley, 'Directors' duties and the interests of creditors' (1989) 10 Co Law 87.
J Birds, (1980) 1 Co Law 67.
LS Sealy, (1987) MLR 164.
F Oditah, 'Wrongful Trading' [1990] LMCLQ 205.
D Milman, 'Personal liability and disqualification of company directors; something old, something new' (1992) NILQ 1.
A Hicks, 'Advising on wrongful trading' (1993) 14 Co Law 16, 55.
A Keay, 'The duty of directors to take account of creditors' interests: has it a role to play?' [2002] JBL 379.
G Scanlan, 'The Criminal Liabilities of Directors to the Creditors of the Company s 458 Companies Act 1985' *The Journal of Financial Crime*, Vol 9, Issue No 4 360.

24 Disqualification of Directors

LEARNING OUTCOMES

By the end of this chapter, you should understand:

- the grounds for disqualification of a director under the Company Directors Disqualification Act 1986;

- the consequences of contravention of a disqualification order.

SCENARIO

The liquidator's report, produced at the culmination of his winding up of the business of Great Expectations Ltd, was extremely critical of the activities of its directors and Company Secretary. Particular reference was made to the appalling way in which the company's records and accounts were maintained in the 12 months prior to liquidation. Despite such a damning report, the committee of creditors had no wish to pursue the directors further, having decided that there was no point throwing good money after bad in funding lengthy civil claims. The liquidator did, however, send an adverse report on his findings to the Department of Trade and Industry.

OVERVIEW

This chapter is concerned with the ways in which directors of failed companies can be prevented from trading in the future, using a limited company as the business medium with the attendant benefit of limited liability. The Company Directors Disqualification Act 1986 was, along with the wrongful trading provision of the Insolvency Act 1986 (see **23.7.2.3** above), an innovation which resulted largely from the recommendations of the Cork Committee. The provision, which deals with disqualifying directors for unfitness, would, it was hoped, work alongside the wrongful trading provision and prevent incompetents from hiding behind the veil of incorporation both where their companies had failed, by making them personally liable, and for the future, by disqualifying them from using the corporate form, for a period of time at least. Statistics to date suggest that few directors of insolvent companies are in fact disqualified.

The statutory provisions relating to the disqualification of directors are contained in the Company Directors Disqualification Act (CDDA) 1986. The Act deals with the disqualification of persons from acting as directors and is therefore applicable to any persons, whether or not they are or have been company directors. If we look at Great Expectations Ltd, any one of the six individuals involved could, in theory at least, be disqualified.

If a person is disqualified from acting as director then he must not, without the leave of the court:

(a) be a director of a company, or

(b) be a liquidator or administrator of a company, or

(c) be a receiver or manager of a company's property, or

(d) in any way, whether directly or indirectly, be concerned or take part in the promotion, formation or management of a company, for a specified period beginning with the date of the order. (CDDA 1986, s1)

It is therefore unlawful for a disqualified person to act as a director, or 'de facto' director, for as long as the order is in place (see *Official Receiver v Hannan* [1997] 2 BCLC 473). However, the court does have a discretion to grant leave to a disqualified person to act in any of the forbidden capacities listed above (this discretion has been exercised in a number of cases, eg, *Re Majestic Recording Studios Ltd* (1988) 4 BCC 519, *Re Lo-Line Electric Motors Ltd* [1988] Ch 477).

24.1 Grounds for disqualification

24.1.1 Disqualification for general misconduct

Sections 2–5 of the CDDA 1986 come under the heading 'Disqualification for General Misconduct in Connection with Companies'. Disqualification under this heading is at the discretion of the court.

Section 2 deals with a person who has been convicted of an indictable offence in connection with the promotion, formation, management or liquidation of a company, or with the receivership or management of a company's property. Management in this section is not limited to the internal workings of a company, and so in *R v Austen* (1985) 1 BCC 99,528 the court held that offences against third parties rather than against the company alone were sufficient to come within the meaning of the phrase 'in connection with the management of a company'. Further, the fact that there is no allegation of mismanagement does not prevent the court exercising its discretion. In *R v Georgiou* (1988) 4 BCC 322, the director of an insurance business, which was being carried on competently but without authorisation, and therefore illegally, was disqualified for five years.

Section 3 deals with the persistent default of directors in completing the returns, accounts or other documents (*Re Arctic Engineering Ltd* [1986] 1 WLR 686 shows that persistent defaults of different types may bring a director within this section).

Section 4 provides that a person may be disqualified if, during the course of winding up of a company, it appears that he has been guilty of fraud under s 458 of the Companies Act 1985, whether or not he has been convicted (CDDA 1986, s 4(1)(a); see *R v Kemp* [1988] QB 645). In addition, any person who, whilst acting as officer, liquidator, receiver or manager, is guilty of any fraud in relation to the company or any breach of duty, may be subject to a disqualification order.

Section 5 provides that the court may make a disqualification order against a person who is convicted of a summary offence for failure to file returns, etc, where during the previous five years that person has had three or more default orders or convictions.

24.1.2 Disqualification for unfitness

Under the heading 'Disqualification for Unfitness', s 6 of the CDDA, 1986 provides for the court to disqualify a person if it is satisfied:

(a) that he is or has been a director of a company which has at any time become insolvent (whether while he was a director, or subsequently); and

(b) that his conduct as a director of the company (either taken alone, or taken together with his conduct as a director of any other company or companies) makes him unfit to be concerned in the management of a company;

Although where the court makes an order where s 6 applies, the court may still grant leave for such a person to act as director (s 1).

The criteria for determining whether or not a person is unfit to act as director seem to vary between the reported decisions. In *Re Bath Glass Ltd* [1988] BCLC 329, Peter Gibson J said (at 333):

> To reach a finding of unfitness the court must be satisfied that the director has been guilty of a serious failure or serious failures, whether deliberately or through incompetence, to perform those duties of directors which are attendant on the privilege of trading through companies with limited liability.

However, the more dominant trend seems to be to require a higher degree of culpability (*Re Dawson Print Group Ltd* (1987) 3 BCC 322; *Re McNulty's Interchange Ltd* (1988) 4 BCC 533; *Re Douglas Construction Services Ltd* (1988) 4 BCC 553). If a director is found to be incompetent, based on the objective test contained in s 214 of the Insolvency Act 1986, the authorities seem to suggest that this may be insufficient for a finding of unfitness. In *Re Lo-Line Electric Motors Ltd* [1988] Ch 477, Browne-Wilkinson V-C said (at 486):

> Ordinary commercial misjudgement is in itself not sufficient to justify disqualification. In the normal case, the conduct complained of must display a lack of commercial probity, although I have no doubt that in an extreme case of gross negligence or total incompetence disqualification could be appropriate.

Phrases such as 'gross negligence' and 'total incompetence' do not fit well with the lower threshold of minimum standards of competence envisaged by the wrongful trading provision (see **23.7.2.3** above). This is undoubtedly good news for Edwina who, having avoided a wrongful trading claim, will be hoping that for the future she will not be prevented from trying to make her fortune using a company as a business medium. Under ss 7(2A) and 8(2A) of the CDDA 1986, the Secretary of State may accept from a person a disqualification undertaking, whereby the party undertakes not to act in any way which would be prohibited under the provisions of a disqualification order.

Section 8 permits the court to make a disqualification order against a person if it is of the opinion that, following a statutory investigation, such person is unfit to be concerned in the management of a company. Section 10 permits the court to disqualify a person who has participated in wrongful trading, but this is contingent upon the making of a contribution order (so far it would seem that in only one of the few cases on s 214 of the Insolvency Act 1986, *Re Purpoint Ltd* [1991] BCLC 491, has a director been disqualified as well as being required to make a contribution to the assets of the company). If no order is made, for example because the directors are men of straw, or because there is no way of financing the claim, then disqualification cannot be applied for.

We have already seen that disqualification for unfitness requires conduct amounting to at least gross negligence, and so is unlikely to protect creditors from the incompetents who fall below minimum standards. However, simply to leave the financial affairs to a co-director, as we saw Bill do in Great Expectations Ltd, will not preclude the disqualification of that director. What would be necessary would be for the court to find that Edwina's behaviour was at least grossly negligent or totally incompetent – which may prove extremely difficult, not least because this is the first company that she has steered into insolvent liquidation (the DTI by their own admission rarely act after one liquidation; more usually *three* liquidations would be the trigger) – and that this reflects on Bill who left matters to Edwina.

24.2 Consequences of contravention

To act in contravention of a disqualification order is an offence triable either way (CDDA 1986, s 13). In addition, if a disqualified person is involved in the management of a company then such person will also incur personal liability for the company's debts (s 15). Any person who acts on the instructions of a disqualified person whom he knows to be a disqualified person, will also incur personal liability for company debts (s 15(1)(b),(3)(b) and (4)).

25 Life After Death – Restoration of Companies to the Register

LEARNING OUTCOMES

By the end of this chapter, you should understand:

- the restoration of a dissolved company to the Register under ss 651 and 653 of the Companies Act 1985;

- the reasons for restoration of a company to the Register.

SCENARIO

Great Expectations Ltd was dissolved and removed from the Register in July 2005. Unfortunately, not all the outstanding matters were dealt with properly before the dissolution took place. In particular, since the dissolution it has become apparent that there are still a number of dissatisfied customers, with complaints dating from 2002-2003 about the quality either of the materials used by the company, or of the workmanship of the company's employees. Although the ex-company has no assets of its own any longer, it did have liability insurance to cover against risks of this kind.

25.1 Restoration to the Register under s 651

Section 651 of the Companies Act 1985 allows for the restoration of a company to the Register in certain circumstances. It is not necessary to show that the application is brought for the purpose of allowing proceedings to be brought against the company, though that will be the most usual reason for the making of an application. Section 651(1) allows for the making of an application by the liquidator or any other person appearing to the court to be interested. Commonly the application is made by a person who wishes to pursue a claim against the company. Section 651(2) provides that on the making of such an order, such proceedings may be taken as might have been taken if the company had not been dissolved.

The application must be brought within two years of the date when the company is removed from the Register, except where the purpose of bringing the application is to allow a claim for damages for personal injury to be brought against the company. Since in most cases the company will have no assets even when it is restored to the Register, the practical context of such applications is usually that the company had liability insurance, and that the applicant desires to bring a claim against the liability insurers under the Third Parties (Rights Against Insurers) Act 1930, which allows such proceedings to be brought directly against the insurers where the company has gone into liquidation. In *Bradley v Eagle Star Insurance Ltd* [1989] 1 All ER 961, the House of Lords held, approving the decision of the Court of Appeal in *Post Office v Norwich Union* [1967] 1 All ER 577, that no action can be brought under the Third Parties (Rights Against Insurers) Act 1930 until the fact and quantum of the insured's liability has been established. Consequently, where a plaintiff brought an action for personal injuries against her former employers, who had by then been wound up, she was unable to proceed directly against the employers' liability insurers since the employers' liability had not been established.

The original form of s 651 of the 1985 Act allowed such petitions only within two years of the dissolution of the company. Often, as in *Bradley v Eagle Star* itself, the two-year period under s 651 proved inadequate, especially in cases of asbestosis which manifested itself only many years after the plaintiff had ceased employment. Section 141 of the Companies Act 1989 made important amendments to s 651 of the 1985 Act. The major change was a matter of timing. In certain specified cases the period of two years from the dissolution of the company, within which an application may be made, was extended to 20 years. The cases to which this change applies are those of claims for damages for personal injury (defined as including any disease and any impairment of a person's physical or mental condition, a definition borrowed from the Limitation Act 1980), or claims under the Fatal Accidents Act 1976.

The restoration of the company to the Register is always a matter for the court's discretion, but a particular problem which may arise in personal injury cases concerns the relevance of limitation of claims. To an extent this issue is important in any case of an application to restore, since it may appear to the court that the claim which it is proposed to bring against the company will be time-barred. The extra dimension in personal injury cases and cases under the Fatal Accidents Act 1976 is that ss 11, 12 and 14 of the Limitation Act 1980 make time run from the date when the cause of action becomes discoverable, rather than from the date when the cause of action accrues, and give the court a discretion to override the primary limitation period if it thinks it just to do so. These two factors make it unusually difficult to tell in advance of a proper exploration of the facts whether the claim can be defeated by a plea of the Limitation Act. This in turn adds to the difficulty faced by the court in exercising its discretion on an application under s 651. The new s 651(5) and (6) attempt to deal with this aspect of the matter, but their drafting is less than clear. Section 651(5) prohibits the making of an order for restoration to the Register if it appears to the court that the proceedings would fail by virtue of any enactment as to the time within which proceedings must be brought. First, it is submitted that the enactments referred to here include all aspects of the Limitation Act 1980 which are relevant to the case, and especially s 33 of that Act, which is the provision giving the court discretion to extend the limitation period. This is a necessary conclusion. If s 33 of the Limitation Act 1980 is ignored, then no order will ever be made once the period of three years from discoverability has expired, since in the absence of s 33 the claim will be bound to fail. The logic of this is that where the three-year period has expired the court will have to consider whether leave under s 33 is likely to be granted, and the hearing of the application will to some extent turn into a discussion of the merits of the s 33 application. That is not the end of the matter, however. Applications under s 651 will normally be made without notice, since at that stage the company is not in existence. Even if it is concluded that the s 33 application has a good chance of success, so that a s 651 order is appropriate, it will still be necessary, once the company has been restored to the Register, to make the s 33 application. These too are sometimes made without notice, but a without notice s 33 order is liable to be challenged at trial, and may be set aside if on the inter partes hearing it appears that the order was wrongly made.

These provisions were considered in *Re Workvale Ltd* [1991] 1 WLR 294, (Hoffmann J) [1992] 2 All ER 627, CA, where it was held that it is generally wrong for the court hearing the application to restore the company to the Register to investigate in any detail the merits of a possible s 33 application. Rather, the proper course is to allow the application for restoration once it is shown that there is an arguable case in favour of granting the s 33 application. Given that there are cases in which s 33 applications have succeeded despite the lapse of over 20 years since the accrual of the cause of action, it is clear that this test will very commonly be satisfied, and that there will accordingly be relatively few cases in which the application for restoration is made for the purpose of bringing a personal injuries claim but should nevertheless be refused. It should be noted that these issues do not arise in anything like the same way where the proposed claim is not in respect of personal injuries. Section 33 is not relevant, and it is in any event much less likely that the claim will be time-barred, since the application for restoration must be brought within two years of the dissolution of the company.

There is another possibility in connection with s 651 applications which requires to be considered. Section 651(6) provides that nothing in s 651(5) affects the power of the court when making a s 651 order to direct that the period between the dissolution of the company and the making of the order shall not count for the purposes of any limitation enactment. This raises the question whether the court has in any event such power under s 651. As appears at **25.2** below, the power has been held to exist under s 653, but there is no express power under s 651 and no direct authority on the point. The draftsman of the new s 651(6) clearly thought that there was power, since the wording of that subsection makes no sense otherwise. However, the draftsman's perception of the law is not binding on anyone. Nevertheless, it is submitted that s 651 ought to be construed as giving such power in view of the width of the general words used to describe the court's power.

25.2 Restoration to the Register under s 653

Section 653 of the Companies Act 1985 also allows for restoration to the Register, but the pre-conditions applicable to this section are somewhat different from those applying under s 651. Section 653 is applicable where the company has been struck off the Register by the Registrar under s 652. This power is exercisable where it appears to the Registrar that the company is no longer carrying on business or in operation. If he wishes to exercise the power, he must first send a letter to the company's address enquiring whether the company is still in operation. If no reply is received within one month, he must then within a further 14 days send a second letter, this time by registered post, referring to the first letter, stating that no reply to it has been received and indicating that unless a reply is received within one month from the date of that letter, a notice will be published in the *Gazette* (The London, Edinburgh or Belfast Gazettes, as the case may be) with a view to striking the company's name off the Register. If no reply is received, or if a reply is received to the effect that the company is no longer in operation, the next stage is the publication of the notice in the *Gazette*. This notice, a copy of which must also be sent to the company, will state that the company will, on the expiry of a further three months, be struck off the Register and dissolved, unless cause is shown to the contrary. At the expiry of the three-month period a further notice will be published in the *Gazette*, and the company will be duly struck off unless cause to the contrary has been shown. The Act does not define 'cause', but it is thought that the Registrar can in practice be dissuaded from exercising this power either by evidence that the company is likely to resume operations, or by evidence that there are claims against the company, or by any other sensible argument.

These rules operate slightly differently in cases where a company is already being wound up, ie where a liquidator has already been appointed. The power to strike the company off the Register may still be a relevant one in such cases if there is no longer a liquidator acting, or if it appears that the company has been fully wound up, and that the returns which the liquidator is required to file with the Registrar have not been filed for a period of six consecutive months. In such cases, s 652(4) provides that the Registrar may proceed directly to issue a notice in the *Gazette* indicating an intention to strike the company off the Register, sending a copy to the liquidator. The striking off of the company does not affect any existing liability of any director, managing officer or member of the company for any debts of the company, or for any misfeasance in the performance of his duties. Thus, claims for wrongful trading (Insolvency Act 1986, s 214; see **23.7.2.3** above) may still be brought if a liquidator is appointed, and members may still be liable for contributions if their shares were not fully paid (Companies Act 1985, ss 79 and 124).

Where the s 652 power has been exercised, s 653 allows the court to restore the company to the Register on the application of the company, or of any member or creditor of the company. The application must be made within 20 years of the date when the notice of striking off was published in the *Gazette*, and the grounds for the making of a restoration order are that the company was in fact carrying on business when it was struck off, or otherwise that it is just to restore the company to the Register. Section 653(3) provides that when the order of the court to this effect is delivered to the Registrar, the company is deemed to have continued in existence as if its name had not been struck off the Register.

An obvious problem arises here, in that there will have been a period, which may be up to 20 years, during which the company could neither sue nor be sued; if the company had the right to sue or the liability to be sued immediately before being struck off, the actions on those claims are likely to have become time-barred, a possibility made all the more likely by the words of the deeming provision, which require the company to be treated as having continued in existence. In an effort to alleviate problems of this kind, s 653(3) goes on to provide that the court may on the making of the order give such directions and make such provisions as seem just for placing the company and all other persons in the same position as if the company had not been struck off. Unfortunately, there are a number of uncertainties surrounding this form of words. If the company had continued in existence, it is clear that time would have continued to run under the Limitation Act 1980, and it is therefore arguable that in this respect no order of the court is needed, since that is what will happen anyway if there is no order. It is suggested, however, that this interpretation fails to give effect to the purpose of the subsection, which is to give the court powers which will enable it to alleviate the unfortunate effects of the company's having been off the Register. On this basis, the court ought to have power to provide, for example, that the period for which the company was off the Register should not count when reckoning limitation periods in claims by or against the company. There might, of course, be cases where the original striking off happened through default on the part of the company's officers in failing to reply to communications from the Registrar, and in these circumstances it might be thought just that time should continue to run in relation to claims *by* the company, but not in relation to claims *against* the company. However, it is well settled that an order restoring the company to the Register under s 653 may include such a provision (*Re Donald Kenyon Ltd* [1956] 1 WLR 1397, though that is a case which pre-dates the first introduction into English law of provisions allowing for the extension of the limitation period in personal injury cases). The point arose again in *Re Advance Insulation Ltd* (1989) 5 BCC 55, though in that case Hoffmann J was able to avoid deciding the substantive point as the appeal from the decision of the Master was so far out of time. The power to include such a provision in a s 653 order is very commonly exercised.

25.3 Advice to the company

It must be remembered that the claim which it is proposed to bring against the company is not a claim for damages for personal injuries. Consequently, the application for restoration to the Register must be brought not later than April 2007, ie within two years of the date on which the company was dissolved. This deadline is not subject to extension by the court. Perhaps the most practical piece of advice which can be given is to try to ensure that the application is not made within this time. If this fails, however, and the application is duly made, then there is likely to be relatively little that can be done to prevent the court from granting it. It may be noted that some of the complaints made by former clients are now quite close to being time-barred, at least in so far as they are based on contract, since contract claims accrue on the happening of the breach and are time-barred six years later (*Gibbs v Guild (1881) 8 QBD 296*). If the claims can be based on tort, it is possible that time will start to run at a later stage, since there must also be damage before the cause of action accrues (see *Pirelli General Cable Works v Oscar Faber & Partners Ltd* [1983] 2 AC 1, HL), and the Latent Damage Act 1986 may further postpone the running of time until the claimants knew, or ought to have known, of the existence of the claim. In any event it seems likely that the court will claim and exercise the power to direct that the period during which Great Expectations Ltd was off the Register will not count in determining the running of the limitation period for the purposes of these claims. Since the claims were certainly not barred in April 2004, it follows that they can be commenced as soon as the company is restored to the Register.

Perhaps the most consoling advice that can be offered to the company (or, more realistically, to Arthur, Bill, Charlotte, Edwina and Frederick) is that for all practical purposes they do not face any additional liability as a result of the restoration of the company to the

26 Choice of Business Medium

The chapter will review the central themes of the book, and the factors that may influence entrepreneurs as to the business medium they will use in conducting their business.

OVERVIEW

This book has sought to examine the consequences of running a business either as a partnership, or as a limited company. Other available business media, such as unlimited companies, limited partnerships and limited liability partnerships, have been largely ignored principally on the ground that they are not commonly encountered at the present day.

Throughout the examination of these consequences it is necessary to bear in mind that all business structures are merely vehicles within which to run a business (see **Chapter 1**). In a developed economy it is the business which is central, not the business structure. The rules relating to business structures can be justified only in so far as they enable economically and ethically sound businesses to flourish, while simultaneously protecting third parties from the activities of unsound and dishonestly or incompetently run businesses. These questions are important in any developed society, and it is not surprising to find that they have arisen in similar, though not identical, form in other European countries. Comparison with these countries is often instructive, since their solutions may be found to be interestingly different from those adopted by English law, no doubt partly because of differences between the common law and civil law modes of thought.

26.1 Protection of entrepreneurs

The greatest protection of entrepreneurs comes through the principle of limited liability, which allows the setting up of businesses without the risk of personal bankruptcy. Unfortunately, this principle has to a large extent been circumvented by the practice of commercial lenders (notably the major banks) requiring directors personally to guarantee the loans made to their companies. Critics of those parts of the 1985–86 insolvency reforms which deal with the disqualification of directors for unfitness and liability for wrongful trading, complain that they lead to businessmen becoming discouraged and afraid to incur the degree of risk required in a growing economy. Arguments along these lines need to be considered in the light of the ways in which other European countries seek to fulfil a function similar to that which was intended for these provisions.

English company law does not have in place any minimum capital rules for private companies, which means that the balance swings more in favour of the entrepreneurs themselves rather than the trade creditors (banks, of course, need to be considered in the light of the personal guarantee requirement, which for a large proportion of private companies is commonplace). Clearly there has to be some mechanism in place which deals with the problems inherent in undercapitalised companies, which can be formed and, it seems, liquidated with comparative ease, to the detriment of their creditors. In attempting to achieve more of a balance between the entrepreneurs and the creditors, the traditional disclosure requirements, which, in theory at least, allowed creditors to obtain pertinent information as to a company's financial position and so take necessary steps to protect their position, appeared to have all but failed in their objective – they were no longer fulfilling this particular function with any degree of credibility (see **Chapter 18**). Disqualification for unfitness and the wrongful trading provision in many ways attempt to redress the balance away from the entrepreneurs in favour of the creditors, although neither provision has proved itself to be terribly convincing in the performance of this function to date (see **Chapter 23**). In unincorporated businesses the absence of limited liability means that there is no effective protection for entrepreneurs (see **Chapter 3**).

A related question is whether the process of disincorporation should be made easier. Although it is relatively easy to transfer an unincorporated business to a company, the reverse process is much more difficult, not least in relation to the taxation consequences. This distinction would appear undesirable in principle, but the attention given to the question over recent years is itself interesting, since it suggests that significant numbers of business people are finding that the structure of a limited company causes more problems than it solves. What is not clear is what these problems are, and whether they are best solved by disincorporation rather than by more imaginative use of the company law rules. If these rules are found to be inherently unsuited to such businesses, it will be necessary to ask whether this reveals a defect in the rules, or whether it reflects some coherent policy about the sort of business for which incorporation is appropriate.

26.2 Protection of shareholders

In this context we mean investors, who must be understood as meaning shareholders who are not directors. It is clear that in practice such shareholders are in a weak position, mainly because of the extensive power given to directors by art 70 of Table A. Although this power can be diluted, it is very often left untouched (to remove it entirely would be impracticable, since it is necessary to give the directors adequate powers to manage the company effectively). However, investors have perhaps the weakest claim of all to protection within the scheme of company law, for they are by definition the risk-takers, who put up venture capital in the hope of making a profit by so doing. They also appoint the directors. The risk of losing money through choosing a bad venture or appointing the wrong directors should fall more on them than on anyone else. In practice the investors are substantially protected against these risks by the principle of limited liability.

Protecting the rights and interests of shareholders is by and large left to an individual company's Memorandum and Articles of Association, and in some instances to shareholder agreements (see **Chapter 7**). Company law does, however, have some part to play in the protection of investors, and to this end the Companies Act 1985 entrenches some shareholder rights – for example s 9, which enables the shareholders to alter the terms of the Articles by special resolution, a right which cannot be contracted out of by the shareholders and the company (see **Chapter 7**). Further examples of the importance of company law in the protection of shareholders are the right to petition for relief from actual or proposed unfairly prejudicial conduct, which is provided by the Companies Act, and, at common law, the availability of the derivative claim which may be permitted where 'fraud' on the minority is being perpetrated by the controllers (see **Chapter 14**).

The development of the law over the last century in respect of ultra vires transactions has involved a perceptible shift in the balance away from protecting shareholders at the expense of third parties, and in the same way that the insolvency reforms sought to render the law more up to date and effective where the protection of creditors was concerned, they better reflect the current needs of commerce.

26.3 Protection of creditors

Creditors appear to be badly served by the existing system. Secured creditors can, of course, enforce their security, and this may give them effective protection, but unsecured creditors will rarely receive more than a nominal amount in a company liquidation or a personal bankruptcy (often they will receive nothing at all). This risk is the inevitable corollary to the availability of limited liability, but a society in which some 35% of new businesses fail within three years of establishment needs to give serious consideration to the question of creditor protection. This may be linked to the issue of the balance between different classes of creditor – in practice secured creditors are in a much stronger position than unsecured creditors, although they have much more information about the company when making lending decisions, and might therefore be thought less deserving of protection. This in turn leads to attempts by unsecured creditors to promote themselves in the order of payment by the use of retention of title clauses (see **Chapter 15**).

It must be accepted that the risk taken by creditors is the natural, indeed inevitable, consequence of the protection afforded to directors and shareholders. Company law has always sought to protect creditors against the risks of fraud, although difficulties in respect of discharging the onerous burden of proof have meant that this protection has never been noticeably successful (see **Chapter 23**). The more recent wrongful trading provision of the Insolvency Act 1986 and the procedure whereby a director can be disqualified for unfitness, seek to provide further protection for creditors, although it must be said that neither of these two provisions has to date proved to be effective (see **Chapter 23**). The disclosure and the maintenance of capital requirements discussed earlier (see **Chapters 17 and 18**) were both conceived as mechanisms designed to protect creditors, although the ineffectiveness of the sanctions for late registration of accounts and the absence of a minimum capital requirement for private companies render both of these concepts virtually impotent.

26.4 Protection of employees

It may be argued that it is not the function of company law to protect employees, and it is certainly true that successive Companies Acts have not given much attention to this area. It is perhaps unfortunate that English law has traditionally observed a marked distinction between company law and employment law, given that they have a large area of interconnection, if not overlap. As an interest group within a company, the employees should be considered by the directors in the performance of their functions (see s 309 of the Companies Act 1985). To ignore the interests of the employees may involve the directors in a breach of their duty to the company, but there is no machinery through which the employees can challenge the directors for such a breach. The only benefit which accrues to the employees under this relatively new provision is that they have at least become a legitimate consideration in company law for the directors, arguably even where this involves a sharp conflict with other interest groups, for example where shareholders are faced with a lower dividend as a direct result of salary increases (see **Chapter 9**).

26.5 Protection of the public generally

In one sense it may be said that the public at large is not in need of protection, since those who do not deal with a business cannot be harmed by its activities. Unfortunately this is untrue, since the circulation of dangerous products and/or environmentally harmful working practices may cause more widespread harm. Legislation has been enacted to deal with these matters, for example the Consumer Protection Act 1987 and the Environmental Protection Act 1990. Considerations of the business's statutory and tortious liability to third parties have lain somewhat outside the scope of the present work, but they are clearly important to those running a business.

26.6 Partnership or company?

The choice between running a business as a partnership or as a company is a complex one. It has been seen that the rules relating to the two structures are different, and a number of arguments are commonly put forward as being relevant to the decision. These include the following.

26.6.1 Limited liability

Shareholders have limited liability for the debts of a company, whereas the liability of partners is unlimited. In practice the apparently great effect of this distinction is significantly reduced by the practice of requiring company directors (who are usually also shareholders) to give personal guarantees for loans and overdrafts from the bank, and by the possibility of directors being made personally liable for the company's debts in the case of an insolvent liquidation (Insolvency Act 1986, ss 212–214), though this risk is probably not great enough to deprive incorporation of all its advantages so far as trade debts are concerned (see also **Chapter 12**). Moreover, the advantage of limited liability may still be real for a non-director shareholder such as Duncan, who would not have been entirely happy to be a mere financier for a partnership, since this would have deprived him of any influence on the management of the business (see **Chapters 3** and **4**).

26.6.2 Finance

Another commonly-held perception is that companies can raise finance more easily than partnerships. This view appears to depend on the belief that companies are necessarily more substantial and creditworthy bodies than partnerships. In the absence of a minimum capital requirement for private companies, such as exists in both France and Germany, this view cannot be considered to be generally justified. Indeed, it may be that some suppliers will be less ready to hand over goods in return for a company cheque than in return for a personal cheque (the supplier could of course sue on either cheque if it were dishonoured, but the action on the company cheque will not yield any return if the company is insolvent, whereas the individual might face bankruptcy if he did not pay). It is not uncommon to find retailers who will not accept company cheques at all, an interesting practical reversal of the assumption that a company is automatically more creditworthy than a partnership or an individual.

Two other more technical points may be raised in relation to finance. The first is that companies may issue shares, whereas partnerships may not. Although this is obviously true, it does not follow that partnerships are thereby placed at a major disadvantage. Given that most small businesses obtain the greatest part of their working capital from lending rather than from equity, the impossibility of issuing shares in a partnership is less of a problem than might be supposed, though there will be some cases, such as that of Duncan, where a financier who wishes to invest in a business will effectively require the incorporation of the business so as to protect his own position. The second technical point concerns floating charges, a financing device available to companies but not to partnerships. This is of particular importance in relation to companies which have few fixed assets but substantial floating assets (primarily stock-in-trade and book debts). This was of course exactly the position of Great Expectations Ltd, and was one of the reasons why the Bank was so anxious to have the business incorporated (see **Chapter 4**). It may be mentioned also that Edwina succeeded in largely negating the value of the charge to the Bank by factoring the book debts.

26.6.3 Corporate personality

The company is a legal person separate from its shareholders. It can own and sell property, employ people (including its owners) and will continue to exist even if all its shareholders die. None of these things is true of a partnership. However, the practical consequences of these distinctions are somewhat limited. The absence of corporate personality in a partnership leads to the rule in the Partnership Act 1890 that any partner may dissolve the firm and claim his share of the property, a rule having no equivalent in company law. In practice, though, any well-drafted partnership deed will contain provisions removing this right and substituting a more commercially convenient alternative.

26.6.4 Corporate substance

The points discussed here are often considered under the heading of corporate personality; the two concepts have deliberately been kept separate here in order to make a distinction between the real legal incidents of incorporation and the psychological consequences – sometimes more apparent than real – which may flow from incorporation.

Beneficial consequences may include the creation of a separate body to which employees may feel a greater sense of loyalty than a partnership might inspire, and which may be helpful in marketing the company's image and products (see also **Chapter 6** on the importance of the company's name). It must be admitted, however, that these consequences rest largely on a convenient illusion, namely, that the business has some real existence apart from those who work in it. The danger is that these people will start to believe in the illusion and will come to see the company as an institution in its own right, which will continue even without their whole-hearted efforts and will continue to pay them a salary even if no profit is made. The directors of Great Expectations Ltd – especially Arthur – have to some extent fallen into this trap, with inevitable negative consequences.

26.6.5 Taxation

It is sometimes said that a company offers the advantage of being able to shelter profits from tax if they are not distributed to shareholders. To a limited extent this is true, but the company would still pay corporation tax on the profits, so the saving would be limited to the difference between the corporation tax rate and the marginal income tax rate of individual shareholders. So far as capital gains tax is concerned, the company may be at a slight disadvantage because it has no annual exemption, unlike individual partners. Overall, there is very little to choose between a company and a partnership from the tax point of view, and it seems unlikely that tax can be a major factor in the decision whether or not to incorporate.

26.6.7 Formality

The formal requirements associated with the creation of a company are sometimes cited as an argument in favour of using a partnership. However, these requirements may be met by the purchase of a ready-formed 'shelf' company. At the same time it is unwise to assume that there will be no formality when a partnership is formed. Although there is no legal requirement of formality, it is usually desirable to have a written partnership agreement, and the absence of any generally acceptable standard form may mean that considerable time and expense is involved in the drafting exercise. Similar problems may of course arise in companies, where Table A is often found unsuitable in certain respects and has to be amended. Every business is different, whatever its legal structure, and it is always important to give attention to the structural and constitutional questions at the outset.

26.6.8 Disclosure

Companies are required to prepare and file annual accounts, as well as disclosing other information at the Companies Registry, whereas there is no such requirement for partnerships. The difference is often cited as a major advantage for partnerships. To the extent that the absence of disclosure protects the privacy of the business and those involved in it, this advantage may be regarded as real. It would be a mistake to assume, however, that partnerships have no need to produce accounts. It is likely that the bank will insist on regular management accounts just as with a private company; and even in the absence of such a requirement, any sensibly-managed partnership would want to produce such accounts for its own purposes. It might even happen that the bank would be more inclined to demand information about the personal finances of partners than of directors, given the unlimited liability of partners for all the debts of the business.

26.6.9 *Ultra vires*

The absence of any ultra vires doctrine from partnership law was traditionally regarded as an important difference between the two types of business. The difference was less striking than it appeared, even before the 1989 reform of the law on ultra vires, because of the tendency for companies to have long and all-inclusive objects clauses (see *Cotman v Brougham* [1918] AC 514, HL). The distinction has all but disappeared since the virtual abolition of ultra vires by the Companies Act 1989.

26.7 **Conclusion**

Questions about the internal and external regulation of businesses are of general interest and importance. Holding the balance between the different interest groups is an essential and complex task. It must never be forgotten that the rules of partnership and company law exist to further socially and economically desirable ends, rather than for their own sake. An important point which emerges from this book is that there appear to be few, if any, advantages in using a partnership rather than a company. On the other hand, there are some advantages in using a company – principally the partial protection against creditors and the possible greater ease of obtaining equity capital from non-managers. In the end, though, the differences in practical effect between incorporated and unincorporated businesses are not so great as is commonly supposed. More than a century after the decision of the House of Lords in *Saloman v Saloman*, it is perhaps time to look for some reconsideration of the rules on corporate structure with a view to serving more effectively and economically the needs of small businesses in the 21st century.

Appendix A

Table A

REGULATIONS FOR MANAGEMENT OF A COMPANY LIMITED BY SHARES

INTERPRETATION

1. In these regulations—

    "the Act" means the Companies Act 1985 including any statutory modification or re-enactment thereof for the time being in force.

    "the articles" means the articles of the company.

    "clear days" in relation to the period of a notice means that period excluding the day when the notice is given or deemed to be given and the day for which it is given or on which it is to take effect.

    "executed" means any mode of execution.

    "office" means the registered office of the company.

    "the holder" in relation to shares means the member whose name is entered in the register of members as the holder of the shares.

    "the seal" means the common seal of the company.

    "secretary" means the secretary of the company or any other person appointed to perform the duties of the secretary of the company, including a joint, assistant or deputy secretary.

    "the United Kingdom" means Great Britain and Northern Ireland.

    Unless the context otherwise requires, words or expressions contained in these regulations bear the same meaning as in the Act but excluding any statutory modifications thereof not in force when these regulations become binding on the company.

SHARE CAPITAL

---

2. Subject to the provisions of the Act and without prejudice to any rights attached to any existing shares, any share may be issued with such rights or restrictions as the company may by ordinary resolution determine.

3. Subject to the provisions of the Act, shares may be issued which are to be redeemed or are to be liable to be redeemed at the option of the company or the holder on such terms and in such manner as maybe provided by the articles.

4. The company may exercise the powers of paying commissions conferred by the Act. Subject to the provisions of the Act, any such commission may be satisfied by the payment of cash or by the allotment of fully or partly paid shares or partly in one way and partly in the other.

5. Except as required by law, no person shall be recognised by the company as holding any share upon any trust and (except as otherwise provided by the articles or by law) the company shall not be bound by or recognise any interest in any share except an absolute right to the entirety thereof in the holder.

SHARE CERTIFICATES

---

6. Every member, upon becoming the holder of any shares, shall be entitled without payment to one certificate for all the shares of each class held by him (and, upon transferring a part of his holding of shares of any class, to a certificate for the balance of such holding) or several

certificates each for one or more of his shares upon payment for every certificate after the first of such reasonable sum as the directors may determine. Every certificate shall be sealed with the seal and shall specify the number, class and distinguishing numbers (if any) of the shares to which it relates and the amount or respective amounts paid up thereon. The company shall not be bound to issue more than one certificate for shares held jointly by several persons and delivery of a certificate to one joint holder shall be a sufficient delivery to all of them.

7. If a share certificate is defaced, worn-out, lost or destroyed, it may be renewed on such terms (if any) as to evidence and indemnity and payment of the expenses reasonably incurred by the company in investigating evidence as the directors may determine but otherwise free of charge, and (in the case of defacement or wearing-out) on delivery up of the old certificate.

LIEN

8. The company shall have a first and paramount lien on every share (not being a fully paid share) for all moneys (whether presently payable or not) payable at a fixed time or called in respect of that share. The directors may at any time declare any share to be wholly or in part exempt from the provisions of this regulation. The company's lien on a share shall extend to any amount payable in respect of it.

9. The company may sell in such manner as the directors determine any shares on which the company has a lien if a sum in respect of which the lien exists is presently payable and is not paid within fourteen clear days after notice has been given to the holder of the share or to the person entitled to it in consequence of the death or bankruptcy of the holder, demanding payment and stating that if the notice is not complied with the shares may be sold.

10. To give effect to a sale the directors may authorise some person to execute an instrument of transfer of the shares sold to, or in accordance with the directions of, the purchaser. The title of the transferee to the shares shall not be affected by any irregularity in or invalidity of the proceedings in reference to the sale.

11. The net proceeds of the sale, after payment of the costs, shall be applied in payment of so much of the sum for which the lien exists as is presently payable, and any residue shall (upon surrender to the company for cancellation of the certificate for the shares sold and subject to a like lien for any moneys not presently payable as existed upon the shares before the sale) be paid to the person entitled to the shares at the date of the sale.

CALLS ON SHARES AND FORFEITURE

12. Subject to the terms of allotment, the directors may make calls upon the members in respect of any moneys unpaid on their shares (whether in respect of nominal value or premium) and each member shall (subject to receiving at least fourteen clear days' notice specifying when and where payment is to be made) pay to the company as required by the notice the amount called on his shares. A call may be required to be paid by instalments. A call may, before receipt by the company of any sum due thereunder, be revoked in whole or part and payment of a call may be postponed in whole or part. A person upon whom a call is made shall remain liable for calls made upon him notwithstanding the subsequent transfer of the shares in respect whereof the call was made.

13. A call shall be deemed to have been made at the time when the resolution of the directors authorising the call was passed.

14. The joint holders of a share shall be jointly and severally liable to pay all calls in respect thereof.

15. If a call remains unpaid after it has become due and payable the person from whom it is due and payable shall pay interest on the amount unpaid from the day it became due and payable until it is paid at the rate fixed by the terms of allotment of the share or in the notice of the call or, if no rate is fixed, at the appropriate (as defined by the Act) but the directors may waive payment of the interest wholly or in part.

16. An amount payable in respect of a share on allotment or at any fixed date, whether in respect of nominal value or premium or as an instalment of a call, shall be deemed to be a call and if it

is not paid the provisions of the articles shall apply as if that amount had become due and payable by virtue of a call.

17. Subject to the terms of allotment, the directors may make arrangements on the issue of shares for a difference between the holders in the amounts and times of payment of calls on their shares.

18. If a call remains unpaid after it has become due and payable the directors may give to the person from whom it is due not less than fourteen clear days' notice requiring payment of the amount unpaid together with any interest which may have accrued. The notice shall name the place where payment is to be made and shall state that if the notice is not complied with the shares in respect of which the call was made will be liable to be forfeited.

19. If the notice is not complied with any share in respect of which it was given may, before the payment required by the notice has been made, be forfeited by a resolution of the directors and the forfeiture shall include all dividends or other moneys payable in respect of the forfeited shares and not paid before the forfeiture.

20. Subject to the provisions of the Act, a forfeited share may be sold, re-allotted or otherwise disposed of on such terms and in such manner as the directors determine either to the person who was before the forfeiture the holder or to any other person and at any time before sale, re-allotment or other disposition, the forfeiture may be cancelled on such terms as the directors think fit. Where for the purposes of its disposal a forfeited share is to be transferred to any person the directors may authorise some person to execute an instrument of transfer of the share to that person.

21. A person any of whose shares have been forfeited shall cease to be a member in respect of them and shall surrender to the company for cancellation the certificate for the shares forfeited but shall remain liable to the company for all moneys which at the date of forfeiture were presently payable by him to the company in respect of those shares with interest at the rate at which interest which was payable on those moneys before the forfeiture or, if no interest was so payable, at the appropriate rate (as defined in the Act) from the date of forfeiture until payment but the directors may waive payment wholly or in part or enforce payment without any allowance for the value of the shares at the time of forfeiture or for any consideration received on their disposal.

22. A statutory declaration by a director or the secretary that a share has been forfeited on a specified date shall be conclusive evidence of the facts stated in it as against all persons claiming to be entitled to the share and the declaration shall (subject to the execution of an instrument of transfer if necessary) constitute a good title to the share and the person to whom the share is disposed of shall not be bound to see to the application of the consideration, if any, nor shall his title to the share be affected by any irregularity in or invalidity of the proceedings in reference to the forfeiture or disposal of the share.

TRANSFER OF SHARES

23. The instrument of transfer of a share may be in any usual form or in any other form which the directors may approve and shall be executed by or on behalf of the transferor and, unless the share is fully paid, by or on behalf of the transferee.

24. The directors may refuse to register the transfer of a share which is not fully paid to a person of whom they do not approve and they may refuse to register the transfer of a share on which the company has a lien. They may also refuse to register a transfer unless—

    (a) it is lodged at the office or at such other place as the directors may appoint and is accompanied by the certificate for the shares to which it relates and such other evidence as the directors may reasonably require to show the right of the transferor to make the transfer;

    (b) it is in respect of only one class of shares; and

    (c) it is in favour of not more than four transferees.

25. If the directors refuse to register a transfer of a share, they shall within two months after the date on which the transfer was lodged with the company send to the transferee notice of the refusal.

26. The registration of transfers of shares or of transfers of any class of shares may be suspended at such times and for such periods (not exceeding thirty days in any year) as the directors may determine.

27. No fee shall be charged for the registration of any instrument of transfer or other document relating to or affecting the title to any share.

28. The company shall be entitled to retain any instrument of transfer which is registered, but any instrument of transfer which the directors refuse to register shall be returned to the person lodging it when notice of the refusal is given.

TRANSMISSION OF SHARES

29. If a member dies the survivor or survivors where he was a joint holder, and his personal representatives where he was a sole holder or the only survivor of joint holders, shall be the only persons recognised by the company as having any title to his interest; but nothing herein contained shall release the estate of a deceased member from any liability in respect of any share which had been jointly held by him.

30. A person becoming entitled to a share in consequence of the death or bankruptcy of a member may, upon such evidence being produced as the directors may properly require, elect either to become the holder of the share or to have some person nominated by him registered as the transferee. If he elects to become the holder he shall give notice to the company to that effect. If he elects to have another person registered he shall execute an instrument of transfer of the share to that person. All the articles relating to the transfer of shares shall apply to the notice or instrument of transfer as if it were an instrument of transfer executed by the member and the death or bankruptcy of the member had not occurred.

31. A person becoming entitled to a share in consequence of the death or bankruptcy of a member shall have the rights to which he would be entitled if he were the holder of the share, except that he shall not, before being registered as the holder of the share, be entitled in respect of it to attend or vote at any meeting of the company or at any separate meeting of the holders of any class of shares in the company.

ALTERATION OF SHARE CAPITAL

32. The company may by ordinary resolution—
    (a) increase its share capital by new shares of such amount as the resolution prescribes;
    (b) consolidate and divide all or any of its share capital into shares of larger amount than its existing shares;
    (c) subject to the provisions of the Act, sub-divide its shares, or any of them, into shares of smaller amount and the resolution may determine that, as between the shares resulting from the sub-division, any of them may have any preference or advantage as compared with the others; and
    (d) cancel shares which, at the date of the passing of the resolution, have not been taken or agreed to be taken by any person and diminish the amount of its share capital by the amount of the shares so cancelled.

33. Whenever as a result of a consolidation of shares any members would become entitled to fractions of a share, the directors may, on behalf of those members, sell the shares representing the fractions for the best price reasonably obtainable to any person (including, subject to the provisions of the Act, the company) and distribute the net proceeds of sale in due proportion among those members, and the directors may authorise some person to execute an instrument of transfer of the shares to, or in accordance with the directions of, the purchaser. The transferee shall not be bound to see to the application of the purchase money nor shall his title to the shares be affected by any irregularity in or invalidity of the proceedings in reference to the sale.

34. Subject to the provisions of the Act, the company may by special resolution reduce its share capital, any capital redemption reserve and any share premium account in any way.

PURCHASE OF OWN SHARES

35. Subject to the provisions of the Act, the company may purchase its own shares (including any redeemable shares) and, if it is a private company, make a payment in respect of the redemption or purchase of its own shares otherwise than out of distributable profits of the company or the proceeds of a fresh issue of shares.

GENERAL MEETINGS

36. All general meetings other than annual general meetings shall be called extraordinary general meetings.

37. The directors may call general meetings and, on the requisition of members pursuant to the provisions of the Act, shall forthwith proceed to convene an extraordinary general meeting for a date not later than eight weeks after receipt of the requisition. If there are not within the United Kingdom sufficient directors to call a general meeting, any director or any member of the company may call a general meeting.

NOTICE OF GENERAL MEETINGS

38. An annual general meeting and an extraordinary general meeting called for the passing of a special resolution or a resolution appointing a person as a director shall be called by at least twenty-one clear day's notice. All other extraordinary general meetings shall be called by at least fourteen clear days' notice but a general meeting may be called by shorter notice if it is so agreed—

   (a) in the case of an annual general meeting, by all the entitled to attend and vote thereat; and

   (b) in the case of any other meeting by a majority in number of the members having a right to attend and vote being a majority together holding not less than ninety-five per cent in nominal value of the shares giving that right.

   The notice shall specify the time and place of the meeting and the general nature of the business to be transacted and, in the case of an annual general meeting, shall specify the meeting as such.

   Subject to the provisions of the articles and to any restrictions imposed on any shares, the notice shall be given to all the members, to all persons entitled to a share in consequence of the death or bankruptcy of a member and to the directors and auditors.

39. The accidental omission to give notice of a meeting to, or the non-receipt of notice of a meeting by, any person entitled to receive notice shall not invalidate the proceedings at that meeting.

PROCEEDINGS AT GENERAL MEETINGS

40. No business shall be transacted at any meeting unless a quorum is present. Two persons entitled to vote upon the business to be transacted, each being a member or a proxy for a member or a duly authorised representative of a corporation, shall be a quorum.

41. If such a quorum is not present within half an hour from the time appointed for the meeting, or if during a meeting such a quorum ceases to be present, the meeting shall stand adjourned to the same day in the next week at the same time and place or to such time and place as the directors may determine.

42. The chairman, if any, of the board of directors or in his absence some other director nominated by the directors shall preside as chairman of the meeting, but if neither the chairman nor such other director (if any) be present within fifteen minutes after the time appointed for holding the meeting and willing to act, the directors present shall elect one of their number to be chairman and, if there is only one director present and willing to act, he shall be chairman.

43. If no director is willing to act as chairman, or if no director is present within fifteen minutes after the time appointed for holding the meeting, the members present and entitled to vote shall choose one of their number to be chairman.

44. A director shall, notwithstanding that he is not a member, be entitled to attend and speak at any general meeting and at any separate meeting of the holders of any class of shares in the company.

45. The chairman may, with the consent of a meeting at which a quorum is present (and shall if so directed by the meeting), adjourn the meeting from time to time and from place to place, but no business shall be transacted at an adjourned meeting other than business which might properly have been transacted at the meeting had the adjournment not taken place. When a meeting is adjourned for fourteen days or more, at least seven clear days' notice shall be given specifying the time and place of the adjourned meeting and the general nature of the business to be transacted. Otherwise it shall not be necessary to give any such notice.

46. A resolution put to the vote of a meeting shall be decided on a show of hands unless before, or on the declaration of the result of, the show of hands a poll is duly demanded. Subject to the provisions of the Act, a poll may be demanded—

    (a) by the chairman; or

    (b) by at least two members having the right to vote at the meeting; or

    (c) by a member or members representing not less than one-tenth of the total voting rights of all the members having the right to vote at the meeting; or

    (d) by a member or members holding shares conferring a right to vote at the meeting being shares on which an aggregate sum has been paid up equal to not less than one-tenth of the total sum paid up on all the shares conferring that right;

    and a demand by a person as proxy for a member shall be the same as a demand by the member.

47. Unless a poll is duly demanded a declaration by the chairman that a resolution has been carried or carried unanimously, or by a particular majority, or lost, or not carried by a particular majority and an entry to that effect in the minutes of the meeting shall be conclusive evidence of the fact without proof of the number or proportion of the votes recorded in favour of or against the resolution.

48. The demand for a poll may, before the poll is taken, be withdrawn but only with the consent of the chairman and a demand so withdrawn shall not be taken to have invalidated the result of a show of hands declared before the demand was made.

49. A poll shall be taken as the chairman directs and he may appoint scrutineers (who need not be members) and fix a time and place for declaring the result of the poll. The result of the poll shall be deemed to be the resolution of the meeting at which the poll was demanded.

50. In the case of an equality of votes, whether on a show of hands or on a poll, the chairman shall be entitled to a casting vote in addition to any other vote he may have.

51. A poll demanded on the election of a chairman or on a question of adjournment shall be taken forthwith. A poll demanded on any other question shall be taken either forthwith or at such time and place as the chairman directs not being more than thirty days after the poll is demanded. The demand for a poll shall not prevent the continuance of a meeting for the transaction of any business other than the question on which the poll is demanded. If a poll is demanded before the declaration of the result of a show of hands and the demand is duly withdrawn, the meeting shall continue as if the demand had not been made.

52. No notice need be given of a poll not taken forthwith if the time and place at which it is to be taken are announced at the meeting at which it is demanded. In any other case at least seven clear days' notice shall be given specifying the time and place at which the poll is to be taken.

53. A resolution in writing executed by or on behalf of each member who would have been entitled to vote upon it if it had been proposed at a general meeting at which he was present shall be as effectual as if it had been passed at a general meeting duly convened and held and may consist of several instruments in the like form each executed by or on behalf of one or more members.

VOTES OF MEMBERS

54. Subject to any rights or restrictions attached to any shares, on a show of hands every member who (being an individual) is present in person or (being a corporation) is present by a duly authorised representative, not being himself a member entitled to vote, shall have one vote and on a poll every member shall have one vote for every share of which he is the holder.

55. In the case of joint holders the vote of the senior who tenders a vote, whether in person or by proxy, shall be accepted to the exclusion of the votes of the other joint holders; and seniority shall be determined by the order in which the names of the holders stand in the register of members.

56. A member in respect of whom an order has been made by any court having jurisdiction (whether in the United Kingdom or elsewhere) in matters concerning mental disorder may vote, whether on a show of hands or on a poll, by his receiver, curator bonis or other person authorised in that behalf appointed by that court, and any such receiver, curator bonis or other person may, on a poll, vote by proxy. Evidence to the satisfaction of the directors of the authority of the person claiming to exercise the right to vote shall be deposited at the office, or at such other place as is specified in accordance with the articles for the deposit of instruments of proxy, not less than 48 hours before the time appointed for holding the meeting or adjourned meeting at which the right to vote is to be exercised and in default the right to vote shall not be exercisable.

57. No member shall vote at any general meeting or at any separate meeting of the holders of any class of shares in the company, either in person or by proxy, in respect of any share held by him unless all moneys presently payable by him in respect of that share have been paid.

58. No objection shall be raised to the qualification of any voter except at the meeting or adjourned meeting at which the vote objected to is tendered, and every vote not disallowed at the meeting shall be valid. Any objection made in due time shall be referred to the chairman whose decision shall be final and conclusive.

59. On a poll votes may be given either personally or by proxy. A member may appoint more than one proxy to attend on the same occasion.

60. An instrument appointing a proxy shall be in writing, executed by or on behalf of the appointor and shall be in the following form (or in a form as near thereto as circumstances allow or in any other form which is usual or which the directors may approve)—

    ".. .. .. PLC/Limited .. .. I/We, ..., of .. .., being a member/members of the above-named company, hereby appoint .. .. of .. .. , or failing him, ... of .. .., as my/our proxy to vote in my/our name(s) and on my/our behalf at the annual/extraordinary general meeting of the company to be held on .. .. 19 .. .., and at any adjournment thereof.
    Signed on .. .. 19 .. .."

61. Where it is desired to afford members an opportunity of instructing the proxy how he shall act the instrument appointing a proxy shall be in the following form (or in a form as near thereto as circumstances allow or in any other form which is usual or which the directors may approve)—

    ".. .. .. PLC/Limited .. .. I/We, ..., of .. .. , being a member/members of the above-named company, hereby appoint .. .. of .. .., or failing him .. .. of .. .., as my/our proxy to vote in my/our name(s) and on my/our behalf at the annual/extraordinary general meeting of the company to be held on 19 , and at any adjournment thereof.

    This form is to be used in respect of the resolutions mentioned below as follows:
    Resolution No. 1 *for *against
    Resolution No. 2 *for *against.
    *Strike out whichever is not desired.

    Unless otherwise instructed, the proxy may vote as he thinks fit or abstain from voting.
    Signed this .. .. day of .. .. 19 .. .."

62. The instrument appointing a proxy and any authority under which it is executed or a copy of such authority certified notarially or in some other way approved by the directors may—

    (a) be deposited at the office or at such other place within the United Kingdom as is specified in the notice convening the meeting or in any instrument of proxy sent out by the company in relation to the meeting not less than 48 hours before the time for holding the meeting or adjourned meeting at which the person named in the instrument proposes to vote; or

    (b) in the case of a poll taken more than 48 hours after it is demanded, be deposited as aforesaid after the poll has been demanded and not less than 24 hours before the time appointed for the taking of the poll; or

    (c) where the poll is not taken forthwith but is taken not more than 48 hours after it was demanded, be delivered at the meeting at which the poll was demanded to the chairman or to the secretary or to any director; and an instrument of proxy which is not deposited or delivered in a manner so permitted shall be invalid.

63. A vote given or poll demanded by proxy or by the duly authorised representative of a corporation shall be valid notwithstanding the previous determination of the authority of the person voting or demanding a poll unless notice of the determination was received by the company at the office or at such other place at which the instrument of proxy was duly deposited before the commencement of the meeting or adjourned meeting at which the vote is given or the poll demanded or (in the case of a poll taken otherwise than on the same day as the meeting or adjourned meeting) the time appointed for taking the poll.

NUMBER OF DIRECTORS

64. Unless otherwise determined by ordinary resolution, the number of directors (other than alternate directors) shall not be subject to any maximum but shall be not less than two.

ALTERNATE DIRECTORS

65. Any director (other than an alternate director) may appoint any other director, or any other person approved by resolution of the directors and willing to act, to be an alternate director and may remove from office an alternate director so appointed by him.

66. An alternate director shall be entitled to receive notice of all meetings of directors and of all meetings of committees of directors of which his appointor is a member, to attend and vote at any such meeting at which the director appointing him is not personally present, and generally to perform all the functions of his appointor as a director in his absence but shall not be entitled to receive any remuneration from the company for his services as an alternate director. But it shall not be necessary to give notice of such a meeting to an alternate director who is absent from the United Kingdom.

67. An alternate director shall cease to be an alternate director if his appointor ceases to be a director; but, if a director retires by rotation or otherwise but is re-appointed or deemed to have been re-appointed at the meeting at which he retires, any appointment of an alternate director made by him which was in force immediately prior to his retirement shall continue after his re-appointment.

68. Any appointment or removal of an alternate director shall be by notice to the company signed by the director making or revoking the appointment or in any other manner approved by the directors.

69. Save as otherwise provided in the articles, an alternate director shall be deemed for all purposes to be a director and shall alone be responsible for his own acts and defaults and he shall not be deemed to be the agent of the director appointing him.

POWERS OF DIRECTORS

70. Subject to the provisions of the Act, the memorandum and the articles and to any directions given by special resolution, the business of the company shall be managed by the directors who may exercise all the powers of the company. No alteration of the memorandum or articles and no such

direction shall invalidate any prior act of the directors which would have been valid if that alteration had not been made or that direction had not been given. The powers given by this regulation shall not be limited by any special power given to the directors by the articles and a meeting of directors at which a quorum is present may exercise all powers exercisable by the directors.

71. The directors may, by power of attorney or otherwise, appoint any person to be the agent of the company for such purposes and on such conditions as they determine, including authority for the agent to delegate all or any of his powers.

DELEGATION OF DIRECTORS' POWERS

72. The directors may delegate any of their powers to any committee consisting of one or more directors. They may also delegate to any managing director or any director holding any other executive office such of their powers as they consider desirable to be exercised by him. Any such delegation may be made subject to any conditions the directors may impose, and either collaterally with or to the exclusion of their own powers and may be revoked or altered. Subject to any such conditions, the proceedings of a committee with two or more members shall be governed by the articles regulating the proceedings of directors so far as they are capable of applying.

APPOINTMENT AND RETIREMENT OF DIRECTORS

73. At the first annual general meeting all the directors shall retire from office, and at every subsequent annual general meeting one-third of the directors who are subject to retirement by rotation or, if their number is not three or a multiple of three, the number nearest to one-third shall retire from office; but, if there is only one director who is subject to retirement by rotation, he shall retire.

74. Subject to the provisions of the Act, the directors to retire by rotation shall be those who have been longest in office since their last appointment or re-appointment, but as between persons who became or were last re-appointed directors on the same day those to retire shall (unless they otherwise agree among themselves) be determined by lot.

75. If the company, at the meeting at which a director retires by rotation, does not fill the vacancy the retiring director shall, if willing to act, be deemed to have been re-appointed unless at the meeting it is not to fill the vacancy or unless a resolution for the re-appointment of the director is put to the meeting and lost.

76. No person other than a director retiring by rotation shall be appointed or re-appointed a director at any general meeting unless—

    (a) he is recommended by the directors; or

    (b) not less than fourteen nor more than thirty-five clear days before the date appointed for the meeting, notice executed by a member qualified to vote at the meeting has been given to the company of the intention to propose that person for appointment or re-appointment stating the particulars which would, if he were so appointed or re-appointed, be required to be included in the company's register of directors together with notice executed by that person of his willingness to be appointed or re-appointed.

77. Not less than seven nor more than twenty-eight clear days before the date appointed for holding a general meeting notice shall be given to all who are entitled to receive notice of the meeting of any person (other than a director retiring by rotation at the meeting) who is recommended by the directors for appointment or re-appointment as a director at the meeting or in respect of whom notice has been duly given to the company of the intention to propose him at the meeting for appointment or re-appointment as a director. The notice shall give the particulars of that person which would, if he were so appointed or re-appointed, be required to be included in the company's register of directors.

78. Subject as aforesaid, the company may by ordinary resolution appoint a person who is willing to act to be a director either to fill a vacancy or as an additional director and may also determine the rotation in which any additional directors are to retire.

79. The directors may appoint a person who is willing to act to be a director, either to fill a vacancy or as an additional director, provided that the appointment does not cause the number of directors to exceed any number fixed by or in accordance with the articles as the maximum number of directors. A director so appointed shall hold office only until the next following annual general meeting and shall not be taken into account in determining the directors who are to retire by rotation at the meeting. If not re-appointed at such annual general meeting, he shall vacate office at the conclusion thereof.

80. Subject as aforesaid, a director who retires at an annual general meeting may, if willing to act, be re-appointed. If he is not re-appointed, he shall retain office until the meeting appoints someone in his place, or if it does not do so, until the end of the meeting.

DISQUALIFICATION AND REMOVAL OF DIRECTORS

81. The office of a director shall be vacated if—

    (a) he ceases to be a director by virtue of any provision of the Act or he becomes prohibited by law from being a director; or

    (b) he becomes bankrupt or makes any arrangement or composition with his creditors generally; or

    (c) he is, or may be, suffering from mental disorder and either—

        (i) he is admitted to hospital in pursuance of an application for admission for treatment under the Mental Health Act 1983 or, in Scotland, an application for admission under the Mental Health (Scotland) Act 1960, or

        (ii) an order is made by a court having jurisdiction (whether in the United Kingdom or elsewhere)in matters concerning mental disorder for his detention or for the appointment of a receiver, curator bonis or other person to exercise powers with respect to his property or affairs; or

    (d) he resigns his office by notice to the company; or

    (e) he shall for more than six consecutive months have been absent without permission of the directors from meetings of directors held during that period and the directors resolve that his office be vacated.

REMUNERATION OF DIRECTORS

82. The directors shall be entitled to such remuneration as the company may by ordinary resolution determine and, unless the resolution provides otherwise, the remuneration shall be deemed to accrue from day to day.

DIRECTORS' EXPENSES

83. The directors may be paid all travelling, hotel, and other expenses properly incurred by them in connection with their attendance at meetings of directors or committees of directors or general meetings or separate meetings of the holders of any class of shares or of debentures of the company or otherwise in connection with the discharge of their duties.

DIRECTORS' APPOINTMENTS AND INTERESTS

84. Subject to the provisions of the Act, the directors may appoint one or more of their number to the office of managing director or to any other executive office under the company and may enter into an agreement or arrangement with any director for his employment by the company or for the provision by him of any services outside the scope of the ordinary duties of a director. Any such appointment, agreement or arrangement may be made upon such terms as the directors determine and they may remunerate any such director for his services as they think fit. Any appointment of a director to an executive office shall terminate if he ceases to be a director but without prejudice to any claim to damages for breach of the contract of service between the director and the company. A managing director and a director holding any other executive office shall not be subject to retirement by rotation.

85. Subject to the provisions of the Act, and provided that he has disclosed to the directors the nature and extent of any material interest of his, a director notwithstanding his office -

    (a) may be a party to, or otherwise interested in, any transaction or arrangement with the company or in which the company is otherwise interested;

    (b) may be a director or other officer of, or employed by, or a party to any transaction or arrangement with, or otherwise interested in, any body corporate promoted by the company or in which the company is otherwise interested; and

    (c) shall not, by reason of his office, be accountable to the company for any benefit which he derives from any such office or employment or from any such transaction or arrangement or from any interest in any such body corporate and no such transaction or arrangement shall be liable to be avoided on the ground of any such interest or benefit.

86. For the purposes of regulation 85—

    (a) a general notice given to the directors that a director is to be regarded as having an interest of the nature and extent specified in the notice in any transaction or arrangement in which a specified person or class of persons is interested shall be deemed to be a disclosure that the director has an interest in any such transaction of the nature and extent so specified; and

    (b) an interest of which a director has no knowledge and of which it is unreasonable to expect him to have knowledge shall not be treated as an interest of his.

DIRECTORS' GRATUITIES AND PENSIONS

87. The directors may provide benefits, whether by the payment of gratuities or pensions or by insurance or otherwise, for any director who has held but no longer holds any executive office or employment with the company or with any body corporate which is or has been a subsidiary of the company or a predecessor in business of the company or of any such subsidiary, and for any member of his family (including a spouse and a former spouse) or any person who is or was dependent on him, and may (as well before as after he ceases to hold such office or employment) contribute to any fund and pay premiums for the purchase or provision of any such benefit.

PROCEEDINGS OF DIRECTORS

88. Subject to the provisions of the articles, the directors may regulate their proceedings as they think fit. A director may, and the secretary at the request of a director shall, call a meeting of the directors. It shall not be necessary to give notice of a meeting to a director who is absent from the United Kingdom. Questions arising at a meeting shall be decided by a majority of votes. In the case of an equality of votes, the chairman shall have a second or casting vote. A director who is also an alternate director shall be entitled in the absence of his appointor to a separate vote on behalf of his appointor in addition to his own vote.

89. The quorum for the transaction of the business of the directors may be fixed by the directors and unless so fixed at any other number shall be two. A person who holds office only as an alternate director shall, if his appointor is not present, be counted in the quorum.

90. The continuing directors or a sole continuing director may act notwithstanding any vacancies in their number but, if the number of directors is less than the number fixed as the quorum, the continuing directors or director may act only for the purpose of filling vacancies or of calling a general meeting.

91. The directors may appoint one of their number to be the chairman of the board of directors and may at any time remove him from that office. Unless he is unwilling to do so, the director so appointed shall preside at every meeting of directors at which he is present. But if there is no director holding that office, or if the director holding it is unwilling to preside or is not present within five minutes after the time appointed for the meeting, the directors present may appoint one of their number to be chairman of the meeting.

92. All acts done by a meeting of directors, or of a committee of directors, or by a person acting as a director shall, notwithstanding that it be afterwards discovered that there was a defect in the appointment of any director or that any of them were disqualified from holding office, or had vacated office, or were not entitled to vote, be as valid as if every such person had been duly appointed and was qualified and had continued to be a director and had been entitled to vote.

93. A resolution in writing signed by all the directors entitled to receive notice of a meeting of directors or of a committee of directors shall be as valid and effectual as if it had been passed at a meeting of directors or (as the case may be) a committee of directors duly convened and held and may consist of several documents in the like form each signed by one or more directors; but a resolution signed by an alternate director need not also be signed by his appointor and, if it is signed by a director who has appointed an alternate director, it need not be signed by the alternate director in that capacity.

94. Save as otherwise provided by the articles, a director shall not vote at a meeting of directors or of a committee of directors on any resolution concerning a matter in which he has, directly or indirectly, an interest or duty which is material and which conflicts or may conflict with the interests of the company unless his interest or duty arises only because the case falls within one or more of the following paragraphs—

    (a) the resolution relates to the giving to him of a guarantee, security, or indemnity in respect of money lent to, or an obligation incurred by him for the benefit of, the company or any of its subsidiaries;

    (b) the resolution relates to the giving to a third party of a guarantee, security, or indemnity in respect of an obligation of the company or any of its subsidiaries for which the director has assumed responsibility in whole or part and whether alone or jointly with others under a guarantee or indemnity or by the giving of security;

    (c) his interest arises by virtue of his subscribing or agreeing to subscribe for any shares, debentures or other securities of the company or any of its subsidiaries, or by virtue of his being, or intending to become, a participant in the underwriting or sub-underwriting of offer of any such shares, debentures, or other securities by the company or any of its subsidiaries for subscription, purchase or exchange;

    (d) the resolution relates in any way to a retirement benefits scheme which has been approved, or is conditional upon approval, by the Board of Inland Revenue for taxation purposes.

    For the purposes of this regulation, an interest of a person who is, for any purpose of the Act (excluding any statutory modification thereof not in force when this regulation becomes binding on the company), connected with a director shall be treated as an interest of the director and, in relation to an alternate director, an interest of his appointor shall be treated as an interest of the alternate director without prejudice to any interest which the alternate director has otherwise.

95. A director shall not be counted in the quorum present at a meeting in relation to a resolution on which he is not entitled to vote.

96. The company may by ordinary resolution suspend or relax to any extent, either generally or in respect of any particular matter, any provision of the articles prohibiting a director from voting at a meeting of directors or of a committee of directors.

97. Where proposals are under consideration concerning the appointment of two or more directors to offices or employment with the company or any body corporate in which the company is interested the proposals may be divided and considered in relation to each director separately and (provided he is not for another reason precluded from voting) each of the directors concerned shall be entitled to vote and be counted in the quorum in respect of each resolution except that concerning his own appointment.

98. If a question arises at a meeting of directors or of a committee of directors as to the right of a director to vote, the question may, before the conclusion of the meeting, be referred to the chairman of the meeting and his ruling in relation to any director other than himself shall be final and conclusive.

SECRETARY

99. Subject to the provisions of the Act, the secretary shall be appointed by the directors for such term, at such remuneration and upon such conditions as they may think fit; and any secretary so appointed may be removed by them.

MINUTES

100. The directors shall cause minutes to be made in books kept for the purpose—
    (a) of all appointments of officers made by the directors; and
    (b) of all proceedings at meetings of the company, of the holders of any class of shares in the company, and of the directors, and of committees of directors, including the names of the directors present at each such meeting.

THE SEAL

101. The seal shall only be used by the authority of the directors or of a committee of directors authorised by the directors. The directors may determine who shall sign any instrument to which the seal is affixed and unless otherwise so determined it shall be signed by a director and by the secretary or by a second director.

DIVIDENDS

102. Subject to the provisions of the Act, the company may by ordinary resolution declare dividends in accordance with the respective rights of the members, but no dividend shall exceed the amount recommended by the directors.

103. Subject to the provisions of the Act, the directors may pay interim dividends if it appears to them that they are justified by the profits of the company available for distribution. If the share capital is divided into different classes, the directors may pay interim dividends on shares which confer deferred or non-preferred rights with regard to dividend as well as on shares which confer preferential rights with regard to dividend, but no interim dividend shall be paid on shares carrying deferred or non-preferred rights if, at the time of payment, any preferential dividend is in arrear. The directors may also pay at intervals settled by them any dividend payable at a fixed rate if it appears to them that the profits available for distribution justify the payment. Provided the directors act in good faith they shall not incur any liability to the holders of shares conferring preferred rights for any loss they may suffer by the lawful payment of an interim dividend on any shares having deferred or non-preferred rights.

104. Except as otherwise provided by the rights attached to shares, all dividends shall be declared and paid according to the amounts paid up on the shares on which the dividend is paid. All dividends shall be apportioned and paid proportionately to the amounts paid up on the shares during any portion or the period in respect of which the dividend is paid; but, if any share is issued on terms providing that it shall rank for dividend as from a particular date, that share shall rank for dividend accordingly.

105. A general meeting declaring a dividend may, upon the recommendation of the directors, direct that it shall be satisfied wholly or partly by the distribution of assets and, where any difficulty arises in regard to the distribution, the directors may settle the same and in particular may issue fractional certificates and fix the value for distribution of any assets and may determine that cash shall be paid to any member upon the footing of the value so fixed in order to adjust the rights of members and may vest any assets in trustees.

106. Any dividend or other moneys payable in respect of a share may be paid by cheque sent by post to the registered address of the person entitled or, if two or more persons are the holder of the share or are jointly entitled to it by reason of the death or bankruptcy of the holder, to the registered address of that one of those persons who is first named in the register of members or to such person and to such address as the person or persons entitled may in writing direct. Every cheque shall be made payable to the order of the person or persons

entitled or to such other person as the person or persons entitled may in writing direct and payment of the cheque shall be a good discharge to the company. Any joint holder or other person jointly entitled to a share as aforesaid may give receipts for any dividend or other moneys payable in respect of the share.

107. No dividend or other moneys payable in respect of a share shall bear interest against the company unless otherwise provided by the rights attached to the share.

108. Any dividend which has remained unclaimed for twelve years from the date when it became due for payment shall, if the directors so resolve, be forfeited and cease to remain owing by the company.

ACCOUNTS

109. No member shall (as such) have any right of inspecting any accounting records or other book or document of the company except as conferred by statute or authorised by the directors or by ordinary resolution of the company.

CAPITALISATION OF PROFITS

110. The directors may with the authority of an ordinary resolution of the company—

(a) subject as hereinafter provided, resolve to capitalise any undivided profits of the company not required for paying any preferential dividend (whether or not they are available for distribution) or any sum standing to the credit of the company's share premium account or capital redemption reserve;

(b) appropriate the sum resolved to be capitalised to the members who would have been entitled to it if it were distributed by way of dividend and in the same proportions and apply such sum on their behalf either in or towards paying up the amounts, if any, for the time being unpaid on any shares held by them respectively, or in paying up in full unissued shares or debentures of the company of a nominal amount equal to that sum, and allot the shares or debentures credited as fully paid to those members, or as they may direct, in those proportions, or partly in one way and partly in the other: but the share premium account, the capital redemption reserve, and any profits which are not available for distribution may, for the purposes of this regulation, only be applied in paying up unissued shares to be allotted to members credited as fully paid;

(c) make such provision by the issue of fractional certificates or by payment in cash or otherwise as they determine in the case of shares or debentures becoming distributable under this regulation in fractions; and

(d) authorise any person to enter on behalf of all the members concerned into an agreement with the company providing for the allotment to them respectively, credited as fully paid, of any shares or debentures to which they are entitled upon such capitalisation, any agreement made under such authority being binding on all such members.

NOTICES

111. Any notice to be given to or by any person pursuant to the articles shall be in writing except that a notice calling a meeting of the directors need not be in writing.

112. The company may give any notice to a member either personally or by sending it by post in a prepaid envelope addressed to the member at his registered address or by leaving it at that address. In the case of joint holders of a share, all notices shall be given to the joint holder whose name stands first in the register of members in respect of the joint holding and notice so given shall be sufficient notice to all the joint holders. A member whose registered address is not within the United Kingdom and who gives to the company an address within the United Kingdom at which notices may be given to him shall be entitled to have notices given to him at the address, but otherwise no such member shall be entitled to receive any notice from the company.

113. A member present, either in person or by proxy, at any meeting of the company or of the holders of any class of shares in the company shall be deemed to have received notice of the meeting and, where requisite, of the purposes for which it was called.

114. Every person who becomes entitled to a share shall be bound by any notice in respect of that share which, before his name is entered into the register of members, has been duly given to a person from whom he derives his title.

115. Proof that an envelope containing a notice was properly addressed, prepaid and posted shall be conclusive evidence that the notice was given. A notice shall be deemed to be given at the expiration of 48 hours after the envelope containing it was posted.

116. A notice may be given by the company to the persons entitled to a share in consequence of the death or bankruptcy of a member by sending or delivering it, in any manner authorised by the articles for the giving of notice to a member, addressed to them by name, or by the title of representatives of the deceased, or trustee of the bankrupt or by any like description at the address, if any, within the United Kingdom supplied for that purpose by the persons claiming to be so entitled. Until such an address has been supplied, a notice may be given in any manner in which it might have been given if the death or bankruptcy had not occurred.

WINDING UP

117. If the company is wound up, the liquidator may, with the sanction of an extraordinary resolution of the company and any other sanction required by the Act, divide among the members in specie the whole or any part of the assets of the company and may, for that purpose, value any assets and determine how the division shall be carried out as between the members or different classes of members. The liquidator may, with the like sanction, vest the whole or any part of the assets in trustees upon such trusts for the benefit of the members as he with the like sanction determines, but no member shall be compelled to accept any assets upon which there is a liability.

INDEMNITY

118. Subject to the provisions of the Act but without prejudice to any indemnity to which a director may otherwise be entitled, every director or other officer or auditor of the company shall be indemnified out of the assets of the company against any liability incurred by him in defending any proceedings, whether civil or criminal, in which judgment is given in his favour or in which he is acquitted or in connection with any application in which relief is granted to him by the court from liability for negligence, default, breach of duty or breach of trust in relation to the affairs of the company.

Appendix B

Articles of GE Ltd

Table A shall apply to the Company except where incompatible with the following provisions

1. On a Resolution proposed at a General Meeting for the removal of a director from the Board of Directors or the company secretary from his office, that director or company secretary shall have three votes for every share held by him/her, and Article 54 in Table A shall to this extent not apply to the Company.

2. There shall be no Chairman of the Board of Directors, and Article 88 in Table A shall not apply to the Company.

3. The minimum number of directors shall be one, and Article 64 in Table A shall not apply to the Company.

4. Directors of the company shall not be required to retire by rotation, and Articles 73–75 in Table A shall not apply to the Company.

5. The directors of the Company may in their absolute discretion refuse to register the transfer of any share in the Company, whether or not it be a fully-paid share, without assigning any reason therefor.

6. Duncan shall have the right to receive notice of and to be present at all meetings of the Board of Directors of the Company, notwithstanding that he is not a director of the Company, but shall not be entitled to speak, to count in the quorum or to vote at such meetings.

7. The directors shall have authority at any time to allot shares in the Company up to the amount of the authorised capital for the time being unissued.

[The following additional Special Articles were added when YOCS became a shareholder.]

8. Ye Olde Curiosity Shoppe plc shall have the right to appoint two non-executive directors to the Board of Directors of the Company.

9. No new shares in the Company shall be issued unless the directors shall first have offered those shares to Ye Olde Curiosity Shoppe plc, and section 89 of the Companies Act 1985 is excluded to the extent necessary to give effect to this Article. Any shares offered to Ye Olde Curisoity Shoppe plc under this Article, but not taken up by that company, may then be offered to the remaining shareholders in accordance with section 89 of the Companies Act 1985.

Appendix C

Memorandum of Association

1. The name of the company is Great Expectations Ltd.

2. The Registered office of the company is situated in England.

3. The share capital of the company shall be five thousand pounds divided into five thousand shares of one pound each.

4. The object of the company is to carry on business as a general commercial company.

5. The liability of the members is limited.

Appendix D

Shareholder Agreement

This Agreement, made the   day of   2001 between Duncan of the first part and Arthur Bill and Edwina of the second part (hereinafter jointly and severally called 'the purchasers') witnesses as follows

1. In consideration of Duncan subscribing for 1,200 £1 ordinary shares in Great Expectations Ltd at par ('the shares') the purchasers agree that they and each of them will upon the written request of Duncan served upon them within three years of the date of this Agreement immediately purchase such of the shares as may be specified in the notice from Duncan.

2. In the event that Duncan serves a written request such as is described in Clause 1 of this Agreement, the price to be paid for the shares shall be fixed by negotiation between the parties. If no price can be negotiated, the price shall be fixed by the company's auditors (acting as experts not as arbitrators).

3. (a) If Duncan wishes to sell the shares, he shall first offer them to the purchasers at a price to be fixed in accordance with the provisions of Clause 2 of this Agreement.

   (b) If Duncan offers the shares to the purchasers under Clause 3(a) but does not serve a notice under Clause 1, the purchasers shall not be bound to purchase the shares.

4. (a) If a contract for the sale and purchase of the shares is entered into pursuant to any of the Clauses of this Agreement, that contract shall be forthwith submitted by the purchasers to the directors of Great Expectations with a request for confirmation that the directors are willing to register the transfer of the shares.

   (b) If the directors of Great Expectations Ltd do not confirm in writing within fourteen days of being asked to do so their willingness to register the transfer of the shares, the contract referred to in Clause 4(a) of this Agreement, shall thereupon lapse.

   (c) The lapse of the contract under Clause 4(b) shall not prejudice Duncan's right to serve further notices under Clause 1 or Clause 3 in respect of some or all of the shares.

Appendix E

Accounts

Accounts of Great Expectations Ltd for the year ending 31 December 2002

Profit and Loss Account

Turnover	510,000
Cost of Sales	295,000
Gross Profit	215,000
Administrative Expenses	110,000
Interest Payable	3,000
Taxation	22,000
Net Profit after Taxation	80,000

Balance Sheet

FIXED ASSETS

Tools & Equipment	3,000
Subsidiary Companies	500
	3,500

CURRENT ASSETS

Stocks	60,920
Work-in-progress	5,750
Debtors	65,530
Cash at Bank	64,830
	245,530
Creditors due within one year	15,030
Net Current Assets	182,000
Total Assets less Current Liabilities	185,500
Debentures	30,000

Provisions for Liabilities	25,000
Net Assets	130,500

CAPITAL AND RESERVES

Called Up Share Capital	3,500
Share Premium Account	1,000
Reserves	1,000
Profit & Loss Account	80,000
Loans and Debentures	45,000
	130,500

Accounts of Subsidiary Company Great Expectations (Ideas) Ltd for the year ending 31 December 2002

Profit and Loss Account

Management Charge	15,000
Interest Receivable	800
Expenditure	15,200
Gross Profit	600
Taxation	150
Net Profit	450

Balance Sheet

CURRENT ASSETS

Cash at Bank	1,400
Creditors due within one year	200
	1200

CAPITAL AND RESERVES

Share Capital	500
Reserves	250
Profit & Loss Account	450
	1,200

Consolidated Accounts for the year ending 31 December 2002

Profit and Loss Account

Turnover	510,000
Cost of Sales	295,000
Interest Receivable	800
Gross Profit	215,000
Administrative Expenses	110,200
Interest Payable	3,000
Taxation	22,150
Net Profit after Taxation	80,450

Balance Sheet

FIXED ASSETS

Tools & Equipment	3,000

CURRENT ASSETS

Stocks	60,920
Work-in-progress	5,750
Debtors	65,530
Cash at Bank	66,230
	198,430
Creditors due within one year	15,230
Net Current Assets	183,200
Total Assets less Current Liabilities	186,200
Debentures	
Provisions for Liabilities	25,000
Net Assets	131,200

CAPITAL AND RESERVE

Called up Share Capital	3,500
Share Premium Account	1,000
Reserves	1,250
Profit & Loss Account	80,450
Loans and Debentures	45,000
	131,200

Report to the members of Great Expectations Ltd:

We have audited these accounts in accordance with auditing standards and in our opinion they give a true and fair view of the position of the company as at the balance sheet date and of the profit and loss for the accounting reference period then ended.

Barnaby, Rudge & Co
Chartered Accountants

Accounts of Great Expectations Ltd for the year ending 31 December 2003
Profit and Loss Account

Turnover	457,000
Cost of Sales	275,000
Gross Profit	182,000
Dividend	80,000
Bad Debts	50,000
Administrative Expenses	100,000
Interest Payable	2,000
Taxation	Nil
Net Profit after Taxation	(50,000)

Balance Sheet

FIXED ASSETS

Tools & Equipment	7,000
Subsidiary Companies	500
	7,500

CURRENT ASSETS

Stocks	81,200
Work-in-progress	10,700
Debtors	127,950
Cash at Bank	51,800
	301,650
Creditors due within one year	18,500
Net Current Assets	253,150
Total Assets less Current Liabilities	260,650
Debentures	65,000
Provisions for Liabilities	100,000
Net Assets	95,650

CAPITAL AND RESERVES

Called Up Share Capital	11,300
Share Premium Account	1,000
Reserves	Nil
Profit & Loss Account	Nil
Loans and Debentures	83,350
Total	95,650

Account of Subsidary Company Great Expectations (Ideas) Ltd for the year ending 31 December 2003

Profit and Loss Account

Management Charge	15,000
Interest Receivable	100
Expenditure	15,100
Gross Profit	Nil
Taxation	Nil
Net Profit	Nil

Balance Sheet

CURRENT ASSETS

Cash at Bank	1,400
Creditors due within one year	200
	1,200

CAPITAL AND RESERVES

Share Capital	500
Reserves	250
Profit & Loss Account	450
	1,200

Consolidated Accounts for the year ending 31 December 2003

Profit and Loss Account

Turnover	457,000
Cost of Sales	275,000
Interest Receivable	100
Gross Profit	182,100
Dividend	80,000
Bad Debts	50,000
Administrative Expenses	100,100
Interest Payable	2,000
Taxation	Nil
Net Profit after Taxation	(50,000)

Balance Sheet

FIXED ASSETS	
Tools & Equipment	7,000
	7,000
CURRENT ASSETS	
Stocks	81,200
Work-in-progress	10,700
Debtors	127,950
Cash at Bank	53,200
	273,050
Creditors due within one year	18,500
Net Current Assets	254,350
Total Assets less Current Liabilities	261,350
Debentures	65,000
Provisions for Liabilities	100,000
Net Assets	96,350
CAPITAL AND RESERVES	
Called Up Share Capital	11,300
Share Premium Account	1,000
Reserves	250
Profit & Loss Account	450
Loans and Debentures	83,350
	96,350

Report to the members of Great Expectations Ltd:

We have audited these accounts in accordance with auditing standards and in our opinion they give a true and fair view of the position of the company as at the balance sheet date and of the profit and loss for the accounting reference period then ended except that we have not been able to form any view as to the accuracy of the figures for the value of stock, which we have taken at the directors' valuation.

Barnaby, Rudge & Co
Chartered Accountants

Appendix F

Share and Financial Structure

Share structure:

1. At formation

Authorised capital £1m, issued £2,000 in £1 shares. Shareholdings:

Arthur	50
Bill	50
Charlotte	25
Duncan	1,200
Edwina	675

2. After introduction of YOCS

Authorised capital £1m, issued £50,000, of which £48,000 only 25% paid. Shareholdings:

Arthur	50 fully paid	+	1,000 25p paid	=	1,050
Bill	50 fully paid	+	1,200 25p paid	=	1,250
Charlotte	25 fully paid	+	175 25p paid	=	200
Duncan	1,200 fully paid	+	15,800 25p paid	=	17,000
Edwina	675 fully paid	+	9,825 25p paid	=	10,500
YOCS plc	20,000 25p paid			=	20,000

Duncan's shares were subsequently transferred to Frederick.

Borrowings

1. At formation

Bank loan	£30,000
Duncan	£20,000

2. From Old Curiosity Shop plc

£25,000

All loans are secured by fixed and floating charges. All are properly registered, and accordingly rank in the chronological order of their creation.

Index